INTRODUCTION TO NETWORKING

FOURTH EDITION

Written by

Barry Nance

Introduction to Networking, Fourth Edition

Copyright© 1997 by Que® Corporation.

Library of Congress Catalog No.: 96-72212

ISBN: 0-7897-1158-3

This book is sold *as is*, without warranty of any kind, either express or implied, respecting the contents of this book, including but not limited to implied warranties for the book's quality, performance, merchantability, or fitness for any particular purpose. Neither Que Corporation nor its dealers or distributors shall be liable to the purchaser or any other person or entity with respect to any liability, loss, or damage caused or alleged to have been caused directly or indirectly by this book.

99 98   6 5 4 3

Interpretation of the printing code: the rightmost double-digit number is the year of the book's printing; the rightmost single-digit number, the number of the book's printing. For example, a printing code of 97-1 shows that the first printing of the book occurred in 1997.

All terms mentioned in this book that are known to be trademarks or service marks have been appropriately capitalized. Que cannot attest to the accuracy of this information. Use of a term in this book should not be regarded as affecting the validity of any trademark or service mark.

Screen reproductions in this book were created using Collage Plus from Inner Media, Inc., Hollis, NH.

Composed in *Stone Serif* and *MCPdigital* by Que Corporation.

Contents at a Glance

Contents

II Building a Network   55

3 Using File Servers   57

4 Using Protocols, Cables, and Adapters   85

5 Using Workstations   123

III Networking Software 143

6 Using Novell NetWare 145

IV Expanding a Network   237

10 Using Network Applications   239

11 Using Electronic Mail   265

12 Managing Your Network   291

Credits

President
Roland Elgey

Publisher
Joseph B. Wikert

Publishing Manager
Fred Slone

Senior Title Manager
Bryan Gambrel

Editorial Services Director
Elizabeth Keaffaber

Managing Editor
Sandy Doell

Acquisitions Editor
Christopher Booher

Product Development Specialist
Erik Daffhorn

Senior Editor
Mike La Bonne

Editors
Jim Bowie
Sean Dixon
Tonya Maddox
Sean Medlock

Technical Editor
Rebecca Campbell

Strategic Marketing Manager
Barry Pruett

Product Marketing Manager
Kristine Ankney

Assistant Product Marketing Managers
Christy M. Miller
Karen Hagen

Technical Support Specialist
Nadeem Muhammed

Acquisitions Coordinator
Carmen Krikorian

Editorial Assistants
Andrea Duvall
Jennifer Condon
Chantal Mees Koch

Book Designer
Ruth Harvey

Cover Designer
Dan Armstrong

Production Team
Maribeth Echard
Christy Hendershot
Heather Howell
Daryl Kessler
Julie Searls

Indexer
Nick Schroeder

This book is for my wonderful family. They gave me both the motivation and the time to do this book.

About the Author

Barry Nance, a columnist for *BYTE* magazine, has been in the computer industry for 25 years. He is the author of *Network Programming in C* and *Using OS/2 Warp*, Special Edition, both published by Que Corporation. Barry is the Category Manager for BIX, where you can reach him as "barryn."

We'd Like to Hear from You!

As part of our continuing effort to produce books of the highest possible quality, Que would like to hear your comments. To stay competitive, we really want you to let us know what you like or dislike most about this book or other Que products.

Please send your comments, ideas, and suggestions for improvement to:

The Expert User Team
Email: euteam@que.mcp.com
Fax: (317) 581-4663

Our mailing address is:

Expert User Team
Que Corporation
201 West 103rd Street
Indianapolis, IN 46290-1097

You can also visit our Team's home page on the World Wide Web at:

`http://www.mcp.com/que/developer_expert`

Thank you in advance. Your comments will help us to continue publishing the best books available in today's market.

Thank You,
The Expert User Team

Introduction

When computers are networked, they can do more work for people. People accomplish entire projects in a short time when they work in teams. You can think of a network as a team of computers, designed to support a team of people. A personal computer (PC) is just that: personal. Using an unconnected, non-networked PC is a solitary effort. The concept of computer networks has been around for decades, but beginning in 1981, the word LAN—short for Local Area Network—crept into the vocabulary of more and more businesses. Many companies use LANs to increase the benefits they receive from their desktop PCs. A network encourages people to share peripherals (like printers and modems), software programs, and an organization's most important asset—data.

Setting up a team of people, coordinating tasks, tracking problems, and monitoring progress are management jobs that help the team work together effectively. Networks similarly involve some management, but the result is worth the effort if management tasks are done correctly and on time. This book helps you understand networks so that you can do your job better as part of your office team.

Networking a group of computers is not as simple as mastering a single computer. And although PCs have become everyday commodities to some extent, they're not quite as simple as a stereo component system or a television set.

Networking computers, like managing a team of people, is a complicated challenge. The vocabulary of LANs is full of acronyms. Products for networks sometimes operate well together and sometimes do not. The cost of networking several PCs can range from less than $100 to several thousand dollars per computer. The benefits realized from networking computers may be none at all—in some unusual instances you may be worse off with the network than without it—or you may find the usefulness transcends the functionality of the individual computers. In spite of the risks, businesses are networking computers at a rapid pace. LANs are one of the fastest growing segments of the computer industry.

Personal computers are replacing mainframes and minicomputers as the tool of choice for processing information. Over the past 10 years, the only serious obstacle to the PC revolution has been sharing information between several PCs. With mainframes and minicomputers, everyone could access the single host computer where the information resided, enabling them to share information. But LANs also let PC users share information—applications and the data on which applications operate—and LANs are now an integral part of personal computing. What will become of the expensive mainframes and minicomputers? You may be surprised to learn that the inexorable trend toward LANs is turning mainframes and minicomputers into repositories of shared data—i.e., file servers.

Why Network Computers?

Networks are primarily used to share costly computer hard disk drives and printers. Early in the 1980s, Apple Computer's very popular Apple II computer was expensive, and so were the large-capacity disk drives for it. Local school systems wanted to purchase Apple II computers, but the cost of the disk drives—even small ones—was prohibitive. And the computers were not nearly as useful without disk drives.

A company named Corvus recognized the need and began selling one of the first LANs to local boards of education. A school system could purchase a single large-capacity disk drive, buy Apple II computers without disk drives, connect the computers and the disk drive through a LAN, and give access to the shared disk drive to each Apple II user. The idea caught on rapidly. School systems found a way to afford computers, and Corvus grew at a fantastic rate.

The economics of desktop computing have changed considerably in the last decade. High-capacity, high-speed disk drives aren't as expensive as they used to be. Today, of course, *high capacity* means hundreds of millions of bytes (*megabytes, or MB*) or even billions of bytes (*gigabytes, or GB*), a far cry from the 5MB and 10MB Apple II disk drives. If you buy computers for your department—let's say 10 people—at current prices, each with a 400MB disk drive, the disk drive component of each computer will cost about $200—a total of $2,000 for all 10 computers. If you buy a single 4GB disk drive, you'll pay only about $1,000. But to network those same 10 computers to it, you'll probably spend more than $1,000 on network cards and software. It's actually *more* expensive. The economics of LANing have changed considerably since the days of Apple II computers and Corvus. So why would you want to network those 10 computers?

There are three answers to this question. The first is that 10 people probably don't need 4GB of disk space because they can share single copies of common files and applications rather than have individual copies on each computer. You can save money by buying a smaller single disk drive that they can share. You can save additional money by using the LAN to give them access to a central printer.

The second answer points to the people costs associated with PC use. If you use a LAN to share a single disk drive, you centralize the administration of the information on the disk. You can easily make backup copies of all the information on the shared disk, for all 10 people. (If each person is responsible for making his or her own backup copies, on the other hand, you'll quickly find that some people ignore guidelines and don't back up their disk drives. The entire department—or perhaps an entire business—thus risks losing some of its valuable information.) Also, those 10 people can use the LAN to share files and information. Without the network, a person must share files by copying them to a diskette and walking it over to another person. (This is sometimes referred to as *sneakernet*.) With a LAN, people can share files simply and easily.

The third answer contains the most sophisticated and complex reason for using a LAN. A growing number of PC software products are multiuser products; they recognize the presence of the LAN. These products are *LAN-aware*: the software coordinates updates to a central file and enables many people to access the same information simultaneously.

Local area networks can save a business money, but the savings in computer hardware costs are less than the savings in personnel expense.

Many times, using a LAN is necessary. Stores that rent videotapes are a prime example. The store needs to keep an accurate record of which videotapes are charged out and which are on the shelf. A minicomputer or mainframe computer with a terminal for each sales clerk would be an expensive solution. Instead, the store uses PCs, networked behind the counter, to track each videotape. Two or three clerks can keep each other informed by simply operating two or three PCs and recording the rentals and returns. The network's file server holds the common database file of videotapes. Each time a clerk enters information, his or her PC updates the common database file on the file server.

Perhaps your company needs to share a CD-ROM disk drive, a plotter, a high-speed modem, or a fax machine. Many (but not all) configurations of LANs support the sharing of these devices.

You can share disk drives and other devices on your LAN. You can share applications and information in a way that formerly was possible only with minicomputers and mainframes. Internet technology lets you use a browser (such as Netscape Navigator) to view information you've published on a network. And you can use a LAN for electronic mail, scheduling (of meetings, for example), and workgroup coordination.

This discussion of sharing files may cause you some concern. You may have files that you consider private and that you don't want to share with other people. Fortunately, most networks provide several levels of security so that you can keep private files from prying eyes. The first level uses a password to verify the identity of the person seeking access to a file server. The next level of security enables you to "hide" files and entire directories of files on a user-by-user basis. If your concern is that the file not be inadvertently modified or deleted, you can mark the file as *read-only* to ensure that it remains intact. Most networks also let LAN administrators designate which people have permissions or rights to look at or modify files.

What Is the Purpose of This Book?

This book introduces you to LANs with illustrations, photographs, and clear, simple explanations. As you read further, you'll learn exactly what a LAN is, how it works, and how to use one. You'll find tips, suggestions, and recommendations for selecting LAN components. You'll become well-versed enough with LANs to avoid costly mistakes. And you'll become acquainted with a number of popular networking products from companies like Novell, Microsoft, IBM, Sun Microsystems, Apple Computer, Digital Equipment Corporation (DEC), Network General, and Xircom.

Who Should Read This Book?

You'll find this book useful and informative if you're curious about networking computers. If you're in the process of selecting a LAN, you can use this book as a comprehensive guide during the selection process.

Perhaps you're getting a LAN in your office. You have some experience using a PC, and you want to know how the LAN will affect your work. If so, you can use this book to prepare yourself for the new LAN. You'll be ready to use it productively when it arrives.

If your computer is already connected to others with a LAN, you can use this book to learn how the network operates. You can familiarize yourself with the different networking products so you can get the most from your LAN.

Perhaps you've been told that your computer at the office is becoming part of a LAN. Perhaps you run an office, small or large, and you wonder whether a LAN would help people in your office do their jobs more effectively. You may have been given the job of recommending a LAN or even installing one. Or perhaps you're just curious about how a network works or what it can do for you. For these and similar situations, you need an introduction to LANs. This book is for you.

What Is in This Book?

Part I of this book, "Understanding Networks," lays the foundation for later chapters and tells you how to benefit from a network. Chapter 1, "A Networking Overview," is an overview of LANs. Chapter 2, "Sharing Computer Resources," discusses the sharing of disks, printers, CD-ROMs, modems, fax machines, applications, and data files.

Part II, "Building a Network," gives you nuts-and-bolts information about how networks function. Chapter 3, "Using File Servers," explains what a file server is and how it differs from other computers on the network. In Chapter 4, "Using Protocols, Cables, and Adapters," you see how the network connects all the computers into a cohesive unit. Chapter 5, "Using Workstations," discusses the PC as a workstation on the network.

Part III, "Networking Software," comprehensively covers the products that bring the network to life—network operating systems. Each chapter discusses specific products and thoroughly acquaints you with their features. Chapter 6, "Using Novell NetWare," leads off with a discussion of Novell NetWare Version 2.2, Version 3.12, and the new Version 4.11, which includes intranet and Internet capabilities along with file and printer sharing features. Chapter 7, "Using Windows NT Server and Warp Server," describes and explains the networking products from IBM and Microsoft. Chapter 8, "Using Windows for Workgroups, Windows 95, and Warp Connect," brings you up to date on products that don't require you to have a separate file server. Chapter 9, "Using UNIX LANs," explores TCP/IP as well as some of the networking alternatives available in UNIX networking environments.

Part IV, "Expanding a Network," gives you a perspective on software and hardware products that help you get the most from your new LAN. Chapter 10, "Using Network Applications," explains how and why some software products are LAN-aware while others are not. Chapter 11, "Using Electronic Mail," explains using the LAN as an office-wide post office for interoffice mail. Chapter 12, "Managing Your Network," thoroughly discusses tools you can use to manage, administer, and diagnose problems on the LAN. Chapter 13, "Analyzing Interoperability," is a critical look at why LAN products from different vendors do not always work well together. And Chapter 14, "Building WANs from LANs," lets you explore the sharing of information across the city, across the nation, or even around the world through Wide Area Networks.

The Appendix, "Understanding LAN Certification," describes the Novell, Microsoft, and IBM programs for your understanding of LANing. Becoming a Certified NetWare Engineer (CNE) through Novell's program, for example, can open up job opportunities and increase your salary.

You will also find a Glossary of Terms in the back of this book.

What Should You Already Know?

This book is not a primer on PCs. You should already have some familiarity with computers to get the most out of this book. In particular, you should know what a PC is, how to start and use an application on a PC, and what a file is. You don't need to know anything about networks themselves.

The first chapter is an overview of LANs that will get you off the ground easily and simply. Turn the page and find out what a LAN can do for you!

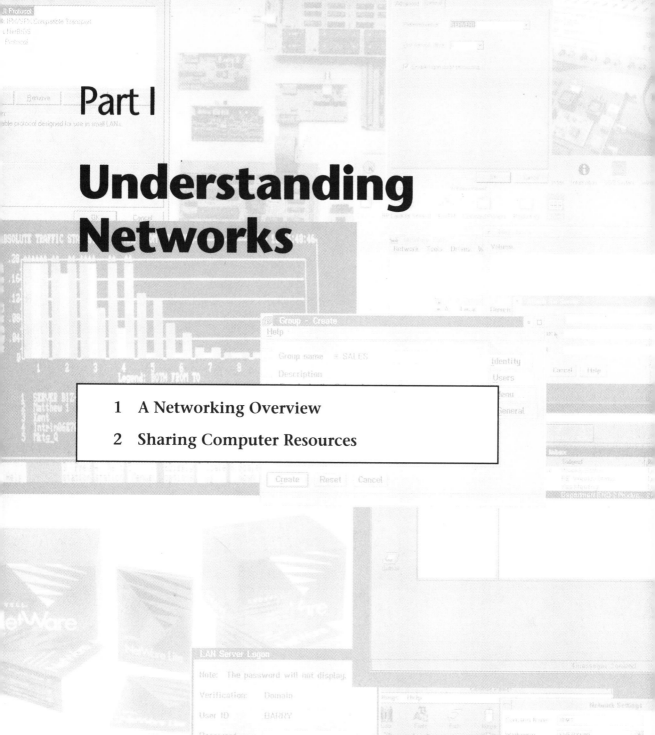

Part I

Understanding Networks

Chapter 1

A Networking Overview

A LAN is a local area network. Within a single building or small geographical area, a LAN enables you to connect a group of personal computers. People using these networked computers can share information. Without a LAN, sharing files means copying them to a diskette and then walking it over to another person (this is sometimes colorfully described as *sneakernet*). This method does not allow several people to access the same file at the same time. But a LAN gives you simultaneous access as long as you use application software designed for multiple users. Even without simultaneous access, a LAN is useful. In addition to easily sharing files, people on a LAN can share a printer, a CD-ROM drive, a modem, or even a fax machine.

In this chapter, you'll first find out what a LAN can do. Next, you'll explore the basics of what comprises a LAN. During your exploration, you'll become acquainted with workstations, file servers, LAN cables, and network adapters such as ARCnet, Ethernet, and Token Ring cards. After discovering what makes up the hardware of LANs, you'll move on to LAN software components. You'll learn about network operating system software products such as Novell NetWare, IBM Warp Server, and Microsoft NT Server. After a brief discussion of application software, you'll learn about security, backing up files on a LAN, data redundancy, and power protection. The chapter concludes with some advice on when to ask for help.

Understanding What a LAN Can Do

A LAN can do virtually everything a mainframe computer or minicomputer can do, at a much lower cost. In each environment, people can share computer resources and information, and they can work together on projects and tasks that require coordination and communication even though they may not be physically close. If a LAN crashes, though, each person may be able to continue working on his or her personal computer. A mainframe or minicomputer crash, on the other hand, brings work to a halt for an entire department or company.

You can do seven things with a LAN that you cannot easily do with non-networked, stand-alone personal computers:

1. *Share files.* A LAN enables many users to share a single copy of a file stored on a central file server, which helps the organization keep its records, documents, and other files consistent. An attorney's office may have a common pool of documents that the various secretaries can access and update, for example.

2. *Transfer files.* A LAN enables you to copy files from machine to machine without having to exchange floppy diskettes. This is especially useful for large files that don't fit on a single floppy disk.

3. *Access information and files.* A LAN enables anyone to run accounting software or other application software from any of its workstations. Employees can access software tools from any LAN-connected desktop computer.

4. *Share applications.* A LAN enables people to use the same copy of the Microsoft Word word processing program, for example. They all know they're using the same version of the software, and a LAN administrator can install software updates that affect everyone immediately. Two people cannot edit the same document simultaneously, however.

5. *Simultaneously key data into an application.* A LAN-aware application program enables two people to key into it at once. Two people can key general ledger transactions at the same time, for example, with the program coordinating their work so they don't interfere with each other. Note that only special LAN-aware versions of programs enable simultaneous data entry. Ordinary computer programs enable only one person at a time to use the program on a given set of files.

6. *Printer sharing.* Using a LAN, you can share one or more expensive printers among several workstations. (If you need only printer sharing, an inexpensive printer switchbox may connect multiple computers to a single printer.)

7. *Electronic mail.* You can use a LAN as a post office to send memos, reports, and typed messages to other people in other parts of the building. The telephone is faster and more convenient, but a LAN e-mail system takes messages when people are away from their phones, and it provides a paperless "interoffice memo" environment.

Understanding the Components of a LAN

A LAN is a combination of computers, LAN cables, network adapter cards, network operating system software, and LAN application software. (You'll sometimes see *network operating system* abbreviated as *NOS*.) On a LAN, each personal computer is called a *workstation*, except for one or more computers designated as *file servers*. Each workstation and file server contains a network adapter card. LAN cables (or other media) connect all workstations and file servers. In addition to DOS, Windows, UNIX, OS/2, or other operating system, each workstation runs network software that enables it to communicate with the file servers. In turn, the file servers run network software that communicates with the workstations and serves up files to those workstations. LAN-aware application software runs at each workstation, communicating with the file server when it needs to read and write files. Figure 1.1 illustrates the components that make up the LAN.

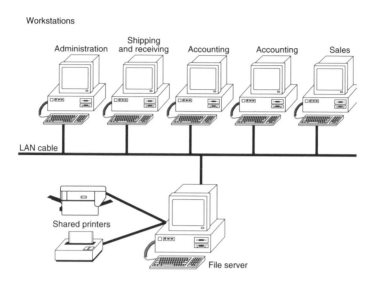

Fig. 1.1   The components on a LAN consist of several computers.

Workstations

A LAN is made up of computers. You'll find two kinds of computers on a LAN: workstations, usually operated by employees; and file servers, usually located in a separate room or closet.

The workstations are the various PCs or terminals connected to the file server. Employees use these PCs on their own or, with network software, link to the file server to access programs, data, printers, etc. Workstations, sometimes referred to as *clients*, are usually intermediate-speed machines with an 80386, 80486, or slow Pentium CPU and 4MB to 16MB of RAM. Workstations often have good quality color or, less often, grayscale VGA monitors as well as high quality keyboards, but these characteristics simply make them easy to use and are not required to make the LAN work. Also, a workstation usually has a smaller, slower hard disk (usually 100MB or less).

Some workstations, called *diskless workstations*, do not have disk drives. Such workstations rely completely on the LAN for their file access.

When you use a workstation, it behaves in almost all respects like a stand-alone PC. If you inspect it closely, though, you'll observe four typical characteristics that set it apart from a stand-alone computer:

   1. Extra messages appear on-screen as the computer starts up. These messages inform you that network software is loading at the workstation.

2. You have to provide your user identification (or account ID) and a password before you can use the LAN. This is the logon procedure.

3. After you log on to the LAN, you see additional drive letters (on a Macintosh, extra folders; on a UNIX computer, extra file systems) that you can access.

4. Your memos or reports may be printed in a remote location on the LAN.

File Servers

In contrast to workstations, a *file server* is a computer that serves all the workstations—primarily by storing and retrieving data from files shared on its disks. File servers are usually fast Pentium or Pentium Pro-based computers, running at 100 MHz or faster and with 16MB or more of RAM. They usually have monochrome monitors and inexpensive keyboards because people don't use them directly. They almost always have one or more large, fast, expensive hard disks, however.

Servers must be high-quality, heavy-duty machines because, in serving the whole network, they do many times the work of an ordinary workstation computer. The server is a repository of data for an entire office or company. In particular, the file server's hard disk(s) must be durable and reliable.

On smaller LANs the file server may double as a workstation. Serving an entire network is a big job that does not leave much spare horsepower for workstation duties, however. Furthermore, if the end-user locks up the workstation that doubles as the file server, the network also locks up.

An application server is a file server that runs additional computer programs alongside the NOS. As an example, consider Oracle, the relational database management software product. Oracle can run on computers that are acting as file servers at the same time. The result is an application server. Some network operating systems are better application server environments than others. In general, DOS-based peer LANs, Windows for Workgroups, and Windows 95 make poor application servers because an application can fail in ways that crash the operating system and thus stop the network. OS/2 Warp, Windows NT, and UNIX are better platforms for application servers. Because writing computer programs for the NetWare environment is difficult, NetWare is not a popular platform for application servers.

The file server may use a different operating system than the workstations use. While the workstation (client) needs an operating system designed for an interactive user, the file server's operating system needs to be especially good at sending, receiving, and accessing files on behalf of the workstation. Novell NetWare is a network operating system that runs only on file servers. (The portion of NetWare that does run on the workstation is there to help the workstation operating system, not replace it.) Because the file server shares its files with the various workstations via LAN data messages that flow through the LAN cables, the server operating system does not have to be the same operating system the workstations use.

If a LAN has 20 workstations and one server, under a heavy load each workstation can use only 1/20th of the server's resources. In practice, though, most workstations are idle most of the time, at least from a "disk file access" point of view. As long as no other workstation is using the server, your workstation can use 100% of the server's resources.

LAN Cables

LAN cables are the nervous system of a local area network. These cables connect everyone to the file server and peripherals such as printers. A LAN can use one of several transmission media: twisted-wire cable, coaxial cable, fiber-optic cable, radio waves, and infrared waves.

LAN cable comes in different varieties. You may use thin coaxial wire (referred to as *Thinnet* or *CheaperNet*) or thick coaxial wire (*ThickNet*). You may use shielded twisted pair (*STP*), which looks like the wire that carries electricity inside the walls of your house, or unshielded twisted pair (*UTP*), which looks like telephone wire. You may even use fiber-optic cable. The kind of wire you use depends mostly on the network adapter cards you choose. The next section discusses network adapter cards.

Each workstation is connected with cable to the other workstations and to the file server. Sometimes a single piece of cable winds from station to station, visiting all servers and workstations along the way. This is called a *bus* or *daisy-chain topology*, as shown in Figure 1.2. (*Topology* simply describes the way the workstations and servers connect physically.)

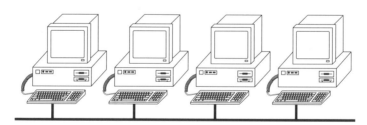

Fig. 1.2 All network devices connect to a common cable in a bus topology.

Sometimes a separate cable runs from a central place, such as a file server, to each workstation. Figure 1.3 shows this arrangement, called a *star*. Sometimes the cables branch repeatedly from a root location, forming the *star-wired tree* shown in Figure 1.4. Buses use the least cable but are the hardest to diagnose or bypass when problems occur. If you have to run cables through walls or ceilings, installing the cable can be the most expensive part of setting up the LAN. At every branching point, special fittings connect the intersecting wires. Sometimes you also need various black boxes such as hubs, repeaters, or access units.

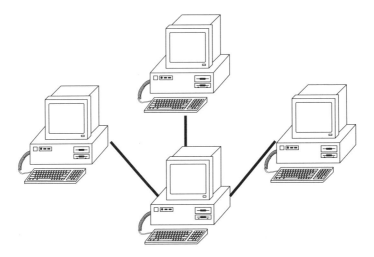

Fig. 1.3 Network devices connect to a central point through separate cables in a star topology.

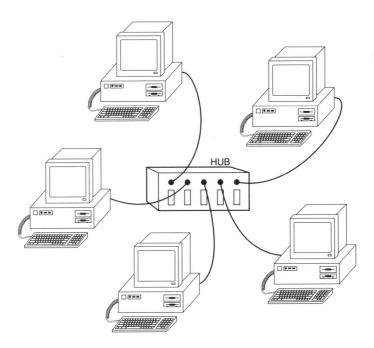

Fig. 1.4 The central point of connection is a hub in a star-wired tree.

Relatively new but growing in popularity are LAN *switches*. These devices, at the center of a star of LAN cables, identify the destination of a LAN data message and quickly route the message directly to that destination.

A few companies, such as Motorola, are pioneering a type of LAN that does not require cables at all. Such a *wireless LAN* uses infrared or radio waves to carry network signals from computer to computer.

Planning the cabling layout, cutting the cable, and installing cables and fittings are tasks best left to experienced workers. If the fittings aren't perfect, you may get electronic echoes (and thus transmission errors) on the network. Coaxial cable costs about 60 cents per foot. This sounds like a big expense, but the cost of installing cable, at about $45 per hour, overshadows the cost of the cable itself. The only circumstance when you might consider installing LAN cable yourself is if you have a group of computers located on adjacent desks so that cable doesn't have to enter the walls or ceiling.

Building codes almost always require fireproof *plenum* cables. Chapter 4, "Using Protocols, Cables, and Adapters," explains LAN cables in detail. For now, you should know that plenum cables are more fire-resistant than other cables. You would be very upset if you installed ordinary cable and were later told by the building inspector to rip out the cable and start over with the proper kind.

Network Adapters

A network adapter card, like a video display adapter card, fits in a slot in each workstation and file server. Your workstation sends requests through the network adapter to the file server. Your workstation receives responses through the network adapter when the file server wants to deliver a portion of a file to you. People often refer to network adapters as Network Interface Cards (NICs).

Only two network adapters may communicate with each other at the same time on a LAN. This means that other workstations have to wait their turn if the network is in use. Fortunately, such delays are usually not noticeable. The LAN gives the appearance of many workstations accessing the file server simultaneously.

Ethernet connectors have a single T connector, a D-shaped 15-pin connector, a connector that looks like a telephone jack, or sometimes a combination of all three. Token Ring adapters have a 9-pin connector and sometimes a telephone jack outlet. Figure 1.5 shows a high-performance Token Ring adapter with both kinds of connectors. Fiber Distributed Data Interface (FDDI) adapters have connectors for fiber-optic cable.

Cards with two or more connectors enable you to choose from a wider variety of LAN cables. A Token Ring card with two connectors, for example, enables you to use shielded twisted-pair (STP) or unshielded twisted-pair (UTP or telephone wire) cable.

The LAN adapter card listens to all traffic on the cable and filters out just the messages destined for your workstation. The adapter then sends them to your workstation when the workstation is ready to attend to them. When your workstation wants to send a request to a server, the adapter card waits for a break in the cable traffic and then inserts your message into the stream. It also automatically verifies that the message has arrived intact and resends it if the message was garbled.

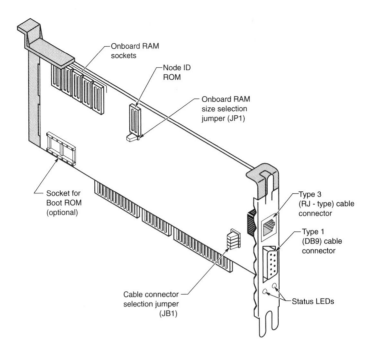

Fig. 1.5   The Thomas-Conrad 16/4 Token Ring adapter has both a 9-pin connector and a telephone wire connector.

Adapters range in price from less than $100 to much more than $1,000. What do you get for your money? Speed, primarily. Faster adapters can push data through the cable faster, which means that the file server receives a request more quickly and responds more quickly.

With a small LAN of four workstations and one server, blinding speed is not that important. If you have 100 or more workstations sharing one cable, however, speed can become a significant issue.

> **Caution**
>
> Electrical engineers and technical people measure the speed of a network in *megabits per second* (mbps). A byte of information consists of 8 bits, so you can divide the megabits per second rating by 8 to find out how many millions of characters (bytes) per second the network can theoretically handle.
>
> Suppose you want to transfer the information on a 3.5-inch, 720KB floppy disk across a LAN. The rated speed of the LAN is 4 megabits per second. Dividing 4 mbps by 8 tells you that the LAN can theoretically transmit .5 megabytes, or 500 kilobytes (500KB), of data per second. This is equivalent to the transfer rate of an average hard disk. The data from the 720KB floppy disk will take at least a few seconds to transfer, as you can see from these rough calculations.

In practice, a LAN is slower than its rated speed. In fact, a LAN is no faster than its slowest component. If you transfer 720KB of data from one workstation's hard disk to the file server, the elapsed time includes not only the transmission time but also the workstation hard disk's retrieval time, the workstation's processing time, and the file server's hard disk and server CPU processing times. The transfer rate of your hard disk, which in this case is probably the slowest component in the copying of the data to the server, governs the rate at which data flows to the file server. Other people's requests will interleave with your requests on the LAN, and the total transfer time may be longer because other people are using the LAN simultaneously.

If you transfer the data from a 720KB floppy disk to the file server, you see that it takes even longer. Floppy disks, as you know, are slow. Your workstation uses the network in small bursts as it reads the data from the floppy disk. In this case, the workstation cannot send data across the LAN any faster than it can read the data from the disk.

ARCnet Adapters. ARCnet is one of the oldest types of LAN hardware. It was originally a proprietary scheme of the Datapoint Corporation, but today many companies make ARCnet-compatible cards. However, ARCnet is waning in popularity. It's slow, but it's known for its solid reliability and it forgives minor errors in installation. Its problems are easy to diagnose, and it costs less than Ethernet. ARCnet operates something like Token Ring but at the slower rate of 2.5 million bits per second (2.5 mbps). The section "Token Ring Adapters" later in this chapter explains the basic principles on which ARCnet and Token Ring work.

Ethernet Adapters. Ethernet-based LANs enable you to interconnect a wide variety of equipment, including UNIX computers, Apple computers, IBM PCs, and IBM clones. You can buy Ethernet cards from dozens of competing manufacturers in three varieties— ThinNet, UTP, and ThickNet. ThickNet cables can span a greater distance, but they're much more expensive than the other kinds. Ethernet operates at a rate of 10 million bits per second (10 mbps) or 100 mbps (*Fast Ethernet*). You cannot mix Ethernet and Fast Ethernet on the same LAN unless you use a router, bridge, or switch between the two types of adapters.

Between *data transfers* (requests and responses to and from the file server), Ethernet LANs remain quiet. After a workstation sends a request across the LAN cable, the cable falls silent again. What happens when two or more workstations (and/or file servers) attempt to use the LAN at the same time?

Suppose that one workstation requests something from the file server just as the file server is sending a response to another workstation. A collision happens. (Remember that only two computers may communicate through the cable at a given moment.) Both computers—the file server and the workstation—back off and try again. Ethernet network adapters use *Carrier Sense, Multiple Access/Collision Detection* (CSMA/CD) to detect the collision, and each computer backs off for a random amount of time. This method effectively enables one computer to go first. With increased traffic, the frequency of collisions rises higher and higher, and response times become worse and worse. An Ethernet network can actually spend more time recovering from collisions than sending data. Recognizing Ethernet's traffic limitations, engineers from IBM and Texas Instruments designed Token Ring to solve the problem.

Token Ring Adapters. Token Ring uses shielded or unshielded twisted-pair cable. It's more expensive than Ethernet, but less expensive than Fiber Distributed Data Interface (FDDI) or Asynchronous Transfer Mode (ATM). Token Ring's cost is justified when there is significant traffic from many workstations. You'll find Token Ring in large corporations with large LANs, especially if the LANs are attached to mainframe computers. Token Ring operates at a rate of 4 or 16 million bits per second (4 mbps or 16 mbps).

On a Token Ring network, all workstations continuously play a game of "hot potato," passing an electronic token among themselves, even when there's no traffic. The token is just a short message indicating that the network is idle.

As soon as it receives the token, a workstation with nothing to send passes the token to the next workstation downstream. Only when a workstation receives the token can it send a message on the LAN. If the LAN is busy and you want your workstation to send a message to another workstation or server, you must wait patiently for the token to come around. Only then can your workstation send its message. The message circulates through the workstations and file servers on the LAN, all the way back to you, the sender. The sender then sends a token to indicate that the network is idle again. During the circulation of the message, one of the workstations or file servers recognizes that the message is addressed to it and begins processing that message.

Token Ring isn't as wasteful of LAN resources as this description makes it sound. The token takes almost no time at all to circulate around a LAN, even with 100 or 200 workstations. It's possible to assign priorities to certain workstations and file servers so they get more frequent access to the LAN. And, of course, the token-passing scheme tolerates higher traffic levels on the LAN than the collision-sensing Ethernet.

ARCnet and Token Ring aren't compatible with one another, but ARCnet uses a similar token-passing scheme to control workstation and server access to the LAN.

Sometimes a station fumbles and "drops" the token. LAN stations watch each other and use a complex procedure to regenerate a lost token. Token Ring is quite a bit more complicated than Ethernet; thus the LAN adapter cards are correspondingly more expensive.

Fiber Distributed Data Interface (FDDI) Adapters. Fiber Distributed Data Interface (FDDI) uses fiber-optic cable (instead of copper cable) to carry LAN data. Operating at a speed of 100 mbps, FDDI uses a technique very similar to that of Token Ring to pass tokens and data between adapters. FDDI adapters are more expensive than Ethernet or Token Ring, but are a worthwhile investment if your LAN traffic consists of large volumes of data, such as large graphics image files.

The Thomas-Conrad company, now a part of Compaq Computer, offers a hybrid between FDDI and ARCnet. Called TCNS, for Thomas-Conrad Network System, its adapters accept ARCNet programming commands from ordinary ARCNet software drivers. However, TCNS sends and receives network traffic at 100 mbps.

Asynchronous Transfer Mode (ATM) Adapters. Asynchronous Transfer Mode (ATM) adapters operate at speeds greater than Ethernet and Token Ring, and as you'd expect, the adapters are correspondingly more expensive. Slower ATM adapters operate at 25 mbps, while the fastest ATM adapters currently available operate at 155 mbps. ATM adapters establish connections among themselves and identify each connection with a unique number. These unique numbers work something like telephone numbers, letting ATM adapters know which adapter a data message is for. ATM adapters send and receive fixed-length data messages called *cells*, with each 53-byte cell containing numbers identifying the connection the message belongs to. ATM can simultaneously carry LAN data, voice, and video images.

Common standards are provided for both private and public networks so that ATM systems can be interfaced to either or both. ATM is therefore a flexible concept that works with data speeds as high as 622.08 mbps. (To put this into perspective, most conventional networks work at 10 mbps.)

All the cells follow the same path through the network, a path determined during the setup of the initial "call." Unlike other networks, ATM has no fixed time slots when other network traffic can occur; any user can access the network when an empty cell is available. Therefore, ATM is like having a yield sign on a country road, rather than a stoplight. Because of its ability to merge into network traffic as needed, ATM is often called "bandwidth on demand."

Apple's LocalTalk

Macintosh computers come with built-in network adapters. Called LocalTalk, the physical network connection you use between Macintosh computers works somewhat like a serial (modem-based) communications link between the computers. LocalTalk is relatively slow, operating at a rate of only 230.4 Kbits per second over a maximum distance of 300 meters. You can easily create a network of Macintosh computers, however, by connecting them with the appropriate twisted-pair cables. The Macintosh operating system contains networking software, called AppleTalk and AppleShare, that lets connected Macintoshes begin sharing files and printers immediately.

Is Token Ring better than Ethernet? Should you use Fast Ethernet? Or do you need high-speed, expensive FDDI or ATM equipment? The answer depends on your message traffic, the adapter cards available for your computers, the distances between the computers, and your budget.

LAN Software

In addition to LAN hardware, you must have a network operating system. The operating system by itself (DOS, for instance) cannot use a network adapter to talk to a file server. The most popular network operating system software is NetWare from Novell. The popular desktop computer operating systems Windows for Workgroups, Windows 95, Windows NT, and OS/2 Warp Connect include various components of network operating system software. When you install one of these operating systems, the installation process asks you what type of network you have, if any, and it configures the network operating system components during the installation of the desktop operating system.

In addition to the network operating system, you probably want application software that takes advantage of your LAN and is LAN-aware.

Network Operating Systems. Just as you need DOS to manage applications on a stand-alone computer, you need a network operating system to control the flow of LAN data messages between stations. In the simplest case, this network software makes the disk drive on the server appear to be an extra drive (perhaps drive F:) on each workstation. The network operating system also may make a LAN printer in another room appear to be locally attached to your workstation. Most ordinary computer programs are thus totally unaware of the LAN, even though they use files on the remote drive F: or print to the LAN printer through the LPT1 port.

On some networks, a separate, unattended computer acts as a file server. This is a *server-based LAN*. On other, smaller LANs, a workstation may be both a file server and a workstation at the same time. This is a *peer-to-peer LAN* (sometimes called a *peer LAN*).

The network operating system (NOS) components on each workstation and on the file server communicate with each other using a computer language called a *protocol*. One common protocol is IBM's NetBIOS, short for *Network Basic Input/Output System*. Several vendors besides IBM use NetBIOS. (Technically, NetBIOS is a programming interface; the actual protocol name is NetBEUI, an acronym for *NetBIOS Extended User Interface*.) Another protocol is Novell's IPX, which stands for *Internetwork Packet Exchange*. TCP/IP, which stands for *Transmission Control Protocol/Internet Protocol*, is a third protocol commonly found on LANs. Chapter 4, "Using Protocols, Cables, and Adapters," discusses these protocols in detail.

Here is a list of some network operating systems and their manufacturers:

Operating System	Manufacturer
AppleTalk	Apple
LANtastic	Artisoft
NetWare	Novell
Network File System (NFS)	Sun Microsystems
Warp Server	IBM
Warp Connect	IBM
Vines	Banyan
Windows NT Server	Microsoft
Windows 95	Microsoft
Windows for Workgroups	Microsoft

In the next few sections, you'll explore the highlights of some of these network operating systems.

Novell NetWare. Novell was one of the first companies to sell network operating system software. It formerly offered both hardware and software, but in recent years has concentrated on the software side of LANs. Novell's NetWare products are popular for several reasons:

- More applications will work on NetWare than on any other kind of network.

- NetWare works with more types of network adapters than any other network operating system. You can select hardware from dozens of vendors, picking the exact amount of power you need. You can use ARCnet, Ethernet, Token Ring, or almost any other type of network adapter with NetWare.

- NetWare LANs can grow to enormous size, with hundreds of workstations.

- NetWare LANs perform well.

- NetWare's security features are more than adequate for most LANs.

Most of the world's file servers run Novell NetWare; Novell's market share is currently about 65%. Novell's programmers have made NetWare work well with a great variety of workstation (client) platforms, including DOS, Windows, Windows for Workgroups, Windows 95, Windows NT, Apple Macintosh, OS/2 Warp, and even UNIX. NetWare version 4 offers NetWare Directory Services (NDS), which allows very large organizations with many file servers to interconnect those servers easily.

NetWare excels at file server tasks such as sharing disk space, files, and printers. The environment inside a NetWare file server is difficult for programmers (other than Novell's) to manage, however. NetWare servers usually don't run additional computer programs alongside the NetWare NOS, thus giving NetWare a reputation as a poor application server environment.

Chapter 6, "Using Novell NetWare," discusses NetWare in more detail.

Warp Server and NT Server. IBM and Microsoft developed OS/2 to be the successor to DOS. They wrote an operating system that can run multiple programs simultaneously, has more than 640KB of RAM available to applications, and performs well in difficult situations. These characteristics make OS/2 a powerful operating system for a file-server environment.

While they developed OS/2, IBM and Microsoft also worked together to create file server software suitable for OS/2. IBM developed IBM Warp Server (formerly called LAN Server), and Microsoft developed NT Server (formerly LAN Manager). You'll find few differences between the products other than cosmetic ones, however. The IBM programmers in Austin, Texas, and the Microsoft programmers in Redmond, Washington, shared their work constantly as they created their almost-twin network operating systems. Both companies want Warp Server and NT Server to outsell Novell NetWare, but so far this has not happened. Novell maintains a commanding lead in the LAN industry, but the IBM and Microsoft products do have an important attribute that makes OS/2-based and NT-based file server software attractive.

Because an OS/2 or NT file server is highly programmable, it can do more than just manage files for workstations. An OS/2 or NT computer, even while it acts as a file server, can run software that aids the workstations in special ways. OS/2 and NT are both excellent application server environments.

In a conventional workstation/server relationship, when a workstation needs to look through a large file for some data, the entire file must travel through the LAN cable to the workstation—in message-sized pieces—to be inspected. This process can cause quite a bit of LAN traffic, slowing other workstations. A better approach, called *client/server technology,* is for the workstation to tell the file server what it's looking for. The search for the data can occur directly in the server. When the server finds the data, it can return just that data to the workstation in only a few LAN messages. Unfortunately, in most cases, client/server requires the efforts of a programmer to implement the special processing that occurs inside the server.

Novell has something similar to OS/2 tasks, called VAPs (value added processes) for NetWare 2.2, and NLMs (NetWare loadable modules) for NetWare Version 3 and NetWare Version 4. But NetWare's file server environment isn't as easily programmed as OS/2 or NT. OS/2 and the file server products Warp Server and NT Server are well-suited to roles as application servers, as well as to client/server technology.

Windows NT Server is the file server version of Microsoft's New Technology operating system (NT). Like IBM's Warp Server, NT Server is a 32-bit network operating system. Unlike Warp Server, NT Server can be run on computers that contain Intel or DEC Alpha CPU chips. Although CPU speed is rarely a bottleneck on file servers, you may choose to run NT Server or Warp Server on a symmetric multiprocessing (multiple CPU) computer. The extra CPU processing power may let you use the file server for additional client/ server applications.

NT Server offers C2-level security; this means that the network operating system has a secure logon procedure, memory protection, auditing, and discretionary access control (the owner of a shared resource can monitor who uses the shared resource). Some corporate and military LANs require C2 or higher security. In terms of reliability, NT Server uses a transaction-based file system that can back out file updates if a series of related updates doesn't finish successfully. NT Server supports RAID level 5 (disk striping with parity), recognizes signals from an uninterruptible power supply, and comes with tape backup software.

Chapter 7, "Using Windows NT Server and Warp Server," describes these Microsoft and IBM networking products more fully.

LANtastic. The LANtastic network operating system from Artisoft is very popular because it is inexpensive, simple to install, and simple to operate. LANtastic supports many kinds of network adapters and uses only a very small amount of the 640KB of conventional DOS memory to do its job, leaving room for you to run larger applications at your workstation. LANtastic's network administration software offers both text mode and Windows interfaces through which you can configure and manage the LAN. LANtastic can work alongside Novell NetWare on the same LAN and offers Apple Macintosh connectivity as well.

LANtastic runs on top of DOS, Windows, or OS/2. In the DOS environment, the file server software consists of a set of DOS programs that remain loaded, alongside DOS, while you run application programs. DOS is quite slow when it tries to manage large files, and LANtastic users suffer some penalty in performance as a result. For light duty on a small network, though, LANtastic can be a cost-effective alternative to more expensive network operating systems.

LANtastic is a peer LAN. On very small LANs, you can even run applications on a LANtastic file server as if it were a workstation. If you're on a tight budget, you can save the cost of a separate file server computer by using LANtastic as a peer LAN. Be aware, though, that performance may not be entirely satisfactory because the file server is using DOS and the server is also acting as a workstation. You also put your data somewhat at risk with a peer LAN. If you use an application at a DOS-based workstation that is also a file server and that application crashes, your network will crash.

NetWare Lite and Personal NetWare. Novell used to offer a peer LAN product called NetWare Lite. Like LANtastic, NetWare Lite could turn a DOS-based PC into both a server and a workstation—with the same risks and performance considerations as with LANtastic. Of course, you could set aside a computer to act as just a file server and avoid some risk. Because it was DOS-based, however, NetWare Lite couldn't perform as well as regular NetWare at serving up files.

NetWare Lite was inexpensive and easy to install, and it operated well within a larger NetWare LAN. In a department of 100 people on a NetWare LAN, you might have used NetWare Lite to connect a small group of five or ten of those people. These people could access the regular NetWare LAN and at the same time share information among their own computers with Lite.

After NetWare Lite, Novell sold a similar peer LAN product called Personal NetWare. Personal NetWare offers many of the same basic features as NetWare Lite, including peer-to-peer file and printer sharing, but Personal NetWare provides better integration with both Microsoft Windows and server-based NetWare products than does NetWare Lite. Novell still sells Personal NetWare to existing Personal NetWare customers, but Novell does not encourage the use of Personal NetWare by new customers.

Windows for Workgroups. Noticing the success of two peer-to-peer network software products—Artisoft's LANtastic and Novell's NetWare Lite—late in 1992 Microsoft released a version of Windows incorporating built-in networking. Called Windows for Workgroups, the Windows-plus-network product enables the sharing of disk space, files, and printers through the point-and-click Windows interface.

Windows for Workgroups is a peer LAN; any PC that can run Windows in 386 Enhanced mode can share resources with other PCs. If a computer on the LAN can run Windows only in Standard mode, that computer can use shared resources but cannot share its own resources across the LAN. Similarly, DOS-only (non-Windows) workstations can use resources shared by Windows PCs running in 386 Enhanced mode. DOS-only workstations need the Windows for Workgroups' companion product, Workgroup Add-On for MS-DOS (formerly called Workgroup Connection), to use the LAN's disk file and printer resources.

Not quite as quick and efficient as LANtastic or NetWare Lite, Windows for Workgroups is generally suitable for small LANs of 2 to 20 PCs. Nonetheless, you'll find that Windows for Workgroups is easy to install and use. The new menu items and toolbar icons in both File Manager and Print Manager make sharing and using resources with Windows for Workgroups almost painless. Windows for Workgroups includes an electronic mail application and a team-oriented scheduling application that can help members of your organization communicate better. If you're already accustomed to using Windows, have PCs that can run Windows in 386 Enhanced mode, and want to share files on a LAN, Windows for Workgroups can be an easy way to get started with networking.

Windows 95. Late in 1995, Microsoft released a new version of its Windows operating environment called Windows 95. It looks very different from its Windows for Workgroups predecessor but offers many of the same networking features. You can create a peer LAN with several Windows 95 computers and use a Windows 95 PC as a workstation on a NetWare, NT, or Warp Server LAN.

Windows version 3 and Windows for Workgroups could run 16-bit DOS and Windows computer programs, but Windows 95 can also run some 32-bit Windows (termed Win32) programs. Similarly, Windows 95 can use the same 16-bit network client software that Windows version 3 and Windows for Workgroups used, such as the Novell NetWare NETX client. On some networks, Windows 95 can also use 32-bit client software to access file servers.

Warp Connect. OS/2 Warp Connect is IBM's peer LAN version of its OS/2 operating system. Warp Connect also includes NetWare, NT Server, and Warp Server client software to allow Warp Connect to act as a workstation on one of these networks. Warp Connect comes with drivers for most popular Ethernet, ARCNet, FDDI, ATM, and Token Ring network adapters.

Warp Connect consists of the OS/2 operating system plus the peer LAN and various NOS client software components. You can access another person's files and shared printer (in a peer LAN) or the file server's files and printer (in a server-based environment) through OS/2 Warp's desktop, called the Workplace Shell. You can also use OS/2 Warp's command line interface to access the drive letters and printers existing elsewhere on the network.

OS/2 Warp runs DOS, 16-bit Windows, 16-bit OS/2, and 32-bit OS/2 computer programs. OS/2 is highly network-aware, giving each DOS or Windows application program an appropriate network environment for sharing files and printers. 32-bit OS/2 computer programs, often written in-house by an organization's own programming staff, are becoming popular "mission-critical" platforms for automating business processes within the organization.

Macintosh System 7 and AppleTalk. Apple Computer designed and developed its own network infrastructure for use by its Macintosh computers. Called AppleTalk, it lets Macintosh computers share files and printers in a peer LAN environment. AppleTalk is both a specification and a collection of hardware products from Apple. People who have multiple Macintosh computers find AppleTalk very easy to set up and use. In fact, Apple decided to offer its own networking environment because the company's designers found that networking products from other vendors did not fit the "ease of use" paradigm established for the Macintosh.

Key among AppleTalk's features are its easy-to-set-up "plug-and-play" architecture, its simplicity, its independence from physical layer protocols (AppleTalk can run on Apple's own LocalTalk protocol as well as Ethernet and Token Ring), and its seamless integration with the Macintosh System 7 operating system's user interface. To log on to a NetWare server that's also running AppleTalk, for example, you merely use the Macintosh Chooser to pick a protocol, indicate which server to log on to, and supply your account identification and password. AppleTalk software responds by displaying new disk drive folders on your Macintosh desktop screen.

Chapter 8, "Using Windows for Workgroups, Windows 95, and Warp Connect," covers peer LAN networks in more detail.

Application Software. To get the most benefit from your LAN, you should buy new application software. If your accounting package isn't LAN-aware, for example, only one person at a time can use the software. Soon you may find this too confining. Consider upgrading to multi-user versions of some applications you use frequently. Word processing software won't become multi-user until some time in the distant future, but developers of spreadsheet software are already designing products for concurrent, multi-user access. Many database management software products allow multiple workstations to share a common database (more than one person can access the database at the same time). And most vertical market software (computer programs written specifically for a particular business or industry) is inherently multi-user.

If you have a word processor—and even if different people cannot edit the same document from different workstations—you need to buy a license for each person who uses the software. The same goes for other kinds of single-user and multi-user applications, including DOS. Companies that buy a single copy of a program and then use the copy on many machines may be in for a rude shock. A programmer can easily design an application to ask other workstations on the LAN if they are running the same copy of the software. This sort of copy protection is used increasingly, while the kind that relies on encrypted diskettes, deliberately damaged diskettes, and parallel port devices (*dongles*) is on the wane.

Communicating Through E-Mail

The most pervasive computer software on local area networks is electronic mail (e-mail). People use e-mail as a substitute for interoffice mail, as well as a company bulletin board. E-mail products from various vendors (or, in some cases, developed in-house by the company's own programmers) have even become part of some organizations' "open door" policies by allowing employees to send employee suggestions and complaints directly to high-level managers.

In the next few sections, you'll learn the basics about e-mail, its components, and its successor—GroupWare. Chapter 11, "Using Electronic Mail," addresses these topics in more detail.

An E-Mail Overview

Electronic mail is simple, yet potent. Used office-wide, e-mail can be more valuable and useful than the telephone for communicating. You can use e-mail to convey information difficult or impossible to read over the telephone, including reports, tables, statistics, charts, and images.

Electronic mail transcends the local area network; the Internet and companies such as MCI Mail and CompuServe offer dial-up e-mail services you can use nationwide or even worldwide. E-mail is not time-zone sensitive. You can carry on an e-mail conversation with someone halfway around the world, someone who may very well be sleeping as you reply to his or her mail.

Understanding E-Mail Components

Various standards exist for exchanging e-mail messages between computers. They include the CCITT's X.400 specification, Action Technologies' Message Handling Service (MHS), and Simple Mail Transfer Protocol (SMTP). Electronic mail gateway software exists to convert e-mail messages from one format to another so that e-mail products based on these or other standards can interoperate.

An e-mail product typically has a post office, often located on a file server, that holds mail in transit. An e-mail product provides e-mail client software for DOS, Windows, UNIX, Macintosh, or OS/2. The e-mail client gives you an in basket, an out basket, a text editor for composing mail messages, and typically a wide range of other features. For example, most e-mail products let you attach a binary file (such as a spreadsheet) to an e-mail note. An e-mail product may come with gateway software for converting mail messages to conform to the format expected by other products, and it may also include modem-based communications software for exchanging mail messages with remote post offices (such as those at other offices) or traveling users.

Defining GroupWare

GroupWare extends the concept of e-mail to encompass tasks such as scheduling meetings or sharing information like price lists and project status. You can easily see how networked computers can help people schedule meetings. Each person maintains a calendar of appointments and available times. A person setting up a meeting runs software that coordinates with the calendars of the interested people. The software finds the available times, lets the person schedule the meeting, and, through the network, updates people's calendars to reflect the scheduled meeting. There's one drawback to automating meeting schedules: people don't always keep their desktop (or computerized) calendars current. Microsoft's Schedule +, included with Windows for Workgroups and also now sold separately, is an example of software that can automate the scheduling of meetings.

Organizations often have price lists, product descriptions, or status information that a group of people (salespeople, marketing people, or engineers) needs to share. The information should be current each time one of the group accesses it. If the group is connected to a network, it can use the network to share the information. Products such as Lotus Notes and Microsoft Exchange enable information sharing. An administrator designs the layout of the information and designates the members of the group. Each member uses client software to access and update the shared information, and each person always sees a current view of the information. A person traveling or at a remote site may have a copy of the information for reference purposes, but the client software doesn't allow the copy to become outdated. It connects to the central site periodically and updates the copy to keep it current.

Reaching Out—Intranets and the Internet

The Internet is not a local area network. It's a collection of geographically dispersed networks connected typically by high-speed phone lines and a common set of communications protocols. People use the Internet to send e-mail, transfer files, discuss diverse topics, run computer programs on distant computers, access databases, and provide navigable screens (pages) of information.

The Internet is a public network that nearly anyone with a computer or even just a terminal can connect to. An *intranet*, on the other hand, is a simulacrum of the Internet that exists just within one organization. When a company creates a version of the Internet strictly for internal use, that company has created an intranet.

Understanding Internet Connectivity

Although people almost exclusively use a local area network to share drive letters (or Macintosh folders or UNIX filesystems) and printers, they use the Internet quite differently. Through the TCP/IP communications protocol, people typically do these tasks on the Internet:

- Remotely log on to a computer via TELNET and run programs

- Transfer files to and from remote computers via FTP

- Send and receive e-mail via a person's Internet address

- Read newsgroup messages via a newsreader (NN, TIN, or other reader)

- Find files and resources via ARCHIE, GOPHER, and VERONICA

- Search indexed databases via WAIS

- Navigate the World Wide Web (WWW) via Mosaic or other browser

If people do these tasks on a network within their organization, they're using an intranet. On the Internet, however, they're interacting with a network consisting of millions of computers in countries all over the world, connected by millions of miles of phone lines.

Using Internet Protocols and Software

Because the Internet consists of diverse computers, operating systems, and people, it needs a common, standard set of protocols, interface specifications, and usage guidelines. Computers manufactured by IBM, DEC, Sun, Hewlett-Packard, and many other vendors are part of the Internet. These computers run UNIX, DOS, Windows, System 7 (Macintosh), OS/2, and other operating systems. The people using the Internet typically haven't met each other in person, and are often unaware of the physical location of the computer resources they use. Internet protocols and software utilities are the key to the Internet's ability to function.

Some Internet information travels through asynchronous modems, but much of it passes through high-speed communications lines that directly connect computers through routers and bridges (see Chapter 14, "Building WANs from LANs"). Over each type of link, the Internet Protocol (IP) carries (encapsulates) messages from one computer to the next. The computers use the Domain Name System (DNS), a naming convention that gives each Internet node a name (such as ncsa.uiuc.edu) that equates to a numeric address (such as 192.112.36.5). A person's Internet e-mail address (fred@ncsa.uiuc.edu) uses the DNS to route Internet e-mail.

The Internet Architecture Board (IAB), a group of volunteers who help administer the Internet, meets regularly to approve standards and guidelines for the Internet. Another group of volunteers, the Internet Engineering Task Force (IETF), meets regularly to discuss technical issues and proposed standards. These groups have established standards for many different Internet activities, from how computers can exchange e-mail to how computer software should behave when a communications link breaks.

Ensuring LAN Security

With a LAN, everyone's files are put in one big container. Unless you provide for security and privacy, anyone can look at—and modify—any file. Any user can easily rifle through the electronic desk and personal papers of any other user, including the president of the company. You may want to set up a security system on a LAN for four reasons:

- *Limiting damage:* Perhaps you know one of those butterfingered types who accidentally types *DEL *.** instead of *DIR *.** and then ends up destroying hundreds of files. Someone typing the wrong thing on a LAN can wipe out everyone's files in addition to his or her own.

- *Protecting confidentiality:* If you know that anyone in the company, including the office gossip, can read any of your files at any time, you can't store important files on the LAN. People who would never dream of rifling through the president's desk will nevertheless browse through others' LAN files.

- *Preventing fraud:* If all employees know they have access to the accounting system's accounts payable files, an unscrupulous person may be tempted to tell the computer to issue a check in his or her name.

- *Preventing malicious damage:* If a disgruntled employee has access to all files on the LAN, he or she may corrupt or modify them. By the time someone detects the damage, the company could be in dire financial straits. The capability to share files is a double-edged sword; it also provides the opportunity to corrupt or destroy files.

Using Passwords

Each LAN user identifies himself or herself with a *password*—a secret word known only to that user. Properly used, passwords verify the identity of the person logging on to the LAN. Proper password administration guidelines include encouraging people to use hard-to-guess passwords, change passwords regularly, and keep passwords secret.

Limiting Access

Another key to security is limiting access within the LAN on a directory-by-directory or server-by-server basis. With NetWare, for example, you can give a person the right to open and read files in a directory but restrict him or her from modifying those files. Or you may make an entire directory off-limits. And to protect important files from even your own typing errors, you can mark files as *read only* so that you cannot delete or modify them.

Protecting Data

File servers, like other computers, sometimes fail. Whether the failure is the result of a loss of electrical power or a hard disk crash, you want to minimize the effect of a server failure. Data is important; it represents an investment of time and energy that you don't want to lose. This means that you need to get serious about file backup, data redundancy, and power protection.

File Backup

The method you use to make backup copies of your data depends mostly on how much data you have. Floppy diskettes may do the job on a very small LAN, but in most cases you'll likely use a tape drive and copy files to a magnetic tape cartridge. If data is critically important, you may forego the tape drive and use a *WORM* (write-once-read-many) drive. (A WORM drive has a laser that burns patterns of pits and holes into a glass/plastic disk; such recordings last a very long time.)

No matter what device you use to make backup copies, you should make frequent and regular copies of your data in case something happens to your computer or its data.

If you're the person in your office who makes backup copies, you can choose one of the following approaches depending on how often your data changes, how important it is, and how much work you have to do to reenter it. The approaches follow:

- *Occasional:* You may get by with occasionally copying individual files to one or more floppy disks. This approach is the least secure, but it's better than nothing. Disorganization is your enemy with this approach. If you use this method, make sure to label disks. And if you have to restore a file, you may find that your backup copy isn't as recent as you would like. If this happens, you must redo work done since the backup copy was made. You may even find that the disk containing the backup copy is damaged and you have to redo *all* the work of re-creating the data.

- *Serious:* If you make backup copies regularly (perhaps more often than once a day), if you use a backup utility such as BACKUP.EXE, and if you use two sets of disks (or two tapes) to do backups, you are in this category. You know exactly how much time has elapsed since the last backup copy was made. You know exactly the disks to use to restore a file.

- *Professional:* Data centers with multimillion-dollar mainframe computers use this method, and you can too. Essentially, you always have three copies of data on three sets of disks (or magnetic tapes). To make backup copies, first identify each set of disks as A, B, or C. (For safety's sake, you should actually have two A sets, two B sets, and two C sets.) Rotate the three sets of disks so that if today's backup is labeled C, you have yesterday's backup copies on B and the previous day's on A. Tomorrow use the A set to make backup copies. You may even extend this approach to a fourth set of disks and make sure that the oldest copy is taken *offsite* (to a different location) just in case something happens to the building in which your computer is located. This backup method is sometimes known as the *grandfather/father/son scheme.*

The Data Storage Products Division of the 3M company recommends a 10-tape grandfather/father/son approach for backing up files. Covering 12 weeks, this concept allows you to restore up to three months' worth of files on your computer's hard disk.

3M's scheme suggests a weekly full backup of your computer for three consecutive weeks. Label the backup sets "Week 1," "Week 2," and "Week 3." Throughout the week, do partial backups to store new or changed files. On the fourth week, do another full backup but label it "Month 1." Repeat this for the second month, but label the fourth week's backup set of the month "Month 2." Repeat this for the third month, creating "Month 3." With this approach, you can recover files stored up to three months ago.

No matter how often you back up, label your backup media clearly. One way to avoid mix-ups is to use a different colored label or floppy disk for each day of the week: Monday backups on red, Tuesday backups on blue, and so on. Monthly backups can be kept on black labels or disks. If you back up weekly, you can also follow a color scheme. For example, use a different-color disk for each week of the month and a black disk for the end-of-the-month backup.

The reliability of your backup depends on the cleanliness of your drive's read/write heads. Have these magnetic heads cleaned regularly. Also rotate in fresh tapes to replace older ones, which become brittle over time.

The best backup plan can be thwarted by fire, flood, theft, and other calamities. To assure the best data protection, always keep a backup set offsite, such as in a safe deposit box or at an employee's house.

Storing tapes in a fireproof safe is not always reliable. Although most safes protect papers from scorching in temperatures above 350°, backup tapes can be damaged by this heat. "Media-safe" safes are available, but cost three to four times as much as conventional fire safes.

Data Redundancy

Backup also means redundancy. You're better off with two medium-size file servers than with one giant server. If a file server breaks down, you can get by temporarily with the other server. Of course, you should make the second server part of your backup procedure.

Manufacturers of file server computers recognize the need for data redundancy and offer models that contain *disk arrays*—multiple hard disks that mirror each other. If one hard disk dies, another one carries on without a moment's hesitation. Note that multiple hard disks and multiple servers aren't a substitute for a good file backup procedure.

Power Protection

Power failures happen unexpectedly. Sometimes they happen during a thunderstorm, but they can happen at other times too.

To some extent, nearly all software will corrupt files it's working on at the time of a power failure. For a word processor, this means that you lose what you've keyed in since the last time you saved the file. For an accounting program, it may mean that you lose everything you keyed in since the last time you backed up the files to tape. To protect yourself, place your servers on an uninterruptible power supply (UPS).

On a UPS, if the power fails, batteries keep the server running for another 10 minutes, enough time to shut down the server without losing files. In addition, a UPS isolates the server from spikes and sags in the supply of commercial electrical power. These spikes and sags may reboot a computer or cause it to malfunction temporarily. Such spikes or sags can cause just as many problems as a full-fledged blackout. Sometimes very large spikes permanently damage a computer. When commercial power fails, a UPS can tell the network operating system to close down the files without human intervention.

You can use a lower-cost standby power supply (SPS) to protect equipment from blackouts, along with a power-line filter to help remove spikes and electrical noise from the supply of commercial power. By itself, however, an SPS does not protect you from spikes and sags.

Asking for Help

If you buy a lemon computer, you will be out at most a few thousand dollars. If you buy a lemon LAN, you may be out tens of thousands of dollars—or more. Even if you buy a first-class LAN, you may buy one that's too complex or that cannot grow with your organization. You may wind up throwing it out and starting all over again. Even if you feel confident enough to choose a LAN on your own, it may be wise to hire someone with experience for just a few hours to verify your plans. The expert also may be able to warn you of costs you forgot to budget.

Installing a LAN can be a humbling experience. Although you need to understand adapter card jumpers, I/O addresses, upper memory blocks, IRQs, page frames, and other esoteric things, most of the work of installing a LAN consists of resolving conflicts between LAN hardware and hardware already installed.

Chapter Summary

You now have a solid understanding of local area networks. You know what a LAN can do, and you know the components of a LAN—workstations, file servers, cables, network adapter cards, and the all-important network operating system. You see security in a new light, and you realize the importance of making backup copies of the information on the LAN. You know why you need an uninterruptible power supply for the file server, and you have some guidelines for when you should ask for advice from an expert. You're well on your way to becoming a LAN expert yourself.

In the next chapter, you'll learn more about sharing disks, printers, CD-ROM drives, modems, fax machines, applications, and application data files on a LAN.

Chapter 2

Sharing Computer Resources

The sharing of computer resources—disks, printers, files, and devices—is the bread and butter of local area networks. Networks come in many sizes, and you can find a configuration to fit virtually every networking situation. You may have two computers that need to share only a single printer. You may have thousands of computers that need to share huge files at the same time that they access on a mainframe computer. Or, more than likely, the combination of computers and devices you want to share is something between these two extremes. In this chapter, you'll find a network that fits your particular needs. You'll see how networks can be configured in a wide variety of ways to solve connectivity problems.

The most popular shared resource is a disk drive, and this chapter begins by explaining the different ways you can share a disk between several computers and people. After you explore the sharing of disks and disk space, you'll move on to printer sharing. From a simple printer switchbox to an array of print servers on a LAN, you'll learn how different printer sharing options enable you to send printouts to a remote printer. You'll discover why you need to be a good neighbor as you use the communal printer.

This chapter then tells how you can share a CD-ROM drive on a network. CD-ROMs require special consideration for successful sharing. And speaking of special considerations, would you like to be able to share a fax machine on your LAN? You can.

Connecting one or more modems to your LAN so that you can share access to other computers (a bulletin board system, a host computer, information system, or the Internet) is the area you'll explore next. Finally, this chapter explains options for communications in the other direction—when remote users want to use your LAN as if they were in the office.

Sharing Disks and Files

Disk-sharing options range from simple PC-to-PC file transfer utilities such as LapLink or Brooklyn Bridge to multiple-server configurations of NetWare and Windows NT Server networks that include Apple Macintosh and UNIX computers alongside the ubiquitous IBM PC and clones. In the next few sections of this book, you'll explore this wide range of options.

Sharing Files Without a LAN

If you want to connect two computers temporarily so that you can copy a few files from one to the other, establishing a simple serial link between the computers does the job nicely. Figure 2.1 shows such a serial link between two PCs. Using the modem port (often labelled *RS-232*, *Serial*, or *COM*) or perhaps the parallel (printer or LPT) port on each computer, products like the following enable you to copy directories and files selected from a menu:

LapLink	"Brooklyn Bridge"
Traveling Software	Symantec Corp.
18702 N. Creek Parkway	10201 Torre Ave.
Bothell WA 98011	Cupertino CA 95014
(800) 662-2652	(800) 441-7234
	(503) 345-3322
	fax: (503) 334-7474

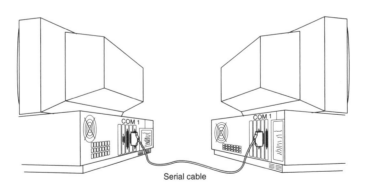

Serial cable

Fig. 2.1   Strictly speaking, a serial link between two computers can let them share files but the link doesn't constitute a LAN.

The software creates directories on the target computer as necessary. If you're transferring several megabytes of files, plan to do something else for a while after you start the transfer. This method of copying files is slow.

Peer-to-Peer Networks

To connect a small group of computers permanently, you need more than a simple file-transfer utility. When you tie computers together on more than a temporary basis, you step up to the first level of local area networks. At this first level, you don't need to set aside a personal computer to act as a file server. In fact, all the computers can be file servers and workstations at the same time; this is called a *peer LAN*. Figure 2.2 depicts a peer LAN environment, in which three desktop computers each act as both file servers and workstations. In a peer LAN, the disk space and files on your computer become communal property. At first it can be unnerving to be working at your computer and see the hard disk activity indicator light blinking as someone else accesses your disk and its files. Or you may be annoyed to find that your computer is slower than usual because you're sharing its resources. Peer LANs, however, are cost-effective for small, lightly loaded networks. And peer LANs have the advantage that users don't have to remember to copy files from their computers to a separate file server for other people to access. Depending on how you set up security, others may be able to access files immediately after you create them.

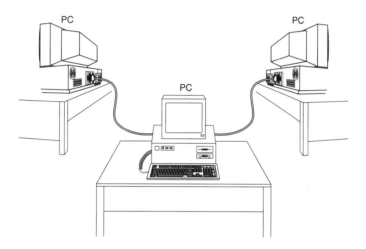

Fig. 2.2 In a peer LAN, computers act as both servers and workstations.

A list of peer LAN products, along with the companies that offer them, follows:

10NetPlus
Digital Communications Associates Inc.
7887 Washington Village Drive
Dayton OH 45459
(800) 358-1010

AppleTalk
Apple Computer
20525 Mariani Avenue
Cupertino CA 95014
(408) 996-1010

EasyNet
LanMark
P.O. Box 246
Postal Station A
Mississauga Ontario
Canada L5A 3G8
(416) 848-6865

GV LAN OS
Grapevine LAN Products
15323 Northeast 90th Street
Redmond WA 98052
(206) 869-2707

LANsmart
D-Link Systems
5 Musick
Irvine CA 92718
(714) 455-1688

LANsoft
ACCTON Technology
46750 Fremont Boulevard
Suite 104
Fremont CA 94538
(415) 226-9800

LANStep
Hayes Microcomputer Products
P.O. Box 105203
Atlanta GA 30348
(404) 441-1617

LANtastic
Artisoft
575 East River Road
Tucson AZ 85704
(602) 293-6363

NET/30
Invisible Software
1165 Chess Drive
Suite D
Foster City CA 94404
(415) 570-5967

Personal NetWare
Novell
122 East 1700 South
Provo UT 84606
(800) 453-1267

Network OSCBIS
5875 Peachtree Industrial Boulevard
Building 100, Unit 170
Norcross GA 30092
(404) 446-1332

POWERLan
Performance Technology
7800 IH 10, W.
800 Lincoln Center
San Antonio TX 78230
(512) 524-0500
(512) 349-2000

ReadyLink
Compex
4055 East La Palma Avenue
Suite C
Anaheim CA 92807
(714) 630-7302

OS/2 Warp
IBM Corporation
One Old Orchard Road
Armonk, NY 10504
(800) 342-6672

WEB
WebCorp
3000 Bridgeway
Sausalito CA 94965
(415) 331-1449

Windows for Workgroups
Windows 95
Microsoft Corporation
One Microsoft Way
Redmond WA 98052
(800) 426-9400

Using Your PC as a Workstation and Server. A peer LAN makes individual computers on the network work much harder than they ordinarily do. Most peer LAN network operating systems are DOS-based, which means that the network software has to use DOS to access the hard disk, just as the applications do. When another user on the LAN runs an application that reads or writes files located on your hard disk, the network operating system steps in and takes momentary control of your computer. After satisfying the other user's file request, the network operating system relinquishes control to the application. With a small file, you may not even notice that your hard disk has been accessed. If the file is large, however, DOS may take several minutes to locate all its portions. DOS is quite slow on large files.

When you start a computer that is a workstation and a server, DOS loads and then the network software loads. Usually the network operating system is one or more TSRs (terminate-and-stay-resident programs). Unless you have an 80386 computer and memory manager software, the network TSRs take up part of the 640KB of conventional memory. You therefore have somewhat less RAM in which to run applications. Memory usage can range from as little as 0KB if you use a memory manager, to as much as 60KB to 110KB of RAM if the network software must use a portion of the 640KB.

On a network, you want to make sure that the SHARE.EXE program loads automatically at all computers. SHARE, which comes with DOS (not with the network operating system), enables file sharing on your computer. If SHARE isn't loaded, you may find that files become strangely corrupted. Chapter 5, "Using Workstations," discusses SHARE.EXE in more detail.

Allowing Others to Access Your Computer. The network operating system enables you to assign names to your disk drives. Then you make these names known to the other users, who use networking commands such as NET USE to access the disks. You can automate this process by putting the networking commands in the AUTOEXEC.BAT files for the computers on the network. If you do this, the network starts up automatically when you power on all the computers.

What happens if you reboot your computer while another user is accessing it? Peer LAN network operating systems do the best they can with such a situation. If you press Ctrl+Alt+Del, the network operating system asks if you're sure you want to reboot. If you answer Yes, the NOS closes any files that other workstations have open, notifies other workstations that the server (which is your computer) is no longer available, and enables the reboot to occur. If you use the power switch to reboot the computer, however, the network operating system has no warning. Another user on the network may be writing a file to your hard disk at that very moment. The power interruption may very well cause that user's file to become corrupted, and you may have to run the DOS CHKDSK or ScanDisk utilities to repair the damage when you power back on. Such utilities probably won't be able to salvage all of the data. The other user will have to redo some or all of his work.

Managing Disk Space. On a peer LAN, other people can use your hard disk as if it were their own. If you don't establish procedures and guidelines for disk space usage, these people can use up your disk space rapidly. You should definitely have procedures in your office for periodic housecleaning.

You can avoid the problem to some degree if you tell DOS to format your hard disk into more than one partition. The extra partition will become a new DOS drive letter (D:, for example). You can publish an alias for just that new drive letter and keep drive C: for your own use. You should, of course, back up all the files on your computer before you run the DOS FORMAT and FDISK commands.

Note that if you simply establish separate directories on the hard disk for public use, you cannot limit disk space usage. One directory can hold files that take up an entire disk.

Backing Up and Restoring Peer LAN Files. Even if people stick to their own hard disks and use the peer LAN lightly or not at all to share files, the network can be the basis for a centralized backup procedure. From one workstation, you can make backup copies of files on all other workstations. Of course, you want to implement the professional file backup scheme mentioned in Chapter 1, "A Networking Overview."

Note that you must publish—and connect to—all the drives on all the computers to do a thorough backup. And note that the workstation performing the backup (the one to which the tape drive is attached) must have permission to access all files in all subdirectories that you want to back up.

Handling Security and Administration on a Peer LAN. Most peer LANs implement security in two ways. First, a network administrator assigns account IDs (sometimes called user IDs) to the computer users on the network. The administrator also sets up passwords for new accounts, but each person can change his or her password to a secret combination of letters and numbers later. To use the LAN, a person logs in by typing the account ID and the password. As it is typed, the password doesn't appear on-screen. Account IDs and passwords ensure that only authorized people use the LAN, and they verify each person's identity so that each person can be given different access rights or permissions on the network.

The second means of providing security is by assigning permissions. Some peer LAN products use default permissions for new account IDs; these enable a user to access everything on the network. The administrator must then specifically name each drive letter (alias) or directory that the new user shouldn't access. Other peer LANs use default permissions that deny a new user any and all access to the LAN, and the administrator must specifically name each drive letter or directory that the new user *can* access. Either way, network administrators are busy people in organizations with a high turnover rate.

A special account ID typically exists to identify the network administrator. This special account ID sometimes is named "Supervisor" or "Manager." Anyone who logs in with this account ID can delete not only files but also other account IDs. The password for this special account ID should be kept highly secret.

The network administrator is responsible for setting up new accounts, deleting old accounts, publishing new aliases for drive letters, and generally troubleshooting all problems. The wise administrator sets up generalized BAT files that can be installed on all workstations to automate much of the access to the network. And he or she keeps handy a special boot diskette containing network software in case a user accidentally renders a workstation unusable.

Server-Based LANs

In contrast to peer LANs, server-based LANs offer better performance and increased reliability. Your first step up from a pure peer LAN environment is to dedicate one computer on the network as a file server and to use the same peer LAN network operating system product to have a server-based LAN. (You should read the license agreement for the peer LAN network operating system to see if you need to pay a different license fee for the software in this situation.)

Naturally, using a peer LAN computer as a dedicated file server means that DOS is still in charge of the files on the server. To go beyond DOS-based LANs, you must take yet another step up. Network operating systems such as Novell NetWare install themselves into the file server and replace DOS entirely. By managing the computer completely as a file server and by organizing the disk in a way that performs well for large files (which DOS cannot do), dedicated server-based network operating systems enable LANs to be larger and to do more work. Figure 2.3 illustrates a server-based LAN. Notice in the figure that the file server is the central resource on the LAN that the other PCs (or workstations) access.

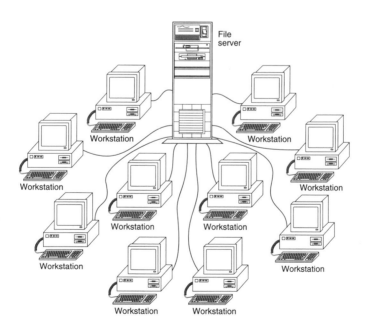

Fig. 2.3   Workstations share files located on a file server on a server-based LAN.

I

Understanding Networks

A list of dedicated-server LAN products, followed by the companies that offer them, follows:

AppleTalk
Apple Computer
20525 Mariani Avenue
Cupertino CA 95014
(408) 996-1010

NetWare
Novell, Inc.
122 East 1700 South
Provo UT 84606
(800) 453-1267

Windows NT Server
Microsoft Corporation
One Microsoft Way
Redmond WA 98052
(800) 426-9400

VINES
Banyan Systems
120 Flanders Road
Westborough MA 01581
(508) 898-1000

Warp Server
IBM Corporation
1 Old Orchard Road
Armonk NY 10504
(800) 342-6672

Using Your Workstation. As you read in Chapter 1, there are four major differences between a stand-alone computer and a computer functioning as a workstation on a LAN. Operating from a LAN, you see extra messages at boot time, you have to use a login process to access the LAN, you have extra drive letters that represent the disk drive(s) on the file server(s), and you can send printouts to a remote printer. You see these differences whether you're on a peer LAN or a server-based LAN.

On a server-based LAN, however, you don't have to share the hard disk on your workstation with other people. In fact, to share a file with someone, you must copy the file to a file server (or create it on the server to begin with) before the other person can access it. You can reboot your workstation without worrying about destroying someone's files. And the disk space on your local hard disk is yours to administer.

Managing Disk Space. Managing the disk space on the file server is another matter. On most server-based networks, a network administrator has tools for controlling disk space usage. On a NetWare LAN, for example, the administrator (supervisor) can limit users to a certain number of megabytes of space. The administrator can easily get reports of disk space usage by account ID. If the administrator needs to, he or she even can use NetWare's built-in accounting system to "charge" for disk space. (In practice, this is rarely done.)

Typically, each user has a directory on the file server, with the account ID as the name of the directory. The user has all rights to this directory and can share files with others by granting them the right to see, open, and read files. These rights may even be the default ones set up by the network administrator as each new account ID is created.

Suppose you're starting a special project with a team at work. The network administrator may create a special directory for you and give the entire team all rights to the directory—rights to see, create, read, write, and delete files as well as to create directories within the project directory.

Backing Up and Restoring Files. The network administrator usually takes care of backing up and restoring files for the entire network. Because server-based networks can be quite large, both in terms of number of users and volume of files, the backup procedure almost certainly falls into the professional category mentioned in Chapter 1. In fact, the LAN may have a computer with the sole purpose of making backup copies of file server files. Such a machine is a *backup server*.

A tape drive that uses 120MB tapes will be out of its league on a large server-based network. On large networks, gigabyte tape drives are more the norm. These companies have products especially for large networks:

Emerald
12230 World Trade Drive
San Diego CA 92128
(619) 673-2161

Irwin Magnetic Systems
(a subsidiary of Archive Corporation)
2101 Commonwealth Boulevard
Ann Arbor MI 48105
(800) 421-1879

Mountain Network Solutions
240 East Hacienda Avenue
Campbell CA 95008
(408) 379-4300

Palindrome
850 Diehl Road
Naperville IL 60563
(708) 505-3300

Palindrome's The Network Archivist (TNA), for example, tracks the last time a file was accessed. If disk space gets low and if a file isn't accessed in a long while, TNA will (at the network administrator's option) delete the old file but leave a marker in its place. If a user accesses the file marker, TNA alerts the network administrator to mount the tape containing the file so the file can be restored to the file server.

Many backup and restore products can even help the network administrator manage the hidden files containing account IDs, passwords, and other network-specific data.

Using Faster, Larger Disks. Network disk drives and old closets have something in common. They tend to fill up rapidly, and they never seem large enough. On a server-based network, large, heavy-duty disk drives are more the rule than the exception. Many companies make disk drives, and almost all of them work just fine on a server-based network. Companies that specialize in larger, sturdier file server disk drives offer additional features such as redundancy (see the discussion on RAID in the next chapter) to accommodate the file server environment.

Handling Security and Administrative Issues. On a peer LAN, the position of network administrator may be a part-time job. On a large server-based LAN, however, the network administrator position may be filled by one, two, or more full-time people. Almost every activity of such an administrator is related to seeing that the resources of the LAN are shared fairly and productively.

In addition to setting up new account IDs (and deleting old ones), an administrator uses his or her supervisory privileges to create new directories as necessary, monitor usage of disk space, make occasional LAN configuration changes, and help people who are having trouble.

Server-based LANs use basically the same approach to security as peer LANs—account IDs, passwords, and permissions—but in a more sophisticated way. The administrator has more flexibility regarding the sharing of LAN resources. On a NetWare LAN, for example, the administrator can assign a greater variety of permissions (rights) among users of the LAN.

Disk space is only one resource a LAN can share—although clearly it is the most important. The next most popular shared LAN device is the printer.

Sharing Printers

In the simplest cases when you need to share a printer among a few computers but you don't want to share files, you don't need a LAN at all; a printer switchbox suffices. At the opposite extreme, you may have multipart forms, address labels, word processing documents, and thousands of pages of reports to print, all produced by dozens of computer users. In this case, you definitely need a LAN. You even may dedicate one or more computers on the LAN to keeping the printers busy.

Using Printer Switchboxes

You can share a single printer among two or three computers quite easily without setting up a LAN. As long as you don't need to share any other computer resource besides the printer, you can install a printer switchbox. The simplest such switchbox is called an A/B Box because a computer user who needs to use the printer just reaches over to the box to flip a switch from the A position to the B position. The switchbox has two or more ports for incoming parallel printer cables from the computers, and it has one outgoing port for the cable to the printer. Figure 2.4 shows three PCs that print to a single printer through a printer switchbox. As a variation on this theme, you can purchase a switchbox that attempts to detect which computer wants to use the printer. As you may expect, when two computers try to print simultaneously, such automatic devices don't always guess correctly which characters go on which page.

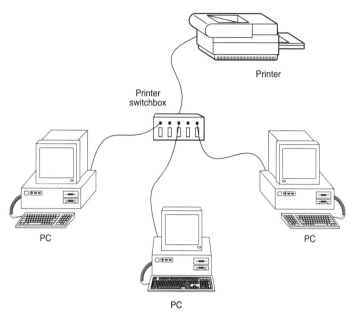

Fig. 2.4 Computers can share a printer through a printer switchbox, but the arrangement is not a LAN.

Using Print Servers

On a peer LAN, your computer can simultaneously be a workstation, a file server, and a print server. A print server, as its name implies, is a computer with an attached printer that shares the printer with other workstations on the LAN. If you find yourself the keeper of the office's printer simply because it's attached to your peer LAN workstation/ server, you become a part-time printer attendant. You clear paper jams, load fresh supplies of paper, change ribbons or toner cartridges, and stack printed pages on a table for others to retrieve. Your workstation performs more slowly because it spends time printing for other people. If this happens to you and the printer is used a great deal, you may suggest that the office arrange a separate, dedicated computer—and an official part-time printer attendant—to take care of the printer.

The separate print server computer can also be a file server. Both peer LANs and server-based LANs can be set up this way. A file server can handle light to occasionally moderate printing chores without affecting its ability to serve files to the workstations on the LAN.

For moderate to heavy printer usage, your LAN needs a dedicated print server. This is especially true if you have more than one printer or if you have a high-speed laser printer (such as the Hewlett-Packard IVsi). Figure 2.5 illustrates a print server PC whose sole purpose is driving a shared network printer.

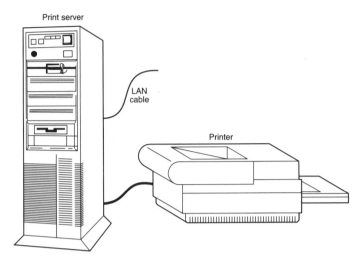

Fig. 2.5 A print server is a computer sharing its printer through a LAN cable with workstations on that LAN.

Redirecting Printouts

Whether or not your print server is dedicated, printing to the network printer is a matter of telling the network software to redirect printouts across the network. With some networks, you issue a NET USE command to accomplish this. On a NetWare LAN, you issue the CAPTURE command.

A personal computer can have up to three printer ports, named LPT1, LPT2, and LPT3. If more than one network printer exists, the NET USE or CAPTURE command can associate these DOS printer port names with different network printers. The system administrator publishes a list of available printers and the printers' alias names. After you set up LPT1, LPT2, and LPT3 to redirect printouts to particular network printers, you simply tell the application software which printer port (and therefore which printer) to use.

Using Laser Printers

Laser printers are fast, heavy-duty, feature-laden devices. They lend themselves to LAN environments because of their speed and versatility. One person may print a memo on the network printer, the next person may print a wide, sideways (*landscape mode*) report or chart, and the third person's print job may consist of a *portrait mode* (upright page orientation) newsletter containing a great number of typefaces (*fonts*). The same printer produces all these printouts fairly quickly without breaking stride.

Page-Per-Minute Ratings. Printer manufacturers rate laser printer speed in terms of pages per minute. The rating is a best-case average; pages containing picture images or many fonts print more slowly. Hewlett-Packard rates its LaserJet IIP printer at 4 pages per minute and the IIIsi at 17 pages per minute. Xerox rates its model 4045 printer at 6 pages per minute and its model 3700 at 24 pages per minute. As you consider the printer to be shared on the LAN, you should conservatively count on actually producing fewer pages per minute, depending on whether you print plain-paper reports (fast) or multiple-font-and-image newsletters (slow).

Duty Cycles. After a laser printer prints about 6,000 pages, the toner cartridge should be changed or the toner compartment refilled. At 100,000 pages (depending on the printer) you may need to return the printer to the factory to be overhauled; a technically oriented employee, service technician, or repair depot may also handle such matters for you. In addition to these limitations, the laser printer needs to rest periodically. A laser printer cannot print continuously 24 hours a day. The period of time the printer can operate without stopping is its *duty cycle,* usually expressed in terms of pages per month. The Hewlett-Packard IIIsi, for example, has a duty cycle of 50,000 pages per month. If you have high-volume print requirements in your office, make sure that you investigate the duty cycle of a printer before you buy it. Because many people share the printer on a LAN, duty cycle and page-per-minute ratings become considerations you may not otherwise need to worry about.

Font Cartridges and Downloadable Fonts. Fonts of different sizes and styles are popular add-ons for laser printers. People like to choose just the right font to make printouts look good. Fonts are available as files that can be downloaded into the printer from a computer and also as cartridges to be inserted into the printer.

On LANs with many users, the number of fonts everyone wants to use may exceed the number supported by the laser printer. You may be able simply to put more RAM into the laser printer, but at some point you should establish guidelines in your office for fonts that are available in the network printer. You should also establish procedures for re-downloading the fonts into the printer in case someone powers off the printer (to clear a paper jam, for example).

Using Dot-Matrix and Other Printers

Because they usually have variable-width paper carriages and pin-feed paper movement mechanisms, dot-matrix printers are excellent for preprinted forms, multipart forms, and address labels. But the process of aligning forms, which isn't always done easily with a locally attached printer, becomes even more of a chore with a remote network printer. You may even find that you have to print a form, go to the printer to make adjustments, and then repeat the process if further alignment is called for.

Dot-matrix printers also have rated speeds and duty cycles.

Practicing Printer-Sharing Etiquette

Unless your office is large enough to warrant hiring a printer operator, sharing a network printer means that each person needs to be a good neighbor so that everyone gets fair use from the printer. When you retrieve a printout, you may discover that the printer is having trouble. The printer may be out of paper, or the paper may have jammed inside the printer. The output tray may be full. The printer may need a new toner cartridge (or a new ribbon). But if everyone in an office agrees to maintain the printer and is taught how to do so, printing can be reliable, fast, and trouble-free.

If you must turn off the printer and then turn it back on again, you may need to download the fonts on the printer again.

You can be a good neighbor in the way you print your output, too. The printer knows the last font it used and, unless told otherwise, continues to use that font for other print jobs. One person may walk away from the printer with a perfectly formatted, sideways-printed, small-font spreadsheet report. The next person, who simply wants to print a plain-paper status report or memo, sighs in disgust to find that the report or memo resembles a spreadsheet. Even on a dot-matrix printer, the way you tear off the last form affects the next person. For the sake of courtesy, leave forms and labels in an aligned state—and reset the fonts to default after you print.

Sharing CD-ROM Drives

CD-ROM drives are popular add-ons for stand-alone personal computers. Naturally, people on a LAN also want to share them. Your LAN may use CD-ROMs containing generally published material such as encyclopedia, dictionary, and almanac information. Or it may use CD-ROM disks containing specialized data particular to your business. On many LANs you can share information via CD-ROM, making access easy for everyone.

Several companies make CD-ROM drives, including Sony, Pioneer, Hitachi, Panasonic, Chinon, and Toshiba. In addition, companies including IBM, Storage Dimensions, Corel, and Racet offer read/write optical drives. A write-once-read-many (WORM) drive, such as the one made by Storage Dimensions, makes a good backup device on a LAN. All these drives use a laser or a laser with magnetism to record data.

Realizing That CD-ROMs Need Special Software

CD-ROMs and other optical drives use an internal data format unlike the format of DOS-based disks or even NetWare file server disks. You need special device drivers that understand this data format, which is sometimes called *High Sierra* but is more formally known as *ISO 9960*.

On stand-alone computers and most peer LANs, you can use the MSCDEX drivers written by Microsoft to understand ISO 9960 data format. These drivers come bundled with all CD-ROM drives. You can obtain a CD-ROM driver from your CD-ROM manufacturer so that you can share a CD-ROM drive on an OS/2 Warp Server or NT Server network. On NetWare version 3 LANs, your options are more limited (it's difficult to make NetWare recognize ISO 9960 format disks). NetWare 4, however, supports the sharing of CD-ROM drives.

Using Optical Drives and Your LAN

CD-ROMs and other read-only optical media hold hundreds of megabytes of data in prerecorded, permanent form (usually about 680MB). WORM disk cartridges are empty when you buy them, but once files are stored on them, the recorded information is etched there permanently. WORM disks typically are guaranteed for 10 years. (These are good reasons to use a WORM drive as a LAN backup device.) A WORM cartridge might hold 800MB (400MB on each side).

A read/write optical drive, on the other hand, behaves like an ordinary disk drive in an important way: you can read and write data on the disk. You can think of a read/write optical drive, such as IOMega's ZIP drives or IBM's 3.5-inch, 128MB drive, as a fast, very high capacity floppy diskette drive. Like a floppy diskette, the R/W optical disk cartridge is easily removed from the drive; you can implement an extra level of security by storing the disk in a safe place when the data isn't in use.

CD-ROM, WORM, and read/write optical media are slower than a personal computer hard disk. You can use them to enhance your LAN but don't use them as a primary means of storing LAN data.

Using Modems and LAN Communications

On a LAN, communication is a two-way street. You can configure your LAN so that people can reach out to other computers from your LAN (the Internet, bulletin board systems, a commercial information service such as Prodigy, CompuServe, or Dow/Jones, or a host computer). And you can set things up so that people outside your office can access your LAN remotely through a communications link.

Occasionally Dialing Out

Perhaps your office needs to share only a modem for occasionally dialing into another computer system. If this is the case, a simple RS/232 switchbox may suffice. An RS/232 switchbox operates like the printer switchbox discussed earlier. Several serial cables lead from each of the personal computers (or workstations; they may be part of a LAN) to the switchbox. A single serial cable connects the switchbox to the modem. When a person wants to use the modem, he or she goes to the switchbox, sets the switch to his or her computer, and uses the modem.

Frequently Dialing Out (Modem Pooling)

If users on a LAN need to access modems more than occasionally, you can establish a pool of modems and use a communications server device from a company such as these:

Cubix
2800 Lockheed Way
Carson City NV 89706
(800) 829-0550

J&L Information Systems
9238 Deering Avenue
Chatsworth CA 91311
(818) 709-1778

Network Products Corporation
1111 South Arroyo Parkway
Suite 450
Pasadena CA 91105
(800) 638-7765

Or you can use a server device from another communications equipment vendor. Such a device connects to your LAN and enables several people to share modems or communications lines to a host computer.

Connecting Through a Gateway Computer

Another option for handling outgoing communications from the LAN is the dedicated *gateway computer*. The gateway computer attaches to a host computer and handles multiple communications sessions at the same time. A person at a workstation runs software that uses one of those sessions. People at other workstations simultaneously use other sessions. Each workstation's software makes it look as if that person's computer is attached directly to the host, but the communications data actually is routed through one of the gateway computer's sessions. Figure 2.6 shows conceptually how each workstation on the LAN can have a host session via a gateway.

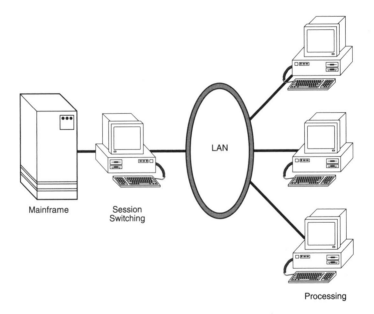

Fig. 2.6 Several LAN workstations can have host sessions through the gateway computer at the same time.

Several companies make gateway software and hardware products:

Attachmate
13231 Southeast 36th Street
Bellevue WA 98006
(800) 426-6283

Digital Communications Associates
1000 Alderman Drive
Alpharetta GA 30201
(800) 241-4762

Eicon Technology
2196 32nd Avenue
Montreal Canada H8T 3H7
631-2592

Gateway Communications
2941 Alton Avenue
Irvine CA 92714
(800) 367-6555

Novell, Inc.
122 East 1700 South
Provo UT 84606
(800) 453-1267

Wall Data
17769 Northeast 78th Place
Redmond WA 98052
(800) 433-3388

Dialing into the LAN

The simplest way to enable remote LAN access is to use remote-control software. The remote user runs one copy of the software on his or her computer; a workstation on the LAN, with a modem attached, runs another copy. The remote user controls the workstation computer remotely, from his or her remote computer. The mirroring of screen and keyboard activity makes the remote user think he or she is logged into the LAN directly. In reality, the LAN workstation does all the work.

The remote-control approach is simple, but it has drawbacks. While the remote user is communicating through the LAN workstation, that workstation cannot be used by anyone else. If the modem is slow, the remote user experiences slow response time. The remote PC becomes merely a terminal mirroring the screen and keyboard activity of the LAN-attached computer. If an application changes the appearance of the screen frequently or if the application uses graphics rather than text (as does Microsoft Windows), a remote-control product is hard-pressed to keep up with the activity.

The following list contains some remote-control software products, along with the companies that offer them:

Carbon Copy
Microcom
500 River Ridge Drive
Norwood MA 02062
(617) 551-1000

Close-Up
Norton-Lambert
P.O. Box 4085
Santa Barbara CA 93140
(805) 964-6767

NETremote
Brightwork Development
766 Shrewsbury Avenue
Jerral Center West
Tinton Falls NJ 07724
(800) 552-9876

PCAnywhere
Symantec Corporation
10201 Torre Ave.
Cupertino, CA 95014
(800) 441-7234

Accessing Remote LANs Frequently

When you're out of the office regularly, either traveling or working at a different location, you want to be able to access the LAN at the office quickly and reliably. Distance limitations won't let you string a LAN cable between your location and the main office; you need to use a modem to connect to the LAN.

There are several alternatives for logging in to the LAN from a remote site. You can use a generalized remote-control product such as Microcom's Carbon Copy; you can use a special LAN remote-control product such as Novell's Access Server; you can buy a LAN-aware modem such as the Shiva NetModem-E; or you might get Remote LAN Node from Digital Communications Associates (DCA). CUBIX also makes an effective product implementing remote access to the LAN. Figure 2.7 shows a PC in a remote office connected via a telephone line to the LAN in the central office; the modems, modem server, and remote LAN software make the remote PC appear as just another workstation on the LAN. Modems are slower than LANs, however, and the remote PC can't access shared LAN files as quickly as can a workstation directly attached to the LAN.

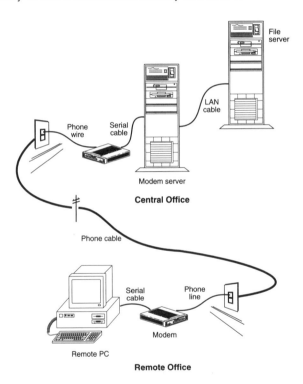

Fig. 2.7 People on business trips can connect to the LAN in the central office through modems and special software.

Generalized remote control software works by echoing keypresses and screen images across the phone line. What you type gets played back by a computer in the office. The screen images that appear on that computer also appear on your remote PC. You need one PC in the office with its own modem for each remote control session. Performance can be sluggish as the remote control software shuttles screen image updates to you. Running Microsoft Windows through a remote control product can also be painfully slow.

A LAN-aware modem eliminates the "smoke and mirrors" to let you actually become a node on the network from your remote site. The LAN-aware modem extends the LAN to you, despite the distance between you and the LAN. Two disadvantages to a LAN-aware modem are that you cannot use existing modems and you're usually limited to the network operating systems supported by the modem. The Shiva NetModem-E, for example, supports only NetWare and AppleTalk.

Novell's Access Server, a popular LAN-based remote-control product, consists of software and special communications adapter boards. You supply an 80386 or faster computer with 8MB to 16MB of RAM. Once installed, Access Server can manage several simultaneous communications sessions with remote users. Each user can use a small part of the Access Server computer. Unlike other workstations, the Access Server computer can perform multiple logins to the LAN, one for each remote user. The applications that are actually run by the remote user execute inside the Access Server computer.

Access Server takes the remote-control design one step further by multi-tasking several mirrored sessions inside the central Access Server PC. From your remote site, you control one session inside the Access Server computer. You can log into an Access Server computer from a VT220 or other terminal or with communications software such as Procomm Plus. With the remote control approach of Carbon Copy or Access Server, transferring files from your remote PC to the file server at the office can be problematic. Your remote PC is only a mirror of the processing occurring in the PC at the office. You can't run Microsoft Windows with Access Server, but you can use Access Server to dial into a NetWare LAN from even a dumb terminal. Access Server works only with NetWare LANs.

Like Access Server, Remote LAN Node from DCA requires a dedicated PC on a network. RLN doesn't work through remote control, though; RLN on the dedicated PC acts as a LAN bridge to give you the same kind of LAN connection as the other, locally attached nodes on the network. Your personal computer does the computational work. File service packets travel across the phone line to give you access to the remote file server. RLN is like a LAN-aware modem in this respect. The RLN server becomes a multi-port LAN bridge that negotiates and distributes virtual network addresses to remote clients.

The RLN server, itself a normal Ethernet node, forwards file request packets from your remote PC to the file server. Because the RLN server contains a single Ethernet card, RLN makes the file server believe that the requests come from the RLN server when in fact they originate in your remote PC. RLN supports a wide variety of network protocols and network operating systems but only through Ethernet cards. You can use Network Driver Interface Specification (NDIS) or Open Datalink Interface (ODI) drivers supplied with RLN to connect to NetWare, UNIX, Banyan, Warp Server, or NT Server networks.

RLN's menu-driven installation and well-written documentation make quick work of getting RLN up and running. Configuration is a simple matter of specifying phone numbers, COM port usage, baud rate, and other communications parameters. On a client PC, the Remote LAN Node TSR takes up 55,872 bytes of RAM, and you can load RLN into high memory with 386MAX.

Performance depends primarily on the speed of the modems used with RLN. Remote LAN Node works with Hayes-compatible modems at speeds from 1,200 baud to 38,400 baud (if the remote workstation and RLN server PCs can handle the higher data rate, of course). At present RLN doesn't work across X.25 links. MNP5 data-compressing modems help performance, and RLN itself implements compression at the packet level.

Because your RLN client workstation is essentially just another node on the LAN, you can copy files to and from the file server with the DOS copy command. To do the same thing with remote control software such as Carbon Copy, PC Anywhere, or Access Server, you must invoke a special mode of the RC software and issue non-DOS commands.

Once you log in to the LAN, your access to the file server and shared network printers becomes almost completely transparent. If you're a Windows user, note that Remote LAN Node modifies SYSTEM.INI and WIN.INI files to load Windows drivers that improve performance of the communications link while Windows is active. The Windows executables, data files, and most certainly the swap file should reside on your local hard disk. You wouldn't want to load these Windows files across a modem-based communications link.

Connecting LANs—Wide Area Networks

Even a multiple-user, dial-in facility like Access Server may not be enough in some cases. If you want a permanent connection between two geographically distant LANs, you need to create a Wide Area Network (WAN) through a *bridge* or a *router*. Chapter 14, "Building WANs from LANs," discusses bridges, routers, high-speed phone links, and wide area networks in detail.

A bridge connects two LANs; each LAN may use a different protocol. You can install a bridge between an EtherNet LAN and a Token Ring LAN, for example. The bridge transfers workstation and file server messages from one LAN to the next, as appropriate. The transfer may take place over phone lines, through modems. Naturally, the speed at which the modems operate governs response times experienced by users on one LAN who access the other LAN. In contrast to a bridge, a router shuttles workstation and file server LAN messages between LANs that use the same protocol (Ethernet-to-Ethernet, or Token Ring-to-Token Ring).

Companies that make LAN bridges and routers include Andrew Corporation, Microcom, Cisco, 3COM, Cabletron, and Bay Networks.

Sharing Fax Machines

Fax machines are essential tools in offices today, just as networks are. Combining the two makes an interesting marriage of technologies.

If you don't have a LAN-based fax server, you typically take these steps to send a document by fax:

- You use a word processor or perhaps other application software to prepare the document to be sent by fax.

- You print out the document pages and fill out a fax cover page.

- At the fax machine, you punch in the telephone number and send the document.

When the fax machine prints an incoming document addressed to you, someone in the office may drop it off at your desk, or you may have to visit the fax machine periodically to retrieve fax correspondence.

A LAN-based fax server saves both steps and paper. You can send fax documents directly from your workstation without printing them first. The LAN-based software prepares much of the cover page for you. The same word processing or other application software creates the document file, but the printout goes to the LAN-based fax server rather than to a printer. Under software control, the document goes into the fax queue to wait its turn for transmission.

For incoming fax documents, the fax server device stores the image in a file on a file server. You or an administrator can route the file to your workstation, where you view the image (the document) at your leisure. You may print the fax, but you don't have to.

If you think a LAN-based fax server would be a useful, time-saving, paper-saving addition to your office, here are three products to investigate:

FAXPress
Castelle
3255-3 Scott Boulevard
Santa Clara CA 95954
(800) 359-7654

FaxWorks LAN
Global Village Communication
1144 East Arques Avenue
Sunnyvale CA 94086
(800) 736-4821 or (408) 523-1000

NET Satisfaxion
Intel
PC Enhancements Division
5200 Northeast Elam Young Parkway
Hillsboro OR 97124
(800) 538-3373

Castelle's FAXPress product, in addition to being a LAN-based fax server, is also a print server for networks using Novell NetWare.

Chapter Summary

In this chapter, you read about sharing computer resources on a local area network. You learned various ways to share disk drives and disk space, from simple file-transfer utilities to peer LANs to server-based LANs. You know why printing on a LAN can be different from printing on a stand-alone personal computer, and you're aware of printer etiquette that makes the office run more smoothly.

You went beyond the sharing of hard disks and printers to explore turning a CD-ROM into an office-wide source of information. You now know ways to make fax documents easier to send and receive.

When people located in a different office need to access your LAN remotely, you understand the communications methods that they can use. And you have a firm grasp of the considerations involved in setting up outgoing communications facilities to access other computers from your LAN.

In Chapter 3, you'll find out more about file servers.

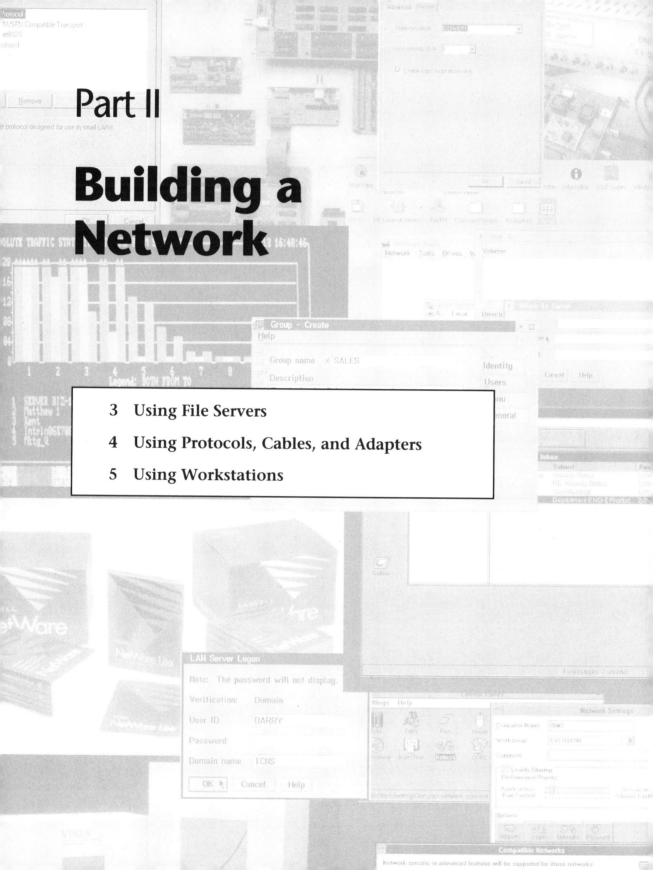

Part II

Building a Network

Chapter 3

Using File Servers

The file server is the Grand Central Station of your network, the only chef on duty at a busy restaurant. These metaphors only hint at how much work the file server has to do. Actually, the file server is a slave to its many masters, the workstations on the network.

In this chapter, you read an overview of file servers. You find out what a file server actually does, and you discover the criteria for a good file server computer. Next, you explore the components of a file server, from both hardware and software points of view. After an introductory discussion of these components, you go over the individual parts in detail: the hard disk, computer CPU chip, RAM (internal memory), the network adapter card, the power supply, the keyboard, monitor, and mouse.

Next, you read about the software that converts the personal computer into a file server, the network operating system. You cover server-based network operating systems, and then you learn about peer-to-peer network operating systems. This chapter treats both kinds of LANs, server-based and peer-to-peer, in depth.

An uninterruptible power supply (UPS) is an important part of a LAN; in this chapter, you find out why.

An Overview of File Servers

In Chapter 2, "Sharing Computer Resources," you looked at a LAN from the viewpoint of sharing disk space and printers. Now it is time to look at the LAN from the perspective of the file server, to see how it shares these resources. First, you see what a server does. Then you examine both hardware and software components of a file server.

What a Server Does

The file server, whether it also acts as a workstation or not, doles out files to the other computers connected to it through the LAN. The server may very well also manage a printer to which everyone can send printing tasks. The file server does this work only on the request of the workstations; it does not behave arbitrarily. You can get unexpected results, however, if two people update the same file at the same time without using LAN-aware, multiuser applications.

Sharing Disk Space and Files. On a peer LAN, your computer can be both a workstation and a file server to the other people on the network. On a server-based LAN, the file server is a separate, unattended computer silently managing disk space and files. Both types of servers perform the same basic functions. On a busy LAN, the following sample dialog of messages happens tens or hundreds of times each minute.

Table 3.1	
Workstation	**File Server**
Open file "SALES.WK1".	Okay; file is open.
Give me the contents of the file.	Okay; here is the data.
Close the file.	Okay; file is closed.

This dialog is typical of about 99% of the activity occurring between workstations and server on an average LAN. The LAN cable carries the messages back and forth from the workstations and file server. The network operating system, with portions running in both the workstation and the file server, carries on the dialog. The network operating system gives the applications running at the workstation the illusion that the file server hard disk is just another drive letter. To enable the workstation to treat the file server hard disk as just another drive letter, the network operating system does all the tasks DOS would. These tasks occur over the LAN cable, rather than locally, inside each workstation.

File-Sharing Collisions. If two workstations both want SALES.WK1 at *approximately* the same time and if the people at the two workstations both have rights to modify the file, trouble can erupt. Suppose that Joe loads the file into his spreadsheet program, types some new data onto the worksheet, and saves the file. You do the same thing, but you type different data. You also type faster than Joe. You write your changes to the file quickly, but Joe—the slower typist—saves his changes a minute or two later. Clearly, Joe's changes take effect while yours are ignored. This is probably not what you intended to happen. You and Joe should coordinate the use of the file to avoid these problems.

If two workstations access SALES.WK1 at *exactly* the same time, the file server opens the file for one workstation but denies access to the other workstation. You may update the file without noticing a problem, but Joe may see the dreaded message:

```
Sharing Violation; Abort, Retry, or Ignore?
```

You can avoid file-sharing problems in a number of ways. The simplest method is to coordinate file updates (communicating via electronic mail can help you accomplish this). Another procedure involves giving people copies of files from one central source and having only one person responsible for updating the central file; or one person may be in charge of files in a manner similar to how a public library is run. When the discussion turns to network operating systems later in this chapter, you see how the NOS can help you enforce good file-sharing techniques.

Sharing a Printer. When you send printouts to the LAN printer, the network operating system stores each one in a temporary *spool file* on the file server. When the printer finishes printing someone's report or memo, the NOS sends the next spool file to the printer as a *print job* and deletes the temporary spool file that already printed. Typically, the network operating system prints a *banner page* or *job separator page* between printouts to identify each one. The banner page shows the user ID of the person who should receive the printout, along with some other information about the print job.

In other words, the file server acts as a buffer for all the printouts, sending each printout to the printer, one by one. On a busy LAN, you may have to wait for other people's printouts to appear before the server prints yours. Unless you disable the banner page, your printout will be preceded by a page that identifies the printout as belonging to you.

Understanding the Components of a File Server

Before you delve into the finer details of file server operation, you need a road map. In the next few sections of this chapter, you get that road map in the form of brief descriptions of file server components. Subsequent sections deal with the parts of a file server in greater detail.

Understanding Hardware. A typical file server consists of a personal computer dedicated to the task of sharing disk space, files, and a printer. On a larger network, you may instead use a personal computer especially built for file server work (a *superserver*), a minicomputer, or even a mainframe. No matter what sort of computer you use as a server, the server and the workstations communicate with each other through the network adapter cards and LAN cables.

Using PC-Based Servers. Personal computers come in all sizes, shapes, and speeds. You can choose exactly the amount of power you need in your file server. Not all network operating systems work with every configuration of personal computer, but the range is wide enough to give you considerable choices. The speed of the computer and the size and speed of the hard disk are primary factors. The amount of memory (RAM) in the computer is an important factor, too. Other components—monitor, keyboard, and mouse—are less important because most file servers operate as unattended machines.

When you set up an ordinary personal computer as a file server, you select a machine with a larger hard disk and more horsepower than other PCs in the office. You follow the directions that came with the network adapter card to install the adapter. You install the server portion of the network operating system on the PC, and you put the machine in a location where people are not likely to trip over its power cord or otherwise interfere with the server's operation. After attaching the LAN cable to the new server, you power up the PC in its new role as file server.

Using SuperServers, Minicomputer Servers, and Mainframes. A *superserver* is a personal computer especially designed to be a file server. It looks and behaves much like a PC, but a superserver may have multiple hard disks that can act in tandem to provide a high degree of data redundancy. Files written to one disk are automatically *mirrored* on the other disk. If the first disk fails, the other disk takes over instantly. This gives the file server a certain level of fault tolerance. A superserver almost certainly has a fast CPU and a good deal of internal memory (RAM).

Your office may choose to use a minicomputer such as a Digital Equipment Corporation VAX computer or an IBM RS/6000 computer to be the file server. In the case of a VAX, you may install the version of NetWare that Novell designed to run on VAX equipment. RS/6000 computers use AIX, IBM's brand of UNIX, as a base operating system. You may install Sun Microsystem's Network File System (NFS) or other UNIX-based network operating system on the RS/6000. No matter what type of minicomputer you use, you probably will be interested in using the minicomputer as a host computer as well as a file server. If the minicomputer's regular workload of application software interacts with the applications running on the workstations on the LAN, you have a client/server environment. In such an environment, some work gets done on the minicomputer and some on the LAN workstations.

You can also use a mainframe computer in a client/server role on a LAN, but of course the programming and administrative costs are greater. At the present time, mainframe computers do not lend themselves very well to being used as file servers. This will change in the future (more than one NOS vendor is developing software to turn a mainframe into a file server), but in the meantime, mainframes require a substantial programming effort to play a role on a LAN.

Using Network Connections. Chapter 4, "Using Protocols, Cables, and Adapters," goes into detail about the network connections you establish to put the file server and all the workstations on the LAN. In brief, you put a network adapter card in the server and attach a LAN cable to the card. You will want to select a network adapter that uses the same protocols as the adapters on the workstations, but you should consider using a more powerful adapter in the server. As the Grand Central Station of the LAN, the server gets more message traffic than the other computers. A network adapter for the file server may have more on-board memory and special controller chips that process messages faster. The adapter may require that you put it into a 16-bit or even a 32-bit slot in the computer.

Understanding Software (Network Operating Systems). Once you set up a personal computer's hardware configuration to make it a server, you install the network operating system (often abbreviated as *NOS*). The NOS may enable the computer to continue to operate as a workstation as well as a server. Or the NOS may "take over" the computer, turning the machine into a dedicated file server.

Using Server-Based or Peer-to-Peer Systems. The network operating system you install on your server may be just one or perhaps a few TSR programs to enable the computer to share itself across the network. Such simple network software usually leaves the computer running DOS and able to act as a workstation at the same time it functions as a server. This is called a *peer-to-peer* network operating system. On the other hand, the network operating system may not be DOS-based at all. The NOS may replace DOS completely once it is loaded into memory, or the NOS may use a high-power operating system such as OS/2 or UNIX instead of DOS. Such a network operating system is a *server-based* NOS.

Of course, you may install a peer-to-peer NOS but choose not to use the server computer as a workstation, enabling the computer instead to concentrate on its role as a file server. This is called a *dedicated server*. The file server still runs DOS, but you do not have to worry about the possibility that an application running on the server/workstation may crash and thus stop the entire network. A server-based NOS, by definition, is a dedicated server.

Deciding Which NOS Is Best for You. Server-based network operating systems are more expensive than their peer LAN counterparts, but they offer better performance, greater reliability, and higher levels of security. A server-based NOS can also enable you to connect more kinds of computers to the network. Novell NetWare, for example, the most popular server-based NOS, supports Macintosh and UNIX computers at the same time that it supports DOS-based and OS/2-based computers.

If you are setting up a small LAN (with perhaps no more than five or 10 workstations), if that LAN will be used only for word processing chores and maybe some light record keeping (database) work, and if you have only DOS-based computers to tie together, you may find that a peer LAN is your best choice. If you have more workstations, if the LAN does more than enable the sharing of word processing document files, or if you have Mac or UNIX computers you want to use on the network, you probably need a server-based network operating system.

Looking at Criteria for a File Server

You need a place to store the files to be shared among the workstations. You may turn one of the office's personal computers into a file server, or you may choose to use a different kind of computer—a minicomputer, perhaps, or what is called a *superserver*—as the file server. Either way, you have four criteria to apply:

- You need fast access to the files on the server.

- You need the file server to have the capacity to hold files and records for many users.

- You need some measure of security for the files.

- You need the file server to be reliable.

II

Building a Network

If you choose something other than a PC to be a file server, you also need to verify that the computer is capable of being connected to the LAN and that it can behave as a file server. You should discuss LAN options with your minicomputer vendor, for example.

On the other hand, if you use one of the PCs as a file server, you should choose a PC that is faster and has larger, faster disks than the other machines. Why do you need the file server to be a faster computer if the software applications run on each of the individual PCs on the LAN and not some central machine? During busy periods, the server receives many requests for disk files and records; it takes a certain amount of CPU effort as well as disk rotation/access time to respond to each request. You want the requests to be addressed quickly so that each user believes that he or she is the only one using the file server at that moment.

You will not want to buy the fanciest color monitor, highest quality keyboard, and most expensive mouse for a dedicated file server. A monochrome monitor will be adequate because you will not interact with the server a great deal once you install the NOS and have the network up and running.

Understanding Server Hardware

You now have a good, basic idea of the components of a file server and know the general procedure you would use to turn a personal computer into a file server. You know the different types of network operating systems and are familiar with the criteria for a good file server. The next sections of this chapter look at each of these components in much greater detail. Begin by thinking about how the reliability of the file server will affect the work in your office.

Evaluating Hardware Reliability

As you read in Chapter 1, a file server does many times the work of an ordinary workstation. You may type on the server's keyboard only a couple of times a day, and you may glance at the server's monitor only a few times. The server CPU and hard disk, however, take the brunt of responding to the file service requests of all workstations on the LAN.

If you consider your LAN an important investment in your office (it is hard to imagine otherwise), you want to get the highest quality computer you can afford for the file server. The CPU should be an 80486 or Pentium chip, one of the faster models. The hard disk should be large and fast. The most important consideration is that the CPU, the motherboard on which the CPU is mounted, and the hard disk should be rugged and reliable. Do not skimp on these components. *Downtime* (when the network is not operating) can be expensive because people cannot access shared files in order to get work done. Higher quality components will keep the LAN running without failure for longer periods of time.

In the same vein, you should set up a regular maintenance schedule for your file server. Over a few weeks, the fan at the back of the computer can move great volumes of air through the machine to keep it cool. The air may contain dust and dirt, which will accumulate inside the computer; you should clean the "dust bunnies" out of the server every month or two. You do not replace components in the server as part of your regular preventive maintenance, but you do want to know if a part is beginning to fail. You may want to acquire diagnostic software and/or hardware to check the health of the file server periodically. (Chapter 12, "Managing Your Network," discusses tools for keeping your file server fit and trim.)

The electricity that the file server gets from the wall outlet may, from time to time, vary considerably in voltage (these are called *sags* and *spikes*). In the interest of making your file server as reliable as possible, you want to install an uninterruptible power supply between the electric company and your server. The UPS will not only provide electricity in case of a power failure; it also will *condition the line* to protect the server from sags and spikes. You will find out more about UPS equipment later in this chapter.

In general, you should do whatever you can to make your network reliable, including placing the server away from public access areas.

Evaluating the File Server Hard Disk

The hard disk is the most important component of a file server. The hard disk stores LAN users' files. Figure 3.1 illustrates a file server hard disk. To a large extent, the reliability, access speed, and capacity of a server's hard disk determine whether people will be happy with the LAN and use it productively. The most common bottleneck in the average LAN is disk I/O time at the file server. The most common complaint voiced by people on the average LAN is that the file server has run out of free disk space.

Evaluating Disk Speed. Disk access speed is determined by a number of factors, including the following:

- Recording method (typically IDE or SCSI)

- Type and on-board intelligence of the controller

- Type of hard disk (stepper band or voice coil)

- Interleave factor

- Location of the files on the disk (location affects how far the read/write head has to move to get to the file)

In general, disk access speed is measured by two things: data transfer rate and average seek time. *Data transfer rate* expresses the number of bytes of data that the hard disk and its controller card can deliver to the computer in one second. *Average seek time* represents the time taken by the disk to move the read/write head a small distance and then wait about a half-revolution of the disk platter for a given sector to appear under the head. For comparison purposes, the type of disk that was installed as standard equipment by IBM in the IBM PC/AT computer gives a data transfer rate of about 180K per second and an average seek time of 40 milliseconds. Third-party disks from companies like Maxtor (Storage Dimensions), Micropolis, Seagate, Connor, and Fujitsu are faster, operating in the 10- to 20-millisecond range for average seek time. And, of course, IBM offers speedy drives in the current crop of high-end PS/2 machines. In general, SCSI disks and controller cards transfer data faster than IDE disks and controllers.

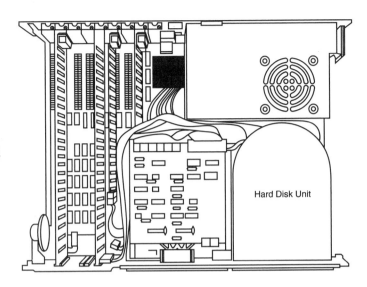

Hard Disk Unit

Fig. 3.1 Everyone on the LAN shares the file server's hard disk.

Evaluating Disk Capacity. Disk capacity tends to go hand in hand with speed; the larger drives are the faster drives. The designers of 1GB and larger drives were obviously thinking in terms of file servers as they engineered their latest technologically advanced products. Some of these huge drives cost as much as the computer you put them in, however. How much space do you need on your file server? How many drives should you buy, and how many file servers will you need?

A significant factor is that you are limited in the number of drives that can be installed in a given file server machine. You can usually install only two hard disks in a personal computer. (SCSI drives are less limiting in this respect.) A related consideration is that it is generally better to have several medium-sized disks, in multiple servers, than one huge disk in one server. You then have more read/write heads, more hard disk controllers, and more CPUs responding to user requests for files. You also can continue to use a second file server to keep the network going if the other one fails.

A very general rule of thumb is that you should allot 50M of disk storage space for each user on the LAN. This is only the roughest of guides because you need to take a look at what you think the LAN will be used for and what type of applications users will run. File server disks are quite a bit like closets and file cabinets: no matter how many you have, they tend to fill up pretty quickly. If you are the LAN administrator, you may want to keep the following tips in mind:

■ Encourage people to use local hard drives for executable files and for applications not shared on the LAN. Applications typically load faster from a local hard drive than from a server.

- Don't buy diskless workstations to save money. Such workstations may not be able to run the operating systems of the future from IBM or Microsoft, and people using diskless workstations cannot work when the file server is down.

- Don't let people store games on the file server.

- Set up a "retention period" scheme for different kinds of files on the network. Houseclean regularly; don't wait for the server to run out of space.

RAID and Data Integrity

Using arrays of three or more disks to form a RAID (Redundant Arrays of Inexpensive Disks) offers two benefits. The first is performance. In a RAID implementation, data is scattered evenly across every disk in the array using a technique called striping. Overall throughput improves because each disk in the array can more or less evenly divide the load of system disk reads and writes.

The second benefit is data redundancy. Every RAID level but one specifies a method whereby data is stored redundantly on the array; it is done so that the failure of one disk does not result in data loss. Six RAID levels are defined, differing in how they implement striping and redundancy.

RAID Level 0: A RAID 0 array consists of a series of disks where striping is the only RAID feature implemented. No provision is made for data redundancy. Because a RAID 0 array provides all the performance benefits of striping and none of the overhead entailed by writing redundant failure recovery data, it is the configuration to choose when performance is important and failure protection is not.

RAID Level 1: RAID 1 arrays implement disk mirroring along with data striping. Each disk in the array is mirrored by another; the second disk in the mirrored pair stores an exact copy of the information on the first disk. In a four-disk RAID 1 array, you have two mirrored pairs and the equivalent capacity of two disks to use for data storage. If all disks perform reads and writes simultaneously, disk mirroring will probably subtly improve disk-read performance because read requests are satisfied by the first drive in the pair to seek the information. Write requests slow performance because they have to be completed for both disks in the pair.

RAID Level 2: RAID 2 sets aside the capacity of one disk to perform data recovery for the remaining ones. Striping is implemented at the bit level. The first bit for a unit of information is written to the first disk, the second to the second disk, and so on. Because multiple error-correcting disks are required in an array, RAID 2 is not commercially implemented for microcomputer systems.

RAID Level 3: In a RAID 3 array, striping is typically implemented at the byte level, and one disk (often called the parity drive) is set aside to store error-correcting information. The error-correcting code stored by the parity drive is calculated by performing bitwise arithmetic on the bytes on the data drives. In a process not unlike finding the value of a variable in a simple algebraic equation, the missing byte on a failed disk is calculated by using a bitwise operation to combine the byte values on the remaining disks and then by comparing that value with the value on the parity drive. Commercial RAID 3 implementations often optimize disk-read performance by synchronizing the spindle rotation of each drive so that parallel reads of a range of bytes can be readily performed. For this reason, RAID 3 units should be particularly fast when doing sequential reads of large files. Because the parity drive must be written to in every write operation, RAID 3 performance suffers when heavy disk writes are done.

(continues)

II

Building a Network

(continued)

RAID Level 4: A RAID 4 array sets aside a single disk in the array as the parity drive. RAID 4 stripes in units of disk blocks rather than bytes, a disk block being the amount of data transferred to or from the disk in one write or read operation.

RAID Level 5: A RAID 5 array spreads the error-correction data evenly across the drives in the array. The data is striped in units of blocks. RAID 5 arrays should handle multiple simultaneous disk writes more quickly than RAID 3 or 4 arrays because no single disk must be written to during every write operation. They stripe in block increments, so RAID 5 arrays should handle multiple simultaneous random reads well because each disk can independently retrieve an entire disk block.

Evaluating Hard Disk Alternatives. Optical disks are another alternative for file servers. They use light to store data or, sometimes, a combination of light and magnetism. With the proper software drivers, optical disks can be made to behave just like any other file server drive. Optical media are extremely durable and reliable. Until recently, optical disks had two major drawbacks that kept them from being more popular: they tended to have slower access times than magnetic disks, and files could not be erased. (The laser-burned holes are permanent. These are called *write-once, read-many—WORM—*drives.) The situation is improving, however; companies such as Corel, Storage Dimensions, and Racet now offer rewritable optical disks that are network-compatible.

Evaluating the File Server CPU

The file server CPU tells the hard disk what to store and retrieve. After the hard disk, the CPU is the next most important file server component. Unless your LAN has only a few users and will never grow, a file server with a fast 80486 or Pentium CPU and plenty of memory (RAM) is a wise investment. The next section in third chapter discusses server RAM.

The CPU chip in a computer executes the instructions given to it by software. Thus, an application runs more quickly if the CPU is fast. Likewise, a network operating system (NOS) runs more quickly if the CPU is fast. Figure 3.2 shows the server's CPU. Note that some NOS products can take advantage of multiple CPUs in the same computer through a technique known as Symmetric Multiprocessing (SMP).

Some network operating systems absolutely require certain types of CPU chips. Novell NetWare Version 2, for example, requires at least an 80286 CPU. NetWare Version 3 requires at least an 80386. IBM Warp Server and Microsoft NT Server require that OS/2 or NT be running on the server computer; OS/2 and NT require an 80486 or better CPU.

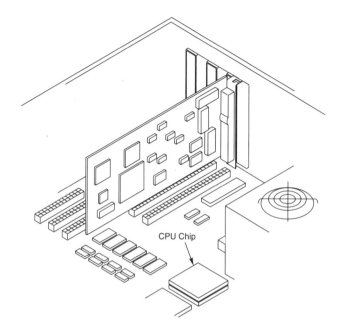

CPU Chip

Fig. 3.2 The file server's CPU processes file requests from all workstations.

Evaluating Server RAM

The network operating system loads into the computer's RAM, just like any other application. You need to have at least enough RAM in the computer for the NOS to load and run.

You can realize significant performance gains with a faster CPU and extra RAM because of something called *caching*. If the file server has sufficient memory installed, it can "remember" those portions of the hard disk that it has previously accessed. When the next user asks for the same file represented by those portions of the hard disk, the server can hand these to the next user without having to actually access the hard disk. Because the file server doesn't wait for the hard disk to rotate into position, the server does its job more quickly.

Evaluating the Network Adapter Card

The server's network adapter card is the server's link to all workstations on the LAN. All the requests for files enter the server through the network adapter, and all the response messages containing the requested files leave the server through the network adapter. Figure 3.3 shows a network adapter you might install in a file server. As you can imagine, the network adapter in the server is a busy component.

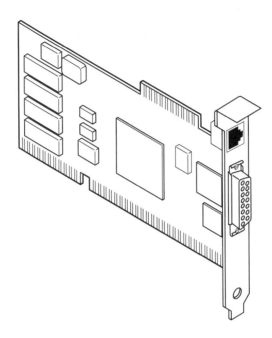

Fig. 3.3 The file server's network adapter sends and receives messages to and from all workstations on the LAN.

All network adapters on the LAN use EtherNet, Token Ring, ARCnet, or some other protocol. Within one of these protocols, however, some network adapters perform better than others. A network adapter may be faster at processing messages because it has a large amount of on-board memory (RAM), because it contains its own microprocessor, or perhaps because the adapter uses one of the larger (longer) computer slots and thus can transfer more data between itself and the CPU at one time. A faster, more capable network adapter is an ideal candidate for installation in the file server. The next chapter, "Using Protocols, Cables, and Adapters," discusses network adapters in more detail.

Evaluating the Computer Power Supply

The innocuous power supply is usually a shiny box inside the computer. The power switch is part of the power supply. Alternating Current (AC) electricity enters the computer through the power cord attached to the power supply. The power supply converts the AC electricity to Direct Current (DC). Inside the computer, small, low-voltage wires carry the current to the motherboard, the floppy disk drives, and the hard disks. The power supply also has one or more fans that move air through the computer to cool the components.

In a file server, the power supply is an important but often overlooked component. Power supply failures and malfunctions cause problems elsewhere in the computer and are difficult to diagnose. Your file server may display a message indicating that a RAM chip has failed and then stop; the cause of the problem may indeed be a failed RAM chip, or the problem may be the power supply.

The fan(s) in the power supply sometimes stop(s) working or become obstructed with dust and dirt. The computer then overheats and either fails completely or acts strange. Cleaning the fan(s)—after unplugging the computer from the wall outlet, of course— should be a part of regular maintenance of the file server computer.

Power supplies vary considerably in quality. Some of the best ones are manufactured by

> PC Power and Cooling
> 31510 Mountain Way
> Bonsall CA 92003
> (800) 722-6555

Evaluating the Keyboard, Monitor, and Mouse

The keyboard, monitor screen, and mouse (if any) are not significant components on a file server computer, so you can often use lower quality components for these parts. A typical file server runs unattended and may go for hours or days without interaction from a user. You can power off the monitor for these long periods.

One caution about the keyboard, however; tuck it away so that falling objects (pencils or coffee mugs, for example) do not harm the network's file server.

Understanding Server Software (Network Operating Systems)

Both server-based and peer LAN network operating systems can share disk space, disk files, and printers. In the next few sections of this chapter, you discover how the network operating system enables you to share these resources.

Learning What the NOS Does

Conceptually, server-based and peer LAN network operating systems have three software components. The actual division of labor among the individual computer programs varies with the network operating system. Some simple products consist of a single computer program that embodies all three components. Other, more complex NOS products divide the work among many computer programs and modules.

The first, lowest-level component that is always present provides connectivity. This network operating system module enables the workstation to communicate, through the network adapter cards and the LAN cable, across the LAN. This lowest level of software consists of network adapter driver computer programs.

Of the other two software elements, one is a workstation component, and the other resides in the file server. The workstation element creates request messages and sends them to a file server. Computers running the file server component can honor those requests.

Most requests from the workstation are file-oriented. Some are administrative, having to do with logging in, logging out, and identifying who's who on the LAN.

Logging in to the Server. When you start up your computer, the network software loads into memory, but you cannot access the file server's hard disk until you log in by typing your user ID and password. On a NetWare LAN, for example, you can change to the file server drive letter (typically F) after loading network software. Then you find yourself in the \LOGIN directory—but you still cannot access any other directory until you log in. One of the few computer programs in the \LOGIN directory is LOGIN.EXE. When you run the LOGIN program, the software asks you for your user ID and password. The password does not appear on-screen as you type it. Figure 3.4 shows the login proce- dure on a NetWare LAN. With the IBM Warp Server and Microsoft NT Server products, on the other hand, the LOGIN computer program resides on your workstation. The server is not even minimally available to you until you log in.

```
F:\LOGIN> login
Enter your login name: joel
Good evening, JOEL.

Drive  A:    maps to a local disk.
Drive  B:    maps to a local disk.
Drive  C:    maps to a local disk.
Drive  D:    maps to a local disk.
Drive  E:    maps to a local disk.
Drive  F: = SERVER1\SYS:  \JOEL
        ------
SEARCH1:   = C:\WINDOWS
SEARCH2:   = C:\DOS

F:\JOEL>
```

Fig. 3.4 Logging in to a NetWare LAN.

The LOGIN program first finds the nearest (or only) file server on the network before prompting you to identify yourself. Even before you type your user ID and password, the workstation sends messages through the LAN cable. The very first of these messages is a *broadcast message*, directed to any and all computers on the LAN. This particular broad- cast message asks file servers to identify themselves. When a file server responds, the workstation knows that it can then request your user ID. If your workstation cannot find a file server, you see an error notification on your computer screen.

During the login process, the file server looks up the user ID in one of its internal tables. Your password, rights and permissions, workgroup ID (the name of the team you are on), default directory, disk space restrictions, and other network restrictions reside in these internal tables. Naturally, the password and other information exists in encrypted form to prevent tampering.

Other network-specific administrative tasks may occur during the log-in process. On a simple peer LAN, these tasks may be called out in the BAT file that turns the computer into a workstation. On a NetWare LAN, a *login script* tells the LOGIN.EXE program how to configure your workstation. NetWare LANs have both system login scripts that apply to everyone as well as individual login scripts.

Mapping Drives. Different personal computers contain different drive letter assignments, even before the network software loads. DOS assigns these initial drive letters based on the number of disk drives (both floppy and hard) in the computer and the number of partitions on the computer's hard disk(s). One computer may have a drive A (floppy) and a drive C (one hard disk partition). On another computer, DOS may assign drives A, B, C, D, and other drive letters.

To complicate matters, the file server may contain multiple disk drives. The network also may have multiple file servers. How should the network software assign drive letters in such cases?

The process of assigning network drive letters is called *mapping drives*. On a NetWare LAN, you run the MAP.EXE utility program to assign drives. By default, NetWare begins assigning drive letters starting with F, or if you already have several DOS-assigned drive letters on your computer, the next available drive letter. Using MAP.EXE, you can change the default assignment and map additional non-default network drives. Typically, a network administrator invokes MAP in the system login script so that everyone gets the same drive letter assignments when he or she logs in. Figure 3.5 shows the use of the MAP utility to map drive J: to directory JOEL on volume SYS on the file server named SERVER1.

```
F:\JOEL> map

Drive  A:    maps to a local disk.
Drive  B:    maps to a local disk.
Drive  C:    maps to a local disk.
Drive  D:    maps to a local disk.
Drive  E:    maps to a local disk.
       -----
SEARCH1:   = C:\WINDOWS
SEARCH2:   = C:\DOS
SEARCH3:   = F:\PUBLIC [SERVER1\SYS:  \JOEL]

F:\JOEL> map root j:=server1\sys:joel

Drive  J: = SERVER1\SYS:JOEL  \

F:\JOEL>
```

Fig. 3.5 Mapping a drive letter to a file server directory.

On a Warp Server or NT Server network, you use a NET USE command to assign drives. Many peer LANs also use a NET USE command to assign drive letters. One peer LAN, WEB (from WebCorp), assigns a single drive W and establishes each different server computer as a directory on this networked drive W. The name of a server's directory is based on the machine name given to the server at installation time.

Macintosh computers do not map drive letters, of course. If you have a Mac, you see additional folders that you can access once you log in. The Chooser enables you to see these additional network resources. A UNIX-based computer, on the other hand, sees the network drive(s) as additional file systems. With Network File System (NFS, developed by Sun Microsystems and offered by many makers of UNIX computers), for example, the UNIX workstation mounts a network drive over an empty directory (thus making the UNIX mount command work almost the same for network drives as for local file systems).

Accessing and Sharing Files. After you log in and map the network drives as drive letters (or folders or file systems), you can access applications and data files on the network. You can also print to the shared LAN printer (as discussed later in this chapter). As you run applications, you should notice little or no difference between using your local hard disk and using the hard disk on the file server.

Depending on how the network operating system implements its security features, however, you may observe that network files and directories behave differently from what you are accustomed to. On a NetWare LAN, for example, you may not have any rights at all in a particular directory. When you use the DOS DIR command, you see no files listed. Or when you try to copy a file into that directory, you see an error message on-screen. You can run the NetWare utility RIGHTS.EXE to find out what rights, if any, you have in a directory.

Some DOS-based utilities and commands do not work on network drives. In particular, CHKDSK and disk diagnostic software such as Norton Utilities and PC Tools that run at a workstation cannot operate on network drives.

The file server itself can help you administer good file-sharing techniques. You can use the rights and permissions capabilities of the network operating system to divide people into teams. Each team may be given its own public directory on the server. Coordination within the team, perhaps in the form of a published procedure and personal assignments of responsibility for certain files, goes a long way toward preventing file-sharing problems.

A server-based network operating system typically uses something other than DOS to access the hard disk. The hard disk in a NetWare file server, for example, uses a fast and reliable method for storing and locating. You cannot boot a NetWare file server with a DOS disk and run the DOS CHKDSK utility on the hard disk because the hard disk does not use a formatting scheme that DOS recognizes. A DOS-based workstation, however, can use NetWare files as if they were DOS files because the workstation and file server conspire to make the server's files look like DOS files. The workstation component transforms the responses from the server into DOS-like files. In contrast, a peer LAN typically does use DOS to access the hard disk.

Disk Sharing—A Technical Perspective. How does the network operating system make the file server's hard disk appear to be just another DOS-assigned drive letter? The answer is *redirection*.

Redirection of DOS function calls makes file sharing possible. An application running on a workstation goes through the motions of asking DOS for some part of a disk file, but the network software intercepts the request and sends it to the file server. The file server does the actual disk I/O to obtain that part of the disk file and returns the result to the workstation. The network software on the workstation hands the disk file contents to the application and, in doing so, makes it look as though the workstation's copy of DOS had obtained the file contents. The application is unaware that the DOS function call it issued was handled by something other than DOS.

The network software performs several steps to send the request to the server and get back the response.

The first thing the workstation's network software does is determine whether the network should handle a DOS file-read request or pass it along to DOS. The workstation network software does this by noting at either file-open or file-creation time whether a network drive letter is in effect for the open or create call. Because the network software maintains an internal table of which drives are network devices, it is fairly easy for the workstation network operating system component to know whether a file-open or a file-create call applies to a network drive. After the file is opened or created, the workstation's network software records the file's identity and knows to send any file-read or file-write requests to the file server. The local copy of DOS running at the workstation never knows about or accesses these files.

Suppose that the network software on the workstation detects that a file-read request is for a file located on the file server. The network software turns the DOS function call into a network message. The format and size of this message varies among the different vendors' protocols, but its basic purpose—to request some file material from the file server—is the same for all network operating systems and protocols. The workstation network software then sends this message to the file server through the network adapter card and LAN cable.

At the server, the receiving network adapter and adapter support software give the message to the file server portion of the network operating system. The NOS recognizes the message as a file-read request.

If another workstation's request is being processed by the server (a common occurrence on a busy LAN), the network operating system puts the file-read request in a queue for later handling. In its turn, the request is processed by the file-service portion of the network software running on the server. The desired sectors of the file are found in the server's cache memory or, if they are not in memory, they are accessed directly from the server's hard disk.

When the file server does the I/O operation, it encounters one of three typical situations for a disk-read: the requested bytes are read, end-of-file is detected, or only some of the requested bytes are read (this happens if more bytes were requested than actually exist). The file server creates a network message that indicates which of these three situations was encountered, appends the file data (if any) to the message, and hands the result to the network support software for transmission to the appropriate workstation.

When the workstation receives the response from the file server, its network software reverses the steps taken to send the file-read request. The network adapter processes the message containing the response by giving the message to the workstation's network software; the network software emulates DOS by putting the file data into the application's buffer. The workstation's network software sets the CPU registers to indicate the number of bytes actually read and returns control of the CPU to the application at the next instruction after the DOS function call.

Sharing a Printer. The network operating system redirects printouts to the shared LAN printer in much the same way the NOS redirects I/O requests from the application file. The stream of print material becomes a series of LAN messages that flow from your workstation to the file server (or perhaps to a separate print server).

Your workstation may have a locally attached printer (a dot-matrix model, perhaps), and the LAN printer may be a high-speed laser printer. The network software enables you to print to either printer. In the next few sections, you explore how printer redirection works and what you need to know about using the LAN printer.

Accessing the LAN Printer. DOS-based computers support up to three printer ports, called *LPT1*, *LPT2*, and *LPT3*. If you have a locally attached workstation printer, it is connected to one of these printer ports (in some instances, your printer may connect to a serial port—COM1 or perhaps COM2). You can print to your locally attached printer as soon as you start up your computer.

Before you print to the LAN printer, however, you must redirect one of your printer ports to the network. With Warp Server, NT Server, and many peer LAN products, you do this with a NET USE command. With NetWare, you use a CAPTURE command to redirect printouts. Figure 3.6 shows using the CAPTURE command to create a connection between a PC's LPT1 port and the network printer named LASERJET. You may want to put the appropriate command into a BAT file, along with the other commands that turn your computer into a LAN workstation, so that you do not forget to issue them. If you send a printout to a printer port that has neither an attached local printer nor a redirected LAN printer, your computer may freeze. Even if it does not freeze, you will not get the printout you expect.

If you have a locally-attached printer, it probably uses LPT1. In this case, you may redirect LPT2 to the LAN printer. If you have no local printer, you can redirect LPT1 to the LAN printer. You may even redirect all three printer ports to different LAN printers if your LAN is large enough to have multiple shared printers.

When you send a printout to the LAN printer, the network software in your workstation considers the current printout a print job separate from other print jobs. The print job is processed by the network spooler.

```
F:\JOEL> capture s=server1 q=laserjet nt nb noff
Device LPT1: re-routed to queue LASERJET on server SERVER1.

F:\JOEL> capture show

LPT1:  Capturing data to server SERVER1 queue LASERJET.
       User will not be notified after the files are printed.
       Capture Defaults:Enabled       Automatic Endcap:Enabled
       Banner  :(None)                 Form Feed       :No
       Copies :1                       Tabs            :No conversion
       Form    :0                      Timeout Count :Disabled

LPT2:  Capturing Is Not Currently Active.

LPT3:  Capturing Is Not Currently Active.

F:\JOEL>
```

Fig. 3.6 Using the NetWare CAPTURE command.

Issuing Print Jobs. The network software at the file server or print server that manages the printer is called a *spooler*. The spooler receives redirected printouts as streams of LAN messages and stores the printouts as temporary disk files. Each printout is a separate print job. Unless you specify otherwise, the network software prints a banner page (sometimes called a *job separator page*) ahead of your printout to identify the printout as belonging to you. A banner page typically contains logon account ID as well as the date and time the printout was produced.

If you print a memo or report from within a word processor application program and then print a subsequent report from a spreadsheet program, how does the LAN know that they are separate printouts? Typically, network operating systems use two methods to identify separate printouts. If the application uses DOS conventions to print, the network software sees the application open the DOS device named LPT1, write to that device, and then close the device. The close operation signals the end of the printout to the network software.

If, on the other hand, the application bypasses DOS to print, the network operating system does not detect the Open LPT1, Write to LPT1, Close LPT1 sequence. The NOS sees only a stream of print material go by, separated by long pauses between the times you tell applications to print. Fortunately, the network operating system can time pauses. If you tell the NOS to consider a pause of 10 seconds or longer as the end of a printout, the NOS dutifully waits those 10 seconds and signals the end of that printout. If you do not specify a time-out period or if the time-out period is too short, the NOS becomes confused about which printout is which. Keeping track of each printout is important to the spooler because the spooler does not want to mix pages of your printout with pages that other people have printed.

II

Building a Network

Using the Spooler. The print spooler module in the network operating system constantly switches its attention between two functions. One function consists of receiving print material in the form of LAN messages and storing that material as temporary disk files. The other function consists of knowing which disk file should be printed next and sending that next printout to the printer. After the spooler prints a file, it deletes that disk file. If you and another person both happen to print reports at the same time, the spooler accumulates each printout into a separate file. After detecting the end of each printout, the spooler prints first one report and then the other. Unless it is confused by time-out periods that are too short, the spooler keeps the pages of each printout separate.

The spooler puts the most recently received printout at the end of a queue. Associated with each printout is information specified at the workstation, such as whether a banner page is to be printed, whether the NOS should eject the last printed page (you may embed a page-eject command at the end of your printout), and the type of paper the NOS should use to print. Each printout, as it is received from a workstation, goes to the end of the queue, where it waits for its turn to print. Most network operating systems provide utility commands to detect how far down in the queue a print job is. Many of these utilities also enable you to cancel a waiting print job or hold the job for later printing.

Using Different Fonts, Modes, and Printer Commands. People like to use different fonts (typefaces) in memos and letters. Most laser printers and some dot-matrix printers support different fonts, of course. Most laser printers can even print reports "sideways," in landscape mode, so that the long edge of the paper is the bottom rather than the side of the page.

Almost all printers stay in the most recently selected mode (portrait or landscape) and use the most recently selected font until told otherwise. On a shared LAN printer, if one person tells the printer to use a Letter Gothic font in landscape mode, the next person's printout may appear in that same mode and font. This may not be what the next person intended.

All printers support commands that reset the printer to a default state. You should make a practice of sending such a reset command to the printer between each printout.

Ensuring Server Security

Chapter 1, "A Networking Overview," mentioned four reasons for implementing security on a LAN: limiting inadvertent damage, protecting confidentiality, preventing fraud, and reducing the chance of malicious damage by a disgruntled employee. The network operating system helps protect information stored on the LAN; it requires people to have user IDs and passwords and allows each person to have different access rights to different directories and files.

Establishing User IDs and Passwords. On the file server, the network operating system tracks each LAN user's log-in name (user ID), password (in encrypted form, of course), directory rights, and other attributes. The network operating system protects the files containing these attributes. You cannot edit these files with a text editor, for example.

On a NetWare LAN, these files are collectively called the *Bindery*. Other network operating systems simply refer to them as *system files*. To modify these files, you must use a utility program supplied with the network operating system.

When a network operating system's log-in process detects an invalid user ID and password, the NOS denies LAN access to the intruder. Some networks even enable the system administrator to specify that a given user ID can log in only once (rather than at several workstations concurrently), can log in only during certain hours of the day, or can log in only from certain workstations.

Granting Rights and Permissions. Even if every person on the LAN has the best intentions as he or she gets work done, mistakes happen. A DIR *.* command may turn into a DEL *.* command. And sometimes a well-intended person overzealously tries to do LAN-management tasks (such as copying a new application's executable files to a public area of the LAN) that can disrupt the office's day-to-day operation. To prevent these and other, similar, situations from happening, most network operating systems enable the system administrator to restrict access rights of each user ID on a directory-by-directory basis.

Novell NetWare, for example, implements the concept of *trustee rights*. The system administrator grants these rights to a person or group of persons to allow or disallow various levels of access to a directory and its subdirectories. Each directory has a *maximum rights mask* that represents the highest level of privilege that any of the directory's trustees can be granted. The eight rights for trustees expressed by the rights mask follow:

- A user may read from open files

- A user may write to open files

- A user may open existing files

- A user may create new files

- A user may delete existing files

- A user may act parentally—he or she may create, rename, or erase subdirectories and set trustee rights and directory rights in the directory and its subdirectories

- A user may search for files in the directory

- A user may modify file attributes

Assigning the Network Administrator

The utility program the system administrator runs to add new user IDs to the LAN or to modify individual access rights requires, as you may expect, that the person running the program has special rights. Such rights by default exist only for a certain user ID. On NetWare LANs, this special User ID is *supervisor*. On Warp Server and NT Server networks, the special user ID is *admin*. The person in the office who knows the password for this special ID can perform network administration tasks on the LAN.

II

Building a Network

Creating New Users. One of the first tasks you perform on a new LAN and one you perform each time your office hires new employees is the adding of user IDs to the network. The utility program that the system administrator runs to create new user IDs is usually menu-driven and simple to use. Figure 3.7 illustrates the NetWare SYSCON utility for adding users and performing other administrative tasks on a Novell NetWare LAN. Vendors of network operating systems know that system administrators are busy people who do not have time to look up complex commands and parameters.

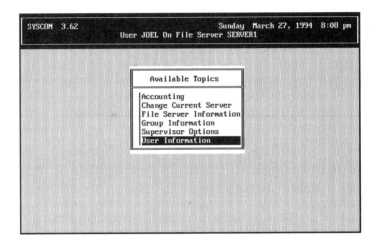

Fig. 3.7 NetWare administrators use SYSCON to manage many aspects of the LAN.

The basic process of adding a user ID, for all network operating systems, involves establishing the ID, its initial password, its directory rights and other security attributes, and perhaps creating a *home directory* for the new user. The home directory usually has the same name as the user ID and is the default initial directory the user sees after logging in.

The process of removing a user from the LAN (for instance, when someone leaves the office) is simply the opposite of adding a new user. The system administrator removes the ID and deletes the user's home directory.

In addition, some network operating systems enable the system administrator to map the root directory for a new user (see the following section).

Mapping Drive Letters. The system administrator assigns the drive letters that everyone uses to access the file server. He or she does this on a user-by-user basis for most peer LAN products. On a NetWare LAN, the administrator usually inserts entries in the network-wide system login script to establish the same drive letters for everyone.

On a large file server with a complex directory structure, the system administrator may find it convenient to map drive letters differently for each user and to provide each user with a different view of the server. By mapping a user's home directory as a root directory, for example, the system administrator can hide the rest of the file server from a user. The fully qualified name of the home directory might be F:\USERS\BARRY, but the administrator may map the root directory for user BARRY so that the user simply uses F:\ to refer to what is actually F:\USERS\BARRY. When one of BARRY's applications writes files to the root directory of drive F, that application is in reality writing to F:\USERS\BARRY.

Tracking Disk Space. The administrator of the network must also track available disk space on the file server. With peer LAN products, the administrator's job is multiplied by the number of workstations on the LAN because every workstation is potentially also a server. On a server-based LAN, the administrator can monitor disk space utilization on the single file server. Fortunately, a simple DOS DIR command is usually all it takes to reveal how much disk space remains on the server.

Most network operating systems do not enable you to limit the disk space that a person's files can occupy. NetWare is an exception; you can specify the maximum disk space that a particular user ID can use.

When available disk space grows tight, the network administrator usually has to house-clean the server's hard disk (even after reminding people to delete obsolete files). To do this effectively takes a surprising amount of time and effort.

Fixing a Failed Server. If the file server runs completely out of disk space, or if it fails as the result of a hardware malfunction, the network administrator is unfortunately respon-sible for putting the server back into service. The administrator may do some housecleaning, reboot the server, or troubleshoot a more difficult problem (which may affect only the file server or a segment of the entire LAN). In this last situation, the administrator will probably have to reconfigure the LAN so that a backup file server computer can be used until the primary server is repaired. Chapter 12, "Managing Your Network," discusses the tools and techniques an administrator can use to solve such problems.

Changing the Server Configuration. From time to time, the network administrator must change the file server configuration. The change may be as simple as adding memory (RAM) chips to the server or as complex as adding a new hard disk or upgrading the network operating system. As you may expect, such tasks require planning and should be scheduled so that they cause the least disruption to the people in the office, typically on weekends or after hours.

Comparing Server-Based and Peer LANs

You now understand the differences between a server-based LAN and a peer LAN. Which is better for your office? You know that a peer LAN is best suited for small, lightly loaded LANs. You should be aware, however, of other considerations.

Lending a File to Someone. On a server-based LAN, people share files by copying them to the file server or by creating them on the file server. The file server directory contain-ing the file must be accessible to people who want to share the file; this involves setting up the proper rights and permissions for those people.

On a peer LAN, where every workstation is also a server, sharing files is somewhat easier than on a server-based LAN. The files can be shared without first being copied to a central file server. As on a server-based LAN, the appropriate rights and permissions must exist for file sharing.

DOS Was Not Designed for File Sharing

DOS was designed more than 10 years ago as a single-user, single-task operating system. It is not useful in a file-sharing environment for several reasons. From the outset, DOS was designed to work well with floppy disks. When hard disks came along, Microsoft programmers simply extended the floppy disk format to apply to hard disks.

Most peer LAN products are DOS-based. A workstation that is also a server is doing much more than DOS was ever designed to do. When you run an application on a workstation/server on a peer LAN, your application and the network operating system compete for the attention of DOS. Depending on the application, you may keep other people in the office from accessing their files on your workstation/server. Or, if the NOS wins the competition, other people in the office can keep you from accessing *your* files.

The simplest example of such a conflict happens when you use a pop-up TSR program such as Borland's SideKick at your peer LAN workstation/server. Without meaning to, you can preempt the peer LAN NOS with such a TSR. The other people in the office will not be happy as error messages appear on their monitors.

Worse yet, you may need to reboot your computer while it is operating as a server on the LAN. The application you are running may have crashed, and the entire network is disrupted as a consequence. If you forget that your machine is a server and use the power switch to turn off your computer when you are not using it, the other people in the office will quickly remind you that your computer is a server.

DOS uses what is called a *file allocation table* (*FAT*) to locate files on a disk. DOS treats hard disks in the same way that it treats floppy disks. Unfortunately, the file allocation table scheme is excruciatingly slow for large files. And DOS is very slow at locating files in a directory containing more than about 100 files. A DOS-based peer LAN server depends on and cannot operate any faster than DOS. If you and another person access your hard disk at the same time, one of you must wait for the other to finish.

Sharing a Printer. On a peer LAN, your locally attached printer also may be a shared, office-wide LAN printer. In this case, you may find yourself the unwitting printer operator for the entire office. Your workload may not permit you the time it takes to attend to the printer.

Managing Your Files. You can, of course, see and access all the files on your computer—even ones belonging to other people on a peer LAN. You can easily see that security on a peer LAN should be administered differently. At the very least, the people on a peer LAN should be cautioned to store private files on their own hard disks and not share directories containing those files with other people on the LAN.

You need to be careful about rebooting your computer on a peer LAN. If no one is writing files to your workstation/server when you reboot, the other people will simply see a notification message telling them that your computer is no longer available as a server. If someone *is* writing a file to your hard disk when you reach for the power switch, you probably need to run CHKDSK before you can use the hard disk again—and the file being written to your hard disk will probably be incomplete or corrupted.

Understanding Client/Server Architecture

If you operate your LAN in the simplest ways, you share disk space on the file server and you share files by making those files available to other people in publicly accessible directories. You can, however, make your LAN work harder. With *client/server architecture*, you integrate the LAN with one or more applications. You may designate one workstation on the LAN as a database server, for example, and use a product such as Oracle, IBM's DB2, or Microsoft's SQL Server to store your records. A file server that runs other computer programs in addition to the NOS is an *application server.*

Understanding Database Servers. Beyond treating a file server as just another drive letter lies a whole area of software technology—that of database servers. A *database server* is an unattended computer on the LAN that serves up records to the application(s) running on other workstations. One goal of a database server is to take some workload away from the file server and the workstations.

An ordinary application that stores or retrieves records on a file server by using a file-indexing method causes a flurry of LAN traffic during each file access. To retrieve a record, the file I/O portion of the application reads through the index to find the desired key. Each read operation becomes a separate request message to the server and, a moment later, a response message back from the server. The network operating system performs this message-passing, completely outside the application. The application is at the mercy of the NOS and the file server.

Looking at Database Server Advantages. The number of requests and responses depends, of course, on the size of the index file. You can get an idea of the number of LAN I/O messages, however, by multiplying the typical number of read operations to locate a key by the number of workstations on the LAN. The traffic adds up fast. Adding or deleting records causes even more traffic. The workstation has to rebalance or coalesce the index by manipulating the file indirectly, piece by piece. The file I/O activity takes place through the network operating system and the LAN cable.

In a database server environment, the application's file access logic (not the network operating system) controls the message-passing. The application retrieves data from the database server by sending the server a LAN message containing Structured Query Language (SQL). For instance, the application might send the SQL message, "SELECT BALANCE_AMOUNT, LAST_PAYMENT_DATE WHERE CUSTOMER_NAME EQUALS 'FRED BROWN'." The database server sends back the desired data, as a sequence of field values (or a record-doesn't-exist indication). In contrast to the way an application reads and writes files on a file server, this process greatly reduces LAN message traffic. More importantly, it puts the indexed file I/O burden on a separate machine.

On a busy LAN, a database server helps distribute the processing evenly and fairly. For the database server, you can select a computer and operating system on different criteria than those used to choose the file server machine. You may even go so far as to use Macintoshes for user workstations and a high-powered superserver as the database server computer. Because the workstation no longer has to contain the actual file I/O logic, the application can be smaller by saving whatever memory those file I/O routines consume. If the application is DOS-based and needs to run within the infamous 640K of conventional memory (minus what DOS and the network use), you will find database server technology tempting for the RAM it saves.

Looking at Database Server Disadvantages. To ensure good performance and to control the LAN environment more closely than a particular network operating system allows, you can build a database server into your LAN architecture. Unfortunately, you almost certainly will need the services of a programmer (or a staff of programmers) to implement a database server. You will incur the cost of programming (or reprogramming) the primary application on the LAN to use the database server. Simply installing a database server product on your LAN is not enough. You must somehow connect the application to your new database server.

Using an Uninterruptible Power Supply (UPS)

You know that rebooting a peer LAN workstation/server can affect other people's work. With a server-based LAN, when the power in your building fails, everyone's work is affected. People writing files to the server at the time of the failure may find their files incomplete or corrupted when power comes back. You may have to use your latest backup to restore some files on the file server after a power failure. An uninterruptible power supply (UPS) helps you to avoid this problem (see the following section).

Defining an Uninterruptible Power Supply (UPS)

An uninterruptible power supply (UPS) runs your computer off batteries all the time. UPSs cost anywhere from $1,000 to $3,500. When power fails, the file server computer just keeps on running, using electricity provided by the UPS batteries. The UPS contains an *inverter* that turns the direct current (DC) power from the batteries into a pure alternating current (AC) sine wave for your computer. The batteries are continuously charged from the AC power. If commercial power fails, the batteries last from a few minutes up to several hours before running down.

A UPS is simpler than a *standby power system (SPS)*. Because a UPS runs continuously, however, it must be much more sturdily built than an equivalently rated SPS. A UPS costs about twice as much as an SPS. Because your file server computer sees only smooth battery power, the server is immune to nearly all forms of AC power problems, such as sags and spikes. A UPS unit may, however, end up costing more than the computer it protects.

Note

Some companies advertise SPS products as UPS systems. Watch out for the term *transfer time* in product information. An SPS must transfer from the AC power to batteries at the time of power failure. A true UPS always runs the computer off the batteries. If the sales literature mentions a transfer time (1 to 18 milliseconds is typical), the literature describes an SPS, not a true UPS.

Understanding How the UPS and Server Work Together

Some network operating systems recognize the presence of a UPS. The UPS may come with a special adapter card you install in the server computer, or the UPS may attach to the server's COM1 or COM2 serial port. The network operating system monitors the information flowing from the UPS. If power to the server fails, the network operating system notifies people on the LAN (if their computers are still operational) of the failure. When the batteries in the UPS begin to run down, the network operating system gracefully closes all files, makes sure that all the data is stored on the hard disk, and quietly shuts itself down.

Chapter Summary

You now have an excellent understanding of the heart of your LAN—the file server. You know what a file server does, and you know what makes a good file server. You examined both hardware and software components of file servers. You recognize the important roles played by the server's hard disk drive and the server's CPU chip. You understand why installing more memory (RAM) chips in a server can result in better performance.

The network operating system in your file server may be a peer LAN product, or it may be server-based. You learned to distinguish between the two, and you know why a server-based LAN can sometimes be a better choice than a peer LAN. You learned how file servers share files and printers. You know what happens when you log in on a LAN. You understand the considerations for security and administration on both peer and server-based LANs. And you realize the importance of using an uninterruptible power supply to protect data stored on the LAN.

In the next chapter, you explore the substrata of the LAN itself. You discover how the workstations and the file server communicate with one another through the network adapters and LAN cables, via a *protocol*.

Chapter 4

Using Protocols, Cables, and Adapters

When a computer program accesses a file server with print, open, read, write, and close operations, the client workstation NOS component turns the file I/O operation into one or more LAN messages. Via layers of protocols, the NOS client then sends messages to the file server, receives the file server's response(s), and delivers results to the computer program running on the client workstation. This chapter explains exactly how the LAN supports these PC-to-PC communications. After exploring the general concepts of protocols and message frames, you become familiar with the OSI Model and discover how different products compare to the OSI standard.

At the lowest layer of protocols, you get an in-depth look at the physical-layer protocols Ethernet, Token Ring, ARCnet, and Fiber Distributed Data Interface (FDDI). The middle-layer protocols operating on top of these low-level protocols are NetBIOS, IPX/SPX, and TCP/IP. At yet a higher level, the file redirection occurs through protocols such as IBM's Server Message Blocks (SMB) standard or Novell's NetWare Core Protocol (NCP). This chapter covers all these layers of protocols.

Once you understand what information your LAN sends from computer to computer, you turn to a discussion of the different types of LAN cables that carry the information. You learn the differences between twisted-pair, coaxial, fiber optic, and other types of cables.

The network adapter enables each computer to send and receive message frames. In this chapter, you find out how network adapters support the various protocols and how each type of network adapter works.

Examining Protocols, Frames, and Communications

The network adapter sends and receives messages among the LAN computers, and the cable carries the messages. The layer of protocols in each computer, however, turns the computers into a local area network.

At the lowest level, networked PCs communicate with one another and with the file server using message packets, often called *frames*. These frames are the foundation on which all LAN activity is based. The network adapter, along with its support software, sends and receives these frames. Each computer has a unique address on the LAN to which frames can be sent.

A network operating system or LAN-aware application sends frames for various purposes, including these:

- To open a communications session with another adapter

- To send data (perhaps a record from a file) to a PC

- To acknowledge the receipt of a data frame

- To broadcast a message to all other adapters

- To close a communications session

Figure 4.1 shows what a typical frame looks like. Different network implementations define frames in different ways, but the following data items are common to all implementations:

- The sender's unique network address

- The destination's unique network address

- An identification of the contents of the frame

- A data record or message

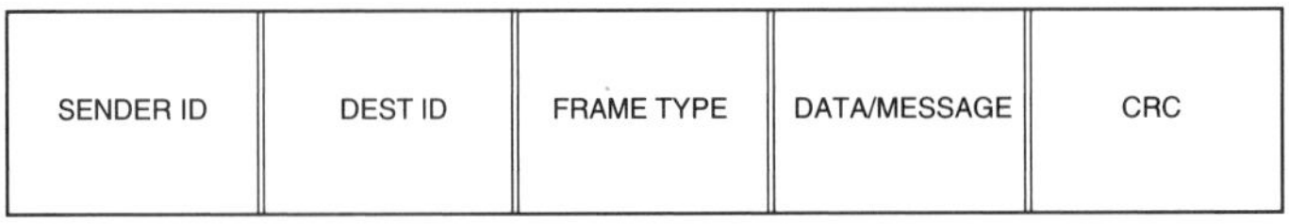

SENDER ID	DEST ID	FRAME TYPE	DATA/MESSAGE	CRC

Fig. 4.1 These data elements are common to frames that travel through LAN cables.

Using Frames That Contain Other Frames

Layering protocols is a powerful concept. The lowest layer knows how to tell the network adapter to send a message, but that layer is ignorant of file servers and file redirection. The highest layer understands file servers and redirection but knows nothing about Ethernet or Token Ring. Together, though, the layers constitute a local area network. Frames are always layered (see Figure 4.2).

When the higher-level file redirection protocol gives a message to a mid-level protocol (such as NetBIOS, for example) and asks that the message be sent to another PC on the network (probably a file server), the mid-level protocol puts an *envelope* around the message packet and hands it to the lowest-level protocol, implemented as the network support software and network adapter card. This lowest layer in turns wraps the NetBIOS envelope in an envelope of its own and sends it out across the network. In Figure 4.2, you see each envelope labeled *header* and *trailer*. Upon reception, the network support software on the receiving computer removes the outer envelope and hands the result upward to the next higher level protocol. The mid-level protocol running on the receiver's computer removes its envelope and gives the message, now an exact copy of the sender's message, to the receiving computer's highest-level protocol.

You learn much more about each layer (including NetBIOS) later in the chapter. For now, you need to remember that lower-level frames can contain higher-level frames and that different protocols exist to deal with each layer.

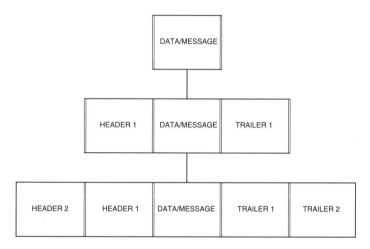

Fig. 4.2   Frames enclose other frames, in layers.

Exploring Frames and Files

Figure 4.3 illustrates how file redirection works. When an application wants to read or write a file located on the file server, the portion of the network operating system at the workstation intercepts the file I/O operation. The workstation NOS software, often implemented as a TSR program (DOS) or a Dynamic Link Library (Windows and OS/2), turns the read or write operation into a LAN message (a frame). The workstation NOS software gives the frame to the LAN support software layer, which adds its own information to the frame and hands the result to the network adapter. The network adapter adds yet more information to the frame and sends it to the file server. The response from the file server travels the opposite route back to the requesting workstation.

The network operating system vendor specifies what each file I/O redirection frame contains. For example, a workstation opening a file sends a frame containing the name of the file to the file server. The file server sends back a frame that contains a reference number the workstation can use in subsequent accesses of that file. The differences between the vendors' layouts of file I/O redirection frames explain why you need to use a particular vendor's client workstation software to connect to file servers running that vendor's NOS.

II

Building a Network

Different vendors split the LAN communications functions in different ways, but they all compare themselves to the OSI Model.

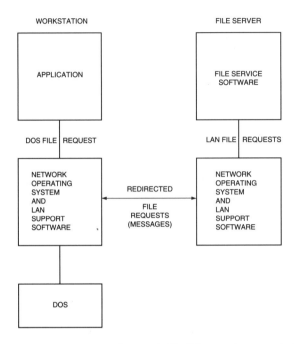

Fig. 4.3 File redirection intercepts an application's file I/O operations, sends them to a file server, and converts the server's responses into what the application would have received from the workstation computer's local operating system (DOS in the example).

Using the OSI Model

ISO, the International Standards Organization, has published a standard called the Open System Interconnection (OSI) Model. Most vendors of LAN products endorse the OSI standard but have not yet implemented OSI fully. The OSI Model divides LAN communications into seven layers. Most network operating system vendors use three or four layers of protocols.

The OSI Model describes how communications between two computers should happen. Sometime in this decade, this theoretical standard will become a practical one as more and more vendors switch to OSI. The OSI Model declares seven layers and specifies that each layer be insulated from the others by a well-defined interface. Figure 4.4 shows the seven layers.

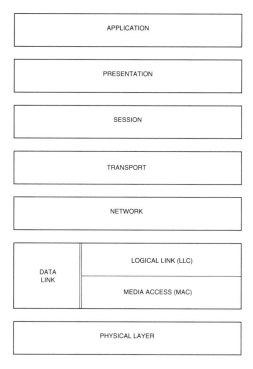

Fig. 4.4 The OSI model has seven layers.

The seven layers of the OSI Model are:

- *Physical:* This part of the OSI Model specifies the physical and electrical characteristics of the connections composing the network (twisted-pair cables, fiber-optic cables, coaxial cables, connectors, repeaters, and so forth). You can think of it as the hardware layer. This layer usually exists as chips, printed circuit boards (network adapters), and cables.

- *Data Link:* At this stage of processing, the electrical impulses enter or leave the network cable. The network's electrical representation of your data (bit patterns, encoding methods, and tokens) is known only to this layer. It is at this point that errors are detected and corrected (by requesting retransmissions of corrupted packets). Because of its complexity, the Data Link layer is often subdivided into a Media Access Control (MAC) layer and a Logical Link Control (LLC) layer. The MAC layer is concerned with network access (either token-passing or collision-sensing) and network control. The LLC layer, operating at a higher level than the MAC layer, is concerned with sending and receiving the user data messages. Chips on printed circuit boards (network adapters) typically implement most or all of this layer, and remaining higher layers are implemented by software (network drivers).

- *Network:* This layer switches and routes packets as necessary to get them to their destination. This layer is responsible for addressing and delivering message packets.

■ *Transport:* When more than one packet is in process at any one time, the Transport layer controls the sequencing of the message components and regulates inbound traffic flow. If a duplicate packet arrives, this layer recognizes it as a duplicate and discards it.

■ *Session:* The functions in this layer enable applications running at two workstations to coordinate their communications into a single session (which you can think of in terms of a highly structured dialog). The Session layer supports the creation of the session, the management of the packets sent back and forth during the session, and the termination of the session.

■ *Presentation:* When IBM, Apple, DEC, NEXT, and Burroughs computers want to talk to one another, obviously a certain amount of translation and byte reordering needs to be done. The Presentation layer converts data into (or from) a machine's native internal numeric format.

■ *Application:* This is the layer of the OSI Model seen by an application program. A message to be sent across the network enters the OSI Model at this point, travels downward toward layer 1 (the Physical layer), zips across to the other workstation, and then travels back up the layers until the message reaches the application on the other computer through its own Application layer.

To use the United States Postal Service as an analogy to explain the functions of these layers, the Application layer would be a plain sheet of paper, folded to fit in an envelope. The Presentation layer is an envelope with windows for the addresses to show through. The Session layer is the envelope with the names of the sender and recipient showing through the windows. The Transport layer is the post office. The Network layer is the mail carrier. The Data Link layer is your mailbox. The Physical layer is, of course, the mail truck.

One factor that makes the network operating system of each vendor proprietary (as opposed to *open architecture*) is the vendor's noncompliance with the OSI Model.

Using Low-Level Protocols

Local area networks work in one of two basic ways: *collision-sensing* or *token-passing*. Ethernet is an example of a collision-sensing network; Token Ring is an example of a token-passing network.

The Institute of Electrical and Electronic Engineers (IEEE) defined and documented standards for the physical characteristics of both collision-sensing and token-passing networks. These standards are known as IEEE 802.3 (Ethernet) and IEEE 802.5 (Token Ring). Be aware, though, that there are minor differences between the frame definitions for true Ethernet and for true IEEE 802.3. In terms of the standards, IBM's 16-megabit-per-second Token Ring adapter card is an 802.5 Token Ring extension. You learn the definitions and layout of Ethernet and Token Ring frames later in this chapter in the sections titled "Ethernet" and "Using Token Ring."

Some older LANs don't conform to either IEEE 802.3 or IEEE 802.5, of course. The most popular of these older, non-standard LANs was ARCnet, available from such vendors as Datapoint Corporation, Standard Microsystems, and Thomas-Conrad. Other types of LANs include StarLan (from AT&T), VistaLan (from Allen-Bradley), LANtastic (from Artisoft), Omninet (from Corvus), PC Net (from IBM), and ProNet (from Proteon).

Fiber Distributed Data Interface (FDDI) is a physical-layer LAN standard that's more re-cent than Token Ring or Ethernet. FDDI uses fiber optic cable and a token-passing scheme similar to IEEE 802.5 (the Token Ring standard) to transmit data frames at a rapid 100 megabits per second. Similarly, Asynchronous Transfer Mode (ATM) is a rela-tively new physical layer LAN standard for high-speed communications. ATM can trans-fer data at rates ranging from 25 mbps to 155 mbps.

Ethernet

In the collision-sensing environment, often referred to with the abbreviation CSMA/CD (carrier sense, multiple access, with collision detection), the network adapter card listens to the network when it has a frame to send. If the adapter hears that another card is sending a frame at that moment, the card waits a moment and tries again. Even with this approach, collisions (two workstations attempting to transmit at exactly the same mo-ment) can and do happen. It is the nature of CSMA/CD networks to expect collisions and to handle them by retransmitting frames as necessary. These retransmissions are handled by the adapter card; neither you nor your applications see or manage them. Collisions generally occur and are handled in less than a microsecond.

Although many people blame poor CSMA/CD (Ethernet) network performance on the number of users sending and receiving message traffic on the network, the truth is that over 90 percent of transmission problems on an Ethernet network are the result of faulty cables or malfunctioning adapter cards.

On an Ethernet network, data is broadcast throughout the network in all directions at the rate of 10 megabits per second. All machines receive every frame, but only those meant to receive a frame (by virtue of the frame's destination network address) respond with an acknowledgment. Figure 4.5 illustrates an Ethernet network.

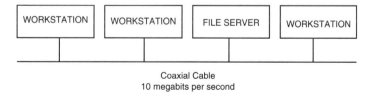

Coaxial Cable
10 megabits per second

Fig. 4.5   An Ethernet LAN sends data at 10 megabits per second.

Digital Equipment Corporation and 3Com Corporation are major suppliers of Ethernet hardware. Other companies that offer Ethernet equipment include AST Research, Data General, Excelan, Gateway Communications, Micom-Interlan, Proteon, RAD Data Com-munications, Thomas-Conrad, Ungermann-Bass, Western Digital, and Zenith.

Ethernet is a LAN standard based on the Experimental Ethernet network designed and built in 1975 by Xerox at the Palo Alto Research Center (PARC). Ethernet operates at 10 megabits per second over 50-ohm coaxial cable; the current version is 2.0, established in November of 1982. A more recent standard, Fast Ethernet, provides for 100-megabit-per-second transfers.

IEEE 802.3, a LAN standard similar to Ethernet, was first published in 1985. The differences between the two Ethernet standards lie in their network architecture and frame formats.

In terms of network architecture, IEEE 802.3 distinguishes between MAC and LLC layers; true Ethernet lumps these layers into a single Data Link layer. Ethernet also defines an Ethernet Configuration Test Protocol (ECTP) that is absent from the IEEE 802.3 standard. Note, however, that the important differences between the two are the types and lengths of the fields that make up a frame. These differences can cause the two protocols to be incompatible. The Ethernet and IEEE 802.3 frames are discussed in the following sections.

Using Ethernet Frames. Figure 4.6 shows the layout and data field definitions for a true Ethernet frame (the original, non-IEEE Ethernet).

Length of each field, in bytes

Fig. 4.6 A true Ethernet frame contains these data elements.

Descriptions for the original Ethernet frame follow:

- *Preamble:* This field is 8 bytes long (the standard refers to a byte as an *octet*, or 8 *bits*; you can call them *bytes*) and is used for synchronization and framing. The Preamble always contains the bit pattern 10101010 in the first 7 bytes, with 10101011 in the last (8th) byte.

- *Destination address:* This field, 6 bytes, contains the address of the workstation that will receive this frame. The first (leftmost) bit of the first byte has a special meaning. If the leftmost bit is 0, the destination address is a physical address that is unique throughout the entire Ethernet universe. As a result of a naming scheme administered by the Xerox Corporation, the first three bytes are a group address assigned by Xerox and the last three are assigned locally. If the leftmost bit is a 1, it represents a broadcast frame. In this case, the remainder of the destination address can refer to a group of logically related workstations or to all workstations on the network (all 1s).

■ *Source address:* This address field, also 6 bytes, identifies the workstation sending the frame. The leftmost bit of the first byte is always 0.

■ *Type:* This field contains 2 bytes of information that identify the type of the higher-level protocol that issued (or wants to receive) this frame. The Type field is assigned by Xerox and is not interpreted by Ethernet. It enables multiple high-level protocols (referred to as *client layers*) to share the network without running into one another's messages.

■ *Data portion:* This portion of the frame can contain from 46 to 1,500 bytes. It is the data message that the frame is intended to carry to the destination.

■ *CRC:* Finally, the frame contains 4 bytes of *cyclic redundancy checksum remainder*, calculated via a CRC-32 polynomial. The workstation that receives this frame performs its own CRC-32 calculation on the frame and compares the calculated value to the CRC field in the frame to find out whether the frame arrived intact or was damaged in transit.

Disregarding the preamble for a moment, you can see that an entire Ethernet frame is between 64 and 1,518 bytes. You also can see that the minimum size of a data message is 46 bytes.

Using IEEE 802.3 Frames. Figure 4.7 shows an IEEE 802.3 frame, which contains the following fields:

■ *Preamble:* This field contains 7 bytes of synchronization data. Each byte is the same bit pattern: 10101010.

■ *Start frame delimiter:* The SFD consists of a single byte that has the bit pattern 10101011. (The Preamble and SFD IEEE 802.3 fields exactly match the single Ethernet Preamble field.)

■ *Destination address:* This field can contain 2 or 6 bytes, depending on which type of IEEE 802.3 network you install; it indicates for which workstation the frame is intended. Note that all addresses on a particular network must be 2-byte or 6-byte addresses. The most popular type of IEEE 802.3, called 10BASE5, specifies 6-byte addresses. The first bit of the destination address is the individual/group bit. The I/G bit has either a value of 0, if the address refers to a single workstation, or 1, if it represents a group of workstations (a broadcast message). If the destination address is a two-byte field, the remainder of the bits form a 15-bit workstation address. If the Destination Address is a 6-byte field, however, the bit following the I/G bit is a universally/locally administered bit (the U/L bit). The U/L bit is a 0 for universally administered (global) addresses and a 1 for locally administered addresses. The remainder of the 6-byte field is a 46-bit workstation address.

■ *Source address:* The 2- or 6-byte address of the sending workstation. The I/G (first) bit is always 0.

■ *Length:* These two bytes express the length of the data portion of the frame.

II

Building a Network

- *Data portion:* From 0 to 1,500 bytes of data. If this field is fewer than 46 bytes long, the next field (PAD) fattens the frame to an acceptable (minimum) size.

- *Pad:* The Pad field contains enough bytes of filler to ensure that the frame has at least a certain overall size. If the data portion is large enough, the Pad field does not appear in the frame (Pad has zero length).

- *CRC:* The *cyclic redundancy checksum remainder* has 4 bytes of remainder from the CRC-32 algorithm—the same as for Ethernet.

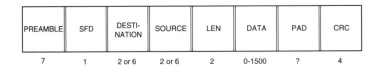

PREAMBLE	SFD	DESTI-NATION	SOURCE	LEN	DATA	PAD	CRC
7	1	2 or 6	2 or 6	2	0-1500	?	4

Length of each field, in bytes

Fig. 4.7 An IEEE 802.3 Ethernet frame contains these data elements.

The size of a frame under both true Ethernet and IEEE 802.3 Ethernet (assuming Type 10BASE5), excluding the Preamble and SFD, is the same—between 64 and 1,518 bytes. Under IEEE 802.3, however, it is permissible for the application (or an upper-layer protocol) to send a data area fewer than 46 bytes, because the frame is padded automatically by the MAC layer. Under true Ethernet, too-small data frames are considered error situations.

Using Token Ring

You can think of a token-passing network as a ring. Even though the network may be wired electrically as a star, data frames move around the network from workstation to workstation in ring fashion, as shown in Figure 4.8. A workstation sends a frame to the *MAU* (multistation access unit), which routes the frame to the next workstation.

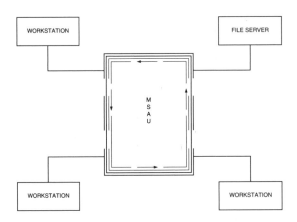

Fig. 4.8 Frames circulate the LAN on a Token Ring network.

Each network adapter card receives a frame from its *upstream neighbor*, regenerates the electrical signals making up the frame, and passes the result along to the next (*downstream*) workstation. The frame may consist of data that one computer is sending to another, or the frame may be a token. A *token* is a 3-byte message, indicating that the LAN is idle.

When a workstation wants to send a frame, the network adapter waits for the token. The adapter then turns the token into a data frame containing a protocol-layered message.

The frame travels along from adapter to adapter until it reaches its destination, which acknowledges reception of the frame by setting certain bits in the frame. The data frame continues its journey around the ring. When the sending station receives its own frame back, and if the frame was properly received, the sender relinquishes use of the LAN by putting a new token into circulation. A token-passing network is designed so that collisions never occur.

IBM currently offers Token Ring products that operate at either 4 or 16 megabits per second. Several other companies make equipment compatible with IBM Token Ring, including Thomas-Conrad, Gateway Communications, Western Digital, 3Com, General Instrument, Harris Data Communications, Madge Networks, NCR, Proteon, Pure Data, Racore, RAD Data Communications, DatAmerica, Siecor, and Ungermann-Bass. A few of these companies, such as Proteon and Siecor, make Token Ring hardware that operates at different rates or that uses fiber optics.

Early Token Release (ETR) is easily misunderstood; Token Ring itself is a fairly complex subject. On a momentarily idle Token Ring LAN, workstations circulate a token. The LAN becomes busy (carries information) when a workstation receives a token and turns it into a data frame targeted at the file server (or targeted back at a file-needy workstation if originated by a server answering a file I/O request). After its target node receives it, the data frame continues circulating around the LAN until it reaches its source node. The source node turns the data frame back into a token that circulates until a downstream node needs it. So far, so good—these are standard Token Ring concepts.

A workstation needs to send only a few bytes to tell the file server that it needs some part of a file. If the signal must go into and out of many workstations to circulate the ring and if the data frame is small, *latency* occurs. Latency is the unproductive delay that occurs while the source node waits to get its data frame returned by its upstream neighbor.

The source node appends idle characters onto the LAN following the data frame until the data frame circulates the entire LAN and arrives back at the source node. The typical latency of a 4-megabits-per-second (mbps) ring is about 50 to 100 idle characters. On a 16-mbps ring, latency may reach 400 or more bytes' worth of LAN time.

With Early Token Release, available on only 16-mbps networks, the originating workstation transmits a new token immediately after sending its data frame. Downstream nodes pass along the data frame and then receive an opportunity to transmit data themselves—the new token. If you had a token ring microscope, you would see tokens and other data frames (instead of a long trail of idle characters) chasing the data frame. You also would know that your 16-mbps token ring LAN is using ETR to keep itself busy.

Using Token Ring Frames. In 1985, Texas Instruments and IBM jointly developed the TMS380 Chipset (IBM doesn't use the chipset; it builds its own proprietary chipset mostly compatible with the TI/IBM set). The TMS380 chipset implements the IEEE 802.5 standards for the Physical layer and the Data Link layer of the OSI Model. The functions of both the MAC sublayer and the LLC sublayer of the Data Link layer are supported. Originally released as a set of five chips, the TI product can now be produced as a single chip. TMS380 functions are as follows:

- *TMS38051 and 38052 chips:* These chips handle the lowest level—the ring interface itself. They perform the actual transmission/reception of data (frames), monitor cable integrity, and provide clocking functions.

- *TMS38020 chip:* This chip is the protocol handler. It controls and manages the 802.5 protocol functions.

- *ROM chip:* This chip has program code burned into it. The permanently stored software performs diagnostic and management functions.

- *TMS38010 chip:* This chip is a 16-bit dedicated microprocessor for handling communications; it executes the code in the ROM chip and has a 2.75K RAM buffer for temporary storage of transmitted and received data.

Although most people think of a token ring as a single piece of cable that all the workstations tap into, a token ring actually consists of individual point-to-point linkages. Joe's workstation sends the token (or a data frame) to your workstation, your workstation sends the token or frame downstream to the next workstation, and so forth. Only the fact that one of your downstream neighbors happens also to be Joe's upstream neighbor makes it a ring. From a communications standpoint, the messages go directly from one PC through a hub to another PC. The hub doesn't modify the messages it passes on to the destination node.

Not all workstations on the ring are peers, although the differences are invisible to the outside world. One workstation is designated as the *active monitor*; it assumes additional responsibilities for controlling the ring. The active monitor maintains timing control over the ring, issues new tokens (if necessary) to keep things going, and generates diagnostic frames under certain circumstances. The active monitor is chosen at the time the ring is initialized and can be any workstation on the network. If the active monitor fails for some reason, the other workstations (*standby monitors*) can decide who becomes the new active monitor.

Three formats are defined for IEEE 802.5 token ring message packets: tokens, frames, and abort sequences. These formats are discussed in the following sections.

Using the Token. Figure 4.9 shows the first format of the IEEE 802.5 message packet: the token. In principle, the token is not a frame but simply a means by which each workstation can recognize when its turn to transmit arrives.

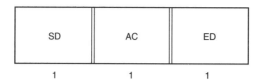

Length of each field, in bytes

Fig. 4.9   A token is a simple 3-byte frame.

A token is three bytes long (24 bits) and contains the following three fields:

- Start Delimiter

- Access Control

- End Delimiter

The Start Delimiter (SD) field appears at the beginning of the token (as well as at the beginning of every message or frame sent across the network). The SD field consists not of just 0s and 1s but of a unique series of electrical impulses that cannot be mistaken for anything other than a Start Delimiter field. Because the SD field contains four nondata symbols (each 1-bit long) and four (normal) 0 bits in the field, the field totals 1 byte in size.

Next comes the Access Control (AC) field. This field is divided into four subfields, as follows:

```
P P P  T  M  R R R
```

in which PPP are the priority bits, T is the token bit, M is the monitor bit, and RRR are the reservation bits.

A network adapter can prioritize a token or frame by setting the priority bits to a value from 0 to 7 (with 7 being the highest priority). A workstation can use the network (that is, change a token into a frame) only if it receives a token with a priority less than or equal to the workstation's own priority. The workstation's network adapter sets the priority bits to indicate the priority of the current frame or token. Refer to the description of the reservation bits for more on how this works.

The token bit has a value of 1 for a token and 0 for a frame.

The monitor bit is set to 1 by the active monitor and set to 0 by any workstation transmitting a token or frame. If the active monitor sees a token or frame that contains a monitor bit of 1, it knows that this token or frame has been once around the ring without being processed by a workstation. Because a sending workstation is responsible for

II

Building a Network

removing its own transmitted frames (by recirculating a new token), and because high-priority workstations are responsible for grabbing a token they have claimed previously, the active monitor detects that something is wrong if a frame or a prioritized token circulates the ring without being processed. The active monitor cancels the transmission and circulates a new token.

The reservation bits work hand in hand with priority bits. A workstation can place its priority in the reservation bits (if its priority is higher than the current value of the reservation bits). The workstation then has reserved the next use of the network. When a workstation transmits a new token, the workstation sets the priority bits to the value that it found in the RRR field of the frame it just received. Unless preempted by an even higher-priority workstation, the workstation that originally set the reservation bits will be the next station to turn the token into a frame.

The final field of the token is the End Delimiter (ED) field. As with the Start Delimiter field, this field contains a unique combination of 1s and special non-data symbols that cannot be mistaken for anything else. The ED field appears at the end of each token. Besides marking the end of the token, the ED field also contains two subfields: the Intermediate Frame bit and the Error-Detected bit. These fields, which pertain more to frames than to tokens, are discussed in the next section.

Using the Data Frame. Figure 4.10 shows the second format of the IEEE 802.5 message packet: The true data frame. Data frames can, of course, contain messages that a network operating system or an application sends to another computer on the ring, and data frames also sometimes contain internal messages used privately among the Token Ring network adapter cards for ring-management purposes.

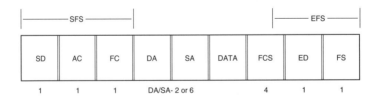

Length of each field, in bytes

Fig. 4.10 A Token Ring data frame contains these data elements.

A frame consists of several groups of fields—the Start Frame Sequence (SFS), the Destination Address (DA), the Source Address (SA), the data itself (DATA), the Frame Check Sequence (FCS), and the End Frame Sequence (EFS). Together, these fields form a message record (envelope) that is used to carry either ring-management information (MAC data) or user data (LLC data). You already know about LLC data; these are the frames that contain application-oriented data such as PC-to-PC messages or a portion of a disk file (from a file server) that is being shared via the network operating system. The network adapters use MAC frames internally, on the other hand, to control and manage the ring.

The IEEE 802.5 standard defines six MAC control frames. The Frame Control field indicates the type of the frame (MAC or LLC); if it is a MAC frame, this field also indicates which one of the six is represented by this particular frame.

Briefly, the six MAC frames are as follows:

- *Duplicate Address Test:* Sent by a workstation when it first joins the ring to ensure that its address is unique.

- *Active Monitor Present:* Circulated periodically by the active monitor to let other workstations know it is still alive.

- *Standby Monitor Present:* Sent by other than the active monitor.

- *Claim Token:* If a standby monitor thinks that the active monitor may have died, it starts sending claim token frames. The standby monitors then go through a process of negotiation with one another to determine which one becomes the new active monitor.

- *Beacon:* Sent if there is a major network problem, such as a broken cable or a workstation transmitting without waiting for the token. By detecting which station is sending the beacon frame, diagnostic software can localize the problem.

- *Purge:* Sent after ring initialization and after a new active monitor establishes itself.

Each frame (MAC or LLC) begins with a start frame sequence, containing three fields:

- *Start Delimiter (SD):* The definition of SD is the same for frames as for tokens.

- *Access Control (AC):* The definition also is the same for frames as for tokens.

- *Frame Control (FC):* This 1-byte field contains two subfields: Frame Type and MAC Control ID, as follows:

      F F C C C C C C

  The two frame type bits (FF) have a value of 00 for MAC frames and 01 for LLC frames (11 and 10 are reserved).

  The MAC control ID bits identify the type of ring-management frame:

CCCCCC	MAC Frame
000011	Claim Token
000000	Duplicate Address Test
000101	Active Monitor Present
000110	Standby Monitor Present
000010	Beacon
000100	Purge

The Destination Address (DA) follows the Start Frame Sequence fields. The DA field can be 2 or 6 bytes long. With 2-byte addresses, the first bit indicates whether the address is a group address or an individual address (just as in the collision-sensing IEEE 802.3

protocol). With 6-byte addresses the first bit also is an I/G bit, and the second bit tells whether the address is locally or globally assigned (the U/L bit, which again is the same as in the IEEE 802.3 protocol). The remainder of the bits form the address of the workstation to which the frame is addressed.

The Source Address (SA) field is the same size and format as the Destination Address field.

The data portion of the frame (DATA) can contain a user data message record intended for (or received from) a mid-level protocol, such as IPX, TCP/IP, or NetBIOS, or the Data field can contain one of the MAC frames just discussed. The Data field has no specified maximum length, although there are practical limits on its size according to how long a single workstation may control the ring.

The Frame Check Sequence (FCS) field is 4 bytes of remainder from the CRC-32 cyclic redundancy checksum algorithm. It is used for error detection.

The End Frame Sequence (EFS) is composed of two fields, the End Delimiter and the Frame Status, as follows:

- *End Delimiter (ED):* You read about this field in relation to tokens; in a frame, however, this field takes on additional meaning. Besides consisting of a unique pattern of electrical impulses, it also contains two subfields, each 1 bit in size. The intermediate frame bit is set to 1 if this frame is part of a multiple-frame transmission, and it is set to 0 if it is the last (or only) frame. The error-detected bit starts off as a 0 when a frame is originally sent. Each workstation's network adapter, as it passes the frame along, checks for errors (verifying that the CRC in the Frame Check Sequence field still corresponds to the contents of the frame, for example). An adapter sets the error-detected bit to 1 if the adapter finds something wrong. The intervening network adapters that see an already-set error-detected bit pass the frame along. The originating adapter notices that a problem occurred and tries again by retransmitting the frame.

- *Frame Status (FS):* This 1-byte field contains four reserved bits (R) and two subfields: the address-recognized bit (A) and the frame-copied bit, as follows:

    A C R R A C R R

- Because the calculated CRC does not encompass the Frame Status field, each 1-bit subfield is duplicated within frame status to ensure data integrity. A transmitting workstation sets the address-recognized bit to 0 when it originates a frame; the receiving workstation sets the bit to 1 to signal that it recognized its destination address. The frame-copied bit also starts out as 0 but is set to 1 by the receiving (destination) workstation when it copies the contents of the frame into its own memory (when it actually receives the data). The data is copied (and the bit set) only if the frame is received without error. If the originating (source) workstation gets its frame back with both of these bits set, it knows that a successful reception occurred.

- If, however, the address-recognized bit is not set by the time the frame gets back to the originating workstation, the destination workstation is no longer on the network; the other workstation must have crashed or powered off suddenly.

- Another situation occurs when the destination address is recognized but the frame copied bit is not set. This tells the originating workstation that the frame got damaged in transit (the error-detected bit in the end delimiter also will be set).

- If the address-recognized bit and the frame-copied bit are both set, but the error-detected bit is also set, the originating workstation knows that the error happened after the frame was correctly received.

Using the Abort Sequence. Figure 4.11 shows the third format of the IEEE 802.5 message packet, the abort sequence. An abort sequence, which can occur anywhere in the bit stream, is used to interrupt/terminate the current transmission.

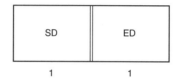

Length of each field, in bytes

Fig. 4.11   A Token Ring abort sequence frame is only 2 bytes.

An abort sequence consists of a start delimiter followed by an end delimiter. An abort sequence signals cancellation of the current frame or token transmission.

Using the Fiber Distributed Data Interface (FDDI)

The Fiber Distributed Data Interface, FDDI, is a much newer protocol than Ethernet or Token Ring. Designed by the X3T9.5 Task Group of ANSI (the American National Standards Institute), FDDI passes tokens and data frames around a ring of optical fiber at a rate of 100 megabits per second. FDDI was designed to be as much like the IEEE 802.5 Token Ring standard as possible. Differences occur only where necessary to support the faster speeds and longer transmission distances of FDDI.

If FDDI used the same bit-encoding scheme employed by Token Ring, every bit would require two optical signals: a pulse of light and then a pause of darkness. This means that FDDI would send 200 million signals per second to have a 100-megabit-per-second transmission rate. Instead, the scheme used by FDDI—called 4B/5B—encodes 4 bits of data into 5 bits for transmission so that fewer signals are needed to send a byte of information. The 5-bit codes (symbols) were chosen carefully to ensure that network timing requirements are met. The 4B/5B scheme, at a 100-megabit-per-second transmission rate, actually causes 125 million signals per second to occur (this is 125 megabaud). Also, because each carefully selected light pattern symbol represents 4 bits (a half-byte, or *nibble*), FDDI hardware can operate at the nibble and byte level rather than at the bit level, making it easier to achieve the high data rate.

Two major differences in the way the token is managed by FDDI and IEEE 802.5 Token Ring exist. In Token Ring, a new token is circulated only after a sending workstation gets back the frame that it sent. In FDDI, a new token is circulated immediately by the sending workstation after it finishes transmitting a frame. FDDI doesn't use the Priority and Reservation subfields that Token Ring uses to allocate system resources. Instead FDDI classifies attached workstations as *asynchronous* (workstations that are not rigid about the time periods that occur between network accesses) and *synchronous* (workstations having very stringent requirements regarding the timing between transmissions). FDDI uses a complex algorithm to allocate network access to the two classes of devices.

Figure 4.12 shows an FDDI token. The token consists of Preamble, Start Delimiter, Frame Control, End Delimiter, and Frame Status fields. These fields have the same definition for tokens as for frames.

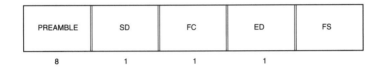

Length of each field, in bytes

Fig. 4.12 A token on an FDDI network contains these data elements.

Figure 4.13 shows the layout of an FDDI frame. Notice the similarity to the IEEE 802.5 Token Ring frames just discussed. An FDDI frame, like its slower cousin, carries MAC control data or user data.

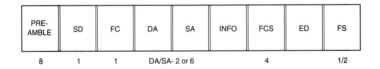

Length of each field, in bytes

Fig. 4.13 A frame on an FDDI network contains these data elements.

The fields in an FDDI frame follow:

■ *Preamble:* This field is used for synchronization. Although initially 64 bits (16 symbol-encoded nibbles) in size, its length can be modified dynamically by subsequent workstations, according to their own clocking and synchronization requirements.

■ *Start Delimiter (SD):* A unique two-symbol (1-byte) field; its pattern identifies the start of the frame.

■ *Frame Control (FC):* A two-symbol (1-byte) field made up of the following subfields:

    C L F F T T T T

The C subfield designates frame class, which tells whether the frame is used for synchronous or asynchronous service. The L bit, frame address length, indicates whether 16-bit or 48-bit addresses are being used (unlike Ethernet and Token Ring, both kinds of addresses are possible on the same FDDI network). The FF bits are the Frame Format subfield, which expresses whether the frame is a MAC frame carrying ring-management information or an LLC frame carrying user data. If it is a MAC frame, the TTTT bits specify the type of the MAC control frame contained in the Info field.

- *Destination Address (DA):* This field, 16 bits or 48 bits long, identifies the workstation to which a frame is being sent.

- *Source Address (SA):* This field, either 16 or 48 bits, identifies the sending workstation.

- *Information (INFO):* This field, the data portion of the frame, contains a MAC control record or user data. This field can vary in length but cannot cause the overall length of the frame to exceed 4,500 bytes.

- *Frame Check Sequence (FCS):* This field contains 4 bytes (eight symbols) of CRC data used for error-checking.

- *End Delimiter (ED):* In a frame, this field is one nibble (one symbol) long. In a token, it is 1 byte (two symbols) long. This field uniquely identifies the end of the frame or token.

- *Frame Status (FS):* Of arbitrary length, this field contains the error-detected bit, the address-recognized bit, and the frame-copied bit. These subfields do the same job on an FDDI network as on a Token Ring network.

Using NDIS and ODI

Network Driver Interface Specification (NDIS) and Open Datalink Interface (ODI) are two competing standards for how the network operating system controls the network adapter. 3Com Corporation and Microsoft jointly developed NDIS, a cornerstone of the Warp Server and NT Server network operating system products. A network adapter manufacturer can make its boards work with these network operating systems by supplying NDIS-compliant software drivers with the boards.

ODI, developed jointly by Novell and Apple Computer, performs many of the same functions as NDIS, but NDIS and ODI are incompatible because they present different programming interfaces to the upper layers of network software. To bridge between NDIS and ODI, Novell, IBM, and Microsoft offer ODI-to-NDIS translation software (sometimes called a *shim*). The computer program software drivers ODI2NDI.SYS and ODINSUP.SYS are such shims. A network adapter manufacturer can make its boards work with NetWare, the most popular network operating system, by supplying ODI-compliant software drivers with the boards.

As you would expect, network adapter manufacturers supply both NDIS and ODI drivers with their products. No matter how the manufacturer designed the network adapter's chip-level programming interface, the NDIS and ODI drivers provide assurance that the network adapter will work successfully with a variety of network operating systems.

II

Building a Network

Understanding the PROTOCOL.INI File

Whereas ODI network drivers use a file named NET.CFG to configure themselves, NDIS drivers use a file named PROTOCOL.INI. The format and content of the two files are quite distinct.

Most installation software for network products automatically creates PROTOCOL.INI (or NET.CFG) files. At times you may need to inspect and perhaps modify the PROTOCOL.INI files on the workstations and at the file server. You might increase the number of NetBIOS names and sessions to provide new connectivity for database management software products, or you might optimize the parameters to improve network performance.

Editing a PROTOCOL.INI file is similar to editing a Microsoft Windows INI file. A PROTOCOL.INI file is a text file containing one or more named sections. Each section is the module name of a protocol or MAC (Media Access Control) driver. Brackets ([and]) surround the section name. Underneath each section name and, optionally, indented slightly (usually by 3 spaces), named configuration entries appear in the format "name = value." Each entry is a configuration value or binding instruction for NDIS. The following is an example of one section of the PROTOCOL.INI file:

```
[XYZNetBIOS]

Drivername = NetBIOS$

Bindings = ETHERFAST

MaxNCBs = 16

MaxSessions = 32

MaxNames = 16
```

NDIS requires a particular syntax for PROTOCOL.INI file entries. Following the NDIS rules as you modify an INI file assures you that the NDIS Protocol Manager (PROTMAN) and the NDIS driver modules can at least parse your changes. The specific keywords and values you use are often unique to the drivers you load. Review the documentation that came with your network adapter (for MAC drivers) or your network operating system (for protocol drivers) to determine what's required.

But how do you deal with products whose documentation sadly lacks a clear, complete description of driver parameters? One approach, of course, is to call the technical support telephone number the vendor should have supplied with the product. A less obvious but sometimes fruitful approach involves using a file browse utility, in hexadecimal display mode, to inspect the file containing the driver software. When you view the contents of the executable file, you can sometimes recognize keyword names of parameters that have meaning inside the PROTOCOL.INI file. Also be aware that NDIS-compliant driver installation software typically uses NIFs (Network Installation Files) to indicate what entries can legally go into the PROTOCOL.INI file. The installation software reads and uses the NIF to find out what configuration choices to present at installation time. You can also explore the NIF with a file browser utility to better understand the parameters for a driver.

Use the following NDIS rules for constructing or modifying a PROTOCOL.INI file:

- The name of each protocol or MAC module must appear in brackets ([XYZNetBIOS] in the earlier example), and the name must contain 15 or fewer characters. You can use either upper- or lowercase because the Protocol Manager converts all entries to uppercase as PROTMAN reads the file into memory.

- The entry "Drivername = <device driver name>" is mandatory in device driver module sections. The Drivername entry defines the name of the OS/2 or DOS device driver that contains the module. Each network device driver can access the in-memory version of the PROTOCOL.INI file, and the network device driver finds its module section by searching for the corresponding Drivername entry. NDIS also uses a Drivername entry for DOS dynamic modules such as TSRs. Even though the TSR technically doesn't represent a .SYS device driver file, the Drivername entry lets the TSR find pertinent sections of the PROTOCOL.INI file. Multiple mentions of the device driver name occur if the device driver contains multiple logical modules.

- Protocol modules (but not MAC modules) can optionally have a "Bindings = <module name>" entry in the INI file. When it is present, the Bindings entry tells the protocol module which MAC modules the protocol will bind to. You can use this attribute to reconfigure a protocol to bind a different MAC module if your protocol supports it. The Bindings entry is unnecessary if the protocol driver is preconfigured to bind to a particular MAC module, or if the protocol stack will consist of only one MAC module and one static protocol module.

- The balance of the PROTOCOL.INI file consists of keyword = value pairs, with each keyword containing 15 or fewer characters. The keyword = value pairs pertain only to the named section in which they appear. Be aware that you can put spaces on either side of the equal sign if the white space makes the INI file more readable; as it processes the entries, Protocol Manager removes white space around the equal sign as well as trailing white space on each line of text in the file. White space characters are spaces, tabs, and formfeeds. A carriage return character and a line feed character mark the end of each line.

- The equal sign has one or more parameters following it on each line of text. The equal sign is optional if there are no parameters. For multiple parameters, you separate the parameters with spaces, tabs, commas, or semicolons. The Protocol Manager doesn't interpret the parameters; only the protocol or MAC module examines the values you specify. For a numeric parameter, the parameter is considered a 32-bit signed quantity. You can express numbers in either decimal or hexadecimal format. To specify a hexadecimal number, you prefix the parameter with either "0X" or "0x," as in "0x0400." String parameters can contain as many characters as necessary. A string parameter as a non-numeric first character or is inside quotation marks (").

- Comments in the PROTOCOL.INI file are lines having a semicolon in the first column. (Installation programs typically do not put comments in the file, but you'll find comments helpful explanations of entries you've inserted with a text editor.) Protocol Manager disregards comment lines and blank lines.

According to NDIS rules, syntax errors in the PROTOCOL.INI file cause Protocol Manager or the software driver to display an error message detailing the exact syntax problem. The module finding the error can, if appropriate, assume a valid (non-fatal) value for the parameter and continue processing. (Not all drivers written by all manufacturers of network adapters follow this rule. Sometimes, modules crash or fail to load when they discover errors in the PROTOCOL.INI file.)

II

Building a Network

Using the IBM PC LAN Support Program

The IBM PC LAN support program is an IBM software product for DOS-based Token Ring LANs. It implements the network adapter support software, as well as NetBIOS, in a set of device drivers (SYS files) that are loaded at boot time. Typically, you use three device driver files. Although memory usage depends on how the drivers are configured, typical memory usage is from 40K to 50K. The file DXMA0MOD.SYS is an interrupt arbitrator for the Token Ring card. The DXMA0MOD device driver acts as a clearinghouse, routing communication requests to the various software modules in the layers of network support software. The DXMC0MOD.SYS file is the layer of adapter support software that talks directly to the IEEE 802.5 chipset on the Token Ring card. The DXMT0MOD.SYS file implements the mid-level protocol, NetBIOS.

Using Mid-Level Protocols

The protocols discussed so far operate at a low level on the LAN. Ethernet, Token Ring, and FDDI reliably carry messages (frames) from computer to computer but know nothing about file redirection and file servers. The low-level protocols do not even provide an easy-to-use scheme for ensuring that a set of messages arrives in the same order it was sent or for identifying applications that need to communicate with one another on the LAN.

The mid-level protocols NetBIOS, IPX/SPX, and TCP/IP—when contrasted with the OSI Model—fall mostly into the Transport layer, with some characteristics of other layers (such as the Session layer). These protocols make computer-to-computer communications easier on a LAN.

Higher-level protocols that do understand file redirection and file servers use mid-level protocols to send message frames from workstation to file server and back again. Later sections of this chapter discuss the higher-level protocols.

Regardless of how each particular vendor's protocol is designed, all have certain common basic functions and features:

- *Initiating communications:* Each protocol provides the means for identifying a workstation by name, by number, or both. This identification scheme is made available to both the file redirection layer and to an application. Point-to-point communications are activated by one workstation identifying a destination workstation (often a *file server*) with which it wants to carry on a dialog. The originating workstation also designates the type of dialog—*datagram*, in which frames are addressed and sent to the destination without guarantee or verification of reception, or *session*, in which a connection (or pipe) is established and which guarantees delivery of message data.

- *Sending and receiving data:* Each protocol provides the means for origination and destination workstations to send and receive message data. A protocol-specific limit on the length of a given message is imposed, and each participant in a session-type dialog is given the means to determine the status of the dialog (for example, a workstation may inadvertently power down in the midst of a dialog—perhaps someone kicks the power cord—and the other participants are notified that an error has occurred).

■ *Terminating communications:* The protocol provides the means for participants to end a dialog gracefully.

The protocols discussed next are IPX, SPX, TCP/IP, and NetBIOS. The actual data messages that fly around the network come from your application software or from the file redirection software that shuttles DOS file-service requests to the file server and back.

Using Datagrams and Sessions

The two types of PC-to-PC or PC-to-server communications are datagrams and sessions.

A *datagram* is a message never acknowledged by the receiver; if verification of message delivery is required, it must be supplied by the receiver in the form of a return message. In other words, the sender and receiver must agree on a protocol to use datagrams safely. Each datagram message stands on its own; if more than one datagram is outstanding, the order in which they are delivered is not guaranteed. In some cases, the maximum size of a datagram is much smaller than that of a session-related message. Most networks can send and receive datagrams faster than session-related messages.

In contrast to datagrams, a *session* is a logical connection between two workstations in which message reception is guaranteed. Datagrams can be sent at will. For messages to be sent during a session, however, more work must be done: the session must be established, data messages sent and received, and at the end of the dialog, the session must be closed.

Using NetBIOS

NetBIOS accepts communications requests from the file-redirection portion of the network operating system or from an application program (such as an electronic mail product). NetBIOS requests fall into four categories:

■ *Name support:* Each workstation on the network is identified by one or more names, which are maintained by NetBIOS in a table; the first item in the table automatically is the unique, permanently assigned name of the network adapter. You can conveniently add optional user names (such as BARRY) to the table to identify each workstation. The user-assigned names can be unique or, in a special case, can refer to a group of users.

■ *Session support:* A point-to-point connection between two names (workstations) on the network can be opened, managed, and closed under NetBIOS control. One workstation begins by listening for a call; the other workstation calls the first. The computers are peers; both can send and receive message data concurrently during the session. At the end, both workstations hang up on the other.

■ *Datagram support:* Message data can be sent to a name, a group of names, or to all names on the network. A point-to-point connection is not established, and there is no guarantee that the message data will be received.

II

Building a Network

■ *Adapter/session status:* Information about the local network adapter card, other network adapter cards, and any currently active sessions is available to application software that uses NetBIOS.

Many years ago, IBM offered NetBIOS as a separate program product, implemented as a terminate-and-stay-resident file named NETBEUI.COM. This program file is now obsolete. If you have an older Token Ring network that uses NetBEUI, you should replace the low-level network support software on each workstation, including NetBEUI, with the device drivers of the later IBM PC LAN support program.

NetBIOS and NetBEUI

Technically, NetBIOS is a programming interface for sending messages on a network, while NetBEUI (an acronym for NetBIOS Enhanced User Interface) is a transport-layer protocol.

Using IPX/SPX

Novell implements a datagram-oriented protocol, IPX, on its NetWare LANs. Novell also implements a session-oriented protocol, SPX. You can also configure Novell NetWare LANs to use TCP/IP rather than IPX/SPX.

Novell has completely redesigned its IPX/SPX software several times in the last decade. Originally included in the same computer program that provided file redirection (ANETX.COM), IPX/SPX later became a separate computer program (IPX.COM) you loaded before the file redirection program (NETX.COM). However, IPX.COM contained hardware-specific information about the network adapter. Still later, Novell produced IPXODI.COM, an ODI-based design that separated IPX from the adapter-specific computer program. More recently, Novell enhanced its IPX/SPX client software to be part of Novell's Virtual Loadable Module (VLM) technology. Many companies still use IPXODI, while some have migrated to VLM technology. Very recently, both Novell and Microsoft released 32-bit IPX/SPX drivers for Windows 95 and Windows NT.

Using IPX. IPX, the Internetwork Packet Exchange, is the underlying protocol used by Novell NetWare's file redirection modules. IPX is an adaptation of a protocol developed by Xerox Corporation called XNS—Xerox Network Standard. IPX supports only datagram messages (it is said to be connectionless). IPX corresponds to the Network layer of the OSI Model; it performs addressing, routing, and switching to deliver a message (packet) to its destination. IPX is speedier than the session-oriented SPX protocol. Although delivery is not guaranteed, Novell indicates that IPX packets are correctly received about 95 percent of the time.

NetWare's file redirection modules use the IPX protocol (not the session-oriented SPX protocol) to send and receive file-service packets to and from the file server. This method is safe and reliable because every such request from a workstation requires a response from the file server. The file redirection modules never assume that a file-service packet (to write data to a file, for example) has been processed by the file server until the proper return acknowledgment response is received.

If you use Novell NetWare, you obviously already have IPX. Depending on your version of NetWare, you may have SPX as well.

Using SPX. SPX, which stands for *sequenced packet exchange*, is a session-level, connection-oriented protocol. Before SPX packets are sent or received, a connection must be established between the two sides that want to exchange information. Once established, messages within a session can be sent in either direction with the guarantee of delivery. SPX also guarantees that packets arrive in the correct order (if multiple packets are sent at once). SPX operates at one layer above the Transport layer of the OSI Model, the Network layer. SPX also has some characteristics of the Session layer. Although Novell NetWare uses IPX to send and receive file service packets, it uses SPX to allow access to its internal diagnostic and network management functions.

SPX is a protocol layer above IPX that uses IPX to actually send or receive message packets. If you have Novell NetWare, IPX exists on your LAN. This is not necessarily true for SPX; early versions of NetWare did not support SPX. If you have Version 2.0a of NetWare, you have SPX only if the version of the file redirection program (ANET3.COM) is 2.01 to 2.04. SPX is present in all later versions of NetWare (2.1 and later).

Using TCP/IP

TCP/IP is like NetBIOS, IPX, and SPX in several ways. TCP/IP stands for *Transmission Control Protocol/Internet Protocol*. The Department of Defense designed TCP/IP for ARPANET, a geographically large network (not a LAN) connecting the various sites of the Department of Defense's Advanced Research Projects Agency. TCP/IP is a layer of protocols, not a LAN operating system. IP provides datagram communications between nodes on a network (like Novell's IPX). TCP is like NetBIOS in that it provides point-to-point, guaranteed-delivery communications between nodes.

A set of fairly standard utilities exist for transferring files (FTP), doing simple remote program execution (TELNET), and sending electronic mail (SMTP) over TCP/IP networks. These utilities do not perform file redirection. You need a product such as Sun Microsystem's NFS (Network File System) or Locus Computing's PC Interface (sold by IBM under the name AIX Access for DOS Users) to do file redirection on a TCP/IP-based network.

Because TCP/IP is a public, not proprietary, protocol, it has become extremely popular as the basis for interconnecting LANs from different vendors. The U.S. federal government decreed in the late 1980s that all major federal computer/network acquisitions after August 1990 must comply with GOSIP, the Government OSI Profile. The government planned that OSI protocols would replace TCP/IP by the late 1990s. The government didn't, however, take into account the growing popularity of TCP/IP. Eventually, the government rescinded its decree—and TCP/IP is replacing NetBIOS and IPX/SPX on many networks. In addition, both IBM and Microsoft offer NetBIOS as an extra protocol layer on TCP/IP networks.

> **Note**
>
> IPX/SPX and TCP/IP are routable protocols because each message identifies the destination network as well as the destination node. A router, which you'll learn more about in Chapter 14, "Building WANs from LANs," can use the destination network information to shunt a message from one network to another. The NetBEUI protocol does not identify the destination network and thus is not a routable protocol.

Using Named Pipes

A *pipe* is a stream of data between two programs. One program opens the pipe and writes data into it; the other program opens the pipe and reads the data from the first program. If this sounds easy and simple to program, that's because it is. A *named pipe* is a file whose name has a particular format, as follows:

```
\PIPE\path\name.ext
```

OS/2 provides functions for opening, using, and closing named pipes. The application that wants to create the pipe (called the *server*—but don't confuse this with a file server) starts the communication session, and another application (called the *client*) joins in. An application can treat named pipes as simple data streams or, if the programmer desires, as message pipes. In the latter case, each read operation fetches one message at a time from the pipe.

Because named pipes do so much work yet require only a programmer to code a few simple program statements, named pipes are extremely popular on OS/2 and NT LANs.

Using File-Redirection Protocols

The file-redirection portions of the various network operating systems use proprietary high-level protocols to accomplish file redirection. In the Warp Server and NT Server products, IBM and Microsoft use server message blocks (SMBs). In NetWare, Novell uses its NetWare Core Protocol (NCP). Peer LANs sometimes use SMBs but often implement their own high-level protocols for file redirection.

The contents of SMB messages and NCP messages are completely different, but both protocols serve the same purpose. File I/O redirection software running on a client workstation sends SMB messages to Warp Server or NT Server, or NCP messages to NetWare, to request file operations at the file server.

Using Server Message Blocks (SMBs)

At the workstation, Warp Server or NT Server client software intercepts an application's file I/O operations and shunts them across the network to the file server. On DOS and some Windows PCs, the workstation software modules that accomplish this redirection are called *DOS LAN Requester* (DLR). DLR uses a Server Message Block (SMB) protocol to accomplish the file redirection. DOS LAN Requester, running on a workstation, opens NetBIOS sessions with the Warp Server or NT Server software running on the file server. DLR then uses NetBIOS to send SMBs to the server. Warp Server or NT Server responds with SMB protocol messages. IBM and Microsoft define four categories of SMBs: session control, file access, print service, and messages. The Windows for Workgroups and Windows 95 operating systems include DLR functionality as part of the operating system.

Using NetWare Core Protocol (NCP)

On a NetWare LAN, the workstation software module that performs file redirection is called the *shell* or *redirector*. Long ago, you needed a different version of the shell program for each different version of DOS. The shell program for DOS 3 was NET3.COM. NET4.COM was for DOS 4, and NET5.COM was for DOS 5. More recently, Novell offered a DOS-version independent shell program, NETX. Currently, Novell suggests that you use Virtual Loadable Modules (VLMs) as a shell to connect to a NetWare file server.

VLMs and all versions of NETX use the *NetWare Core Protocol (NCP)* to send and receive file service message packets. The inner workings of NCP are considered a trade secret by Novell. Although IBM has published the SMB protocol for programmers and network administrators to understand, Novell offers the NCP protocol exclusively to developers for an expensive license fee.

Using LAN Cables

Cabling systems for LANs vary widely in appearance, characteristics, intended purpose, and cost. This chapter discusses the three most popular ways to tie computers together on a LAN: the IBM cabling system, the AT&T premises distribution system, and the Digital Equipment Corporation cabling concept called DECconnect.

Generally speaking, the cabling systems described in the next few sections use one of three distinct cable types. These are twisted-pair (shielded and unshielded), coaxial cable (thin and thick), and fiber optic cable.

Using Twisted-Pair Cable

Twisted pair is just what its name implies—insulated wires with a minimum number of twists per foot. Twisting the wires reduces electrical interference (*attenuation*). *Shielded twisted pair* refers to the amount of insulation around the wire and therefore its noise immunity. You already are familiar with the unshielded twisted pair; it is often used by the telephone company. Shielded twisted pair, however, looks entirely different; it looks somewhat like the wire used to carry house current (110 volts) throughout your home or apartment. Appearances are deceiving, though, because shielded twisted pair actually carries a relatively low voltage signal. The heavy insulation is for noise reduction, not safety. Figure 4.14 shows unshielded twisted-pair cable, while Figure 4.15 illustrates shielded twisted-pair cable.

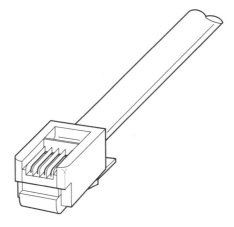

Fig. 4.14   An unshielded twisted-pair cable.

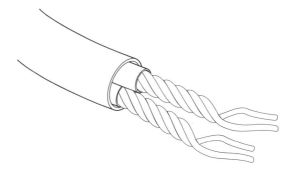

Fig. 4.15   Shielded twisted pair.

Using Coaxial Cable

Coaxial cable is fairly prevalent in everyday life; you often find it connected to the backs of television sets and audio equipment. Thin and thick, of course, refer to the diameter of the coaxial cable. Standard Ethernet cable (thick Ethernet) is as thick as your thumb. The newer ThinNet (sometimes called *CheaperNet*) cable is about the size of your little finger. The thick cable has a greater degree of noise immunity, is more difficult to damage, and requires a *vampire tap* (a piercing connector) and a drop cable to connect to a LAN. Although it carries the signal over shorter distances than the thick cable, ThinNet uses a simple BNC connector (a bayonet-locking connector for thin coaxial cables), is lower in cost, and has become a standard in office coaxial cable. Figure 4.16 is a picture of an Ethernet BNC coaxial connector, and Figure 4.17 illustrates the design of coaxial cable.

Fig. 4.16   An Ethernet coaxial cable connector has a T shape.

Note

10Base-2 and 10Base-T are technical terms for LAN cabling. 10Base-2 refers to coaxial cable, which is similar to the cable used for cable TV. With 10Base-2, the maximum cable distance is 200 meters (607 feet). 10Base-2, also called thin Ethernet or sometimes "CheaperNet," uses twisted-pair cable. 10Base-2 attaches to a computer through an RJ-45 jack. With 10Base-T, the maximum cable distance is 100 meters (328 feet).

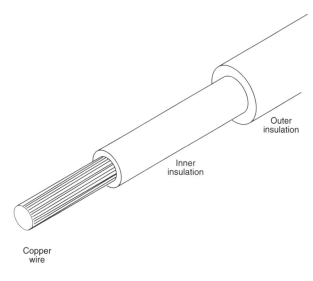

Outer
insulation

Inner
insulation

Copper
wire

Fig. 4.17   Coaxial cable.

Using Fiber-Optic Cable

Fiber-optic cable, as its name suggests, uses light rather than electricity to carry information. Fiber can send data over huge distances at high speeds, but it is expensive and difficult to work with. Splicing the cable, installing connectors, and using the few available diagnostic tools for finding cable faults are skills that very few people have.

Fiber-optic cable is simply designed but unforgiving of bad connections. Fiber cable usually consists of a core of glass thread whose diameter is measured in microns, surrounded by a solid glass *cladding*. This, in turn, is covered by a protective sheath. The first fiber-optic cables were made of glass, but plastic fibers also have been developed. The light source for fiber-optic cable is a light-emitting diode (LED); information is usually encoded by varying the intensity of the light. A detector at the other end of the cable converts the received signal back into electrical impulses. Two types of fiber cable exist: single mode and multimode. Single mode has a smaller diameter, is more expensive, and can carry signals for a greater distance.

Figure 4.18 illustrates fiber-optic cables and their connectors.

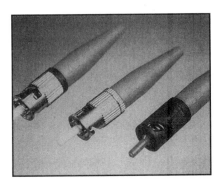

Fig. 4.18 Fiber-optic cables use light to carry LAN messages. The ST connector is commonly used with fiber-optic cables.

Using the IBM Cabling System

The IBM cabling system, ironically neither manufactured nor sold by IBM, consists of a published IBM standard that defines cabling system components and different cable types for wiring systems in office buildings. When the cabling system was first introduced in 1984, IBM described it as the intended backbone for its Token Ring network. The first such cables to be manufactured by third-party companies were tested by IBM, verified to IBM specifications, and actually given IBM part numbers. At present, however, cable manufacturers have to rely on the ETL or UL independent testing laboratories or industry-standard manufacturers such as AMP to verify compliance with the specifications published by IBM.

The IBM specifications define workstation faceplates, adapters/connectors, access units, and wiring closet termination methods. The standard also defines the following cable types:

- *Type 1 data cable:* Copper-based, for data connections only, and available in non-plenum, plenum, and outdoor varieties. It consists of two twisted pairs of 22-gauge solid conductors, shielded with both foil and braid and covered with a polyvinyl-chloride (PVC) sheath. Type 1 data cable is used for connecting terminal devices located in work areas to distribution panels located in wiring closets and for connecting between wiring closets. The plenum cable is installed in plenums, ducts, and spaces used for environmental air; in case of fire, it gives off less toxic fumes than the non-plenum cable. The outdoor cable is protected in a corrugated metallic shield with a polyethylene sheath, and the core is filled with a jelly-like compound to prevent moisture from entering.

- *Type 2 data and telephone cable:* For both data and voice (telephone) applications. This cable is similar to Type 1 but has four additional twisted pairs (22-gauge). Type 2 cable comes in plenum and non-plenum varieties.

- *Type 3 telephone twisted-pair cable:* Consists of four-pair, 24-gauge wire in polyvinyl-chloride plastic. This cable is equivalent to the IBM Rolm specification and is available in plenum. It is unshielded and not as immune to noise as Type 1 cable when it is used for data.

- *Type 5 fiber optic cable:* Contains two 100/140-micron multimode optical fibers (100-micron core surrounded by 140-micron cladding layer). This cable is not defined by IBM.

- *Type 6 patch panel cable:* For connecting a workstation to a wall faceplate, or for making connections within a wiring closet. More flexible than Type 1 cable (hence its use as patch cable). This cable consists of two twisted pairs of 26-gauge stranded conductors.

- *Type 8 undercarpet cable:* An undercarpet cable useful for open office or workstation areas where there are no permanent walls. Type 8 cable consists of two pairs of 26-gauge solid conductors in a flat sheath.

- *Type 9 low-cost plenum cable:* An economy version of Type 1 plenum cable with a maximum transmission distance of about two-thirds that of Type 1 cable. Type 9 cable consists of two twisted pairs of 26-gauge stranded conductors. This cable is not defined by IBM.

Using the AT&T Premises Distribution System

The AT&T premises distribution system (PDS) is similar in many ways to the IBM cabling system, but it relies more heavily on unshielded telephone twisted pair. PDS also integrates voice and data wiring. Connections are based on modular jacks/plugs and the cross-connect techniques originally designed for voice PBX and telephone-set wiring, which use multipair cable. With its strong roots in the telephone company's existing wiring systems, PDS obviously builds on the huge installed base of telephone cable. Generally, the AT&T PDS parts costs are lower than the IBM system but more labor-intensive to install.

II

Building a Network

Using DECconnect

The DECconnect cabling concept is based on the use of ThinNet 50-ohm thin coaxial cable, commonly used in Ethernet networks. The DECconnect system has standardized much of the connecting hardware used in major DEC installations of VAX systems. DECconnect also defines a line of protocol converters, line drivers, and *satellite closet* rack and termination hardware. A satellite closet is a small room in your office set aside just for communications equipment. Many DECconnect installations consist of an Ethernet *backbone* (a central cable to which all other cables connect) wired throughout a building with *taps* (connection points) provided at VAX computer sites and the satellite closets.

Connecting the Cables

In a token-passing network, cables from the workstations (or from the wall faceplates) connect centrally to a multistation access unit (abbreviated MSAU, or sometimes just MAU). The MAU tracks which workstations on the LAN are neighbors and which neighbor is upstream or downstream. It is an easy job; the MAU usually does not even need to be plugged into a electrical power outlet. The exception to this need for external power is an MAU that supports longer cable distances or the use of unshielded twisted-pair (Type 3) cable in high-speed LANs. The externally powered MAU assists the signal by regenerating it.

An IBM MAU has eight ports for connecting from one to eight Token Ring devices. Each connection is made with a genderless data connector (as specified in the IBM cabling system). The MAU has two additional ports labelled *RI (Ring-In)* and *RO (Ring-Out)* that daisy-chain several MAUs together when more than eight workstations are on the LAN.

It takes several seconds to open the adapter connection on a Token Ring LAN (something you may have noticed). During this time, the MAU and your Token Ring adapter card perform a small diagnostic check, after which the MAU establishes your workstation as a new neighbor on the ring. Once it is established as an active workstation, your computer is linked on both sides to your upstream and downstream neighbors (as defined by your position on the MAU). In its turn, your Token Ring Adapter card accepts the token or frame, regenerates its electrical signals, and gives the token or frame a swift kick to send it through the MAU in the direction of your downstream neighbor.

In an Ethernet network, the number of connections (taps) and their intervening distances are limiting factors. Repeaters regenerate the signal every 500 meters or so. If repeaters were not used, *standing waves* (additive signal reflections) would distort the signal and cause errors. Because collision detection depends partly on timing, only five 500-meter segments and four repeaters can be placed in a series before the propagation delay becomes longer than the maximum allowed time period for the detection of a collision. Otherwise, the workstations farthest from the sender would be unable to determine whether a collision had occurred.

The people who design computer systems love to find ways to circumvent limitations. Manufacturers of Ethernet products have made it possible to create Ethernet networks in star, branch, and tree designs that overcome the basic limitations mentioned. You can have thousands of workstations on a complex Ethernet network.

Local area networks are local because the network adapters and other hardware components cannot send LAN messages more than about a few hundred feet. Table 4.1 reveals the distance limitations of different kinds of LAN cable. In addition to the limitations shown in Table 4.1, keep in mind that you can't connect more than 30 computers on a ThinNet Ethernet segment, more than 100 computers on a ThickNet Ethernet segment, more than 72 computers on unshielded twisted-pair Token Ring, or more than 260 computers with shielded twisted-pair Token Ring cable.

Table 4.1. Network Distance Limitations

Network Adapter	Cable Type	Maximum	Minimum
Ethernet	Thin	607 ft.	20 in.
	Thick (drop cable)	164 ft.	8 ft.
	Thick (backbone)	1,640 ft.	8 ft.
	UTP	328 ft.	8 ft.
Token Ring	STP	328 ft.	8 ft.
	UTP	148 ft.	8 ft.
ARCnet (passive hub)		393 ft.	depends on cable
ARCnet (active hub)		1,988 ft.	depends on cable

Using Network Adapters

Network adapters are generally collision-sensing or token-passing. A network adapter's design ties it to one of the low-level protocols—Ethernet, Token Ring, FDDI, ARCnet, ATM, or some other protocol. Figure 4.19 is a photograph of ARCnet network adapters. Figure 4.20 shows the network adapters and hub for the Thomas-Conrad TCNS product, a high-speed network operating at 100 megabits per second. Figure 4.21 shows some typical Ethernet network adapters.

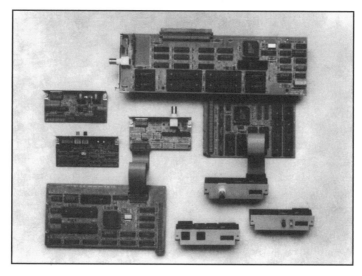

Fig. 4.19 ARCnet adapter cards.

Fig. 4.20 The high-speed TCNS network adapters and hub.

Fig. 4.21 Popular Ethernet adapters.

If you have fast workstations and a fast file server, you want a fast network. Even 16 megabits per second may be too slow if your applications are data-intensive. TCNS, from Thomas-Conrad, operates at 100 megabits per second and doesn't cost a lot more than Token Ring. TCNS gives you all the advantages of FDDI without FDDI's high price tag. NetWare, NT Server, POWERLan, LANtastic, and other ARCnet-compatible network operating systems work well with TCNS. The only catch is that you have to use fast computers to realize performance gains with TCNS.

Chips & Technologies makes a hybrid network adapter that works on both Ethernet and Token Ring LANs, but you should be aware that Ethernet and Token Ring cards cannot operate together on the same LAN cable. You may have a dual-purpose network adapter, but your LAN can use only one type of low-level protocol. To mix two LANs that use different low-level protocols, you must install a bridge between the two networks.

A *bridge* connects different LANs, enabling communication between devices on separate LANs. Bridges are protocol-independent, but hardware-specific. Bridges connect LANs with different hardware and different protocols. An example would be a device that connects an Ethernet network to a Token Ring network. With a bridge, messages can be sent between the two networks.

Collision-sensing and token-passing adapters contain sufficient on-board logic to know when it is permissible for them to send a frame and to recognize frames intended for themselves. With the adapter support software, both types of cards perform seven major steps during the process of sending or receiving a frame.

Outbound (when data is being sent), the steps are performed in the order presented in the following list. Inbound (when data is received), however, the steps are reversed. The steps are:

1. *Data transfer:* Data is transferred from PC memory (RAM) to the adapter card or from the adapter card to PC memory via DMA, shared memory, or programmed I/O.

2. *Buffering:* While it is being processed by the network adapter card, data is held in a buffer. The buffer gives the card access to an entire frame at once, and it enables the card to manage the difference between the data rate of the network and the rate at which the PC can process data.

3. *Frame formation:* The network adapter has to break up the data into manageable chunks (or on reception reassemble it). On an Ethernet network, these chunks are about 1,500 bytes. Token Ring networks generally use a frame size of about 4K. The adapter prefixes the data packet with a frame header and appends a frame trailer to it. The header and trailer are the Physical layer's envelope, which you learned about earlier in this chapter. At this point, a complete, ready-for-transmission frame exists. (Inbound, upon reception, the adapter removes the header and trailer at this stage.)

4. *Cable access:* In a CSMA/CD network such as Ethernet, the network adapter ensures that the line is quiet before sending its data (or retransmits its data if a collision occurs). In a token-passing network, the adapter waits until it gets a token that it can claim. (These steps are not significant to receiving a message, of course.)

5. *Parallel/serial conversion:* The bytes of data in the buffer are sent or received through the cables in serial fashion, with one bit following the next. The adapter card does this conversion in the split second before transmission (or after reception).

6. *Encoding/decoding:* The electrical signals that represent the data being sent or received are formed. Most network adapters use *Manchester encoding*. This technique has the advantage of incorporating timing information into the data through the use of *bit periods*. Instead of representing a 0 as the absence of electricity and a 1 as

its presence, the 0s and 1s are represented by changes in polarity as they occur in relation to very small time periods.

7. *Sending/receiving impulses:* The electrically encoded impulses making up the data (frame) are amplified and sent through the wire. (On reception, the impulses are handed up to the decoding step.)

Of course, executing all these steps takes only a fraction of a second. While you were reading about these steps, thousands of frames were sent across the LAN.

Network adapter cards and the support software recognize and handle errors, which occur when electrical interference, collisions (in CSMA/CD networks), or malfunctioning equipment cause some portion of a frame to be corrupted. Errors are generally detected by using a cyclic redundancy checksum (CRC) data item in the frame. The CRC is checked by the receiver; if its own calculated CRC doesn't match the value of the CRC in the frame, the receiver tells the sender about the error and requests retransmission of the frame in error. Several products perform network diagnostic and analysis functions on different types of LANs. Chapter 12, "Managing Your Network," covers these tools in detail.

The different types of network adapters vary not only in access method and protocol, but also in these ways:

- Transmission speed

- Amount of on-board memory for buffering frames and data

- Bus design (8-bit, 16-bit, 32-bit, or MicroChannel)

- Bus speed (some fail when run at high speed)

- Compatibility with various CPU chipsets

- DMA usage

- IRQ and I/O port addressing

- Intelligence (some adapters use an on-board CPU)

- Connector design

Most network adapters install in a slot on the motherboard of your personal computer. In support of the rapidly growing number of laptop and notebook computers that do not have slots, however, some companies offer network adapters that simply plug into the parallel printer port. These devices are called *pocket network adapters*. Xircom makes the most popular pocket network adapters, offering models for Ethernet, Token Ring, and ARCnet LANs. Figure 4.22 shows the Xircom Pocket Ethernet Adapter.

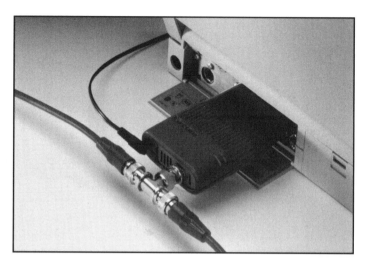

Fig. 4.22   The Xircom Pocket Ethernet Adapter connects to the computer's parallel (printer) port.

Xircom's address follows:

> Xircom
> 26025 Mureau Road
> Calabasas, CA 91302
> (818) 878-7600

Chapter Summary

In this chapter, you took a detailed look at the inner workings of a LAN. You learned about the OSI Model. You explored the Ethernet, Token Ring, and FDDI low-level protocols, and you learned how these protocols carry information from computer to computer on a network. This chapter discussed how the IPX, SPX, NetBIOS, and TCP/IP mid-level protocols work and how they relate to the OSI Model. You learned that each network operating system vendor uses a file-redirection protocol that makes one vendor's products generally incompatible with other network operating systems. This chapter also explained different types of LAN cable and how they carry information. Finally, you looked at how network adapter cards (or pocket adapters) work.

In Chapter 5, "Using Workstations," you learn about the role your own personal computer plays on the LAN: that of a client workstation.

II

Building a Network

Chapter 5

Using Workstations

If local area networks were perfect, you would not need this book. You could use a computer as a workstation without knowing that the LAN was present. An administrator would set up the file server, and people using their computers would not know anything had changed. Local area networks have a long way to go, however, before they are actually this easy to use.

AppleTalk LANs come close to making workstations seem like stand-alone computers that happen to have enhanced capabilities. Other LANs also come close, but with any LAN you should be aware of certain differences between your computer as a stand-alone tool and your computer as a workstation on a LAN.

DOS-based computers constitute the majority of workstations on local area networks. Most LAN designers' efforts go into making DOS-based access of file servers as transparent as possible. If you use Microsoft Windows on your DOS-based computer, your view of the LAN is different than without Windows. If you use OS/2's capability to give you both multiple DOS and multiple OS/2 sessions, your view also differs.

Your computer may boot from a local hard drive (or floppy disk), or your PC may get a copy of the operating system from a file server. If you have the latter type of PC, you have a *diskless workstation*—and your computer behaves differently when it is not connected to the LAN.

If you use a Macintosh, your view of the LAN is also different. Or if your computer uses the UNIX operating system, you see the LAN in yet a different way.

This chapter is divided into sections that address each of these types of computers and operating systems. Each section discusses the practical aspects of how your particular combination of computer, operating system, and operating environment behaves on a LAN, with particular emphasis on what you need to know when your computer is a LAN workstation.

Using DOS-Based Computers

Your DOS-based computer can access extra drive letters and print to the LAN printer (if one exists, of course). In addition, you have new commands and utilities you can run. Some DOS commands behave differently on a LAN. Applications may have less memory in which to run. The DOS PATH statement for your computer almost certainly changes as a result of your connection to the LAN. You may find it necessary to change entries in your CONFIG.SYS file because your computer is attached to the LAN. And, unless you have a diskless workstation, you have new network-related files stored on your computer.

The next sections of this chapter address these issues for DOS-based computers.

Drive Letters

At boot time, DOS assigns drive letters whose values depend on the number of floppy-disk drives, hard-disk drives, and DOS-formatted partitions on those hard-disk drives. DOS always reserves drives A and B for floppies, even if you do not have a drive B. DOS assigns drive C to your first hard disk; it uses drives D, E, and other drive letters to refer to the second hard disk, additional DOS partitions, and additional floppy-disk drives.

The network operating system (NOS) also assigns drive letters but not until you perform the login sequence. With many network operating systems, you can choose which drive letters you want the NOS to assign. By default, Novell NetWare assigns drive F as the file server hard disk. You can use the NetWare MAP utility to assign other server hard disks, if they exist, or to change the drive letter assignment. An example of the NetWare MAP utility follows:

```
MAP G:=SYSTEMPRO\SYS:
```

This example tells NetWare to refer to the SYS: volume (hard disk) on the server named SYSTEMPRO as drive G.

The LASTDRIVE parameter, which you may place in your CONFIG.SYS file, influences how some network operating systems assign drive letters. Usually, the NOS assigns drive letters that follow LASTDRIVE. For NT Server and Warp Server, however, LASTDRIVE encompasses local and network drives. You may see an entry such as the following in the CONFIG.SYS file of a workstation on a Warp Server network:

```
LASTDRIVE=Z
```

You may have applications that write to the root directory of the current drive. On a LAN, you may not have sufficient rights to the root directory of the file server's disk to run such applications (not to mention the confusion that would reign if the application put such files in the root directory for every person on the LAN). In such a case, you would be interested in NetWare's MAP ROOT feature. With MAP ROOT, you set up a drive letter whose root directory is really another directory on the file server: G:\, for example, may refer to the directory SYS:\USERS\BARRY. An application thinks it is writing files in the root directory of drive G when, in fact, it is writing them in \USERS\BARRY.

> **Note**
>
> With some network operating systems, it is possible to assign a drive letter to a file-server disk drive that is the same as that of a local disk drive. If you do this, your local disk drive becomes "invisible," and you cannot use the files on that disk drive until you undo the overlapped drive letter mapping.

The LAN Printer

In Chapter 2, "Sharing Computer Resources," you learned the basics of LAN printer sharing, and you learned the etiquette you should use in a shared printer environment. In Chapter 3, "Using File Servers," you looked at printer sharing from the file server's point of view. From your workstation's point of view, you print to the LAN printer in almost the same way you print to a locally attached printer.

Your computer can have up to three printer ports: LPT1, LPT2, and LPT3. If you have a locally attached printer, it probably uses LPT1. In this case, you can assign (redirect) LPT2 to the LAN printer. If you do not have a locally attached printer, you can assign LPT1 to the LAN printer. With most network operating systems, you can assign all three printer ports to one or more LAN printers. You do not have to have a physical parallel printer port on your computer to use the LAN printer; the network operating system enables you to pretend that you have an LPT1 port.

With Novell NetWare, you use the CAPTURE command to redirect your printouts. With Warp Server and NT Server, you use the NET USE command. NetWare's CAPTURE command has more options and capabilities than printer redirection commands of other network operating systems. However, all printer redirection commands provide the same basic function: making your applications think they are printing to a real printer. The application software does not know the print data becomes LAN messages that transfer to the server and into the print queue before the server's spooler modules print the data.

An example of a NetWare CAPTURE command follows:

```
CAPTURE NT NFF NOTIFY TI=10 NB Q=LASERJET
```

Descriptions of the command elements follow:

Element	Function
NT	Tells the spooler module not to expand tabs into spaces.
NFF	Tells the spooler not to add a form feed to the end of the printout.
NOTIFY	Tells the spooler to send a notification message to your workstation when the printout finishes.
TI=10	Tells the print redirector portion of your workstation's network software to interpret a 10-second pause of silence to mean that the application has completed printing.

NB	Indicates not to print a banner page.
Q=LASERJET	Indicates that you want your printout to go to the print queue named LASERJET.

The following is an example of a LANtastic printer redirection command:

```
NET USE LPT1 \\SERVER1\@LASERJET
```

Where LPT1 is the printer port to assign, SERVER1 names the file server to which the printer is attached, and @LASERJET specifies the printer.

When you send a printout to the LAN printer, you do not lose control of the data. With most network operating systems, you can manipulate the queue entry before it actually prints. You can delete (cancel) your own entry or hold it for later processing. You can modify some characteristics of the queue entry, such as how many copies you want printed. People with system administration authority can modify the queue attributes of other people's printouts, or cancel them. You cannot change the contents of the printout once it's in the queue, however.

Note

Just as with drive letter assignments, you can tell the network operating system to override the printer port assignments that DOS uses. If you have a locally attached printer on LPT1, and you assign LPT1 to the LAN printer, you lose the use of your local printer until you undo the assignments.

Network Commands and Utilities

Once you log into the LAN, you have new commands and utilities for managing your workstation's relationship with the network. Besides giving you a way to redirect printer output, the network commands enable you to turn off printer redirection and do a number of other useful things. The following is a list of many NetWare commands and their purposes:

Command	**Function**
CAPTURE/ENDCAP	Starts/stops printer redirection.
CHKDIR, CHKVOL, VOLINFO	Displays file-server disk data.
FLAG	Manages file attributes.
GRANT/REVOKE	Changes a user's rights.
MAP	Assigns and redirects drive letters.
NCOPY	Copies files.
NETBIOS	Provides NetBIOS emulation.
NPRINT	Prints files.
NVER	Shows network version data.

PCONSOLE	Manages print queues.
SALVAGE	Undeletes a file.
SLIST	Lists file servers.
SMODE	Sets file-sharing mode.
SYSCON, FILER, SESSION	Manages users, files, and sessions.
USERLIST	Shows who is logged on.

Other network operating systems offer similar commands and utilities, although not quite as many as NetWare. Three popular commands on a LANtastic network follow:

NET COPY	Copies a file.
NET PRINT	Prints a file.
NET WHO	Shows who is logged on.

DOS Commands and Utilities

For the most part, DOS commands and utilities operate on your LAN workstation just as they did on your stand-alone personal computer. Be careful, however, about sharing DOS commands through a public directory. If some users on the LAN use a different version of DOS than the version you put on the file server, they see this message when they try to use a DOS command:

```
Incorrect DOS Version
```

The DOS TSR program SHARE.EXE is especially important on a LAN. Because the SHARE command enables file sharing, you should run SHARE immediately after you log in. You probably should make SHARE part of the BAT file that loads the network software.

On a Windows for Workgroups computer running in 386-Enhanced mode, a replacement for SHARE.EXE (called VSHARE.386) takes over and manages concurrent file access and record locking. VSHARE is a Microsoft Windows *virtual device driver*. You might want to ignore the existence of VSHARE and load SHARE.EXE anyway, especially if you use a memory manager to load SHARE.EXE into upper memory (which means SHARE.EXE doesn't take up even its sparse 6K of conventional RAM). If Windows for Workgroups does not run in 386-Enhanced mode on your PC, VSHARE will not work and so you must still load SHARE.EXE to enable file sharing.

The following DOS commands do not work on a file-server hard disk across the LAN:

ASSIGN

CHKDSK

DISKCOMP

DISKCOPY

FDISK

> FORMAT
>
> LABEL
>
> RECOVER
>
> SYS
>
> UNDELETE
>
> UNFORMAT

Note also that most third-party disk diagnostic and maintenance utilities do not work on a file-server hard disk, including utilities such as Norton Utilities and PC Tools.

The following DOS commands, however, do operate on a file server disk just as well as they do on your local hard disk:

> ATTRIB
>
> BACKUP
>
> COMP
>
> COPY
>
> FC
>
> RESTORE
>
> SORT
>
> TREE
>
> XCOPY

Memory Constraints

The network software that loads at your workstation is usually a TSR program or a combination of device drivers (SYS files loaded by statements in the CONFIG.SYS file) and TSRs. If your workstation's CPU chip is an 8088, 8086, or 80286 model, network software (such as NetWare's IPX.COM and NETX.COM) probably takes up some portion of the 640K of conventional memory in your computer, which leaves less memory in which to run application software.

If your workstation uses an 80386 or higher CPU with more than 1M or 2M of RAM, you can usually use a memory manager to load some or all network software into upper memory. The following is a list of memory manager products and their manufacturers that should help you reduce the network's use of your conventional memory:

> 386MAX and BlueMAX
> Qualitas
> 7101 Wisconsin Avenue
> Suite 1386
> Bethesda, MD 20814
> (800) 733-1377

QEMM-386
Quarterdeck Office Systems
150 Pico Boulevard
Santa Monica, CA 90405
(213) 392-9851

If NetWare is your network operating system, Novell also offers special versions of its shell (redirector) module. The plain version, NETX.COM, loads into and uses a portion of conventional memory. EMSNETX, however, loads into expanded memory, and XMSNETX loads into upper memory.

DOS Version 5.0 and Version 6.x contain 80386/80486/Pentium memory-management capabilities. Depending on how much conventional memory you need for applications, you may be able to use DOS and not have to purchase a separate memory manager product.

OS/2 doesn't use conventional memory to load network driver software, and the UNIX and Macintosh System 7 operating systems do not distinguish between conventional and extended memory. Windows 95 uses conventional memory for 16-bit network drivers and extended memory for 32-bit network drivers.

A DOS Memory Management Dictionary

The following definitions of DOS memory management terms will help you understand how computer programs, including network operating-system client software, use computer memory.

Conventional memory: Memory directly addressable by an Intel CPU in real mode. The upper boundary is ordinarily the infamous 640K limit, but some memory managers raise that ceiling.

DOS-Protected Mode Interface (DPMI): Developed by Microsoft, DPMI offers functions similar to VCPI (see below) but enforces control over extended memory access.

Expanded memory: Invented jointly by Lotus, Intel, and Microsoft, expanded memory enables an application to bank-switch RAM, in 16K blocks, from an EMS memory card into conventional or upper memory. (*Bank-switching* is the mapping of a given page of memory into an address space the application can reach.) The specification is the Lotus/Intel/Microsoft (LIM) Expanded Memory Specification (EMS). Version 4.0 of the EMS is the most recent. On 80386 and 80486 machines, memory managers can transform extended memory into expanded memory.

Extended memory: Memory above the 1M threshold, addressable only in protected mode.

Extended Memory Specification (XMS): Also developed by Lotus/Intel/Microsoft, this standard provides a rudimentary means for DOS applications to use portions of extended memory.

High-memory area (HMA): The first 64K of extended memory, minus 16 bytes, beginning at the 1M threshold. Through a quirk in the design of the 80286, 80386, and 80486 CPU chips, it is possible to address these 65,520 bytes in real mode.

Protected mode: 80286, 80386, and 80486 CPU chips can operate in protected or real mode. In protected mode, the CPU can address more than 1M of memory.

Real mode: Default mode of Intel CPU chips; only mode available for 8088 and 8086 CPU chips. In real mode, the CPU can address up to only 1M of memory.

Upper memory: The memory between 640K and 1M. Video adapters, ROM BIOS chips, hard disk controller ROMs, and network adapters live in this region, but there are *holes—* upper memory blocks—that some memory managers can map as regular memory.

Virtual Control Program Interface memory (VCPI): Quarterdeck Office Systems and Phar Lap Software developed the VCPI standard to enable DOS applications to share extended memory without conflict.

The DOS PATH Statement

Naturally, you want to extend your DOS PATH statement to enable you to load applications and utilities from network drives as well as from your local hard disk. The PATH statement functions the same on a network, but its maximum length is only 128 characters. On a large LAN, it is easy to make the mistake of trying to exceed this limit.

STACKS

With DOS Version 3.2 (released at the same time IBM began offering its Token Ring LAN products), it was necessary to insert a special statement in the CONFIG.SYS file that looked like this:

```
STACKS=9,128
```

The parameters told DOS to create 9 separate stacks within itself, each 128 bytes, to handle hardware interrupts. DOS version 3.2 needed the STACKS entry in the CONFIG.SYS file because DOS could not keep up with the rapid occurrence of hardware interrupts in a Token Ring environment.

With DOS Version 3.3 and later, however, this entry is not necessary. You can save a very small amount of conventional memory (the separate stack areas) by inserting the following statement into your CONFIG.SYS file:

```
STACKS=0,0
```

New Files

On a NetWare LAN, you may have one or more device drivers (SYS files that you load with statements in the CONFIG.SYS file) to help turn a DOS-based computer into a workstation. You typically have two TSRs: IPX.COM and NETX.COM (or EMSNETX or XMSNETX). For NetWare, these files are all you need to gain access to the LAN. You may have a NET.CFG or SHELL.CFG file to help configure IPX and NETX at log-in time. All told, these files take a little over 100K of space on your local hard disk.

Many peer LAN products add from 200K to 2M of new files on a workstation's hard disk after a product is installed. For Warp Server and NT Server, the installation procedure puts about 3M of files on your computer.

Using Diskless Workstations

Imagine a PC consisting of just a keyboard, network adapter, and a monitor—no floppy drives or hard disk. Turn the computer on and it attaches itself immediately to the network. This type of computer is fairly low cost.

Sounds like a great way to save money on LAN workstations, doesn't it? Don't be fooled; it isn't. A diskless workstation must rely completely on the file server's hard disk and therefore increases network message traffic dramatically. Furthermore, a diskless workstation is a single-purpose computer that you cannot upgrade later. Such a machine cannot run OS/2 or Windows NT and cannot be used as a stand-alone computer. Diskless workstations do not save money in the long run, but there is a reason for using them: security. If you have a LAN environment in which it is important that files cannot be copied to disk and transported, diskless workstations may give you just the security you need.

If you do use a diskless workstation, you may be curious to know how the workstation appears to run DOS just like all other workstations with their own disk drives. The network adapter in a diskless workstation contains a special boot ROM chip. When you start up the computer, this ROM chip automatically receives control at the end of the power-on self test. The chip contains software that knows how to find a file server, look for a special copy of DOS on the server, and load DOS across the LAN cable.

Using DOS and Microsoft Windows

Installed on individual computers, Version 3.x of Microsoft Windows occupies from 5M to 7M of disk space on each computer's hard disk. Windows for Workgroups needs about 15M. Windows 95 uses even more hard disk space. On a large LAN with many Windows users, the total disk space consumed by Windows files is considerable. You can, however, share certain Windows files from one or more file servers if you configure things properly.

You can use Windows' built-in menuing facilities to create application menus for individuals and groups. The object-oriented Windows menus can, of course, use file-server search paths if you want. If, however, a person logs into the network from a computer with a different kind of monitor, keyboard, or mouse, that person may run into problems running Windows. You should design log-in scripts with this possibility in mind.

> **Note**
>
> Windows for Workgroups and Windows 95 have networking software built into them. Both versions of Windows consist of a network operating system and Microsoft Windows combined. Chapter 8, "Using Windows for Workgroups, Windows 95, and Warp Connect," discusses Windows networking in detail.

Installing Windows on a File Server

Installed in stand-alone mode on a personal computer, all Windows software—including executables, fonts, initialization files, customization files, and dynamic link libraries (DLLs)—resides entirely on your local hard disk.

Windows cannot actually run on the server, but you can store some of its files there. Windows (through the network operating system) transfers these files into local workstation memory as needed. On a LAN, you can store the files that Windows reads (but not the ones it writes to) in a central, public directory on the file server. These files include the executables, fonts, DLLs, and help files. You should store each user's initialization and customization files (the INI files, for example) on the personal computer's local hard disk or perhaps in a private server directory for each user.

If your LAN has diskless PCs that need to run Windows, you definitely should create private, user-specific server directories for Windows initialization and customization files.

Sharing Windows files from a file server has several advantages. The most important advantages to people on the LAN are the access and management of LAN resources through the Windows interface. You can connect and disconnect remote printers with the Control Panel, view and manage remote files with the File Manager, and view or change the status of print jobs on LAN printers with the Print Manager. Probably the next most important advantage is the savings in disk space, savings that become even more significant if the LAN workstations consist of personal computers with relatively small hard disks.

As you contemplate storing Windows files on your LAN, you should look closely at the mix of software applications, users, and hardware configurations that make up your LAN. If only a few people in your office use Windows, putting Windows on the file server is not cost effective. Installing Windows on a network is usually difficult and tedious. The effort is worthwhile only if Windows is a popular operating environment in your office. You should also choose whether Windows should begin running automatically on workstations or whether it should be an option for users on the LAN. Study how people in the office use Windows and whether most applications used there are DOS or Windows applications.

Microsoft Windows requires computers and adapter cards extremely compatible with the IBM PC standard. And Windows requires a computer with a certain amount of speed and internal memory. These requirements become key issues if you integrate Windows with your network.

Keep in mind that Windows executes in the workstation, not in the server. You cannot improve the performance of Windows on a slower personal computer by installing Windows on a high-performance file server. The server acts only as a place to store files that make up the Windows environment.

Sharing Windows from a Server

As it runs, Windows reads and writes each user's initialization and customization files frequently. You can save some local workstation hard-disk space by putting these files on the file server, but performance will suffer. When Windows accesses files on the server, the Windows file requests must be redirected across the LAN like all other such file requests. A diskless workstation does not generally offer a speedy Windows environment.

As the LAN becomes easier to use, the network administrator's job gets harder. This is doubly true for Microsoft Windows on a LAN. If you are (or become) a network administrator, you should document and keep detailed records of Windows configurations on the LAN.

If you plan to install and run Windows from a shared directory on the LAN, be sure to give all files in this directory a read-only attribute so that every user can access but not write to the files. You can do this with the Windows File Manager, with the ATTRIB command at a DOS command line prompt, or with a network utility such as NetWare's FLAG command. Most Windows applications must have read-only status before they can be shared.

Printing with Windows on a LAN

With Windows Version 3.x, you can access network queues directly from within Windows Print Manager. You can see which print jobs are in the queue, delete print jobs, and reselect printers easily. Set the LAN printer defaults by running the printer redirection command (CAPTURE, for example) before starting Windows.

If you have a large LAN, you probably have several LAN printers to share. Any user printing from within Windows then chooses a printer from a list of configured printer devices. Because such lists can sometimes be unwieldy, you should set up and configure Windows for those printers used most often. Most people do not like to scroll through multiple printer selections to find the one they want to use.

Identifying Problems with Windows on a LAN

When you load network operating-system software into upper memory, Windows sometimes fails to start or behaves strangely. If this happens, try loading the network software in conventional memory (the first 640K bytes).

The Windows SETUP program modifies the PATH statement in your AUTOEXEC.BAT file. Review SETUP's modifications to make sure that the PATH statement appears before the statements that load the network software. Also make sure that network drives are mapped properly for your Windows environment. Changing the drive-letter mappings may require changes to the Windows customization and initialization files for each LAN user.

If SETUP has problems running on a workstation, try specifying SETUP /I when you run SETUP. The /I parameter disables SETUP's hardware detection. You may need to do this on an ARCnet LAN, for example. The SETUP program tries to detect an IBM 8514 video adapter by using certain machine instructions. Because these instructions use addresses that also exist on an ARCnet network adapter, SETUP becomes confused.

If printing to the LAN printer is difficult (incorrect page breaks, incorrect fonts, or extra blank lines), you may need to change your LAN print job configuration. Under NetWare, for example, use the PRINTCON utility to choose the No option for the Auto Endcap and Enable Timeout settings. Chapter 6, "Using Novell NetWare," explains these commands and parameters in more detail.

II

Building a Network

If any Windows INI files become corrupted when Windows is accessed from the file server, make sure that each person uses a unique, user-specific directory (or local hard disk) to store his or her customization and initialization files.

While you are at a DOS prompt in a Windows Enhanced Mode DOS session, you should never attempt to log in, log out, or attach to the network server. Doing so will crash your workstation. Always perform these functions before you start Windows or while you are in Windows—from the Windows Control Panel.

If you see file-error messages on a NetWare LAN, you should probably increase the maximum number of file handles from the NetWare default of 40 files to 60 files. Do this by adding the following line to the SHELL.CFG file:

```
FILE HANDLES = 60
```

Identifying Networks Recognized by Windows Setup

At SETUP (installation) time, Windows enables you to choose from several network operating systems, including:

- 3Com 3+Open LAN Manager (XNS only)

- 3Com 3+Share

- Banyan Vines

- IBM PC LAN Program

- LAN Server

- Warp Server

- LAN Manager 1.x (or 100-percent compatible)

- LAN Manager 2.x Basic (or 100-percent compatible)

- LAN Manager 2.x Enhanced (or 100-percent compatible)

- Windows NT Server

- Microsoft Network (or 100-percent compatible)

- Novell NetWare 2.10 or above, or Novell NetWare 386

Microsoft Windows 3.x operates a bit differently for each of these network operating systems, so choose your network carefully.

NetWare Considerations. On a NetWare LAN, make sure to use recent versions of the NetWare Shell and the NetWare Utilities. The NetWare shell must be Version 3.01 or higher.

In enhanced mode, Windows can do some additional adjusting of NetWare drive mappings. In standard mode, all drive mappings changed from inside Windows are reset to original mappings when you exit Windows. Changing drive G, for example, from USER USER1 to represent PUBLICWINAPPS will be reset to USER USER1 on exit. In enhanced mode, you can make all drive mappings stay in place even when you leave Windows by adding this line in the [NETWARE] section of the SYSTEM.INI file:

```
RESTOREDRIVE=FALSE
```

The default for each virtual machine in enhanced mode is to have its own (local) set of drive mappings—thus changing mapping in one machine does not affect the other. To have mapping (or any mapping change) affect all virtual machines (global), use the following setting in the [NETWARE] section of SYSTEM.INI:

```
NWSHAREHANDLES=TRUE
```

Microsoft LAN Manager Considerations. Windows is incompatible with early versions of LAN Manager version 1. To use Microsoft Windows, you may need to upgrade your LAN Manager software. LAN Manager 1.*x* includes pop-up services that enable you to see incoming broadcast messages. This feature causes problems with the Windows graphical user interface, for instance.

The LAN Manager workstation software cannot be loaded into upper memory (with one of the memory manager products mentioned earlier) if you want to run Microsoft Windows.

To have pop-up services (the ability to view broadcast announcement messages), use the LAN Manager WinPopup utility, which is designed to work with Windows. The utility should be located in the LAN Manager NETPROG directory and included in your DOS PATH statement.

To start the utility automatically with Windows, use the LOAD option in the [WINDOWS] section of WIN.INI, as shown by the following entry:

```
LOAD=WINPOPUP.EXE
```

For LAN Manager 2.0 Enhanced, Windows needs the two DLLs NETAPI.DLL and PMSPL.DLL in the LAN Manager NETPROG directory and in your PATH.

Note that NT Server, LAN Manager's replacement, does not impose these restrictions on Windows-based PCs.

Other Network Operating Systems. With networks that support MS-NET and NetBIOS, be aware that the Print Manager cannot handle multiple print queues, so print jobs may be listed improperly.

To run Banyan Vines 4.0 with Windows in enhanced mode, you should obtain the software update Banyan refers to as *patch OH*. When you run Windows in enhanced mode, you can run only one application that uses NetBIOS at a time. If, for example, you print to a LAN printer from a Windows application or you run an application that uses NetBIOS, be sure to close all other virtual DOS sessions. Also keep in mind that you must load NetBIOS to use Windows printing functions and to run nonWindows applications with VINES.

II

Building a Network

Configuring Windows on a LAN. You should create a different SYSTEM.INI file for each Windows user, putting the file in a personal Windows directory unique to that user. This means that you will have to change many separate files to modify configuration settings, but Windows will not operate properly otherwise. To save time and effort, you create a template SYSTEM.INI file first and then customize this file for each user.

As you create the template file, you must know the configuration parameters that the network uses. These network-related parameters are as follows (if you want further information about these parameters, refer to your Microsoft Windows manuals):

- *AllVMsExclusive=:* A Boolean setting that controls whether a DOS application can run in a window or must run in exclusive full-screen mode, regardless of settings in the program information file. The default setting is FALSE. If the setting is TRUE, network users see an increase in time for Windows sessions to be completed.

- *[Boot] Section Network.drv=:* Specifies network driver file name you are using; default is NONE. Most network driver choices are available using SETUP. Modify this setting by choosing the SETUP icon located in the Main group window and modifying network choice. To install a network driver not provided with Windows, run SETUP again.

- *FileSysChange=:* A Boolean setting that controls whether File Manager automatically receives messages from nonWindows applications when those applications create, delete, or rename files. If the setting is FALSE, a virtual machine can manipulate files while it runs independently of File Manager. If it is TRUE, all messages automatically go to File Manager, and system performance is degraded.

- *InDOSPolling=:* A Boolean setting determining whether other applications can run when memory-resident software has the InDOS flag set. The default setting is No. Change the setting to Yes if your memory-resident software needs to be in a critical section to perform operations. A Yes setting degrades system performance.

- *INT28Critical=:* A Boolean setting specifying whether a critical section is required to handle INT28h interrupts for a memory-resident software application. Default setting is TRUE. If you do not need a critical section, change this setting to FALSE to improve Windows' task switching.

- *INT28Filter=:* A numeric setting that determines the number of INT28 hexadecimal interrupts generated for use by software loaded before Windows while your system is idle. Default value is 10. Increasing this value improves Windows' performance but can cause conflicts with memory-resident software such as network shells. Changing the setting to 0 eliminates interrupts. Users of communication applications on a network should be aware that the lower the value of INT28Filter, the higher the system overhead—and this can cause conflict with the communication application.

- *NetAsynchSwitching=:* Controls whether Windows provides the capability to switch away from an application after it makes an asynchronous NetBIOS call. The default value of 0 indicates that task switching is not available. With a value of 1, task switching is available. Network users should determine whether any applications will receive network messages while switched to other applications; if an application does receive messages, and you have a setting of 1, the system may fail.

■ *NetHeapSize=:* A numeric setting (in kilobytes) that determines the size of the buffer pool allocated in conventional memory (640K bytes) for moving data over a network. The default value is 8, but many networks require a bigger buffer size. The larger the buffer size, the smaller the amount of memory provided to applications.

■ *NetAsynchFallback=:* A Boolean setting that can require Windows to try to save a NetBIOS request if it is failing. The default setting is FALSE. Windows has a global network buffer to handle data; if sufficient space is not available in this buffer when an application makes a NetBIOS request, Windows fails the request. If you change this setting to TRUE, Windows tries to save the request by creating a buffer in local memory and preventing all virtual machines from processing until the data is received properly and the timeout period passes. The timeout period is controlled by NetAsynchTimeout.

■ *NetAsynchTimeout=:* A setting (in seconds to one decimal place) that determines the length of a timeout period if Windows attempts to save a failing NetBIOS request. The default, 5.0 seconds, applies only if NetAsynchFallback is set to TRUE.

■ *NetDMASize=:* Determines buffer size (in kilobytes) for NetBIOS transport software. Buffer size always represents the largest value established by this setting or the value established by DMABuffersize.

■ *Network=:* Represents the 386 enhanced-mode synonym for Device. The default is None; it is controlled by SETUP.

■ *PSPIncrement=:* A setting (from 2 to 64) that tells Windows to reserve, in 16-byte increments, additional memory for each successive virtual machine if UniqueDOSPSP is TRUE.

■ *ReflectDOSINT2A=:* A Boolean setting that tells Windows to run through or reflect DOS INT 2A signals. The default is FALSE, which instructs Windows to run through this type of signal, providing more efficiency. If you have memory-resident software that requires knowledge of INT2A messages, change the setting to TRUE.

■ *TimerCriticalSection=:* A setting (in milliseconds) that tells Windows to go into a critical section around any timer interrupt code and use the timeout period specified. A value greater than 0 guarantees that only one virtual machine at a time receives time interrupts. Some network memory-resident software fails if a value greater than 0 is not used; using this setting slows system performance.

■ *TokenRingSearch=:* A Boolean setting instructing Windows to look for a Token Ring network adapter on machines with IBM AT architecture. The default is TRUE. This search can interfere with another device.

■ *UniqueDOSPSP=:* A Boolean setting telling Windows to start every application at a unique memory address (PSP). Default setting is FALSE. If the setting is TRUE, each time Windows creates a new virtual machine to start a new application, a unique amount of memory below the application is reserved. PSPIncrement controls this amount. This approach guarantees that applications in different virtual machines start at different addresses. In some networks, the load address of the application identifies each process on the network.

Using OS/2 Computers

IBM's newest edition of OS/2, named Warp, has a number of LAN-aware features not found in DOS, early versions of OS/2, or Windows. Because IBM designed and developed OS/2 after networks became popular, this latest version of OS/2 understands networks and requires less tweaking and fine-tuning than other environments.

When you use Novell's NetWare Requester for OS/2 to turn your OS/2 computer into a workstation on a NetWare LAN, you notice the extra drive letters, the capability to print to the LAN printer, and many other differences noted earlier for DOS-based workstations. The network software, however, does not use conventional memory under OS/2. You do not have the same memory issues to deal with, and you do not need a memory manager product to reclaim usable memory.

Multiple OS/2 and DOS Sessions

OS/2 Warp provides several operating environments: multiple OS/2 sessions (full-screen or windowed), multiple DOS sessions (full-screen or windowed), Microsoft Windows sessions, and Presentation Manager sessions. You manage these operating environments from your OS/2 desktop, called the *Workplace Shell*. The Workplace Shell is LAN-aware, and you can manipulate *remote objects* (those that are LAN-attached rather than local to the workstation) the same way you manipulate local objects.

Once you log into the network and map file server drives as drive letters, each new DOS session or OS/2 session you create has equal access to the file server drives. A CAPTURE command issued in one DOS or OS/2 session affects all other sessions. After you issue the printer redirection command, you can print from any environment in OS/2.

Ordinarily, each workstation should attach itself to the LAN each time the computer boots. Under OS/2, do this with batch file statements in the file STARTUP.CMD. You may, for example, create a STARTUP.CMD file with statements like these:

L:

CD OS2

LOGIN BARRY

PASSWORD: *<type your password here>*

MAP F:=SYSTEMPRO\SYS:

Multitasking

OS/2 is a multitasking operating system. You may start a long-running print job in one session under OS/2 and switch your attention to another session to complete other work. The print job continues in the background while you work. If you start another print job in a different session, the OS/2 spooler and the network spooler work together to keep printouts separate.

OS/2 and the LAN also work together to protect the integrity of data files. If, for example, you edit a document with a word processor in one session and try to edit that same document from another session, you receive a Sharing Violation error message from OS/2. The same mechanism that protects multiple users on the LAN from editing the same file at the same time also protects your multiple OS/2 and DOS sessions from colliding.

Using Macintosh Computers

If you use a Macintosh as a workstation on the LAN, you probably have a NetWare LAN or an AppleTalk LAN. Both are good platforms for Macintosh connectivity. You probably notice very few changes in your Mac's behavior when it is on the LAN. The current version of the Mac operating system, System 7.x, contains some significant networking enhancements.

System 7 and AppleTalk

System 7's new LAN-related capabilities include peer-to-peer file sharing, ethernet and Token Ring drivers, Interapplication Communication (IAC), and Apple events messaging.

System 7 provides peer-to-peer-based file sharing. File transfers occur directly between computers; a file server does not have to be an intermediary. You can easily share a Mac's folders, hard-disk drives, CD/ROM drives, or any combination of all three resources.

From the Finder's File menu, simply click objects to be shared and select Sharing. File sharing has little effect on your Mac's performance unless another LAN user copies files to or from a shared object; then the slowdown lasts only for the duration of the transfer.

Three Macintosh Control Panels (CDEVs—Mac configuration utilities) enable you to start or stop file sharing, arrange access rights to your Mac and shared objects, and monitor user access. The Sharing Setup CDEV switches file sharing on or off. It also sets a network name and password for your Mac, and it determines whether other users can use the IAC function to link applications. The Users & Groups CDEV enables you to configure access privileges for your Mac and the shared objects. Finally, a File Sharing Monitor CDEV shows shared objects and a list of users currently accessing your Mac.

When file sharing is active, your Mac appears as an AppleShare file server to other LAN users. Those people use the Chooser desk accessory to connect to your Mac; shared objects appear as volumes in the Items window.

For the network administrator, configuring file sharing is similar to setting up an AppleShare server. AppleShare users access shared objects the same way they access other objects. Peer-to-peer file sharing makes it easy for Mac users to exchange or distribute files. Security may be a problem, however; remember that security on a peer LAN can be difficult to enforce. To prevent unauthorized access to confidential or sensitive information, you must plan carefully. Be especially careful when you configure parameters in the Users & Groups CDEV.

You can share Apple's CD/ROM drive on a System 7-based LAN, but you should upgrade the CD/ROM software driver to Version 3.1. In addition, be aware that you must upgrade to AppleShare 3.0 to run System 7 client/server applications on your LAN. Electronic mail or group-scheduling software needs the later version of AppleShare to support System 7-specific features, such as the IAC Publish/Subscribe mechanism.

Interapplication Communication is a System 7 feature that enables applications to exchange information by forwarding document updates across the network or by exchanging commands and information with other LAN-aware applications. IAC links applications running on different AppleTalk workstations.

The simplest form of IAC is the Publish/Subscribe mechanism. One Mac user (the person who "owns" the information and who has responsibility for updating it) tells an application to "publish" all or part of the information. IAC automatically makes this data available to another Mac user on the LAN, who "subscribes" to that data through the Standard File dialog box that appears when he or she chooses Subscribe from the Edit menu. Each time the information changes, System 7 passes the information to the subscribers through an edition file, created by the application that publishes the data.

In System 7, applications can share information by using special messages called *Apple events.* With this feature, one Mac application can request the services of another Mac application on the LAN (or within the same computer, for that matter). Apple events are a form of client/server architecture.

System 7 comes with both ethernet drivers and Token Ring drivers. AppleTalk, which operates at the relatively slow rate of 230K per second, supports a recommended maximum of 32 networked computers. The new drivers enable you to connect your Mac to larger, faster ethernet and Token Ring networks.

Macs on a NetWare LAN

Novell offers Macintosh connectivity in the form of two distinct products for the NetWare 2.*x* and NetWare 3.*x* server-based network operating systems. These products are NetWare for Macintosh 2.2 and NetWare for Macintosh 3.0. NetWare 4.1 includes Macintosh connectivity support. In addition, the Dayna, Asante, and Xircom companies also sell Macintosh hardware and software to allow Macs to access a NetWare LAN.

NetWare for Macintosh Version 2.2 is server software that enables Mac users to access NetWare 2.*x* file and print services. NetWare for Macintosh Version 2.2, a value-added process (VAP), loads each time a NetWare 2.*x* server starts. At your Mac workstation, you use the same AppleShare workstation software that is part of the System 7 Macintosh operating system. NetWare for Macintosh Version 2.2 comes bundled with the NetWare 2.*x* network operating system.

The server portion of NetWare for Macintosh Version 3.0, which runs on NetWare 3.*x* servers, is a NetWare Loadable Module (NLM). The workstation portion is a desk accessory (DA) you install on your Mac. The desk accessory enables you to manage the print queue, send messages, and perform administrative functions such as granting file-access rights and adding new users. For file sharing and printing, you use your System 7

AppleShare workstation software. NetWare for Macintosh Version 3.0 must be purchased separately from the NetWare 3.x network operating system.

Use the Chooser to access NetWare file servers. With either product, at your Mac workstation you retrieve and update files exactly as you did before you became part of the LAN. You also print in the same manner. You have the resources of the network at your disposal, however, and people at other workstations on the LAN (including DOS, OS/2, and UNIX computers) can share files with you on a NetWare LAN.

Some software makers offer versions of their applications that run on DOS and Mac computers and use a common file format. These applications include WordPerfect, Aldus PageMaker, Microsoft Excel, and Microsoft Word. DOS and Mac users can share such files without first converting the files from one format to another.

Using UNIX Workstations

You can use a UNIX-based computer as a workstation on a LAN, and you can share files with DOS and Mac users. A DOS user sees the file server as a drive letter, directories, and files. The Mac user sees objects and folders. On a UNIX workstation, you see additional file systems, directories, and files. If you use something like X-Windows on your UNIX machine, you, too, see icons and folders. Your new commands and utilities include such tools as RLOGIN, RCOPY, and RWHO, which are network versions of their UNIX counterparts. You also get TELNET (for executing programs remotely on other computers), FTP (for transferring files), and SMTP (for sending electronic mail).

Most UNIX networks are based on the TCP/IP protocol, discussed in Chapter 4, "Using Protocols, Cables, and Adapters." TCP/IP is not a network operating system. You must get additional software to be able to access a file server.

Sun Microsystems' Network File System (NFS) product is a popular way to connect UNIX-based computers. Several other computer manufacturers have licensed NFS, including IBM. Locus Computing offers PC Interface, a network operating system for UNIX environments. Chapter 9, "Using UNIX LANs," describes each of these products in detail.

The Santa Cruz Operation's SCO Open Desktop is a UNIX operating system based on SCO UNIX System V release 3.2 for 386 and faster computers. Open Desktop includes ODTNet, which enables you to tie into other computers on your company's network, as well as an X client application called Desktop Manager that has an icon-based interface. Desktop Manager enables you to copy, move, execute, print, and delete LAN files simply by moving your mouse. Open Desktop enables you to work with computers connected with Xenix-NET, NT Server, Warp Server, Windows 95, Warp Connect, or even the IBM PC LAN Program. For more information on Open Desktop, contact:

> The Santa Cruz Operation, Inc.
> 400 Encinal Street
> P.O. Box 1900
> Santa Cruz, CA 95061
> (408) 425-7222

II

Building a Network

Chapter Summary

You now understand how your workstation views its role on the network. Your desktop computer may be based on the DOS, Windows, OS/2, Macintosh System 7, or UNIX operating systems. No matter what kind of personal computer and operating system you use, this chapter explains how the network changes your computer into a workstation. You read about the practical aspects of how your workstation behaves on the LAN, and you know what to expect from your personal computer when you log on to the LAN.

In the next few chapters, you explore several specific network operating system products. Chapter 6 gives you a close look at Novell NetWare.

Part III

Networking Software

Chapter 6

Using Novell NetWare

People like NetWare because it performs well, it runs on several types of hardware, and it offers useful, comprehensive security features.

Novell offers several LAN-oriented products, but its flagship products are its two server-based network operating systems, NetWare 3.12 and 4.11, described in this chapter. Novell used to sell a peer LAN product, Personal NetWare, a DOS-based network operating system product for smaller workgroups. However, Novell stopped promoting Personal NetWare a few years ago. Novell discontinued sales of the entry-level NetWare 2.2 in 1996.

In addition to its server-based and peer LAN network operating systems, Novell sells other network-oriented products. Novell's 3270 communications software package enables workstations to have 3270 terminal-emulation sessions with a host (mainframe) computer. Access Server, a communications hardware and software product, enables multiple remote workstations to dial up and log in to the file server. A Novell hardware and software product called LANalyzer diagnoses certain kinds of network problems. Chapter 12, "Managing Your Network," explains more about LANalyzer.

In this chapter, you learn about Novell's three server-based network operating systems. You survey both versions of NetWare from a general perspective, and then you read about the utility software Novell supplies with NetWare. After exploring many NetWare commands to see what they look like and what they do, you focus on NetWare's design objectives. You discover how a NetWare file server operates. You learn about NetWare security and fault tolerance. You look at NetWare's administrative functions and the software that turns a personal computer into a NetWare workstation. This chapter also discusses previous versions of NetWare, which many people still use. First, though, you should know a few things about Novell.

Understanding Novell's History

In 1982, in Orem, Utah, Ray Noorda, Judith Clarke, Craig Burton, and a talented set of programmers from a firm called Superset, Inc. started Novell, Inc.

The company's first facilities consisted of a small office near the local steel plant. Novell began selling its first file server product in 1983. In its 15 or so years of operation, Novell has grown to more than 7,000 employees worldwide. In 1985, sales totaled $55 million; in 1990, sales soared to $497 million. Novell's mission statement is simple: accelerate the growth of network computing. Clearly, Novell is accomplishing its mission.

Novell was the first distributed-processing vendor to support heterogeneous computing platforms as client workstations. Novell also was the first to support multiple topologies and to provide routing facilities among those topologies. Novell was the first to support OS/2 and all versions of DOS. And Novell provides connectivity options for IBM, Apple, UNIX, Digital Equipment Corporation, and other computer types. You could say, with quite a bit of accuracy, that Novell invented file server technology. Prior to Novell's 1983 launch of NetWare, network software allowed the sharing of disk space but not the sharing of files.

NetWare works with more than 200 network adapters and more than 100 disk storage subsystems, backup devices, and server computers. Novell maintains certification laboratories to test its products with other vendors' hardware and software components. In one of its laboratories, Novell has 1,368 personal computer workstations to test software.

Novell has contracts with some of the largest and most capable independent service organizations to provide support for NetWare. These organizations include Bell Atlantic, DEC, Hewlett-Packard, Intel, IBM, Prime, Unisys, and Xerox. Major system integrators and resellers of Novell products include Electronic Data Systems (EDS), Boeing Computer Services, NYNEX Business Centers, and Sears Business Centers. And in 1990, IBM became a reseller of Novell NetWare.

Novell has sometimes encountered a rocky road in its quest for the high ground of networking. At one time, it sold file server computers and network adapter cards along with its network operating system software. It owned UNIX (purchased from Bell Labs and later sold to SCO UNIX) and Word Perfect (acquired from WordPerfect Corporation and later sold to Corel). The company has given up its hardware and non-network-related software businesses in favor of its strength, the network software market.

Reviewing NetWare Products

Novell NetWare is the most popular network operating system for a good reason. Its performance, reliability, and security appeal to almost everyone. You should be aware, however, that NetWare is one of the more expensive network operating systems for small networks. It is sometimes complicated to install and administer. And NetWare's TSR workstation components require about 60K of RAM, leaving less of the workstation's 640K for running applications. (On an 80386 or 80486 workstation with 1MB or more of memory and a memory manager, such as DOS 5.0, QEMM, or 386MAX, it is usually possible to locate Novell's TSR workstation components outside the 640K of conventional memory.)

A NetWare *file server* is a personal computer that uses the NetWare operating system to control the network. The file server coordinates workstations and regulates the way they share network resources. The file server regulates who can access which files, who can change data, and who can use the printer first. All network files are stored on a hard disk in (or attached to) the file server, instead of on floppy or hard disks in individual workstations.

Novell offers two versions of NetWare. The recently discontinued version 2.2 worked on computers with an 80286 CPU chip, which is now obsolete. Novell sold version 2.2 licenses for 5, 10, 50, or 100 concurrent users, with version 3.12 server licenses allowing up to 20, 100, or 250 connections. NetWare 4.11 supports up to 1,000 users, and you can buy licenses for NetWare 4.11 in additive quantities—you use a license diskette to increase the number of users the server supports. For instance, Novell now allows you to combine a 150-user license and a 25-user license to create a 175-user installation of NetWare 4.11. The license you buy depends on the number of workstations that should be able to log onto the LAN at the same time (i.e, concurrent connections). If you have 7 users, you need to buy a 10-user license, and if you have 67 users, you should buy a 100-user license. On the other hand, you might have only 100 out of 120 employees logging on at the same time; in that case, a NetWare license for 100 connections would suffice.

Version 3.12 and Version 4.11 run on 80386, 80486, or Pentium-based servers. Novell has also prepared special editions of NetWare 4.1 to run on UNIX-based and OS/2-based computers. On 80386 or better CPUs, versions 3.12 and 4.11 of NetWare use 32-bit technology for extra speed.

You will not have a problem if you have NetWare 4.11, 3.12, or even 2.2 servers on the same network; most NetWare utilities (the files in the PUBLIC directory) are the same for these versions, and utility programs are smart enough to recognize NetWare versions and behave accordingly. NetWare 3.12, for example, has eight file access rights; NetWare 2.2 has only seven. Both SYSCON and RIGHTS (NetWare utility programs for administering logon accounts) show the correct information, depending on which kind of server you're viewing. Later sections of this chapter cover SYSCON and RIGHTS in more depth.

NetWare 3.12 is faster and more powerful and offers more connectivity options than the entry-level NetWare 2.2. And NetWare 4.11 extends the limits of NetWare 3.12 to allow more workstations and more servers to exist on the same LAN, and also makes it easier to administer logon accounts across multiple file servers. NetWare 4.11 features NetWare Directory Services (NDS), integrated messaging in the form of an integrated multi-mail-protocol MHS (Message Handling System), multiprotocol routing, network management, security, and the usual file- and print-sharing services. In addition, 4.11 includes several important functions for large, mission-critical LANs: TCP/IP or IPX for transmitting file service packets, NetWare Link Services Protocol (NLSP), NetWare for Macintosh, and new VLMs (Virtual Loadable Modules) for client workstations. Version 4.11 includes support for NetWare for OS/2 and mirrored file servers via Novell's SFT III technology. While Version 3.12 typically works best for LANs with one or a few file servers and fewer than 250 workstations, Version 4.11 is best for networks with many servers, networks with more than 250 workstations, and networks consisting of geographically dispersed LANs (i.e., wide area networks). Figure 6.1 shows the NetWare family of products.

III

Networking Software

Fig. 6.1 The NetWare family of network software products.

Using NetWare Utilities

You use NetWare utilities to perform network tasks. Two types of utilities are available: menu utilities and command-line utilities. Menu utilities enable you to perform network tasks by choosing options from menus. Command-line utilities enable you to perform tasks by typing commands at the DOS command line.

Using Menu Utilities

When you run a NetWare menu-based utility such as FILER, you see the utility's main menu along with a screen header that shows the following information:

- The full name of the utility
- The current date and time
- The directory path of your current directory (most utilities)
- Your user name on your file server (most utilities)
- Your connection number (most utilities)

Press Esc or the Exit key (usually Alt+F10) to leave a NetWare menu utility. Pressing Esc saves changes; the Exit key enables you to abandon changes.

The F1 (Help) key displays a help screen that applies to the task you're working on. The help screen describes all options on-screen. To get help on a specific option, highlight the option and press Enter.

If you press F1 twice, the menu utility lists your computer's function-key assignments.

Using Command-Line Utilities

NetWare commands enable you to do single-purpose network tasks that do not need a menu. NetWare offers a multitude of such utilities. The installation process puts these program files into a standard NetWare directory named PUBLIC.

To show the similarity between NetWare and DOS commands, an explanation of two simple NetWare commands, NPRINT and TLIST, follows.

The NPRINT command, which sends a text file to a LAN printer, is the NetWare equivalent of the DOS PRINT command. TLIST shows you the list of trustees for a directory. Examples of the command formats for the NPRINT and the TLIST utilities follow:

```
NPRINT path [option...]
TLIST [path [USERS ¦ GROUPS]]
```

The *path* parameter for NPRINT specifies the path and file name of the file you want to print. Use the *option* parameter to specify how you want the file treated as it prints. These options let you specify whether you want a banner page and what it should contain, whether the spooler should append a formfeed (page eject) to your printout, the number of copies to print, the server and the queue that should service the printout, and other similar print queue attributes. For TLIST, the *path* parameter specifies the directory for which you want trustee information. You can use USERS or GROUPS to tell TLIST whether you are looking for single-user information or group information.

Using the NetWare Login Command. To log into your default server, type

```
LOGIN servername/username
```

LOGIN is a NetWare command. Replace *servername* with the name of the file server you want to log into. For *username*, use your login name. The LOGIN command prompts you for your password. To log out of your default server, type *logout*.

If you have multiple NetWare servers on the same LAN, use the ATTACH command to connect your workstation logically to each server after the first. You then log in to the attached servers.

You would attach to another file server to do any of the following tasks:

- Send messages to users on that file server
- Map a drive to that file server
- Copy a file or directory to (or from) that file server

NetWare Commands. You change your NetWare password with the SETPASS command. SETPASS asks you to type your old password (once) and your new password (twice, for verification).

To find out who is logged into a workstation, use the WHOAMI command. You see a response like this:

```
You are user BARRY attached to server SERVER1, connection
12 Server SERVER1 is running NetWare v3.12. Login time:
Wednesday January 15, 1997 8:05 am
```

III

Networking Software

You can find out the names of the file servers on your network with the SLIST command. To learn the user IDs of the other people who are logged into the LAN, use the USERLIST command to produce a USERLIST display that looks something like this:

User Information for Server SYSTEMPRO

Connection	User Name	Login Time	
1	THOMAS	1-06-1997	8:17 am
2	SUSAN	1-06-1997	8:19 am
4	* BARRY	1-07-1997	8:42 am

An asterisk (*) appears next to your user name.

Creating Your Login Script

Your *login script* is a program that sets up the workstation's environment each time you log in. Two kinds of login scripts exist in a NetWare environment: the system login script, global for every user, and individual user login scripts. The script maps network drives, executes programs, starts applications, and attaches you to different file servers. You cannot, however, run terminate-and-stay-resident (TSR) programs from your login script. This section introduces you to some basic login script commands.

To edit your individual login script, run the NetWare SYSCON menu utility. After you choose User Information, your user ID, and login script from the menus, you are ready to configure your script. To execute your new login script, first log out of the network and then log in again.

Typically, the NetWare commands you include in your login script are ATTACH, MAP, and SET. You can also use IF...THEN statements in your script. On a large LAN, you may put script commands into the system login script rather than into your personal login script. The MAP command can establish your network drive letters and augment the DOS PATH facility for locating executable files (applications and utilities). The latter type of mapped drive is called a *search drive*. An example of a MAP command you may place in your login script follows:

```
MAP F:= SERVER1/SYS:
```

You learn more about drive mapping with the MAP command in the following section.

The # (pound sign) script command runs an executable file (a file with an EXE or COM extension). Note that you must be careful not to load TSRs within your login script. An example of the # script command follows:

```
#SYSCON
```

This example runs the SYSCON NetWare utility each time you log into the LAN.

The ATTACH command enables you to connect logically to other file servers while you remain logged in to your current file server. If your second NetWare server is named SERVER2, the ATTACH command that you insert in the login script (or perhaps type at a command line prompt) would be:

```
ATTACH SERVER2
```

The SET script command sets DOS variables. You might use SET as in the following example:

```
SET user="jwilson"
```

In a login script, IF...THEN executes certain commands if a specified condition is met. An example follows:

```
IF DAY_OF_WEEK = "Monday" THEN WRITE "AARGH . . . "
```

The WRITE login script command, as you can see, writes messages to your screen as the login script executes.

Mapping Network Drives

You can map an entire NetWare file server hard disk as a drive letter, and you also can map a subset of the hard disk (a directory and its subdirectories).

Mapped drives point to particular locations in the directory structure. In NetWare, three type of drives exist: *local drives*, *network drives*, and *search drives*. Local drives are physically attached to a workstation. Network drives are the disk drives in the file server (often referred to as *volumes*). Like the DOS PATH facility, a search drive enables you to execute programs (applications and utilities) in a directory other than the current directory.

To view the present status of your drive mappings, type the MAP command with no parameters. You see information similar to this:

```
DRIVE A: maps to a local drive
DRIVE B: maps to a local drive
DRIVE F:= SERVER1/SYS: /HOME/FRANK
DRIVE G:= SERVER1/SYS2: /
DRIVE H:= SERVER2/SYS: /APPS

SEARCH1:=Z: [SERVER1/SYS: /PUBLIC]
SEARCH2:=Y: [SERVER1/SYS: /PUBLIC/UTILS]
SEARCH3:=X: [SERVER1/ACCT: /APPS]
```

Suppose that you want to map a network drive to a directory in which you have files. To see which network drive letters are available, type the MAP command. After you choose a drive letter not in use (such as J), run MAP again. This time give MAP parameters that instruct the command to set up the new drive mapping. Suppose that your user name is FRANK and you want to map drive J to your home directory, which is on file server SERVER1 in volume SYS. You would type the following command:

```
MAP J:= SERVER1/SYS:HOME\FRANK
```

Suppose that your search drives appear as follows:

SEARCH1:=Z: [SERVER1/SYS: /PUBLIC]

SEARCH2:=Y: [SERVER1/SYS: /PUBLIC/UTILS]

The next available search drive is SEARCH3 (S3). To map a search drive to directory APPS on volume SYS2:, type this:

```
MAP S3:=SERVER1/SYS2:APPS
```

When you type MAP again, the new search drive appears as follows:

SEARCH1:=Z: [SERVER1/SYS: /PUBLIC]

SEARCH2:=Y: [SERVER1/SYS: /PUBLIC/UTILS]

SEARCH3:=X: [SERVER1/SYS2: /APPS]

Sending Messages to Others

You can communicate with other users on your network by sending messages from your workstation command line. Suppose that you want to send the following message to users MARK and HOLLY:

Meeting at 1:30 today.

Also suppose that MARK and HOLLY are logged into your default server. Use the SEND command, as shown in the following example, to notify Mark and Holly of the meeting:

SEND "Meeting at 1:30 today." MARK, HOLLY

NetWare displays a confirmation message, telling you that it sent the message success-fully to the two people.

If HOLLY is logged into another file server called SERVER2, you would attach to that file server and type

SEND "Meeting at 1:30 today." SERVER2/HOLLY

As another example of NetWare's simple, one-line messaging facility, suppose that you are your company's accountant (or president) and want to tell all employees that the paychecks are ready. Because the NetWare group EVERYONE includes all users, you can type

SEND "Paychecks are ready." EVERYONE

If you do not want to receive messages sent to you from any network stations, you can use the CASTOFF command. You see the following NetWare message:

Broadcasts from other stations will now be rejected.

To allow your workstation to receive messages from other network users again, use the CASTON command.

Understanding Files, Directories, and Attributes

You can manage files and directories in a variety of ways: you can copy, delete, rename, view, write to, share, and print them. NetWare's system of file and directory rights and file attributes ensures that only authorized network users can access and update LAN files.

Both files and directories can have attributes on a NetWare file server. These attributes override the rights granted to users on the LAN. Suppose that you have the right to rename files (the Modify right). The file you want to rename, however, is flagged with the Rename Inhibit attribute. The attribute prevents you from renaming the file, even though you have the right to do so.

Knowing Your Rights

To see what rights you have in the current directory, use the RIGHTS command. If, for example, you have all rights in the directory, you see the following display:

```
SYSTEMPRO\SYS:BARRY

        Your Effective Rights for this directory are [SRWCEMFA]
        You have Supervisor Rights to Directory.     (S)
        May Read from File.                          (R)
        * May Write to File.                         (W)
        May Create Subdirectories and Files.
        May Erase Directory.
        May Modify Directory.                        (M)
        May Scan for Files.                          (F)
        May Change Access Control.                   (A)

    * Has no effect on directory.

    Entries in Directory May Inherit [SRWCEMFA] rights.

    You have ALL RIGHTS to Directory Entry.
```

Using the NCOPY Command

The DOS COPY command is an inefficient way to copy files on the LAN if the same file server is both the source and recipient of the files. Because the DOS COPY command executes at your workstation and because of the way file redirection works, the source file must flow into your workstation as a series of LAN message packets and then flow back to the server as yet another series of packets when you use COPY. The incoming packets represent the COPY command's read-file operations. The outgoing packets are the write-file operations. Why not tell the file server to do the copy operation and avoid the LAN traffic?

The NetWare NCOPY command does exactly this. When NCOPY determines that a file server is both the source and target of a file copy, the command sends a special message packet to the server instructing the server to do the file copy. If the copy operation involves different file servers or a file server and a workstation, NCOPY does its job exactly like the DOS COPY command.

Suppose that you want to copy a file called REPORT.DOC from your current, default directory on drive F to the MANAGERS directory. Both directories exist on volume SYS on the file server named SERVER1. You type this:

```
NCOPY REPORT.DOC F:\MANAGERS\REPORT.DOC
```

Note that you can use the NetWare menu utility FILER to copy, delete, and rename files on the network.

Salvaging Deleted Files

You can undelete files on a NetWare LAN with the SALVAGE utility. From the utility's menu, select View/Recover Deleted Files and specify to undelete a single file, multiple files selected from a list, or multiple files based on wild cards you supply. You can give the resurrected file a new name during the salvage operation if you want. SALVAGE lets you "regret" accidental deletions of files. Note that running the PURGE utility actually removes deleted files from the NetWare server. SALVAGE can't recover deleted files after you've run PURGE.

Using the NetWare NDIR Command

Like the DOS DIR command, the NetWare NDIR command lists files in a directory. NDIR is NetWare-aware and knows how to display the additional file information that NetWare stores for each file and directory. NDIR also can traverse the file server directory tree to look for a file. The NDIR utility searches all directories you have rights to for a misplaced file. A typical NDIR *.EXE display looks like this:

```
SYSTEMPRO/SYS:BARRY

Files:         Size     Last Updated     Flags      Owner
LANXPERT EXE   91,078   12-06-96 8:39p   [Rw-A]     BARRY
SHOW EXE        7,338    6-06-96 8:17p   [Rw-A]     BARRY

 98,416 bytes in 2 files
102,400 bytes in 25 blocks
```

Printing with NetWare

Printing on a NetWare workstation is similar to printing on a stand-alone personal computer. When you send a print job to a network printer, however, the job first is routed through the file server and then delivered to the printer by the print server. The file server and print server may very well be the same computer.

Using CAPTURE to Print Screens

After you issue a CAPTURE command to redirect printer output to the shared LAN printer, you can use that printer port just as if a local printer were attached to it. You even can use your PrtSc key to print screens to the LAN printer.

Examining CAPTURE Options

These are some of the most common CAPTURE options:

Option	Function
L=*n*	Indicates which of your workstation's LPT ports (local parallel printing ports) to capture. Replace *n* with 1, 2, or 3. The default is L=LPT1.
Q=*queuename*	Indicates the queue to which the print job should be sent. If multiple queues are mapped to a printer, you must include this option. Replace *queuename* with the name of the queue.
TI=*n*	Indicates the number of seconds between the last time the application writes to the file and the time it releases the file to the queue. You normally include this option to print from an application without exiting it. Replace *n* with a number of seconds (1–1,000). The default is TI=O (time-out disabled).

As an example, you may put the following CAPTURE command in a batch file that you run after you log in:

```
capture ti=10 q=laserjet
```

ENDCAP, a NetWare command, undoes the printer redirection of the CAPTURE command. If you send something to the printer, ENDCAP sends your print job to the print queue without waiting for the time-out period to elapse. ENDCAP also ends the capture of your LPT port. You must then issue another CAPTURE command to re-enable printing to the LAN printer.

Managing Your Print Jobs

A *print queue* is a special directory where print files are stored while they wait to print. To see which jobs are waiting in a queue to print, use the PCONSOLE NetWare menu utility. After you select Print Queue Information and the name of the print queue, select Current Print Job Entries from the Print Queue Information list. The print job entries are displayed.

You can cancel your print job by deleting it from the print queue even after the job has started printing. You can delete a print job only if you own the job or are the print queue operator. Print job removal is a function of the PCONSOLE utility supplied with NetWare. Highlight your print job in a menu displayed by PCONSOLE, press the Del key, and confirm the deletion of the print job.

Understanding NetWare's Design

NetWare was the first network operating system to enable users to share files, as opposed to merely providing multiple users the capability to store private files on a central hard disk. In the early days of networking, the Corvus Systems company sold many hard disks to organizations such as local school boards. With Corvus software and network adapters, people could share space on a large, expensive hard disk, but each person's files were separate. No one could access the same file at the same time. Thus, when Novell designed and developed NetWare, it set a new standard for file sharing.

Until Novell created NetWare, network operating systems were entirely proprietary. Then, if you wanted a LAN, you had no choice but to purchase the vendor's hardware and software together. Novell designed NetWare to be hardware-independent so that it could be run on several types of networks and with a variety of network adapters. Novell has always adhered to an open standard regarding its software products. An example of its commitment to open architecture is its Open Datalink Interface (ODI) standard. Any network adapter manufacturer can make an adapter that works with NetWare simply by including a device driver that implements ODI.

NetWare's fault tolerance is another characteristic that sets it apart from other network operating systems. The basic design of the NetWare file system (the way data is written to the hard disk), the Transaction Tracking System (TTS), disk mirroring, and disk duplexing all contribute to data integrity on a NetWare file server. You learn more about fault tolerance and the Transaction Tracking System in "Understanding NetWare Fault Tolerance," later in this chapter.

Using the NetWare Server and File System

Although it looks like a regular IBM AT, IBM-compatible, or IBM PS/2 computer from the outside, a NetWare file server is really a minicomputer in disguise. The hard disks in the file server are formatted with a file system structure completely foreign to DOS. It's impossible, for example, to boot a NetWare file server with a DOS disk and then access the hard disk with DOS commands. A user at a workstation, however, can view the file server as just another DOS disk drive. The magic that allows this, of course, is the redirection of DOS function calls that you read about in Chapter 3, "Using File Servers." Novell simply carries the principle further than other NOS vendors.

The proprietary format of a NetWare file server disk contains more information about files and subdirectories than is possible under DOS. Not only can a file have the DOS attributes read-only, hidden, and modified-since-last-backup, but it also can be marked as shareable or nonshareable (properties that enable or disable simultaneous access to the file by more than one user). NetWare also tags each file with its original creation date, identification of the user/owner who created the file, date on which the file was last accessed, date last modified, and date/time last archived. Directories, too, have special properties described in the following section.

From this description of the file system on a NetWare file server, you can tell that the operating system software running on the server is not DOS. NetWare operates the CPU in protected mode (something that OS/2 also does) and takes control of the entire computer. Protected mode enables the 80286 CPU chip to address 16MB of memory and 4 gigabytes (4 billion bytes) with an 80386, 80486, or Pentium CPU. NetWare uses any extra memory installed in the file server for file-caching purposes.

Understanding NetWare Security

Office-wide (or company-wide) information, consisting of data files and programs, all resides on the same file server hard disk. Not all people in the office or company, however, should have access to all the company's information. Certain files containing confidential data (such as payroll files) should be available only to certain users. And in applications that are not LAN-aware, you probably have data files that multiple people can update, one person at a time. If two people access the same file at the same time, they may overwrite each other's work.

To prevent problems like these, NetWare provides an extensive security system to protect data on the network. NetWare security combines these factors:

■ Login security, including user names, passwords, and workstation, time, and account restrictions.

■ Trustee rights controlling which directories and files a user can access and what the user can do with those directories and files—such as creating, reading, erasing, or writing to those files.

■ Directory and file attributes that determine whether the directory or file can be deleted, copied, viewed, or written to. These attributes also mark a file as shareable or nonshareable.

Each directory has a *maximum rights mask* representing the highest level of privilege that can be granted to any directory trustees. Each trustee may have these rights, expressed by the rights mask:

■ A user can read from open files.

■ A user can write to open files.

■ A user can open existing files.

■ A user can create new files.

■ A user can delete existing files.

■ A user can act parentally—creating, renaming, or erasing subdirectories—and can set trustee rights and directory rights in the directory and its subdirectories.

■ A user can search for files in the directory.

■ A user can modify file attributes.

Understanding NetWare Fault Tolerance

Realizing that reliability is an important trait of a file server, designers and programmers at Novell have tried to make sure that data stored on the server is protected. NetWare 3.12 and 4.11 incorporate Novell's System Fault Tolerant (SFT) technology. *Fault tolerance* refers to the file server's ability to continue functioning without missing a beat. Both versions of NetWare employ basic strategies and techniques to minimize any failure of the disk surface to record data correctly; SFT goes a step further and provides *disk mirroring* and *disk duplexing*, software and hardware mechanisms for maintaining duplicate copies of disk data. Chapter 3, "Using File Servers," explains mirroring and duplexing.

The NetWare operating system recognizes signals from an uninterruptible power supply through UPS monitoring. The operating system knows when the UPS is supplying power, it notifies users of how much time they have left before the UPS batteries run down, and if commercial power is not restored within that time period, NetWare closes any open files and shuts itself down gracefully.

Finally, SFT NetWare offers the NetWare Transaction Tracking System (TTS). An application programmed to use TTS can treat a series of database updates as a single operation—either all updates take place or none of them does. A system failure in the middle of a multiple-file update does not cause inconsistencies between files.

Assigning NetWare Users

You can assign four levels of responsibility to users on a NetWare LAN:

- Regular network users

- Operators (file server console operators, print queue operators, print server operators)

- Managers (work group managers, user account managers)

- Network supervisors

Regular network users work on the network. They can run applications and work with files according to the rights assigned them.

Operators are regular network users who have been assigned additional privileges. A file server console operator, for example, is a network user given specific rights to use FCONSOLE or the Remote Management Facility (RMF). The discussion of the specific features of NetWare 3.12, in the section of this chapter titled "Using NetWare 3.12," addresses RMF in more detail.

Managers are users with responsibility for creating groups or managing other users. Work group managers can create and manage users. User account managers can manage, but not create, users. Managers function as supervisors over a particular group, but they do not have supervisor equivalence.

Network supervisors are responsible for the smooth operation of the whole network. They maintain the system, reconfiguring and updating the LAN as necessary.

Understanding a NetWare Workstation

Workstations typically use two pieces of software to communicate with a version 2 or version 3 NetWare file server: the Shell (redirector) and a protocol. The Shell must be loaded into each workstation before that workstation can function on the network.

Two software components run on each Novell NetWare workstation, both of which are terminate-and-stay-resident programs (TSRs). IPX manages the PC-to-PC and PC-to-file-server communications by implementing Novell's IPX/SPX communications protocol. NETX (or perhaps NET2, NET3, NET4, or NET5, if you use the older, DOS-version-dependent programs) is the Shell/redirector that shunts DOS file requests to and from the file server by issuing commands to IPX. Together, NETX and IPX make the file server's disks and printers look like DOS-managed peripherals. IPX takes about 19K of memory; NET3 takes about 38K.

The NETX.COM NetWare shell directs workstation requests to DOS or NetWare. When a workstation makes a request (asks to do a file I/O task), the shell decides whether the task refers to the workstation's local hard disk (to be directed to DOS) or to a network file server (to be directed to NetWare). If the request is a local workstation task (such as using the DOS DIR command to list files in a local directory), NetWare lets DOS handle the request. If the request is a network I/O task (such as printing on a LAN printer), NetWare handles the request. The Shell sends the request to the appropriate operating system—DOS or NetWare—like a railroad track switcher sending trains to the proper destination.

The workstation shell uses another file, IPX.COM, to send network messages to the file server and in some cases directly to other network stations. This IPX protocol is the language the workstation uses to communicate with the file server.

You don't have to run NetBIOS on a NetWare workstation (unless, of course, you have applications that use its protocol) because the NetWare Shell software uses IPX to communicate with the file server. Novell supplies a NetBIOS emulator that can be loaded on top of IPX; this emulator converts NetBIOS commands into IPX commands for transmission across the network if you want both protocols—thus adding roughly 20K of memory to the resident portion of NetWare.

You can use the same IPX/NETX pair of programs on a NetWare 2.2 LAN just as well as you can on a NetWare 3.12 LAN. For NetWare 4.11, you use Novell's newest client software.

Novell has recently updated its client software using 32-bit architecture. The 32-bit components work with Windows 95, Windows NT, and OS/2. They offer the same file- and print-sharing functions found in earlier NetWare client software, and the components provide new features that network administrators can use. For instance, to migrate or upgrade a group of network clients, administrators can use the new Automatic Client Upgrade (ACU) feature. ACU offers the following benefits:

- Distribution of client software automatically from the server

- Detection of workstation network environment changes and restoration of network connections

- Caching of frequently used data, such as file content and network information, for faster client response times

III

Networking Software

- Multiple directory tree access within NetWare Directory Services
- Use of 32- or 16-bit LAN drivers

Macintosh clients can communicate with a NetWare server without using AppleTalk. Additionally, the client software for OS/2 supports full NDS connectivity during global DOS and Windows sessions.

Previous Versions of NetWare

Originally developed as the network operating system for the now obsolete Novell S-Net LAN, NetWare quickly migrated to the Intel 80x86 CPU chip. In 1985, Novell introduced Advanced NetWare 1.0; Version 1.2, released later that same year, was the first operating system to take advantage of the 80286 CPU chip's special protected mode operating environment.

Advanced NetWare 2.0

Version 2.0 of Advanced NetWare, released in 1986, increased LAN functionality, improved performance, and added internetworking capability to NetWare. A NetWare 2.0 milestone was its capability to connect as many as four different networks with a single file server.

NetWare 2.1x, SFT NetWare, and NetWare 386

In 1987, Novell reworked NetWare yet again to provide significant levels of fault tolerance and data integrity in its SFT NetWare product. Features such as FCONSOLE (which enabled an administrator at a workstation to control the file server across the LAN remotely), new resource accounting, and improved security enabled network managers to control the LAN better.

To make its products appeal to the cost-conscious, small-LAN market, Novell also created 5- and 10-user versions of NetWare called NetWare ELS (Entry Level System) I and ELS II.

Version 2.15 of NetWare and NetWare for Macintosh made their debut in December, 1988. Providing Mac connectivity was an important step for NetWare, but customer complaints regarding the complexity of NetWare reached new heights during this time. One bitter complaint dealt with the COMPSURF utility, which ran automatically as part of the installation process. COMPSURF is a disk surface diagnostic program designed to reveal flaws in a hard disk. People complained that COMPSURF was *too* thorough; typically it ran for a full day or even two days. In addition to the time it required, the entire installation process required a high level of expertise to accomplish correctly.

NetWare 386, a full 32-bit edition of the network operating system, shipped in September, 1989. Concentrating on data integrity and reliability, Novell provided significant enhancements in security, performance, and flexibility to NetWare in the NetWare 386 product.

NetWare 2.2

Novell consolidated all earlier versions of 80286-based NetWare (NetWare 2.15, SFT Advanced NetWare, ELS I and ELS II) into a single product when it released NetWare 2.2. As with NetWare 3.12, price differences for NetWare 2.2 relate only to the number of users supported. Version 2.2 is quite similar to SFT Advanced NetWare. All 2.2 editions provide exactly the same features; for example, a 5-workstation LAN has the same system fault tolerance (SFT) level as a 100-user LAN. Version 2.2 is available for 5, 10, 50, or 100 users.

The installation process for NetWare 2.2 is almost as simple as that of NetWare 3.12; Novell responded to customers' feedback by redesigning the installation process for the two products. In the basic installation mode, you answer just three questions about your file server and your local area network, wait a brief moment while the ZTEST disk test runs, and then insert several floppy disks. The long-running COMPSURF program is still there but only as an optional step.

NetWare 2.2 also supports value-added processes (VAPs)—separate program modules linked with NetWare—which enable the file server to provide extra services. Novell's BTRIEVE file-access method is a good example of a VAP. Instead of using DOS redirection to ask the file server for various portions of a file, an application running on a workstation sends the key of the record it wants directly to BTRIEVE, which looks up the record on the server and returns the appropriate record to the application.

Current NetWare Versions

In 1991, Novell released NetWare 2.2 and 3.11; in 1993 Novell enhanced version 3.11 to become version 3.12. 1993 also saw the release of NetWare 4.1. During 1996, Novell discontinued NetWare 2.2 and began shipping NetWare 4.11. The two server-based LAN software products, NetWare versions 3.12 and 4.11, are currently Novell's flagship offerings. While versions 3.12 and 4.11 are current, you can understand that many organizations have not yet upgraded to these current versions. They've found the older version stable and reliable, and they don't feel the new features of later versions warrant an upgrade. For example, NetWare 3.11 is still commonly in use.

Using NetWare 3.12

NetWare 3.12 takes advantage of the 80386, 80486, or Pentium CPU chip to extend the limits of NetWare. Version 3.12 supports up to 4 gigabytes of memory for caching: up to 250 users can be logged into a server; up to 32 terabytes (32 trillion bytes) of disk storage can reside on a single server; each file may be up to 4 gigabytes; and a file can span multiple physical drives. As many as 100,000 files can be open concurrently. NetWare 3.12 includes the features of SFT NetWare and adds enhanced security facilities. Also new is the concept of *NetWare loadable modules* (NLMs)—software modules that can be loaded into (or unloaded from) the file server even while the server is running. NLMs are much easier to use than VAPs.

As a client/server platform, NetWare 3.12 is not as good as the NT Server or OS/2-based Warp Server network operating systems (discussed in the next chapter). Novell does, however, offer a set of programmer-oriented tools for developing client/server applications. If you're a programmer or if you have access to a staff of programmers, you may use Novell's NetWare developer tools for writing applications to reside in both the file server and the client workstations, including a memory-protection NLM and several relatively easy-to-program transport protocols.

To help programmers manipulate this new environment more easily, Novell offers The Professional Developer's Program. Programmer tools from Novell consist of a C compiler, linker, symbolic debugger, libraries of LAN-related code, and NetWare RPC. RPC stands for *Remote Procedure Code*, a distributed processing concept in which different parts of an overall program or process execute on different kinds of networked computers.

Version 3.12 of NetWare fulfills Novell's promise to support several workstation environments. The server can store files from DOS, Macintosh, OS/2, UNIX, and OSI-based client workstations transparently. To do this, NetWare 3.12 sets aside special name spaces on the server. You load optional server modules (NetWare loadable modules) to manage these name spaces. Each directory entry for a file holds a DOS-style name. The corresponding name space entry (two 128-byte areas) contains machine-specific name information. A file that originates on an OS/2 workstation, for example, can retain its extended attributes (long name, creation date, and so forth). A Mac file uses the name space to hold the long name and Mac Finder (resource fork) information. An application running on a DOS workstation can access a file created by a Mac workstation, and vice versa.

The Mac, DOS, and OS/2 file-sharing features work well. After you load the NetWare for Macintosh NLM, you can create a Microsoft Word document on a Mac, revise the same file with Microsoft Word for Windows on a DOS-based computer, and perform a final revision under Word/PM on an OS/2 workstation. In each case, you won't know that the file originated on a different kind of computer. NetWare for Macintosh complies with Apple File Protocol (AFP) 2.0 and with AppleTalk Phases I and II.

NetWare's open architecture extends beyond its file system to include new transport layer interfaces, based on Novell's Open Data Link Interfaces (ODI). These interfaces provide a wide range of connectivity options, including IPX/SPX, NETBIOS, LU 6.2 (APPC), named pipes for DOS and OS/2 workstations, TCP/IP, a Berkeley 4.3 Sockets interface, and AT&T UNIX System V Streams/Transport Layer Interface (TCI).

If you store files from many kinds of workstations on your server, you're probably concerned about backing up these files. NetWare 3.12's SBACKUP utility enables you to back up and restore all server files, regardless of origin, to an internal server tape drive. The name space information goes onto the backup tape too. You can back up and restore DOS, Macintosh, and OS/2 high performance file system (HPFS) files all in a single operation.

With the TCP/IP NLM included with NetWare 3.12, you can, for example, put a UNIX machine such as the IBM AIX-based RS/6000 on a Token Ring segment of the LAN; you can then use a NetWare 3.12 server with NetWare TCP/IP loaded to route IP packets internally from a DOS workstation to the separate RS/6000 segment. NetWare TCP/IP's IP tunneling feature enables NetWare 3.12 LANs to communicate across TCP/IP internetworks. To get IPX packets from one NetWare server to another across a TCP/IP link, NetWare wraps the IPX packets in an IP envelope and transfers them across the internetwork. In essence, the TCP/IP portion of the LAN becomes a natural extension of the IPX (NetWare) LAN.

To enable a UNIX workstation to use a NetWare file server, you load an NFS implementation on a UNIX machine (such as an RS/6000) and NetWare NFS on the NetWare file server. After you make the proper entries in the /ETC/HOSTS and other setup files on the UNIX computer, you create an empty directory and use the standard UNIX MOUNT command to turn the empty directory into a remote view of the NetWare 3.12 file server. You then access the NetWare file server from the UNIX workstation using ordinary UNIX commands, utilities, and application programs.

The NetWare FTAM NLM is a file-transfer facility that connects NetWare 3.12 servers to OSI-based networks. It is fully GOSIP 1.0-compliant; GOSIP workstations can use FTAM to share NetWare print services and to send files back and forth.

NetWare 2.15's FCONSOLE workstation utility monitored server activity. The first few versions of NetWare 386 did away with FCONSOLE. Now it is back, thanks to the Remote Management Facility (RMF) utility. You can use RMF to monitor a server or to upgrade NetWare at a second server. Remote installation works well, but you must follow the steps in the manual carefully.

NetWare 3.12 includes all the features and capacities of its NetWare 386 predecessors in terms of reliability, security, RAM usage, disk size, and file size. Installing NetWare 3.12 is easy.

The NetWare 3.12 online help system can use improvement. The data is there—all 1.7MB of it—but the NFOLIO user interface is non-intuitive and makes finding what you need difficult. You can move around the screen with cursor-movement keys and scroll the screen with the PgUp and PgDn keys. You press Tab to move the cursor to a subtopic name. Then you press Enter to get help for that subtopic.

NetWare 3.12 is a good performer, in part because of the new Turbo file allocation table (FAT). Each volume contains a *FAT*—an index to one or more disk allocation blocks in which a file resides. NetWare keeps the entire FAT in server memory and creates a Turbo FAT for files larger than 64 entries; this provides faster access for larger files.

Another NetWare 3.12 feature, *dynamic memory allocation*, parcels out cache buffers for file buffering, NLM memory requests, FAT buffering, and directory table buffering. NetWare 3.12 can have more file service process (FSP) threads running concurrently than is possible under NetWare 2.2 because of its memory management, and this translates to faster workstation response times.

Long, HPFS-style names are not supported by NetWare 2.2. AppleTalk was only emulated by Version 2.2 but is directly supported by Version 3.12.

Using NetWare 4.11 (IntraNetware)

NetWare version 4.11, IntraNetware, consists of network software for enterprise-wide file and printer sharing, as well as Internet (and intranet) World Wide Web connectivity.

III

Networking Software

From your DOS, DOS/Windows, Macintosh, or OS/2 workstation, you may not notice that your organization upgrades to NetWare 4.11. Novell carefully designed NetWare 4.11 to be completely compatible with Versions 2.2 and 3.12. If you're a network administrator, however, you'll notice several changes right away.

NetWare 4.11 Basics. Novell began selling the core NetWare 4.1 product in March, 1993, after showing it at the Interop/Spring trade show in Washington, D.C. In 1993, Novell released NetWare System Fault Tolerance (SFT) III—a version of NetWare 4.1 that incorporates software techniques to ensure failsafe LAN operation. Novell also offers NetWare 4.1 for UNIX and OS/2 2.x. The versions of NetWare 4.1 for UNIX and OS/2 are completely rewritten network operating systems, based more on the core NetWare 4.1 product than on the older Portable NetWare. NetWare for UNIX relies on technology provided by UNIX System Laboratories (USL), which Novell acquired from AT&T late in 1992. Late in 1996, Novell began offering NetWare 4.11. No matter what OS platform you prefer, Novell wants to be the supplier of your network software.

You install NetWare 4.11 from CD-ROM. The CD-ROM installation method quickly and painlessly creates a NetWare 4.11 server. NetWare 4.11 requires at least 6MB of RAM and, depending on features installed, from 12 to 60MB of disk space. For a server with large-capacity hard drives, NetWare needs more RAM because NetWare maintains an in-memory cache of server disk directories.

The 4.11 shell software that enables a DOS client to access a NetWare file server is smaller (53K versus 59K for Version 3.12) but otherwise provides the same I/O redirection functions as the 3.12 shell software. Workstations can continue to use the older shell software; you don't have to upgrade all workstations at once. Novell supplies the 4.11 DOS client software in modular form as Virtual Loadable Modules, or VLMs. You can log in from within Windows, just as you can from within OS/2 PM (see Figure 6.2). People who use the Windows or PM interfaces get new tools for managing network sessions.

NetWare 4.11 also has built-in packet-burst support, provides the ability to back up DOS and OS/2 workstations, and offers a smaller RAM footprint for designated remote printer machines. Packet-burst is a LAN performance technique for helping workstations get faster responses from a file server.

NetWare Directory Services (NDS). The most significant feature of NetWare 4.11, however, is Novell's NetWare Directory Services (NDS), a hierarchically organized database that replaces the old bindery. Much 3.12-aware network utility software uses the Novell API to access the bindery. By default, NetWare 4.11 turns on bindery emulation, so you don't have to throw those utilities away. Version 4.11 includes a new named directory service that Novell says works with software written to the X.500 specification. The new named service is the key that lets people log onto local servers in a single operation. People also can easily access servers located in geographically dispersed LANs.

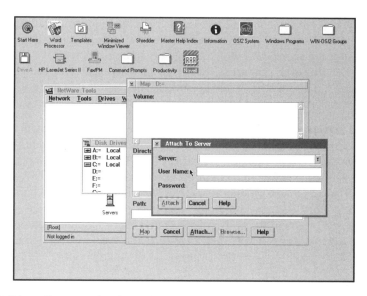

Fig. 6.2 NetWare offers a graphical interface in addition to its command line interface.

NDS is more than just a replacement for the bindery files where earlier versions of NetWare stored logon accounts, passwords, server names, and other administrative data. Whereas bindery files were a keyed, hierarchical set of named properties and their values, NDS is a relational database of network administrative data that 4.11 servers automatically keep up to date by periodically exchanging replicative status information.

NDS treats all network resources as tree-structured objects in the distributed NDS database. Network managers run NetWare Administrator on Windows, or OS/2 workstations or NetAdmin on DOS workstations, to change the network configuration. (NetAdmin doesn't yet run on NT workstations.) Note that NDS uses a period (".") to denote levels of the NDS tree; before you upgrade to NetWare 4.11, you should identify and change any logon account names containing periods.

With NDS, an administrator can manage multiple directory trees—such as the directories for the New York and Los Angeles offices—in the NetWare Administrator at the same time. To reflect the transfer of employees from New York to Los Angeles, the administrator simply opens browse windows for the two trees and uses the mouse to drag-and-drop directory objects between windows. This results in the users losing network permissions in New York and gaining network permissions in Los Angeles. Novell is extending this object motif in various ways to make NetWare work well with object-based scripts and computer languages such as Java.

To support the single logon function, a user "object" contains information about access rights to a range of servers and applications, each of which might have its own unique password and access controls. Administrators can give users access to authorized servers and applications without requiring them to go through the individual logon process for each different server.

You can add 3.12 servers to a 4.11 NDS tree, which gives client workstations easier access to the 3.12 servers. Attaching to a version 3 server by simply mapping its volumes is also possible. A utility called NetSync, which integrates 3.12 servers with the NDS, is a standard part of 4.11. However, don't run NetSync until you're ready for your 4.11 primary server to assume full responsibility for the bindery files in the 3.xx servers. The version 3 servers become slaves to the 4.11 NDS once you run NetSync.

Internet and Intranet Connectivity. The Internet and intranet components of NetWare 4.11 give the product its name, IntraNetware. They add several Internet technology features to NetWare, including improved TCP/IP protocol support and access to World Wide Web and distributed computing functions. Although earlier versions of NetWare required an add-on product to use the TCP/IP protocol—the communications protocol many companies have chosen for their networks—IntraNetware offers built-in support for TCP/IP. NetWare/IP is a set of server and client modules that provide access to a NetWare network using TCP/IP instead of IPX, and is now integrated into IntraNetware. NetWare/IP lets an administrator do the following:

- Transparently extend IntraNetware services and applications to nodes on an existing IP network

- Migrate current NetWare users from IPX to TCP/IP

- Interconnect TCP/IP and IPX networks, allowing all users to access IntraNetware resources on either network

- Manage TCP/IP address using the Dynamic Host Configuration Protocol (DHCP)

- Provide access to network printers attached to UNIX hosts using the lpr protocol

For administrators who want to avoid the expense of enabling the TCP/IP protocol for every client, IntraNetware also provides an IPX/IP gateway that allows the IPX-based NetWare network to communicate with a TCP/IP network. Because only the server has an IP address (rather than each user), the gateway can lower network costs and improve performance.

The NetWare Web Server component of NetWare 4.11 makes an IntraNetware server a Web server as well. For data integrity, NetWare and TCP/IP security functions work together to provide HTML document access protection. NDS authentication provides secure access to the server and directories, while access controls let the administrator control document access.

The NetWare Web Server includes Netscape Navigator (the client-side browser application), and it supports common Web features, including forms, Java applets, JavaScript, remote and local CGI, access controls and logging, and both Basic and Perl script interpreters. CGI, or Common Gateway Interface, is a standard for running computer programs on a Web server; CGI programs process form data entered onto Web pages. Perl is a computer language typically found in UNIX environments. Administrators can also browse the NDS directory through the Web Server to aid the administration process.

Other NetWare 4.11 Features. Many NetWare-compliant utilities and network extensions use the older bindery APIs. Until third-party utility vendors and Novell itself replace their bindery API calls with NDS API calls, Novell provides "bindery emulation"— an insulating layer of functions that internally translates bindery API calls such as SetPropertyValue( ) to NDS equivalents.

VLM clients can also support bindery emulation mode connections to both 3.12 and 4.11 servers. Be careful about VLMs, however. VLM client software behaves somewhat differently from the earlier NETX software. Performing a change directory (CD) command in a DOS session under Windows on a NetWare LAN causes all DOS sessions to change to the new directory. Under NETX, DOS sessions retain their individual current directories.

New in Version 4 of NetWare is a read-ahead cache to help performance, along with two features to help you conserve server disk space—data block suballocation and on-the-fly data compression. You can configure the data compression to operate off-hours, when most people have left the office, if you're afraid that on-the-fly compression will bog the server down. When you access a compressed file in the middle of the day, however, NetWare 4.11 has to do extra work to fluff the file to its uncompressed form. You can enable both sub-allocation and compression on an upgraded 3.12 server simply by loading INSTALL after you complete the upgrade. Select Maintenance/Selective Install/ Volumes Options and then the volume you want to modify. Move down to the Block Sub-allocation & Compression fields and turn them on. The only thing you can't change with an in-place upgrade is the block size. To change block size, you must make a backup copy of the volume, delete it, re-create it with the new features, and restore the data.

NetWare 4.11 supports up to 1,000 simultaneous connections (Version 3.12 supports only 250 connections to a server), and Novell sells licenses in strata of 5, 10, 20, 50, 100, 250, 500, and 1,000 users. NetWare 4.11 offers up to 54,000 server connections if you use the new shell (Version 3.12 allowed a workstation to have only 8 server connections). You can run NetWare 4.1 in nondedicated mode with the UNIX and OS/2 versions, but the core 4.11 product remains a dedicated server environment. A future version of NetWare (perhaps 4.12), says Novell, will offer nondedicated OS/2 and UNIX support like Version 4.1 did.

NetWare 4.11 supports symmetric multiprocessor machines (computers with more than one CPU chip). In response to a frequent criticism of Version 3.12, Version 4.11 distinguishes between ring 0 and ring 3 memory protection. These rings are protection mechanisms the Intel 80386, 80486, and Pentium CPUs make available to operating system software. Software running in a particular ring has a specific privilege level, and the CPU doesn't let software in one ring interfere with software running in a different ring.

NetWare Link Services Protocol (NLSP), the new link state router for IPX that is part of NetWare 4.11, helps IPX use WAN links wisely and frugally. NLSP is based on a routing strategy termed Open Shortest Path First (OSPF) that overcomes the limitations and high WAN traffic of the older Routing Information Protocol (RIP) and Service Advertising

III

Networking Software

Protocol (SAP). NLSP is faster than RIP at determining alternate routing paths between servers and networks, supports Simple Network Management Protocol (SNMP), balances routing loads across multiple paths, and causes much less WAN traffic than RIP does. NLSP acts as a superset of RIP, accommodating mixed RIP/SAP and NLSP traffic on the same network.

NetWare 4.11 has the same limits on number of volumes and total disk space as Version 3.12. Version 4.11 offers RSA Public/Private Key cryptography for better security, along with NDS and file system event-logging. You also get remote console session security and remote session modem callback. NetWare 4.11 can use a time server to synchronize clocks of multiple servers (even in different time zones). Novell's enhancements to Version 4.11 include Image Enabled NetWare, based on Kodak technology, and document-management services, based on content document architecture technology. NetWare 4.11 also offers the High Capacity Storage System (HCSS), which lets you share large optical media jukeboxes on NetWare 4.11 LANs.

NetWare 4.11 is a logical, practical step up from previous versions. If you've outgrown the 250-user or 8-server limits of NetWare 3.12 or if you have several LANs connected in a WAN, you'll find that Version 4.11 injects new life into your network. However, if your network hasn't yet grown enough to need NetWare 4.11, you'll be glad to know that Novell continues to sell and support the popular Version 3.12.

The table below shows the list prices for NetWare 4.11. They're the same as version 3, and about 25% less than the previous version 4.0 prices. A new additive licensing verification scheme in 4.11 allows you to combine items in the table in creative ways. For 275 users, you might buy the 250-user version and the 50-user version. Novell doesn't require you to buy the 500-connection license if you need only 275 concurrent connections.

Number of Connections	Price
5	$1,095
10	$2,495
25	$3,695
50	$4,995
100	$6,995
250	$12,495
500	$24,995
1,000	$47,995

Chapter Summary

The server-based NetWare network operating systems come in enterprise (NetWare 4.11) and high-performance (NetWare 3.12) versions. Both NetWare versions offer excellent security and reliability. Both are easy to install, and NetWare versions 3.12 and 4.11 deliver long-awaited connectivity options to Novell customers who have DOS, OS/2, Mac, Windows NT, Windows 95, and UNIX computers. NetWare 2.2, on the other hand, was an expensive solution for creating a small, entry-level LAN.

A large LAN or one with a diverse mixture of workstation types is a good candidate for NetWare 3.12. Version 3.12 is the first network operating system to support DOS, Macintosh, Windows, OS/2, and UNIX file and print services. NetWare 4.11 is appropriate for the largest of LANs—those with more than 250 workstations or more than eight file servers.

For more information about NetWare, you can contact Novell at the following address:

Novell, Inc.
122 East 1700 South
Provo Utah 84606
(800) 346-7177

In Chapter 7, you learn about Warp Server and Microsoft's Windows NT Server, the (almost) twin network operating systems from Microsoft and IBM.

Chapter 7

Using Windows NT Server and Warp Server

While Novell NetWare is the most popular server-based network operating system at the present time, NetWare doesn't lend itself well to a relatively new software technology called client/server computing. Client/server architecture, as Chapter 3, "Using File Servers," pointed out, integrates the LAN with one or more applications. The next step beyond mere file and printer sharing, client/server provides an environment in which a file server performs additional roles on the LAN, such as running a database management product. The applications running on the client workstations expect more services than simple file sharing. NetWare has difficulty in a client/server environment because programming NetWare Loadable Modules (NLMs), computer programs that run inside the file server alongside NetWare, is just too difficult a task. The server-based network operating system products from Microsoft and IBM, on the other hand, allow programmers to easily develop software that takes advantage of client/server technology. If all you need is the sharing of files and printers, Novell NetWare may be the product you should buy. But if you're interested in going beyond the sharing of files and printers on your LAN, you'll want to be aware of what Microsoft and IBM have to offer.

This chapter focuses on Microsoft NT Server and IBM Warp Server. These products are growing in sales somewhat, but still lag behind Novell NetWare by a wide margin. The network operating systems from Microsoft and IBM let people create client/server environments as well as share files and printers. As local area networks migrate toward client/server technology, you may find that Microsoft and IBM will someday sell more network software than Novell. However, the history of Microsoft's and IBM's file server software products is somewhat checkered. Both companies will have difficulty overcoming their reputations in the networking software arena.

It may seem odd that two companies would work together to create two virtually identical products with different names and slightly different sets of features. Therefore, the first subject you cover in this chapter is the genesis of these fraternal-twin network operating systems. You discover why OS/2 and

NT are such rich environments for network operating systems in general and for client/server applications in particular.

You learn what NT Server and Warp Server look like, how they operate, and what functions and features they offer. You explore, in depth, the procedures for logging in and mapping drives. You learn about OS/2 and Windows NT files, directories, and attributes. You see how your workstation behaves on an OS/2- or Windows NT-based LAN, and you find out how print redirection works with these products.

After you become familiar with print job management under NT Server and Warp Server, you look critically at the levels of security offered by these network operating systems. If you are thinking of installing NT Server, Warp Server, and NetWare on the same LAN but on different file servers, you find out about the potential problems you face. You complete the chapter by covering a detailed list of the similarities and differences between NT Server and Warp Server.

Exploring the IBM and Microsoft Team Effort

IBM and Microsoft have worked together on OS/2 since 1985. Each company markets its version of OS/2 differently, and each company has made slight changes to the operating system to customize it somewhat, but MS-OS/2 and IBM-OS/2 are essentially the same product. In 1985, the two companies added the writing of the OS/2 file server software to their Joint Development Agreement. IBM's product was called LAN Server and Microsoft's was LAN Manager. Both share a common *codebase*, meaning that, like OS/2 itself, the network operating systems are the same software with only minor differences.

The first few versions of OS/2 were not greatly popular, despite the fact that OS/2 does not have a 640K limitation or many of the other problems associated with DOS. Microsoft and IBM envisioned that OS/2 would replace DOS, but this did not happen. Application developers did not rush to market an OS/2 version of every DOS application as Microsoft and IBM expected they would. The emulation of DOS in early versions of OS/2 was limited in significant ways, and not every DOS application would run in the DOS box under OS/2. People kept using their DOS applications, purchasing memory managers such as QEMM and 386MAX to give them more conventional memory in which to run their applications. Such purchases prolonged the life of the DOS applications, but people still complained when they ran out of room by bumping into the 640K DOS limitation.

The 32-bit versions of OS/2, starting with Version 2.x, rectify the situation by giving you multiple concurrent DOS sessions, each with about 620K of available conventional memory free for running your software. OS/2, now known as Warp, includes the Microsoft Windows environment, and, of course, you can run OS/2 applications under OS/2 2.x. IBM calls OS/2 "a better DOS than DOS, a better Windows than Windows, and a better OS/2 than ever before."

In the latter part of 1991, Microsoft and IBM split up and decided to go their own ways with OS/2 and their jointly developed network operating systems. Microsoft's LAN Manager ran on OS/2, but Microsoft began in 1993 to also sell a new operating system product, called Windows NT, and a complementary network operating system product called Windows NT Advanced Server. Microsoft later dropped "Advanced" from the name of the product. Microsoft's network operating system is now NT Server, while IBM's product is Warp Server.

IBM remains firmly committed to OS/2. IBM believes that, with its new features, OS/2 may yet replace DOS as the dominant operating system for personal computers. At the same time, Microsoft believes that Windows NT will someday dominate desktop computers. IBM, Microsoft, and Novell compete fiercely to sell network operating systems to connect those desktop computers.

The History of OS/2 and NT

Software developers and end users had complained about DOS almost from Version 1. Through the late 1980s, DOS did not keep up with people's needs for personal computers that did more work and were more reliable. Specifically, people said they did not have enough memory in which to run their applications (the infamous 640K limitation), DOS did not support multiple concurrent applications, DOS was too fragile, DOS was too simple and rudimentary, and DOS was too slow when applications accessed large files. In short, DOS was not industrial-strength. People's biggest complaint about DOS, however, was that each DOS application had its own user interface and required too much training to make the DOS environment truly productive.

Version 1.0 of OS/2 shipped in December 1987. The first implementation of OS/2 had a single, small DOS *compatibility box*—a special version of DOS within OS/2—for running DOS applications along with OS/2 applications. This first version of OS/2 did not contain or support a graphical user interface. It did, however, offer up to 16MB of memory to applications rewritten to run under OS/2 instead of DOS.

Version 1.1 of OS/2, essentially the 1.0 product with the addition of Presentation Manager, appeared in the last quarter of 1988. Still saddled with a small DOS compatibility box, OS/2 1.1 was nonetheless a technical marvel. OS/2 1.1 enabled software developers to transcend the limitations of DOS if they would rewrite their software. Unfortunately, few did.

At the same time that IBM and Microsoft released a Presentation Manager version of OS/2, IBM published a set of guidelines and standards, called *Systems Application Architecture* (SAA), to help the computer industry achieve some measure of consistency and coherence. IBM mentions its own products in the guidelines, but otherwise freely offers the guidelines as a set of suggested methods, interfaces, computer languages, and design techniques software developers can follow. IBM reasons that consistency and coherence among software applications will encourage more people to use computers in more ways, more productively, and thus indirectly help IBM sell more hardware and software.

Microsoft and IBM also began offering an extended edition of OS/2. Called OS/2 EE 1.1, this special version contained a communications manager for computer-to-computer data transfer, a database manager based on IBM's *Structured Query Language* (SQL) standard for record keeping, and special support for local area networks. The regular version of OS/2 was called OS/2 Standard Edition (SE).

In December 1990, IBM and Microsoft released Version 1.3 of OS/2. Slimmed down considerably from earlier versions, OS/2 1.3 got the nickname OS/2 Lite. You could run OS/2 1.3 on a computer with as little as 2M or 3M of memory (although you would need more RAM if you wanted to use the machine as a file server). Version 1.3 did many things well for applications rewritten for OS/2, but it still had only a single, small (in other words, limited memory available for running applications) DOS compatibility box. Unlike for earlier versions, IBM did most of the development work for Version 1.3. OS/2 1.3 was small, fast, reliable, and had printing capabilities. Its only drawback was its small DOS box.

IBM released Version 2.0 of OS/2 in March, 1992. In late spring of 1993, Version 2.1 of OS/2 became available. The current version, OS/2 Warp 4.0, has the following key features:

Simple, graphical-user-interface installation

System integrity protection

Virtual memory

Preemptive multitasking and task scheduling

Fast, 32-bit architecture

Overlapped, fast disk file access

DOS compatibility

More available memory for DOS applications (typically about 620K of conventional memory)

Capability to run concurrently OS/2, DOS, and Windows 2.1, 3.0, and 3.1 software

Multiple concurrent DOS sessions

High Performance File System (HPFS)

Presentation Manager (PM) graphical user interface

Object-oriented Work Place Shell (WPS)

National Language Support (NLS)

Interactive online documentation and help screens

Capability to run OS/2 on IBM and IBM-compatible hardware

Support for popular Super Video Graphics (SVGA) adapters

Support for additional printers

Personal Computer Memory Card International Association (PCMCIA) support

Support for popular SCSI CD-ROM drives

Advanced Power Management (APM) support

Almost all the items in this list help make OS/2 a good file server platform.

As Microsoft and IBM codeveloped the OS/2 operating system, they realized OS/2 could form the basis for a new, full-featured network operating system. With OS/2 running at the file server, the software modules of the network operating system could service file and print requests in a multi-tasking, *threaded* environment. (Threads are a software technique employed by some operating systems that enable different parts of the file server software to execute concurrently. Threads enable the server to give the appearance of doing more than one thing at a time.) The workstations, which might be using DOS, OS/2, or some other operating system, would see the benefit of the new high-performance environment. OS/2 file servers and DOS workstations seemed like a natural, popular combination. Microsoft and IBM planned that customers would get an extra benefit, too. It is relatively easy to program an OS/2 computer, even one that is already running as a file server. If you have a staff of programmers, or if the application software you buy already supports it, client/server architecture becomes a possibility.

In 1989 and again in 1990, Microsoft and IBM announced that the companies would merge their network operating system products into a single product. This has not happened, and the split between Microsoft and IBM makes it extremely unlikely the products will ever merge.

After developing OS/2 and the similar LAN Manager and LAN Server (now called Warp Server), Microsoft and IBM in 1991 stopped working together. Then, in 1993, Microsoft released yet another operating system, Windows NT, and a new network operating system based on Windows NT, called Windows NT Advanced Server. The three products are, not surprisingly, somewhat similar.

With a history such as this, you begin to see why NT Server and Warp Server have not preempted Novell NetWare as the most popular network operating system. Novell has always sharply focused on building a better network operating system. People perceive IBM and Microsoft as being not quite as focused. On the (client) desktop, OS/2 Warp has outsold NT about 13 to 1. But, at the file server, NetWare continues to give both OS/2 and NT strong competition.

NT and OS/2 File Servers

NT Server runs on Windows NT and Warp Server runs on top of OS/2. NT Server 4.0 and Warp Server 4.0 are the most current versions as this book went to press. For client workstation connectivity, NT Server supports Intel-CPU workstations running Windows and Macintosh workstations running System 7. Warp Server Intel-CPU client workstations can run DOS, Windows, or OS/2, and Warp Server also supports Macintosh System 7 workstations. You can use an OS/2 or NT file server as both a workstation and a server—in a peer-to-peer arrangement—but you probably will want to keep the file server isolated and unattended for security reasons. Practically speaking, no one uses Warp Server or NT Server as the basis for a peer LAN.

Learning NT Server and Warp Server Basics

You install NT Server or Warp Server after first installing the base operating system on the file server computer. For Warp Server, you'll want to disable OS/2's capability to emulate DOS when you install OS/2, because Warp Server consists purely of non-DOS software. A DOS box would just take up memory; you can give the network operating system more memory by disabling DOS emulation. The installation documentation for NT Server or Warp Server will give you other configuration changes you can make to provide a better file server environment.

On the server computer, NT Server and Warp Server run as tasks managed by the base operating system. The network operating system software (NT Server or Warp Server) does most of its work in the background. The work, as you know from earlier chapters, is the sharing of files, disk space, and, perhaps, a LAN printer across the network. The network operating system also performs administrative tasks, such as recognizing workstations as LAN users log in and forgetting about workstations when those users log out.

Like Windows for Workgroups, Windows 95, Warp Connect, and the PC LAN Program, NT Server and Warp Server use the SMB file I/O redirection protocol. Chapter 4, "Using Protocols, Cables, and Adapters," describes the SMB protocol.

You can use command-line entries or menus to do administrative tasks on the network, including logging in and setting your shared drive letters and printers. NT Server and Warp Server also include graphical interfaces that let you point and click through LAN administrator tasks.

Using the High Performance File System

When you install OS/2 on the file server computer, the installation process asks you if you want to use the High Performance File System. Because the computer is going to become a file server and you want the server to be as efficient as possible, you should answer "yes" to the question. If you answer "no," OS/2 uses the same type of file system that DOS uses, known as the FAT (file allocation table).

The file allocation table scheme was designed to work with the small disks popular when DOS was first released. Performance suffers when applications access FAT files, especially large files. DOS and OS/2 have to read and process long chains of physical disk location information to satisfy application requests for files.

OS/2 offers a High Performance File System (HPFS) designed for hard disks. OS/2 can access files in an HPFS partition more rapidly than files in a FAT partition. As Chapter 3 mentioned in the "DOS Was Not Designed for File Sharing" section, the FAT file system was designed for floppy diskettes. The difference in performance is most dramatic for large files.

Outside of OS/2, DOS cannot recognize files on an HPFS partition. If you use the OS/2 System Editor to create a text file on an HPFS drive, then reboot your computer with DOS (perhaps by using Dual Boot to switch from OS/2 to DOS, or by using a system-formatted floppy diskette), DOS will not show you the HPFS disk drive. DOS will reassign your computer's drive letters and the HPFS drive will be invisible. However, if you use the DOS that is built into OS/2, your DOS applications can use files on an HPFS partition.

HPFS lets you use long file names, up to 254 characters, which can include spaces and periods. OS/2-based computers—either the file server or OS/2 workstations—can see and use these files; DOS workstations cannot.

NT Server offers an alternative file system, called New Technology File System (NTFS), that has features similar to those of HPFS. NTFS and HPFS are better suited for file server use than the FAT file system. These file systems offer faster access, they're more robust (they contain extra information that lets NT or OS/2 recover damaged files), and HPFS and NTFS provide for administering access rights and permissions.

Using Client/Server Architecture

NT Server and Warp Server provide good environments for client/server applications. Chapter 3 explains client/server architecture and discusses why you may want to take advantage of it on your LAN.

Programmability is the biggest reason people talk about client/server in connection with the two OS/2-based network operating systems, NT Server and Warp Server. OS/2 and NT are easily programmed, perhaps more so than DOS. NT Server and Warp Server can share the network adapter with other OS/2 application software running on the file server computer. OS/2 and NT *multitask*, which means they can run several computer programs concurrently. One program is the network operating system, of course. Another may be a database server application. The workstations can see and use the extra drive letters provided by the network operating system. Your programming staff also may program the workstations to send and receive special requests and responses to and from the file server (or a separate computer). These custom-programmed requests and responses may, for example, carry SQL statements and relational database records.

OS/2 and NT provide *named pipes* to programmers. The programmer treats a named pipe almost as he or she would a file, but the named pipe contains message records. These message records travel from the workstation to the file server. On the file server, a custom-written application may handle records and perform other tasks before responding to the workstation through the named pipe.

SQL Server is a Microsoft product that enables programmers to create client/server applications. SQL Server provides a relational database "engine" that you install on an OS/2 computer on the network. Programmers write workstation software that sends SQL statements to SQL Server. SQL Server honors each request by sending back the appropriate records from within its database. Some database management products, such as Microsoft's FoxPro and Borland's Paradox, can work with SQL Server to give you the

III

Networking Software

ability to update and query your data without hiring programmers or studying the syntax and commands of Structured Query Language. Microsoft SQL Server runs only on NT, but other relational database manager products, such as Oracle and DB2, run on both NT and OS/2.

Lotus Notes is yet another client/server application. Notes offers intelligent, group-oriented electronic mail services. Notes enables sophisticated storage and retrieval of messages; an index contains the subject, author, recipients, and other key data items related to the messages. Notes is particularly useful for large, geographically dispersed organizations in which people need to exchange information frequently but do not work in the same time zone or have conflicting schedules or work styles. Notes stores data on a central personal computer on a LAN. Workstations on the LAN or on a remotely attached LAN, through a wide area network, can interact with the central Notes computer. Notes runs on both NT and OS/2.

Working with NT Server and Warp Server

In the following sections, you see how to operate NT Server or Warp Server.

You first cover the menu interface these products offer, followed by the command-line interface. You learn what it means to log in on an NT Server or Warp Server network. You discover how to map drive letters, use files and directories, and print on the LAN. You explore how your computer behaves when it becomes a workstation on an NT Server or Warp Server network, and you learn about the security features of these products. You also get a comparison of the two network operating system products.

Administering the LAN Graphically

The Warp Server and NT Server administration tools are Presentation Manager (OS/2) and Windows (NT) graphical software. The screens these tools present are CUA-compliant, which means you use standard keystrokes or mouse actions to interact with the network operating system's menu. CUA stands for *Common User Access*, and CUA is part of IBM's recommended standards for information processing, SAA (Systems Application Architecture).

Where does the IBM standard for consistency and ease of use come from? An IBM team spent several years investigating user interfaces. The team's findings parallel the findings of the Xerox company at the Palo Alto Research Center (PARC) and Apple, makers of the Macintosh computer. IBM published these findings as suggested standards and called them Common User Access. The standards, Systems Applications Architecture, cover communications, programming, database design, and user interfaces.

The graphical tools you use with Warp Server encompass more sophisticated features of the CUA standard, including drag-and-drop mouse operations and folders, than does NT Server. Nonetheless, the actions performed by NT Server's administrative tools and Warp Server's administrative tools are similar in terms of their effect on the network operating system.

The first time you use Warp Server, you'll want to set up one or more named groups into which you'll put log-on accounts. To create a group, use mouse button 2 to drag the Group Template icon onto an empty area of the Groups folder. Before manipulating the Group Template icon, you should resize the borders of the Groups folder to make room for the new group's icon. When you release the mouse button, the template opens and you see a settings notebook on your screen. Figure 7.1 shows an example of a new group, with the Group name and Description fields filled in. Note that OS/2 and Warp Server give you several ways to accomplish the same operations. In addition to the template method of adding a group, you can choose Create Another from an existing group's pop-up menu.

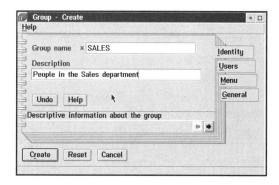

Fig. 7.1   Creating new groups with Warp Server lets you put log-on accounts into separate categories.

With the Warp Server Administration graphical tool, you establish named shared re-sources that workstations on the LAN can access. The already-installed objects in the domain folder are templates, in OS/2 terms, and have the titles Printer Template, Serial Device Template, and Directory Template. You create shared resources by dragging-and-dropping one of these templates onto an empty area of the folder. Alternatively, you create a shared resource by choosing Create Another from an existing resource's pop-up menu. Figure 7.2 shows the settings notebook for a shared directory resource named "Drive-E."

When you use a shared resource template or the Create Another menu option, a settings notebook opens. You see an Identity tab and two other tabs, Menu and General, that offer ways to customize the shared resource object. The Identity tab of the settings note-book for a shared resource is the administrator's primary means of establishing and con-figuring the resource.

On the Identity tab of a shared directory resource, the administrator specifies the De-scription, Server Name, and Path (server drive letter and directory name). The adminis-trator can designate whether the resource becomes available at server startup, by administrative action, or only when requested. The administrator can also limit the number of concurrent connections to the shared resource by using the Number of Con-nections entry on the Identity tab.

III

Networking Software

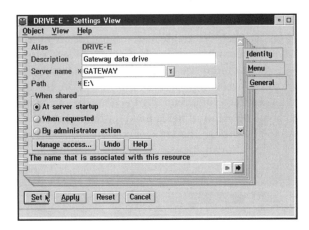

Fig. 7.2 Shared resource administration with Warp Server is a matter of manipulating icons within a folder.

The Identity tab's Manage Access push-button displays a screen, titled Access Control Profile, on which an administrator can grant or restrict access to the shared resource. The Auditing tab of the notebook lets an administrator turn auditing on or off for the shared resource. When auditing is on, Warp Server can put entries in the audit log when access to the resource fails, when access succeeds, or when any access occurs.

Using the Command-Line Interface

You may feel more comfortable issuing network commands at the DOS prompt of your workstation, or at the command line prompt at the file server, after you have gained some experience with NT Server or Warp Server. You invoke the network commands by running the NET command, but you avoid the menu screens by typing parameters after the word NET. The following is a list of the most important and most frequently used NET commands, with their parameters, that you use at a basic or enhanced workstation:

Command	Function
Net Access	Views permissions
Net Continue	Continues a paused service
Net Copy	Copies network files
Net Help	Gets help for a command
Net Name	Assigns a computer name
Net Pause	Pauses a connection to a network service
Net Print	Controls print jobs and prints files
Net Share	Assigns shared resources that others can connect to
Net Start	Starts a workstation or learns what workstation connections exist
Net Time	Synchronizes the workstation's clock with the server's clock
Net Use	Displays shared resources or assigns a drive letter or device name to a new shared resource
Net View	Displays a list of servers and server resources
Net Who	Sees who is logged on

Using Utilities

The NET command performs most of your administrative duties on an NT Server or Warp Server network; however, the network operating system comes with additional utilities. These utilities enable you to schedule commands or programs, back up the network's administrative (passwords and permissions) files, restore these files, verify a connection to a remote computer, and do other odd jobs on the LAN.

Logging In

You use the LOGON command to log into the network. This command establishes the user ID, password, and domain for a workstation. The user ID and password identify you in a particular domain and grant you access to shared resources. You can use shared resources in other domains once you have logged on. Figure 7.3 shows the graphical interface that appears if you type the LOGON command without command-line parameters.

Fig. 7.3   You use the LAN Server Logon screen to gain access to the network.

If you forget your password your account may be locked out. If you make repeated un-successful tries to enter your password, the system will disable your account, and you will have to ask the network administrator to re-enable your account. This security feature helps keep intruders from gaining access to the LAN.

Mapping Drives

You use the NET USE command, or the graphical interface, to map drive letters. Depending on how the network administrator has set up the file server's shared resources, you may find that your workstation's new drive letter refers to an entire server disk drive or only to a directory. The administrator decides the extent to which the file server's resources are shared. The distinction between sharing an entire disk and just a directory is invisible from a workstation.

The following NET USE command sets up drive F. The network administrator has published the shared resource with the name NORTHEAST on the server named \\SALES.

```
NET USE F: \\SALES\NORTHEAST
```

You also issue a form of the NET USE command to delete, or cancel, the use of a drive letter. The same NET USE command that sets up your network drive letters also redirects your printed output to the LAN printer, as you will see later in the section "Printing with NT Server and Warp Server."

After you establish the network drive letters your workstation can use, you work with your applications as you ordinarily would. Files on the LAN now are available to the computer programs you run, as long as you have permission to use those files. If you do not have permission at least to read a file, you cannot access that file. Be aware that you may have read permission but not write permission on some files. This means you cannot save new data in that file. If you encounter strange error messages from the applications you run, you may want to visit your network administrator to make sure your permissions are correct.

Using Your Workstation

One of the biggest reasons that Novell NetWare is more popular than NT Server or Warp Server is the disk space taken up by the NT Server or Warp Server executable and configuration files. You generally need to use only from two to six relatively small files on a NetWare workstation to gain access to a file server. On an NT Server or Warp Server workstation, however, you need from 1M to 3M of workstation disk space. You can easily create a bootable floppy diskette that gets you onto the network with NetWare. With NT Server or Warp Server, you might not be able to create a bootable diskette to access the LAN.

The memory used by the NT Server and Warp Server workstation software is also greater than that for a NetWare-based workstation. Memory requirements vary according to the type of network adapter card and associated software drivers, but you can expect NT Server or Warp Server workstation software to occupy about 90K of RAM. NetWare workstation software, on the other hand, usually occupies only 50K to 60K. On a workstation with an 80386, 80486, or Pentium CPU chip, you may be able to use a memory manager to load some or all of the network software into high memory. Chapter 5, "Using Workstations," discusses memory managers.

The workstation installation program will copy files to your computer's hard disk and put statements in your CONFIG.SYS and AUTOEXEC.BAT files to load the network software when you boot your computer. You can put your NET USE statements into a BAT file so that you do not have to retype them each time you reboot.

Printing with NT Server and Warp Server

Besides giving you network drive letters, the NET USE command also redirects your printed output to the shared LAN printer. The network administrator gives a name to the LAN printer in the same way he or she gives names to the file servers and to the shared resources that become drive letters at your workstation. The administrator may set up a printer named HP_LASER on the SALES file server, for example. In this case, your NET USE statement for your printed output would look like the following:

```
NET USE LPT1: \\SALES\HP_LASER
```

When you copy a file to the LPT1 device or when you tell one of your applications to print, the network operating system creates a print job. The print job goes into the server's print queue, to be printed after other pending print jobs when the printer becomes available.

You can configure the network operating system to notify you when the print job is finished. If you are impatient and want to see where your job is in the queue, you can view the items in the print queue. You can hold, release, and delete print jobs in the queue (but only your own print jobs, of course).

Security

You organize file servers and workstations into *domains*. A domain is a group of file servers and workstations with similar security needs. You can set up several domains on a large NT Server or Warp Server network. Domains provide a simple way for you to control user access to the network and its resources. A user can have accounts in multiple domains, but he or she can log on in only one domain at a time.

User-level security on an NT Server or Warp Server network consists of log-on security and permissions. Each user account has a password; the user specifies a user ID and the password to gain access to the network through a domain. A network administrator can limit a user's access to certain times or to certain workstations. Permissions limit the extent to which a user can use shared resources. The network administrator, for example, can create a COMMON directory everyone can use, and the administrator can create an UPDATE directory with files only certain people can modify but everyone can read.

You can assign the following permissions for files and directories:

Change Attributes	Flags a file as read-only or read/write.
Change Permissions	Grants or revokes access to other people.
Create	Creates files and directories.
Delete	Deletes files and removes directories (if the user has this permission).
Execute	Executes a program file (EXE, BAT, or COM file) but does not read or copy that file. Only workstations running OS/2 or DOS 5 recognize this permission, which is a restricted version of the read permission.
Read	Enables you to read and copy files, run programs, change from one directory to another, and use OS/2's extended attributes for files.
Write	Lets you write to a file.

These IBM and Microsoft network operating systems also let you control access to the file server's keyboard and computer screen. In a special unattended mode, the file server lets people view and manage print queues without letting them modify user accounts or other administrative data. You must specify a password in order to use other screens.

NT Server also provides share-level security, which you learn about in "Comparing NT Server, Warp Server, and NetWare" later in this chapter.

III

Networking Software

The IBMLAN.INI File. Warp Server uses entries in the IBMLAN.INI file to configure itself for the size and type of network your organization needs. NT Server uses similar information embedded in the NT registry file. Like the PROTOCOL.INI file mentioned in Chapter 4, "Using Protocols, Cables, and Adapters," the IBMLAN.INI file is a text file you can modify with a text editor. Make sure you have backup copies of the file prior to editing it, in case your changes don't work. As a rule, you should always run MPTS, the OS/2 LAN Services Installation/Configuration utility, or the Tuning Assistant to alter the IBMLAN.INI file. Using a text editor to make changes is riskier than using the installation and tuning software.

The commonly found section headings within the IBMLAN.INI file are: NETWORKS, REQUESTER, MESSENGER, NETLOGON, REPLICATOR, SERVER, and SERVICES. The following sections of this chapter explain these components of the IBMLAN.INI file. For further information, refer to the Performance Tuning manual that comes with Warp Server. Be aware the IBMLAN.INI file on your file server might not have exactly the same headings and entries as the examples in this chapter.

The NETWORKS Section. The NETWORKS section usually has a single entry identifying the network protocol that Warp Server uses to send information through the LAN cable. Other entries in IBMLAN.INI refer to the network protocol by name (net1 in the following example). In the following example, that protocol is NETBEUI. The redirector portion of the Warp Server software uses this entry to configure itself. Running MPTS is the best way to change the protocol your LAN uses.

```
net1 = NETBEUI$,0,LM10,102,175,14
```

The REQUESTER Section. The REQUESTER section of IBMLAN.INI contains parameters that Warp Server uses to manage access to the LAN. As shown in the following example, the REQUESTER section identifies the name of the computer, the name of the domain, and several values that control how the components of Warp Server behave. The useallmem entry, for instance, determines whether 386HPFS should use memory above 16 MB, and the charcount parameter sets the number of characters, in bytes, that the requester stores before sending data to a modem via a serial device queue.

REQUESTER Entry	Brief Description
COMPUTERNAME=Z-SERVER	Network name of this computer
DOMAIN = EVERYONE	Domain name
charcount = 16	Modem buffer character count
chartime = 250	Milliseconds before emptying modem buffer
charwait = 3600	Seconds to wait for a modem to become available
keepconn = 600	Seconds an inactive shared resource connection lives
keepsearch = 600	Seconds an inactive file search request is maintained
maxcmds = 16	Maximum number of concurrent file service operations
maxerrorlog = 100	Maximum error log entries
maxthreads = 10	Maximum threads Warp Server can start
maxwrkcache = 64	Maximum size (KB) of large-transfer buffers

REQUESTER Entry	Brief Description
numworkbuf = 15	Number of file service network message buffers
printbuftime = 90	Seconds before truncating a DOS print job
sesstimeout = 45	Seconds before stopping a non-responsive connection
sizworkbuf = 4096	File service buffer size
useallmem = Yes	Whether 386HPFS should use memory above 16 MB
WRKSERVICES = MESSENGER	The messenger service lets your workstation receive broadcast announcement messages
wrknets = NET1	The name by which Warp Server refers to the network protocol
wrkheuristics = 111111112131111111000101112011122100121111	

The `wrkheuristics` parameter in the IBMLAN.INI file is a set of one-character options for tuning and controlling Warp Server. Most of the options have a value of 0 or 1, with 0 signifying "off" and 1 signifying "on." Each character controls a different characteristic of Warp Server. The manual titled *Warp Server Network Administrator Reference Volume 2: Performance Tuning* contains more detail regarding `wrkheuristics` entries. The following explanation of these entries begins numbering the characters at 1.

Character 1 is the opportunistic locking of files option (default is 1). The server can use opportunistic locking to provide faster file access to a workstation by assuming that workstation is the only one using a given file. Turn opportunistic locking OFF in environments that use LAN-aware application software.

Character 2 specifies performance optimization for batch (CMD) files (default is 1).

Character 3 controls asynchronous unlock and asynchronous write-unlock:

> 0 = Never

> 1 = Always (default)

> 2 = Only on a Warp Server virtual circuit

Character 4 controls asynchronous close and asynchronous write-close:

> 0 = Never

> 1 = Always (default)

> 2 = Only on a Warp Server virtual circuit

Character 5 determines whether named pipes and serial devices are buffered (default is 1).

Character 6 controls combined read-lock and write-unlock:

> 0 = Never

> 1 = Always (default)

> 2 = Only on a Warp Server virtual circuit

A value of 1 in character 7 specifies open and read optimization (default is 1).

Character 8 is reserved.

Character 9 controls the use of the chain-send NETBIOS NCB:

0 = Never

1 = When a server's buffer is larger than the workstation's buffer

2 = Always (default)

Character 10 indicates whether to buffer small read and write requests until the buffer is full:

0 = Never

1 = Always (default)

2 = Only on a Warp Server virtual circuit

Character 11 specifies buffer mode:

0 = Always read buffer size amount of data if the request is smaller than the buffer size and data is being read sequentially

1 = Use full buffer if file is open for reading and writing

2 = Use full buffer if reading and writing sequentially

3 = Buffer all requests smaller than the buffer size (default)

A value of 1 in character 12 specifies RAW read and RAW write SMB protocols (default is 1).

A value of 1 in character 13 specifies the use of a RAW read-ahead buffer (default is 1).

A value of 1 in character 14 specifies the use of a RAW write-behind buffer (default is 1).

A value of 1 in character 15 specifies the use of read multiplexing SMB protocols (default is 1).

A value of 1 in character 16 specifies the use of write multiplexing SMB protocols (default is 1).

A value of 1 in character 17 specifies the use of big buffers for large (non-RAW) reads (default is 1).

A value of 1 in character 18 specifies the use of a same-size read-ahead or read-to-sector boundary (default is 1).

A value of 1 in character 19 specifies the use of a same-size small record write-behind or write-to-sector boundary (default is 0).

Character 20 is reserved and must be 0.

Character 21 specifies how pipes and devices are flushed (emptied) on a `DosBufReset` or `DosClose` operation:

0 = Flush only files and devices opened by the caller. Wait until flushed. Wait for confirmation before processing with other tasks (default).

1 = Flush only files and devices opened by the caller. Flush only once. Do not wait for confirmation.

2 = Flush all files and all input and output of short-term pipes and devices. Wait until flushed.

3 = Flush all files and all input and output of short-term pipes and devices. Flush only once.

4 = Flush all files and all input and output of all pipes and devices. Wait until flushed.

5 = Flush all files and all input and output of all pipes and devices. Flush only once.

A value of 1 in character 22 specifies the encryption of passwords (default is 1).

Character 23 controls log entries for multiple occurrences of an error:

0 = Log all occurrences (default)

1–9 = Limit occurrences that are logged (1–9 defines size of table used to track errors)

Character 24 indicates whether to buffer all files opened with deny-write sharing mode (default is 1).

Character 25 directs Warp Server to buffer all files opened with the read-only attribute set (default is 1).

A value of 1 in character 26 specifies read-ahead when opening a program file for execution (default is 1).

Character 27 specifies how to handle the interrupt (Ctrl C) keypress:

0 = Allow no interrupts

1 = Allow interrupts only on long-term operations

2 = Always allow interrupts (default)

Character 28 forces correct open mode when creating files on a server (default is 1).

Character 29 specifies NETBIOS `NoAcknowledgement` mode:

0 = `NoAck` disabled

1 = `NoAck` set on send only (default)

2 = `NoAck` set on receive only

3 = `NoAck` set on send and receive

Character 30 specifies whether to send data along with SMB write-block RAW requests (default is 1).

Character 31 controls whether Warp Server displays a message when the requester logs an error:

0 = Never

1 = On write-fault errors only (no time out) (default)

2 = On write-fault and internal errors only (no time out)

3 = On all errors (no time out)

4 = Reserved

5 = On write-fault errors only (time out)

6 = On write-fault and internal errors only (time out)

7 = On all errors (time out)

Character 32 is reserved.

Character 33 controls the behavior of DosBufReset on a redirected file (not pipes or devices). DosBufReset handles the data in the buffer as follows:

0 = Changed data in the buffer was sent from the requester to the server. The server has written the data to disk.

1 = Changed data in the buffer was sent from the requester to the server. The server has not yet written the data to disk.

2 = DosBufReset was ignored (default).

Character 34 specifies the time interval for performing logon validation from the domain controller:

0 = 5 seconds

1 = 15 seconds (default)

2 = 30 seconds

3 = 45 seconds

4 = 60 seconds

5 = 90 seconds

6 = 2 minutes

7 = 4 minutes

8 = 8 minutes

9 = 15 minutes

Character 35 controls date validation between workstations and the server:

   0 = PC LAN Program date format (default)

   1 = MS NET date format

   2 = No validation; assume date is correct

Character 36 determines the free disk space reported to DOS and Windows applications:

   0 = Return true value (default)

   1 = Return a value less than 2 gigabytes

A value of 1 in character 37 specifies time and date synchronization with the domain controller at logon (default is 1).

Character 38 controls the type of verification for the Warp Server logon:

   0 = No verification

   1 = Verify against local NET.ACC

   2 = Verify against domain NET.ACC (default)

Character 39 specifies how Warp Server displays warning messages for a Warp Server logon:

   0 = Do not display warning messages

   1 = Display all warning messages (default)

   2 = Do not display Warp Server specific warning messages

Character 40 specifies how Warp Server buffers files opened in compatibility mode:

   0 = Buffer only files opened for read access in compatibility mode

   1 = Buffer all files opened in compatibility mode (default)

A value of 1 in character 41 allows multiple logons by a person in the same domain (default is 1).

The MESSENGER Section. The MESSENGER section's two parameters express the name of the message log file and the size, in bytes, of the buffer used to receive network messages. The logfile parameter is a file name within the \IBMLAN\LOGS subdirectory for the message log. The sizmessbuf parameter is the size of the buffer.

```
logfile = messages.log
sizmessbuf = 4096
```

The NETLOGON Section. The NETLOGON section supplies Warp Server with directions that specify how Warp Server makes backup copies of your NET.ACC file. The NET.ACC file is an important file in the Warp Server environment because it contains logon account information, group information, shared resource information, and other significant network data.

The scripts parameter is the path where the Netlogon service searches for logon scripts. The update parameter indicates whether to synchronize the Netlogon service with the primary domain controller at the next pulse. The pulse parameter value is the number of seconds between backup copy operations.

```
SCRIPTS = D:\IBMLAN\REPL\IMPORT\SCRIPTS
pulse = 60
update = yes
```

The REPLICATOR Section. The REPLICATOR section of the IBMLAN.INI file contains instructions that control how frequently Warp Server automatically backs up your files and directories. Using these parameters, Warp Server can replicate files and directories onto another file server or onto a workstation. The server sending the data is called an exporter, while the workstation or server receiving the data is called an importer. Any number of exporters and importers can exist in a domain. A server can be both an exporter and an importer, while a workstation can only be an importer.

You specify an export path on the exporter (server) and an import path on the importer beneath the REPLICATOR section heading. The replicator service within Warp Server periodically examines the specified export directory. The replicator service notifies the importer PC of file or directory changes and sends the importer information that lets the importer PC mirror the operation.

The replicate parameter specifies whether the workstation is an importer, an exporter, or both. The parameter can have one of the following values:

import

export

both

If a server is an exporter, the value can be export or both. If a server is an importer, the value can be import or both.

The importpath parameter specifies the path of the top-level import directory on the PC acting as importer. Warp Server replicates files into the directory structure within the path specified by this parameter. The logon parameter is the logon account the replicator service uses to log on (if no one is already logged on at that computer). The password parameter is the password that the Replicator service uses when connecting to the exporter when no one is logged on at the importer.

The tryuser parameter indicates how the importer should automatically attempt logging on to the exporter even if a logon is already active at that workstation. If the parameter is yes, the importer tries connecting to the exporter using the logon account and password of the person logged on at the importer PC. The attempt succeeds if the logon account has read and attributes permissions for the directories to be replicated. If the logon attempt fails, no replication takes place until the person logs off.

The interval and pulse parameters indicate how often the data replication operation should take place.

```
replicate = IMPORT

IMPORTPATH = D:\IBMLAN\REPL\IMPORT

tryuser = yes

logon = GUEST

password =

interval = 5

pulse = 3
```

The SERVER Section. The SERVER section provides parameters and options that specify file server component behavior. The entries in this section work much like those in the REQUESTER section, discussed earlier in this chapter.

The parameters in the Server section affect the server's basic functioning. If a parameter has a too-high or too-low value, the server may fail to run and will display an error message indicating the failure. Some of the parameters in the Server section of the IBMLAN.INI file work differently for the 386-HPFS server. The Server section parameters that function differently on a server running 386HPFS are maxconnections, maxlocks, maxopens, maxsearches, numbigbuf, and srvheuristics.

SERVER Entry	Brief Description
alertnames =	Logon accounts to receive server error messages
auditing = no	Which events, if any, to audit
autodisconnect = 120	Minutes before disconnecting inactive workstations
maxusers = 101	Maximum concurrent logons on a 386HPFS server
guestacct = guest	An optional general-usage logon account
accessalert = 5	Alert threshold for resource-access attempts
alertsched = 5	Minutes between checking for alert conditions
diskalert = 5000	Minimum free disk space (KB) before alert sent
erroralert = 5	Error count at which server sends an alert message
logonalert = 5	Logon attempt threshold for alert messages
maxauditlog = 100	Maximum size (KB) of the audit log file
maxchdevjob = 6	Maximum concurrent serial device requests
maxchdevq = 2	Maximum serial device queues
maxchdevs = 2	Maximum shared serial devices
maxconnections = 300	Maximum connections to shared resources
maxlocks = 64	Maximum concurrent file locks
maxopens = 256	Maximum files/devices the server can open
maxsearches = 350	Maximum concurrent directory searches
maxsessopens = 256	Maximum shared resources a requester can use
maxsessreqs = 50	Maximum requests for shared resource operations

III

Networking Software

(continues)

(continued)

SERVER Entry	Brief Description
maxsessvcs = 1	Maximum virtual circuits a workstation can create
maxshares = 192	Maximum resources the server can share
netioalert = 5	Network error threshold for sending alerts
numbigbuf = 12	Number of 64KB buffers for large data requests
numfiletasks = 1	Number of concurrent file/print server processes
numreqbuf = 250	Number of server buffers for workstation requests
sizreqbuf = 4096	Size of each server buffer
srvanndelta = 3000	Milliseconds used to vary handshaking interval
srvannounce = 60	Seconds between server/workstation handshaking
SRVSERVICES = NETLOGON, LSSERVER,ALERTER,GENALERT, NETRUN	Network services the server should provide
srvnets = NET1 ·	Server's internal reference name for the network protocol
autopath = D	Drive letter for network services
srvheuristics = 111101411113110013311	

Like the `wrkheuristics` parameter discussed earlier in this chapter, the `srvheuristics` parameter sets a variety of server fine-tuning options. Each character of `srvheuristics` controls a different aspect of Warp Server.

A value of 1 in character 1, the first digit of `srvheuristics`, specifies opportunistic locking of files (default is 1).

Character 2 controls read-ahead when the requester is performing sequential access:

> 0 = Do not use read-ahead
>
> 1 = Use single read-ahead thread (default)
>
> 2 = Use asynchronous read-ahead thread

A value of 1 in character 3 specifies write-behind (default is 1).

Character 4 specifies use of the chain-send NETBIOS NCB (default is 1).

Character 5 turns on or off checking of incoming SMBs for validity (default is 0).

A value of 1 in character 6 specifies support for FCB opens (default is 1).

Character 7 sets the priority of server (default is 4); 0 is highest priority, while 9 is lowest priority.

Character 8 automatically allocates additional memory for directory searches (default is 1).

Character 9 controls whether audit log records get written on a timed basis (default is 1) by the server watchdog process.

Character 10 specifies full buffering when a file is opened with deny-write sharing mode (default is 1).

Character 11 sets the interval for the running of the server watchdog process:

    0 = 5 seconds

    1 = 10 seconds (default)

    2 = 15 seconds

    3 = 20 seconds

    4 = 25 seconds

    5 = 30 seconds

    6 = 35 seconds

    7 = 40 seconds

    8 = 45 seconds

    9 = 50 seconds

Character 12 controls compatibility-mode opens of certain types of files by translating them to sharing mode opens with a mode of deny-none:

    0 = Always use compatibility-mode opens.

    1 = Use deny-none sharing mode for read-only access to programs.

    2 = Use deny-none sharing mode for write-only access to programs.

    3 = Use deny-none sharing mode on all compatibility-mode opens (default).

A value of 1 in character 13 allows the use of a second NETBIOS session by DOS LAN Services workstations for printer requests (default is 1).

Character 14 indicates the number of 64K buffers to be used for read-ahead (default is 1; maximum is 9).

A value of 1 in character 15 specifies the conversion of incoming path specifications into their most basic format (default is 0).

Character 16 specifies various combinations of Oplock Timeout and NETBIOS Acknowledgment Timeout (default is 0):

    0 = 35 second Oplock Timeout; 34 second NETBIOS Acknowledgment Timeout

    1 = 70 second Oplock Timeout; 69 second NETBIOS Acknowledgment Timeout

    2 = 140 second Oplock Timeout; 127 second NETBIOS Acknowledgment Timeout

    3 = 210 second Oplock Timeout; 127 second NETBIOS Acknowledgment Timeout

    4 = 280 second Oplock Timeout; 127 second NETBIOS Acknowledgment Timeout

    5 = 350 second Oplock Timeout; 127 second NETBIOS Acknowledgment Timeout

    6 = 420 second Oplock Timeout; 127 second NETBIOS Acknowledgment Timeout

III

Networking Software

7 = 490 second Oplock Timeout; 127 second NETBIOS Acknowledgment Timeout

8 = 560 second Oplock Timeout; 127 second NETBIOS Acknowledgment Timeout

9 = 640 second Oplock Timeout; no NETBIOS Acknowledgment Timeout

A value of 1 in character 17 specifies the validation of IOCTL API calls (default is 1).

Character 18 specifies how long the server maintains unused, dynamic, big buffers before freeing the buffer memory:

0 = 0 seconds

1 = 1 second

2 = 10 seconds

3 = 1 minute (default)

4 = 5 minutes

5 = 10 minutes

6 = 20 minutes

7 = 40 minutes

8 = 1 hour

9 = indefinitely

Character 19 specifies how long the server waits after failing to allocate a big buffer before trying again:

0 = 0 seconds

1 = 1 second

2 = 10 seconds

3 = 1 minute (default)

4 = 5 minutes

5 = 10 minutes

A value of 1 in character 20 specifies the use of RAW read and RAW write SMB protocols (default is 1).

Character 21 specifies whether the server responds to announcement requests (default is 1).

The SERVICES Section. The SERVICES section identifies the location of the Warp Server program files that provide services on the file server. Each entry gives the path of the executable program file for that named service.

```
alerter = services\alerter.exe
dcdbrepl = services\dcdbrepl.exe
genalert = services\genalert.exe
lsserver = services\lsserver.exe
messenger = services\msrvinit.exe
```

```
netlogon = services\netlogon.exe
netrun = services\runservr.exe
replicator = services\replicat.exe
requester = services\wksta.exe
server = services\netsvini.exe
timesource = services\timesrc.exe
```

Windows NT Server

Like Warp Server, NT Server is a 32-bit network operating system. Unlike Warp Server, you can run NT Server on Intel or DEC Alpha platforms. While CPU speed is rarely a bottleneck on file servers, you might run NT Server on a symmetric multiprocessing (multiple-CPU) computer. The extra CPU processing power might let you use the file server for additional client/server applications.

For reliability, NT Server uses a transaction-based file system that can back out file updates if a series of related updates don't finish successfully. NT Server supports RAID level 5 (Redundant Array of Inexpensive Disks—disk striping with parity), recognizes signals from a UPS, and comes with tape backup software.

NT Server adds an interesting dimension, Trusted Domains, to the way domains work in Warp Server and NT Server. Suppose your LAN has separate domains for Engineering and Marketing. People in Engineering have developed a new product and want to allow product managers in the Marketing department to see the specifications for the new product. Engineering can authorize access to the files by making the Marketing domain "trusted" and giving read-only permissions to the Product Manager group. The product managers don't have to separately log in to the Engineering domain to view the files. When the file server holding the documents senses a request from a Marketing-domain product manager, the file server verifies access permission, through the Engineering domain controller, with the "trusted" Marketing domain controller. However, if you want to use the Trusted Domains feature on a LAN with existing NT Server or Warp Server file servers, you need to add an NT file server to each domain on your LAN. Figure 7.4 show the NT version 4 *network neighborhood* user interface for viewing domains and shared resources.

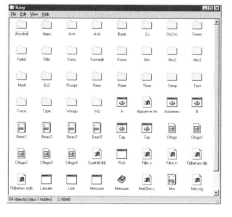

Fig. 7.4 The NT Server version 4.0 network neighborhood shows network resources graphically.

A Performance Monitor utility helps administrators manage NT Server, and the NOS is also SNMP- and NetView-aware. Desktop and LAN management products such as OpenView, LANlord, LANDesk, and Frye's Utilities should soon support NT Server. (You explore LAN management concepts in Chapter 12, "Managing Your Network.") Microsoft says NT Server will someday comply with the Desktop Management Task Force (DMTF) specification for the management of LAN-connected desktop computers, but at present NT Server lacks such support. Other utilities you get with NT Server include User Manager, Disk Administrator, Event Viewer, and an enhanced Control Panel.

If you prefer not to establish permanent drive letter mappings for each workstation, but would rather let each workstation browse lists of shared resources to create connections to shared directories and printers, you can use NT Server's BrowseMaster feature. Each PC with resources to share periodically reports a list of those resources to the BrowseMaster server. When a person at a workstation clicks the Browse push-button (for example, in Windows for Workgroups File Manager or Print Manager), the workstation gets the list of available resources from the central BrowseMaster computer. This technique keeps LAN traffic down because servers and workstations don't have to continually broadcast resource lists to each other.

NT Server uses SMBs, on NetBIOS, to send and receive file I/O redirection requests over the LAN cable (you learned about these protocols in Chapter 4, "Using Protocols, Cables, and Adapters"). This means that NT Server interoperates with Warp Server, Windows for Workgroups, Windows 95, and even the older PC LAN Program (PCLP). NT Server also supports TCP/IP and Novell's IPX/SPX transport layer protocols. Figure 7.5 shows NT Server's list of available protocols.

Fig. 7.5   These are typically available NT Server protocols on most networks.

You get several other connectivity options with NT Server: Windows Sockets, Named Pipes, Network Dynamic Data Exchange (NetDDE), IBM's data-link control (DLC) for host sessions, and Remote Procedure Calls (RPCs). This last interface is compatible with the Open Software Foundation Distributed Computing Environment (OSF/DCE) specification and SNA Server. The version of Remote Access Server for NT Server handles up to 64 concurrent connections over dial-up, leased, X.25, and ISDN lines.

Comparing NT Server, Warp Server, and NetWare

The Microsoft programmers in Redmond, Washington, and the IBM programmers in Austin, Texas, worked together to create NT Server and Warp Server. The network operating systems use virtually the same basic approach to networking throughout both products. With a few limitations and restrictions, noted in the next section, you can install NT Server and Warp Server on file servers on the same LAN and have workstations connect to both kinds of servers.

NT Server and Warp Server support Macintosh workstations as well as DOS and Windows workstations, but Microsoft does not officially support connecting OS/2 workstations to NT Server.

Server Optimization and Performance. You optimize Warp Server—make it more efficient for the information processing you do in your office—by running a tuning utility IBM supplies with Warp Server. The Warp Server Tuning Assistant can help you adjust your Warp Server configuration (including the IBMLAN.INI file). When you double-click the Tuning Assistant program object in the Warp Server folder, you see a settings notebook. The first tab, Server, displays information about the file server. You see Server Name, Domain Name, Server Type, Server Software Package Type, File System Type, and Server Hardware data. Click the Setting, Supports, and Application tabs across the bottom of the settings notebook to reveal more information. The tabs across the bottom are subcategories of the main Server tab (which appears on the right).

The Installation and Configuration program runs the tuning utility each time you use Installation and Configuration to change your Warp Server configuration. In contrast, NT Server features *autotuning*, whereby the file server software monitors its own activity and changes its initialization files automatically. To take advantage of autotuning, you merely have to stop and restart an NT Server file server periodically.

NT Server and Warp Server are 32-bit software. As the numbers "16" and "32" imply, these two products should better manage the 32-bit CPU chips you find in the faster, more capable computers you can buy today. The Warp Server product is a good performer, but Windows NT uses an operating system architecture that insulates the network software from the network adapter with many layers of intervening software. The result, according to benchmarks published by *PC Week* and *PC Magazine*, is that Windows NT is slower and takes up more disk space and memory than NetWare or Warp Server. Microsoft is working to make Windows NT a faster, smaller network operating system.

Remote Administration and Resource Security. NT Server also offers remote administration. If you have administrative privileges, you can add users, delete users, and do other administrative tasks from any OS/2 or NT Server Enhanced workstation. You don't have to visit the file server to make your changes.

With share-level security, a feature of NT Server, you can set up a single password to limit access to a shared resource or device. Warp Server doesn't support share-level security.

III

Networking Software

Domains, Aliases, and Directory Services. NT Server and Warp Server both use the concepts of domains and logon security, but in slightly different ways. If you want to use NT Server and Warp Server on the same physical network, you should set up separate domains for each network operating system. In one domain, all file servers should run NT Server or all file servers should run Warp Server. You should ensure that workstations in a Warp Server domain log into a Warp Server domain before trying to access NT Server file servers. Workstations in an NT Server domain, however, can log on in any domain.

Warp Server can use *aliases* (nicknames) for shared resources, but NT Server cannot. NT Server workstations must refer to the shared resources by their full name, not by the alias. Suppose that you have a Warp Server machine named PRODUCTION that shares a printer with an alias of REPORTS. The full name of the shared printer is \\PRODUCTION\PRINTER1. Warp Server workstations can share REPORTS, but NT Server workstations must use the full name \\PRODUCTION\PRINTER1 to access that printer.

In contrast to Windows NT, Warp Server does not have a BrowseMaster feature. While Microsoft believes people should be able to point-and-click to share and use network resources, IBM believes a LAN administrator should designate those disk drives and printers that are shared on the network and that people should use just those designated shared resources. As mentioned earlier in this chapter, Microsoft's resource-browsing feature lets you point-and-click to create a connection between your workstation and a shared disk or printer resource. Browsing for shared resources might seem handy and useful, but the browsing can cause confusion when people forget which drive letter they've mapped to a file server directory. Browsing for resources can also result in a workstation exhausting the number of NetBIOS commands and NetBIOS sessions available to that workstation.

NT Server scales better than its predecessor, LAN Manager, did, but comes up short when compared with NetWare and Warp Server. In this context, scalability denotes the network software's ability to work equally well for small, medium, and large groups of people. NT is a good application server, but NT's shortfalls—primarily in the areas of directory services, dynamic IP assignments, network management, and network administration—make it less scalable than its competition.

Directory services and domains are two ways to find a needle in a haystack. A directory service, such as NetWare 4's NDS, hands you the needle when you ask for it. NT Server uses domains, which tell you to look in a smaller haystack.

In Microsoft LAN Manager, a domain was an independent, nonhierarchical database of account information; it didn't have a mechanism to tie independent domain databases together. To overcome this design limitation, Windows NT introduced trust relationships between domains. In a trust relationship, a domain grants access to users if those users have rights in a trusted domain. Trust relationships provide users with a single login to their home domain and access to resources in other domains that trust the user's home domain.

But management of relationships can be difficult. A trust relationship doesn't grant users access to resources in trusting domains. Instead, it permits an administrator in the trusted domain to grant access rights to resources in the trusting domain. Only after a trust relationship is established between domains can an administrator grant rights to resources in the trusting domain. Worse, the number of two-way trust relationships grows geometrically. Mathematically, it's N times (N-1), where N is the number of domains. Ten domains require 90 trust relationships while 50 domains require 2,450 trust relationships and 100 domains require 9,900. That's a lot of relationships to set up and administer.

In contrast, a directory service gives users, administrators, and their computers transparent access to all network resources. The CCITT has defined a standard for directory services—X.500. This international standard says a directory service should provide network name functions that map all network resources and that give them unique identities for easy reference. The name functions should supply access to network resources regardless of their location, offer extensible attribute information (in other words, detail about a resource that its name alone can't convey), and allow searches for network resources by attribute, such as a printer's type or location. NT doesn't offer X.500-compliant, NDS-like directory services.

NT replicates domain information across servers to provide some degree of fault tolerance. Every Windows NT server that contains a copy of the domain is known as a domain controller. There are two types of domain controller, the Primary Domain Controller and the Backup Domain Controller. Each domain must have at least one PDC and can have multiple BDCs. Each Windows NT server may participate as a domain controller in a single domain.

An NT Server Primary Domain Controller synchronizes across the domain, periodically communicating with the Backup Domain Controllers to distribute account information and ensure the integrity of the domain database. The Primary Domain Controller contacts the Backup Domain Controllers at definable intervals and sends mirrors of recent updates. While users can use either the Primary Domain Controller or a Backup Domain Controller for login authentication, all changes to the domain occur on the Primary Domain Controller. If the Primary Domain Controller is down or unreachable, administrators cannot update domain information until they manually intervene to "promote" a Backup Domain Controller to become the Primary Domain Controller. This makes the Primary Domain Controller a single point of failure.

The replicated directory services database provided by Novell's NetWare Directory Services (NDS) does not have this limitation. Administrators can partition and replicate the NDS database among many NetWare file servers, and can update NDS on any server that contains a read/write copy of the database. As long as any server that contains a replica of the partition is available, all administrative functions are possible, including adding or deleting users, groups, profiles, file servers, printers, print servers, message servers, and organizational units.

III

Networking Software

Because NDS replication doesn't depend on a single, primary database, there is no single point of failure within NDS. Any server that contains either the master or a read/write replica of the NDS database communicates with all other servers with similar replicas. Any server may exchange NDS information with any other server that shares a common replica. If a server is unavailable for synchronization, updates will continue among the remaining servers, permitting full NDS administration of the NDS tree, regardless of the state of any single server.

Here's another limitation to NT's domains: to move an NT server from one domain to another you must reinstall the operating system. To move a NetWare server to a different branch of the directory tree, you merely indicate your change in Novell's NWAdmin software—a point-and-click operation. Similarly, you move resources (users and printers) in NT by deleting the entry in one domain and adding the entry in the other domain. NWAdmin makes such chores a drag-and-drop operation. Since NDS groups can include user objects from any portion of the NDS tree, a transferred user retains all of his prior group memberships and immediately inherits all rights granted to his new home on the NDS tree.

Automatic IP Address Assignment. Everyone wants to get on the Internet. For an administrator, that can mean assigning all desktop systems their own IP addresses, and then tracking them. Intelligent network operating systems assign and track them for you. In this respect, NT is better than NetWare, but not as intelligent as IBM's OS/2 Warp Server.

The technology for automatic IP address assignment and tracking is Dynamic IP, which is composed of the Dynamic Host Configuration Protocol (DHCP) and Dynamic Domain Naming System (DDNS). DHCP and DDNS are complementary open networking standards developed by the IETF (Internet Engineering Task Force). Each protocol implements half of the TCP/IP "plug-and-go" network solution. The DHCP protocol centralizes and automates the configuration of IP hosts, including IP addresses, while the DDNS protocols automatically record the association between IP hosts and their DHCP-assigned addresses.

Using DHCP and DDNS, a host automatically configures itself for network access wherever it connects to the IP network. Users can locate and access that host using its permanent, unique DNS host name. Mobile hosts, for example, can freely move about a network without knowledge of the local IP network addresses or services and without end-user or administrator intervention.

Microsoft ships partial support for dynamic IP in NT Server. Dynamic assignment of IP addresses in Windows NT, which Microsoft calls Windows Internet Naming Service (WINS), only works with NetBIOS-based systems. Microsoft says the Internet standard for dynamic IP is not yet final and Microsoft didn't want to attempt support for a moving target.

However, IBM decided to implement the not-yet-final draft standard in OS/2 Warp Server. Warp Server includes an IETF-compliant integrated Dynamic Host Configuration

Protocol/Dynamic Domain Naming System package that lets any computer configure itself for IP network access whenever it plugs into the IP network. All DNS addresses are updated, not just the subset of NetBIOS addresses. The OS/2 Warp Server software package includes a Dynamic IP client, a DHCP server, and a Dynamic DNS Server. The Dynamic IP client consists of a DHCP and a Dynamic DNS client component. The DHCP client may be configured to operate as a simple DHCP client or as a Dynamic IP client, integrating Dynamic DNS client services with the DHCP client. The Warp DHCP clients and servers support DHCP user classing, a new DHCP extension for administering groups of network hosts with common configuration requirements (for example, an accounting department), independent of where the hosts in the network are located. IBM's Dynamic IP is a general IP networking solution that has broad application, works with UNIX, Windows, Mac OS, and OS/2 clients, and scales easily to an entire Internet.

Other Differences. NT Server doesn't offer per-user disk space limits (a feature that NetWare and Warp Server do provide), and it cannot send alerts to network management products such as OpenView or NetFinity. NT Server also does not yet support the Desktop Management Interface (DMI), a network management standard designed and agreed upon by virtually every LAN vendor. The DMI specification, along with sample driver source code, has been available since 1994.

Through Hierarchical Storage Management (HSM), NetWare allows seamless migration of unused files to a near-line (as opposed to off-line) storage facility, such as a read/write CD-ROM jukebox, after a configurable period of inactivity. Microsoft's NT Server does not support HSM.

NetWare offers C2-level security, which means the network operating system has a secure logon procedure, memory protection, auditing, and discretionary access control. (The owner of a shared resource can monitor who is using the shared resource.) Some corporate and military LANs require C-2 or higher security.

NT Server 4 takes advantage of a new dial-up protocol for connecting to a server through the Internet. Called Point-to-Point Tunneling Protocol (PPTP), it won't alleviate data routing delays on the Internet but will allow remote LAN access via a local Internet Service Provider (ISP). 3Com and Microsoft jointly developed the PPTP specification, which they hope ISPs and other network software vendors will support.

StreetTalk Access for Windows NT

StreetTalk, the resource-naming convention embodied in the Banyan Vines network operating system, has an excellent reputation for ease of use. StreetTalk predates X.500, yet offers most of the same benefits. For sites that use Novell NetWare, Banyan sells Enterprise Network Services (ENS) for NetWare. For NT-based LANs, Banyan licenses its StreetTalk Access for Windows NT File and Print. StreetTalk Access provides location-independent resource names administrators can use, for instance, to migrate a print server from one domain to another without updating user profiles.

(continues)

III

Networking Software

(continued)

StreetTalk Access is a directory services add-on for NT Server that supplies features missing in NT Server itself. Through StreetTalk Access, administrators can forget about domain-based resource maintenance. StreetTalk Access allows users to log on to the network even if the server holding the user's profile is inaccessible. StreetTalk also has Simple Network Management Protocol (SNMP) support for integration with network management products such as Hewlett-Packard's OpenView. StreetTalk Access, which replaces the Microsoft redirector network client on NT machines, can run on either the Vines IP or TCP/IP protocols.

In addition to supporting NetWare, Banyan's Enterprise Network Services product works with Solaris, AIX, HP-UX, and SCO UNIX. StreetTalk Access targets NT Server environments.

NT Server and Warp Server Vendors

For more information about Microsoft's NT Server product, contact

Microsoft Corporation
One Microsoft Way
Redmond, WA 98052
(800) 426-9400
www.microsoft.com

For more information about IBM's Warp Server, contact

IBM
Old Orchard Road
Armonk, NY 10504
(800) 426-2468
www.ibm.com

Chapter Summary

You looked at the fraternal twins NT Server and Warp Server in this chapter. These two network operating systems from Microsoft and IBM behave alike but have subtle differences you're now aware of. You understand why these products lend themselves to client/server architecture, you know why NetWare sells better, and you are familiar with the principles and concepts on which NT Server and Warp Server are based. You have explored what these products look like, how they operate, and what they can offer in the way of advantages and benefits for your office.

Chapter 8

Using Windows for Workgroups, Windows 95, and Warp Connect

Many more peer LAN network operating system products exist than server-based products. If you think a peer LAN will meet your needs, you have a wide range of products to choose from. This chapter looks at three of the most popular of these network software products: Windows for Workgroups, which is a combination of Microsoft Windows and a peer LAN; Windows 95, the latest version of Windows from Microsoft; and IBM's Warp Connect, which consists of OS/2 Warp plus peer networking services. If you want to explore other peer LAN products, the list of peer LAN vendors in Chapter 2 is an excellent starting place.

A peer LAN enables every workstation to be a file server, and vice versa. As Chapter 1, "A Networking Overview," explains, you don't need to dedicate a separate computer to be the file server on a peer LAN, which makes it comparatively inexpensive. You will notice slower performance, however, if you have more than a few workstations or if the work consists of more than word processing and light record keeping. Peer LANs are great for small workgroups that put only a light workload on the network. Naturally, some peer LAN network operating systems perform better than others.

Slow performance isn't the only problem you might encounter on a peer LAN. If someone runs an application on a PC that's acting as both server and workstation, and that application locks up the PC, other people on the LAN (who are using that PC as a file server) may lose their work and will have to wait until the PC reboots before they can resume using the network. Backing up files on a peer LAN can be a problem, too. If files are scattered on several different server/workstation PCs, you risk omitting important files from your daily backups.

Which Workstation Is Which?

You can organize a peer LAN in myriad combinations of shared drives and printers. Keeping track of workstations, cable connections, and drive letters helps you avoid confusion on any LAN (peer or server-based). On a peer LAN, such good habits are especially important. You want your efforts and expense to be well spent. Organization is the key.

Unfortunately, peer LANs are not completely self-documenting. In other words, the burden for knowing which drive letter is which workstation's hard disk is solely yours. You can help yourself by naming each workstation and attaching a label to each computer that shows its name. Because many peer LAN products let you refer to workstations by name, you can use the labels you attach to the workstations to tell you where your information resides.

Using Windows for Workgroups

Windows for Workgroups is a combination of Microsoft Windows 3.1, a peer-to-peer network operating system, an electronic mail application, and an appointment book application. The network operating system software is built right into Windows. The electronic mail software is Microsoft Mail, and the appointment book software is Schedule+. The Windows SETUP program installs the latter two software products into the Main program group.

If you are part of a small team of people, and if the other members of the team are accustomed to using applications in a Windows 386 Enhanced mode environment, Windows for Workgroups can help the team share information. This means the members of the team can store files in public directories everyone can access. A common directory might be on one of the team members' PCs or on a separate, unattended PC used for file storage. With most applications, however, only one team member at a time can access a given file. You need to purchase multi-user software to have concurrent access to files.

People who use Windows for Workgroups can share printers as well as disk files. Through File Manager and Print Manager, you designate the PCs that should share disk directories and those that should share printers. When you share a disk directory or printer from a PC, you give the shared resource a name by which other team members can refer to that resource. Other members establish connections to shared resources by also using File Manager and Print Manager. Establishing the connection assigns a new drive letter to a shared directory and, for a shared printer, redirects the parallel printer port (LPT1) across the LAN to the shared printer. You can tell Windows for Workgroups to remember the connections you've established. Windows for Workgroups automatically re-creates each connection when you start Windows.

With your new drive letter(s) and printer(s), you can work with files on other PCs as if those files were on your PC's hard disk. When you print, the pages appear on the shared printer. You have access to shared directories and printers from within Windows and the DOS applications you run in a Windows DOS session, through either the MS-DOS Prompt icon or a PIF file.

Windows for Workgroups is somewhat compatible with Novell NetWare. You might use Windows for Workgroups to supplement an existing NetWare LAN. For example, a small team of people can use Windows applications and Windows for Workgroups for the team's work, yet retain access to the NetWare file server. You can also use Windows for

Workgroups on a LAN running Microsoft NT Server. On a server-based NetWare or NT Server network, Windows for Workgroups adds convenient peer-to-peer networking functions. Figure 8.1 shows the Windows for Workgroups screen you use to change your network settings and load support for a server-based network such as NetWare.

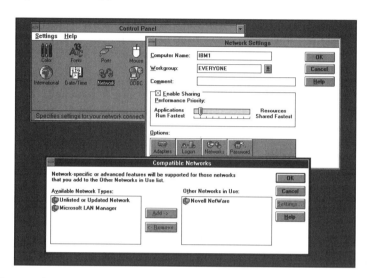

Fig. 8.1   You use the Windows for Workgroups network configuration to change your network settings.

Windows for Workgroups runs best on an 80486 or Pentium-based computer with at least 8MB of RAM. (Microsoft suggests at least 4MB, but you'll see better performance with 8MB or more.) On a lesser CPU chip or without sufficient memory, Windows for Workgroups executes in Standard mode instead of 386 Enhanced mode. You can share files only if Windows is running in Enhanced mode. In Standard mode or outside Windows, your computer cannot share its files with other people on your team.

Your PC needs MS-DOS or PC DOS Version 3.3 or later to run Windows for Workgroups. DOS Version 6.0 is best. You should have about 15MB of free disk space to install Windows for Workgroups, plus 10MB to 20MB of free disk space for the Windows swap file. To take advantage of Windows' graphical user interface, you need a VGA, SuperVGA, 8514/A, or XGA video adapter and an appropriate color monitor. And, of course, it's easier to use Windows if you have a mouse.

Microsoft offers a Windows for Workgroups Starter Kit containing two EtherNet network adapter cards, 25 feet of LAN cabling, a videotape that shows how to install and use the Starter Kit, and a two-license copy of Windows for Workgroups software. You can buy User Kits that provide additional licenses and network adapters.

The Workgroup Connection for DOS package consists of non-Windows, DOS-only software. Workgroup Connection for DOS permits PCs that can't or don't run Windows to access resources shared by computers running Windows for Workgroups. The converse isn't true, however; Workgroup Connection for DOS machines can't make their disk drives and printers available to other machines on the LAN.

Sharing and Using Files

On each of the computers you designate as file servers, you tell Windows for Workgroups the name of the directory to be shared and give each shared directory a Share Name—the name by which a shared resource will be known on the LAN. At a workstation that will use the shared directory resource, you connect to the resource by referring to its Share Name.

You use File Manager to share a directory on a PC running Windows for Workgroups in 386 Enhanced mode. Click the Main program group and double-click File Manager. Choose the Share As menu item from the Disk menu. The Share Directory dialog box is displayed, which you use to give others access to the entire hard drive, a directory, a CD-ROM drive, or a floppy disk drive.

In the Share Directory dialog box, you enter a Share Name. The Path field specifies the drive letter and directory of the shared resource. To indicate whether the resource should be automatically shared when Windows for Workgroups starts, you check the Re-share at Startup check box. You have three options for setting up security for the resource: Read-only, Full, and Depends on Password. Read-only access grants people at other workstations the right to view files but not to delete or change them. Read-only access also prevents someone from creating directories below the shared resource directory name. Full access allows other people to view, edit, and delete files and to create or remove directories. If you use the Depends on Password option, you can give Read-only access to some people and Full access to others. A person at another computer on the LAN obtains the appropriate level of access by entering a password that matches the Read-only or Full access password you designate. The default Share Name is the current directory name. The default Path is the current drive and directory. By default, the Re-share at Startup and Read-only options are selected.

The Connect Network Drive dialog box has a Drive field, Path field, and Reconnect at Startup check box. With these items, you can create new drive letters to use in your application software programs. This process is called mapping a network drive letter.

You indicate in the Drive field the DOS drive letter you want to use. Normally, you should use the next available drive letter after those already assigned by DOS and those already mapped. Don't attempt to map a drive letter that is already assigned (or mapped). The range of drive letters extends from A: to the value of LASTDRIVE as specified in your CONFIG.SYS file. The DOS default for LASTDRIVE is usually E:, but the Windows for Workgroups SETUP program modifies the CONFIG.SYS file to contain the entry LASTDRIVE=Q. If you like, you can change your CONFIG.SYS file with a text editor to show LASTDRIVE=Z, but this means you won't be able to map drives on a NetWare file server, if one is present. The Drive field shows File Manager's suggestion for a drive letter you can map. In the Path field, you specify the computer name and the network name of the resource you want to map to a drive letter.

Printing with Windows for Workgroups

Print Manager is your tool for sharing and connecting to printers. When you install Windows for Workgroups on PCs with printers attached, you identify the printer to the SETUP program. When you click Print Manager (in the Main group), it displays the list of attached printers. To share a printer in the list across the network, click the printer and choose the Share Printer As menu item from the Printer menu.

The resulting Share Printer dialog box contains the name of the printer, which you can change if you highlighted the wrong printer in the Print Manager list. This dialog box also contains a suggested network name in the Share As field, a Comment field, a Password field, and a Re-share at Startup check box. The available pushbuttons are OK, Cancel, and Help. You can change the network name, and the Comment field is a good place to describe the typical kinds of printouts the printer will produce. If you want the PC to be a dedicated print server, click the Re-share at Startup check box so that Windows for Workgroups makes the printer available whenever it's running. Click OK to finish making the printer a LAN resource.

From a Windows for Workgroups workstation, you use Print Manager to create the connection to a shared printer. Choose the Connect Network Printer menu item from the Printer menu. Print Manager displays the Connect Network Printer dialog box.

The Connect Network Printer dialog box contains a Device Name field, Path field, and Reconnect at Startup check box. Also included is a list of workgroups and computers that are sharing resources. As you click in the first list the name of a computer that is sharing a printer, the name of the printer appears in the second list. Clicking the name of the printer causes Print Manager to construct the network name of the printer in the Path field. If the printer is a resource that is usually available on the network, you should click the Reconnect at Startup check box.

Learning Other Windows for Workgroups Features

Windows for Workgroups lets you reduce or eliminate paper interoffice mail. As Chapter 11, "Using Electronic Mail," explains, you can use Microsoft Mail to send and receive computer files that take the place of handwritten or typed notes. If you simply want to ask someone a quick question and you know the person is using Windows at his or her desk, you can use the Chat program within Windows for Workgroups to get your answer.

The Schedule+ software included with Windows for Workgroups lets you maintain an electronic appointment book. The software can display the appointments for a particular day, general tasks (your to-do list), and the blocks of time represented by your scheduled activities. You can share your appointment book across the LAN. Sharing appointment books makes it possible for Schedule+ to automatically coordinate the times when people on the team can get together for a meeting.

The Windows for Workgroups SETUP program installs Schedule+ in the Main program group. To use Schedule+, double-click the Schedule+ icon and, if you're not running the Mail program, sign in with your mail account name (mailbox name) and password.

III

Networking Software

The main Schedule+ screen is a graphic representation of a page of your appointment book. The page shows section tabs on the left side of the screen, a list of time slots containing entries for the day's scheduled activities in the center of the page, a calendar page in the upper-right corner, and a place to write notes in the lower-right corner.

You or someone you designate can use the displayed pages of the appointment book to maintain your daily schedule, make notes about meetings, and request meetings with other Schedule+ users. An appointment (meeting) can be a single, recurring, or tentative event. If you set aside blocks of time for your own work, Schedule+ won't allow other people to set up meetings with you during those times.

In addition to the main screen, Schedule+ provides a task list and planner views. You use the task list to categorize your work into projects and tasks, and you give the projects and their tasks priorities and due dates. As tasks are completed or they change priority or become overdue, you update the task list accordingly.

The planner view shows blocks of time for several days running—a week or two, depending on the width of the planner screen. The easiest way to schedule a meeting with other people who use Schedule+ is through the planner view. As you select the names of people you want to attend a meeting, information from their appointment books flows onto your planner view. You see at a glance when all the people are available for a meeting.

Windows for Workgroups also comes with WinMeter and NetWatcher. WinMeter monitors how much of your computer's processing power other people are using. With NetWatcher, you can see who is connected to your PC and which of your files other people are accessing.

For more information about Microsoft Windows for Workgroups, contact:

Microsoft Corporation
One Microsoft Way
Redmond, WA 98052
(800) 426-9400

Using Windows 95

Like Windows for Workgroups, Windows 95 has peer networking built in. To the basic peer networking ability of Windows, Microsoft added a new user interface, better network adapter identification, and new network management features. However, Microsoft doesn't include Schedule+ with Windows 95. Figure 8.2 shows Windows 95's network neighborhood screen, an icon-based graphical interface for dealing with shared resources.

Windows 3.x is often difficult for LAN administrators to manage. The 3.x versions of Windows aren't easily integrated into corporate LAN management infrastructures and don't provide system access interfaces to PC inventory and configuration information. Third-party LAN management products from vendors like Saber can't provide complete, open solutions to LAN management problems with Windows 3.x. In the design of Windows 95, Microsoft set out to provide an environment that would easily mesh with current and future LAN management technologies and that would make LAN administration easier. The following sections explore Microsoft's latest version of Windows.

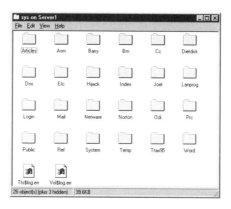

Fig. 8.2   The Windows 95 network neighborhood shows network resources you can connect to.

LAN management encompasses several functions: taking inventory, monitoring traffic, detecting viruses, distributing software, monitoring applications, metering software licenses, mapping the network, notifying administrators when errors (alerts) occur, and creating trouble tickets for help desk resolution (you learn more about LAN management in Chapter 12, "Managing Your Network"). Remote access to the LAN management functions is a plus, as is the ability to globally modify workstation configuration files from a central site. Windows 95 offers features, some built into Windows and some available as APIs (application programming interfaces) that third-party LAN management software vendors can use, that touch on almost all of these categories of LAN management functions.

Networking and the Windows 95 Registry

Windows 95 uses its Registry to store LAN management details, and Windows 95 includes programming interfaces that can present the Registry information that is LAN-oriented in formats LAN management products expect. The Registry is a hierarchical system file containing configuration information, driver settings, operating system parameters, user option choices, and other data. The Registry takes the place of the 3.x-style INI files, although Windows 95 keeps INI files for backwards compatibility with 3.x applications. The heart of Windows 95's new resource management features, the Registry supplies information about network hardware (both Plug-and-Play devices and legacy devices), authorization levels (permissions), user profiles, network protocols, installed software packages, recent backups, and shared resources (including drive letter mappings, printer queue preferences, and whether the workstation can act as a peer to share its resources with other PCs). Figure 8.3 shows Windows 95's graphical interface for configuring network settings.

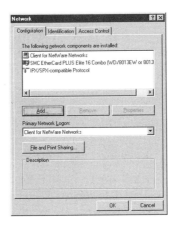

Fig. 8.3 Windows 95 network configuration lets you change your network configuration.

The information the Registry stores is exactly the kind of information LAN administrators need to manage LAN-attached Windows-based PCs. To help administrators get at the information, Windows 95 lets administrators remotely view and modify a PC's Registry, through the LAN cable or through a dial-up telephone connection. For management through the LAN cable, Windows 95 offers a Remote Procedure Call (RPC) interface that LAN management products can use to access the Registry. An administrator can even set (or reset) a Windows 95 PC's configuration, including screen colors, from a central console. If you have hundreds or thousands of PCs, and if you upgrade those PCs to Windows 95, you'll be able to set what Microsoft calls System Policies. With the System Policies editor or a third-party administrative tool, you set up configurations, restrictions, and other global corporate standards you want to apply to all PCs. When a Windows 95 PC logs on to the LAN, Windows 95 looks on the network for the policies you've set up. Windows 95 retrieves the administrator's policies from the network, applies those policies, and continues with the log-on. An administrator can, for example, selectively remove system capabilities, such as peer resource sharing, from a group of PCs. People using those PCs won't be able to make their hard disks available to others.

Through user profiles stored in the Registry, Windows 95 makes it possible for different people to share a pool of desktop computers and see a consistent Windows configuration no matter which machine the person uses. With its user-level pass-through security features, Windows 95 restricts the ability to make configuration changes to the LAN administrator and to people designated by the administrator.

Windows 95 software components (Plug-and-Play configuration manager, applications, operating system shell, device drivers, and operating system services) store system configuration information in the hierarchical structure of the Registry. A separate structure within the Registry, user profiles, holds information about each user. Windows 95 interfaces (RPC, SNMP, DMI, peer services, and backup services) allow over-the-wire access to the information in the Registry. The RPC interface enables remote access, the peer services interface controls resource sharing within the PC, and the backup services interface lets administrators perform remote backups of Windows 95 PCs.

Managing Windows 95 on a LAN

To make installing and configuring new PC hardware components simple and almost foolproof, Plug-and-Play tracks system resources (DMA channels, IRQs, base I/O addresses, and upper memory block usage) as well as device driver configuration settings. The Plug-and-Play configuration manager stores the information in the Registry. For the new Plug-and-Play hardware you buy, the obvious benefits are quick, easy configuration and the extra confidence you feel when you first turn on a newly upgraded PC. For LAN administrators, the Plug-and-Play information becomes a valuable source of inventory detail, detail that's available over-the-wire to LAN management software products.

Different LAN management products accept over-the-wire resource information in different formats, using different protocols. Using the information stored in the Registry, interfaces built into Windows 95 provide resource management information in a variety of ways to third-party LAN management products. For those management products expecting data through the Simple Network Management Protocol (SNMP), Windows 95 includes an SNMP agent. SNMP is a popular Internet protocol for sending network management information from one computer to another. The Windows 95 SNMP agent is patterned after the Windows NT SNMP agent and consists of a 32-bit Windows software module. Network management products such as Hewlett-Packard's OpenView and Novell's Network Management System (NMS) can accept data via SNMP. Windows 95 can send the SNMP messages over the Internetwork Packet Exchange (IPX) transport layer or the Transmission Control Protocol/Internet Protocol (TCP/IP) transport layer.

Windows 95 invokes a "MIB handler," which converts the information in the Registry into Management Information Block (MIB) format. The SNMP agent then transmits the MIB data to the requesting remote management console. Because each LAN component can have a different MIB format, Windows 95 needs a different MIB handler for each component. The MIB handler extracts data from the Registry, puts the data for that component into the appropriate format, and hands the data to the SNMP agent for transmission across the LAN cable. Microsoft says that hardware and software manufacturers should find writing MIB handlers an easy programming task.

The Desktop Management Interface (DMI) is an emerging standard for how LAN management products describe and control the components in a desktop computer. DMI doesn't address how the information crosses the LAN cable, but rather how the management products interface to and describe the PC components. Microsoft will supply a DMI Service Layer (SL) interface to the Registry. That interface will reformat information in the Registry into DMI's Management Information Format (MIF).

The DMI specification defines the contents of the MIF files produced by the component-level modules, describes the Management Interface (MI) through which software can issue commands to query, reset, or control components, provides a Service Layer that implements the Management Interface and which directs the activities of the various DMI modules, and identifies the Component Interface (CI) that a LAN product vendor can use to provide querying and controlling access to its product. The Component Interface not only responds to commands but also generates event notifications (called alerts

III

Networking Software

in some LAN management products). Microsoft supplies the Service Layer; third-party vendors will have to supply the other pieces of DMI.

Microsoft did not initially offer DMI support in Windows 95. However, Microsoft has said you'll be able to get Windows 95 DMI support by downloading Windows 95 patches and updates from a variety of electronic sources (Compuserve, for instance). Microsoft has yet to add DMI support to Windows 95. The group of companies promoting the DMI, called the Desktop Management Task Force (DMTF), have already created DMI software components for DOS, Windows 3.x, and OS/2 workstations. An alternative management protocol that's part of the Open Systems Interconnection (OSI) standard, Common Management Information Protocol (CMIP), doesn't appear in Windows 95.

One of the complaints LAN administrators have about Windows for Workgroups is that it's too easy for people to share disk drives and printers across the LAN. With Windows 95, Microsoft lets administrators clamp down on the indiscriminate sharing of disk drives and directories. For instance, a person using a Windows 95 workstation might want to make his or her entire hard disk available to others, on a read/write basis, and thus avoid using a central file server to share files. Windows 95 would prohibit the operation if the LAN administrator had restricted peer sharing. Even after the fact, an administrator can close files and delete inappropriate peer connections (from a central console). Windows 95 gives administrators virtually the same control over peer resource sharing that those administrators have over departmental file servers. An enhanced version of the Windows for Workgroups NetWatcher module gives administrators remote control and management of peer resource sharing.

Windows 95 includes backup agents for Cheyenne's ARCserve and Arcada's Backup Exec. A backup agent is a specially designed peer sharing function that makes a workstation's files available, just for backup purposes, across the LAN. The backup agents lets administrators back up a workstation's files via a central backup scheme. Cheyenne and Arcada have modified their products to interface with the backup agents in Windows 95.

Backup agents are bidirectional, which means that remote software distribution and installation can occur through the backup agent interface. With yet-to-be-developed third-party software distribution utilities, administrators will be able to install (or upgrade) software on a workstation through the backup agent interface just by instructing the backup agent to pull files from a central file server. Windows 95 also has provisions for configuring the installed software, including new program groups, icons, and application-specific entries in the Registry.

Windows 95, at least in its initial release, won't offer the Licensing Services API (LSAPI) developed by Brightwork, DEC, Gradient Technologies, Microsoft, and Novell. However, future versions of Windows will likely contain LSAPI components. The LSAPI will let LSAPI-enabled application software products monitor and control the number of concurrently-in-use instances of those applications. Through the LSAPI, an application can register itself with a "license server." When run on a workstation, the application asks the license server if the license agreement recorded in the license server permits another instance of the application to run.

LAN administrators often complain that people perceive a performance problem at their workstations. Windows 95 includes a Performance Monitor, an enhanced version of the WinMeter utility in Windows for Workgroups, that administrators can use to see the resources being used at a workstation in real time. Performance Monitor can show a graph of file I/O and CPU usage at a workstation, for example. The administrator can run Performance Monitor at a central console, indicate which workstation to monitor and which statistics to graph, and then analyze that workstation's workload in real time.

The resource management features of Windows 95 are several orders of magnitude richer than those provided by earlier versions of Windows. Rob Price, Program Manager in Microsoft's Personal Operating System Division, says, "Microsoft wants Windows 95 to be just another asset on your network that's simple to manage and well-integrated." LAN administrators know that's a tall order, one that isn't achieved overnight.

The new features, in the form of code modules on your hard disk, will naturally consume disk space. An upgrade to Windows 95 requires a hard disk housecleaning or purchase of additional disk space. As you load and run Windows 95, you'll notice that its features—especially the new agent modules—use up additional RAM. You may need to buy memory for those workstations on which you install Windows 95. And you may notice that workstations don't seem quite as peppy when running Windows 95; the new features will need to use some CPU time to get their work done.

Perhaps the biggest cost of these new resource management features is the risk that not all third-party LAN management product vendors will embrace the new interfaces right away. Companies such as Arcada and Cheyenne have provided Windows 95 support, but several others have bypassed support for Windows 95 in favor of Windows NT. You may find yourself waiting for a new version of your preferred backup software that supports the Windows 95 backup agent technology, or you may find that the hardware component vendors you deal with don't write Windows 95 MIB handlers so you can take advantage of the SNMP agent interface. If you do get MIB handlers on a timely basis, some of them may contain bugs that keep Windows 95 from running. Windows 95 offers a lot of potential in the area of LAN management, but some time may pass before you can realize that potential in your organization. Compounding the problem is Microsoft's positioning of Windows 95 as a personal operating system and Windows NT as a business-oriented operating system.

The resource management interfaces and resource data organization Microsoft has designed into Windows 95 represent a strong reaction to the complaints from LAN administrators about Windows 3.x. If third-party vendors rise to the occasion, Windows 95 PCs will become easily managed assets on a LAN. To take advantage of Windows 95's new management features, a PC will likely need more RAM and more CPU power. However, the benefits of the rich set of Windows 95's management facilities may make the extra cost worthwhile.

Windows 95 and NetWare

In general, Windows 95 client workstations connect well to NetWare file servers. Both Microsoft and Novell have released client (requester) software for Windows 95, and both

III

Networking Software

companies are making further improvements to the client software. Figure 8.4 shows one of the screens you use to configure Windows 95 on a NetWare LAN.

Fig. 8.4 You use the Windows 95 NetWare configuration to connect to NetWare file servers.

Windows 95 clients can cause some problems on NetWare LANs. One of the most significant issues with Windows 95 is its ability to crash NetWare-based LANs with just a few clicks in the Control Panel. If you configure the Microsoft NetWare client for printer sharing through the Network icon in the Control Panel, and if you inadvertently enable SAP Advertising on the File and Printer Sharing for NetWare Networks screen, your Windows 95 PC will broadcast LAN messages that tell other clients your PC is a NetWare file server. People who try to log on to your PC as a NetWare server will fail, of course. Microsoft has already released a patch for this bug; you'll find it at:

www.windows.microsoft.com.

The new 32-bit NetWare NDS (Network Directory Services) client from Novell fixes this problem by preventing Win95 from emulating a NetWare server or otherwise doing file/printer sharing via IPX. Microsoft's NetWare NDS client software, however, continues to exhibit the problem. Furthermore, the Microsoft NDS client implements only a few NDS functions.

In several other respects, Microsoft's NetWare client is well-written and thorough in its cloning of the NetWare environment. While Microsoft's 32-bit NetWare client doesn't yet support NDS fully, it nonetheless presents virtually all the NetWare APIs that NETX previously did. In a Windows 95 command line session, you can run NetWare utilities such as RIGHTS, USERLIST, and NDIR. These utilities, which you'll find in your NetWare PUBLIC directory, are unaware that the "real" NETX isn't loaded.

Incidentally, you'll probably want to use Windows 95's long file names on your NetWare server. To do so, make sure you've applied Novell's patches to the network operating system (they're at www.novell.com) and then enable OS/2 namespace support on the file server. Also, use uppercase characters in your login scripts, replace commas in scripts with the word "AND," and don't try to load TSRs via a login script (Windows 95 doesn't support them).

Windows 95's internal representation of "shortcuts" to network resources is a problem on NetWare networks, especially large ones. A Windows 95 shortcut points to a specific file server, through a Universal Naming Convention (UNC) machine name address. When it creates the shortcut, Windows 95 resolves a NetWare drive mapping (R:, for instance, mapped to volume SYS1 on server SERVER1) into the UNC equivalent \\SERVER1\SYS1. If a LAN administrator changes the drive mapping, perhaps to achieve load balancing across multiple servers, Windows 95 ignores the change and continues to use the shortcut's embedded UNC. Windows 3.1 behaves better; because Windows 3.1 clients refer to the server's volume through the drive mapping, rather than UNCs, they adhere to the change the next time they log in. The administrator has to manually update the shortcuts on all the Windows 95 PCs. Opportunity knocks… Novell or a LAN software utility vendor should develop and market a shortcut repair tool.

Integrating Windows 95 on a LAN

Third-party companies need to help Windows 95 produce usable network statistics and application tracking information. LAN software, written specifically to network APIs that were available in DOS and Windows 3.1, typically fail to function in the Windows 95 environment. Frye Computing's DOS/Windows utilities are just one example. Frye NodeTracker, Frye Utilities for Networks, and Frye Statistics Display Rack for NetWare show incomplete network diagnostic statistics under Windows 95, and Frye Software Metering and Resource Tracking can't reliably meter file use under Windows 95. The problem isn't the quality of the programming by Frye Computing (or any other utility vendor), it's the new network driver code that's part of Windows 95. To help Windows 95 client PCs become part of a managed network, utility vendors and Microsoft should resolve the differences between the old and new APIs.

The automatic detection of frame type (802.3, TOKEN RING, TOKEN RING_SNAP, etc.) doesn't often work properly in Windows 95. Incorrect detection typically happens on very quiet or very busy multi-protocol networks. LAN administrators must configure frame type manually, using the Control Panel.

If you want to access a Lotus Notes server from a Windows 95 client, you must configure Windows 95 to use IPX as the default protocol. If you don't, your Notes client will complain that the NetBIOS unit number is too large and it will fail to find the Notes server. There are two solutions to this problem. The first entails the use of 16-bit real mode ODI drivers along with Novell's NETBIOS.EXE, and the second—if you're using 32-bit network drivers—involves clicking the checkbox labeled "Set this protocol to be the default protocol" on the Advanced tab of the Network Control Panel's IPX/SPX Compatible Protocol property sheet. Perhaps Lotus will treat this sort of problem as an opportunity to enhance its installation and configuration software for Notes to automatically make the appropriate property sheet changes under Windows 95.

Security can be a big problem in Windows 95. For example, Windows 95 stores network and dial-up passwords (for NetWare, Warp Server, NT, and SLIP/PPP access) in world-readable .PWL files. The files are named C:\WINDOWS\<USERNAME>.PWL. Decoding these .PWL files isn't terribly difficult. In effect, anyone with physical or network access to a Windows 95 machine has access to all network passwords on that machine. This default password caching behavior is inappropriate for many sites. To turn it off for Windows 95, use Policy Editor or insert a value of 1 into the following Registry entry:

```
HKEY_LOCAL_MACHINE\SOFTWARE\Microsoft\Windows\CurrentVersion\Policies\
Network\DisablePwdCaching
```

To make Windows 95 password caching more secure, Microsoft has released a patch that increases the size of the encryption key from 32 bits to 128 bits. The patch is on Microsoft's Web site (www.microsoft.com). Applying the patch updates existing .PWL files and replaces the MSPWL32.DLL and NET.EXE files. The new command-line NET.EXE utility no longer uses the password cache, prompting you instead to type a password.

For more information about Windows 95, contact:

Microsoft Corporation
One Microsoft Way
Redmond, WA 98052
(800) 426-9400

Using Warp Connect

Warp Connect combines the product known as OS/2 Warp with WIN-OS/2 peer-to-peer networking capabilities, connectivity hooks to many different kinds of servers, advanced remote access capabilities, and enhanced TCP/IP support to provide dial-up or LAN connections to the Internet and other online services.

Small businesses and workgroups within larger organizations can use OS/2 Warp Connect's built-in peer-to-peer capability, which lets users share applications, printers, modems, and files located on any PC in a network without special hardware. On a peer network, OS/2 Warp Connect does not require a dedicated server or a LAN administrator, making it particularly attractive to small companies lacking in-house technical resources.

OS/2 Warp Connect's bundled LAN requesters link desktop systems to each other and to network operating systems such as OS/2 Warp Server, Novell NetWare, Microsoft NT Server, Lotus Notes, and a variety of Internet servers. OS/2 Warp Connect supports communication via NetBIOS, TCP/IP or IPX on Ethernet, Token Ring and FDDI networks, which eliminates the need to buy separate transport protocols or client requesters. Warp Connect also supports wireless LAN connections via infrared, cellular devices, and serial port connectivity. Figure 8.5 shows a partial list of the network adapters Warp Connect supports.

IBM's latest edition of its 32-bit operating system, OS/2 Warp Connect, adds a wide range of network software and other applications to the basic OS/2 Warp product. Competitively aimed at both Windows 95 at the low end (client) and Windows NT at the high end (server), Warp Connect gives you LAN requesters (client network software), peer-to-peer networking, groupware and e-mail, Internet access, a full-featured word processor, a spreadsheet, a personal information manager (PIM), a FAX utility, remote access, communications programs, and other software. IBM reasons that if OS/2's technical superiority doesn't persuade you to get Warp, you'll buy OS/2 for the volume of networking and application software IBM bundles with Warp Connect. In fact, Warp Connect consists of so much software it only comes on CD-ROM (three CD-ROMs, to be precise).

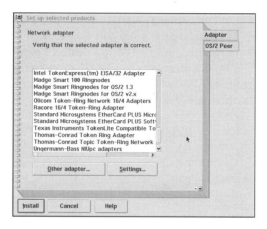

Fig. 8.5 Warp Connect network adapter list.

Warp Connect costs quite a bit more than the base Warp product and, for a full install, requires more disk space and RAM. One of the reasons for the higher price is the network requester license fee; another reason is the royalty IBM pays its subsidiary Lotus Development for the Notes Express client application you get with Warp Connect. OS/2 Warp Connect takes from 25 to 90 MB of disk space and at least 12MB of RAM, depending on which features you choose to install. IBM recommends at least 8 MB of RAM, but Warp Connect performs better in 12 MB.

Warp Connect augments the base OS/2 Warp with IBM and third-party network client technologies such as NetWare Requester 2.11, Warp Server 4.0 Requester, OS/2 Peer to Peer, LAN Distance Remote 1.1, Lotus Notes Express, and support for TCP/IP, IPX, and NetBIOS/NetBEUI. IBM says it's collaborating with Novell to produce a 32-bit NetWare Requester for OS/2. There's also a comprehensive TCP/IP LAN and SLIP/PPP dial-up client that can replace the Bonus Pack's TCP/IP client. IBM TCP/IP Version 3 can maintain a dial-up Internet connection and a network card connection at the same time. Version 3 also includes ftp and telnet server software.

In general, Warp Connect is robust, reliable, and responsive. The base operating system is OS/2 Version 4 plus voice recognition software (Voice Type). The past three years have seen OS/2 mature into an excellent platform for running DOS, Windows, and native OS/2 applications. Some companies use OS/2 at the server as well as on the desktop. One of Warp's greatest strengths is its ability to straddle the line between server and client.

Almost all of Warp Connect's features, including the requesters, LAN Distance, CID (Configuration, Installation, and Distribution), and the Bonus Pack of applications, have been around for a while. Warp Connect simply brings them together in the same box. The peer-to-peer networking within Warp Connect is new, as is the installation program that lets you pick the features you want to install.

III

Networking Software

The peer-to-peer networking services work well and offer better security and network reliability than Windows for Workgroups. The peer networking and Warp Server requester features let Warp Connect access files, printers, and CD-ROM drives on computers running Warp Server, Windows for Workgroups, NT Server, PC LAN Program, LANtastic, and, of course, Warp Connect. Warp Connect peers and Warp Server clients can even share modems, through shared serial port access, with PCs running OS/2-based communications software. Figure 8.6 shows Warp Connect's graphical interface for managing shared resources. Warp Connect Peer Services is a superset of the LAN Requester in all ways except one—to run the Warp Server graphical administration tools, you must use the LAN Requester rather than Peer Services.

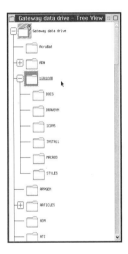

Fig. 8.6   The Warp Connect drives object is an object-oriented view of your files and directories.

When you add the NetWare Requester to the Warp Server Requester, the resulting dual protocol stack consumes extra extended memory but still leaves nearly 640KB of conventional memory for each DOS and Windows session. Trying to use multiple protocols in a DOS or DOS-plus-Windows machine often leaves you with insufficient memory to run applications. Drive mappings can be established through the NetWare Tools utility or the MAP command.

For smaller networks (typically 10 or fewer PCs), or for a decentralized campus environment, OS/2 Warp Connect's Peer Services environment is useful and productive. Beyond eight to ten clients, you'll need a separate file server running a product such as NetWare or Warp Server.

Notes Express is a useful e-mail tool that comes with six ready-to-use groupware application templates. Notes Express is an entry-level Notes client for organizations that have (or plan to buy) Lotus Notes.

The networking utilities in OS/2 Warp Connect include Network SignOn Coordinator, a help database, and LAN Distance Remote. Network SignOn holds all your logon names and passwords and sends them to the various services. Thus, you only need to log on once, even when you connect to a variety of other computers. The help database lets you perform keyword searches for frequently asked questions, set-up guides, and descriptions of known problems. LAN Distance Remote is a client for a LAN Distance Server that lets your PC work through a modem to access files on a server, just as if your modem were a LAN adapter.

Warp Connect's Peer Services also offers auditing, logging, and a REXX interface. You can monitor access to your shared peer resources, and you can write REXX scripts to automate routine tasks. REXX is a scripting language that IBM includes with OS/2. The Network Clipboard/DDE lets you cut and paste clipboard data across the LAN or, if you use NetBIOS over TCP/IP, across the Internet. You can use the OS/2 Chess application to play chess across a network. And the Person to Person application lets you do workgroup and video conferencing across a network.

You have three ways you can install Warp Connect... easy, tailored, and hands-off. This last installation method, CID (Configuration, Installation, and Distribution), is appropriate for large organizations that want to seed Warp onto many LAN-connected PCs quickly and painlessly. CID is an IBM-designed over-the-wire software distribution mechanism that creates a redirected installation environment. To quickly install a CID-enabled product such as Warp Connect across a LAN, you modify a template script supplied with Warp Connect and run the LAN CID utility. A component called the Service Installable File System (SRVIFS) handles the file redirection between the server and the client workstation. We found the CID scripts easy to set up and run. A server-based LAN CID REXX program identifies the products you want to install and contains REXX language statements for performing the installation. Individual product response files contain the menu selections and choices of features that you otherwise would provide interactively. A SRVIFS configuration file sets up the code server. And a SRVIFS authorization list file gives clients access to the product files on the code server. You can install Warp Connect (or other CID-enabled product) on several hundred PCs in a single day with CID.

Warp Server has a unique feature that Warp Connect clients can use. A LAN administrator can store applications on a server, create icons for those applications, and centrally—without visiting each Warp Connect PC—cause those icons to appear in the Network Applications folder on each Warp Connect machine. The icons, complete with settings specified by the LAN administrator, are available to Warp Connect users at logon.

For more information about Warp Connect, contact:

IBM
Old Orchard Road
Armonk, NY 10504
(800) 426-2468

III

Networking Software

Chapter Summary

In this chapter, you learned about three popular peer LAN products: Windows for Workgroups, Windows 95, and Warp Connect. If you would like to research other peer LAN products, Chapter 2, "Sharing Computer Resources," provides a list of vendors, addresses, and telephone numbers you can use. The criteria and features presented in this chapter can form the basis of your evaluation of other products from other vendors, and you should certainly consider one of the three products mentioned in this chapter during your research. All three offer good performance, features, reliability, and ease of use.

In Chapter 9, you learn about networks built around computers that use UNIX for an operating system.

Chapter 9

Using UNIX LANs

Networks built around computers that use the UNIX operating system are different from DOS, Windows, or OS/2-based peer LANs. They are different from NetWare, NT Server, and Warp Server networks, too. In this chapter, you explore these differences.

If you were to take the best qualities of a peer network, a NetWare network, and an NT Server/Warp Server network, you would have most of the characteristics of a network based on a UNIX file server. The only thing holding UNIX back from being a predominant part of networks is UNIX itself. UNIX and the computers it runs on are sometimes expensive, and people think of UNIX as an operating system for engineers and scientists. UNIX commands are cryptic. Too many programmers, many of them college students, have modified and enhanced UNIX over the years. It is large and bulky; it is a general-purpose operating system that is not designed for networking. Nonetheless, UNIX can be an effective basis for a LAN. So-called RISC computers (such as the IBM RS/6000) perform extremely well and enable UNIX to be a good host for a network operating system.

UNIX is an old operating system, as operating systems go. It is a popular operating system for minicomputers, but not for PCs or mainframes. You will learn the basics of UNIX and you will find out why UNIX is popular on minicomputers as you read the next few sections of this chapter.

If you are unfamiliar with UNIX and want to learn more, you will find Que's *Introduction to UNIX* an invaluable tool to help you understand this arcane but useful operating system.

UNIX networks often use *TCP/IP* (Transmission Control Protocol/Internet Protocol) to send data among computers. Technically, TCP/IP refers to a pair of protocols. Unofficially, TCP/IP is a generic term for a set of protocols and utility software. TCP/IPs are covered early in this chapter, and you will discover why TCP/IP is frequently used on UNIX networks. You soon will understand how TCP/IP works.

Defining UNIX, the Operating System

UNIX is a general-purpose, multitasking, multi-user operating system. A computer running UNIX can support more than one computer program at a time, typically for more than one logged-in computer user. You may be using a database application at the same time your coworker is using a word processor, on the same computer. Both of you would be using terminals to access the central "host" UNIX machine. To use the computer, you first log in. UNIX supports the grouping of user accounts; the system administrator assigns your UNIX account to one of the groups.

The following sections explain the fundamentals of the UNIX environment.

Defining the Characteristics of UNIX

At Bell Laboratories in 1969, a group of AT&T employees created the first version of UNIX on a small DEC PDP-7 computer. In 1973, Ken Thompson and Dennis Ritchie rewrote the UNIX operating system in the C programming language. This made it somewhat easy to make UNIX run on different kinds of computers. The core of UNIX has not changed much since 1973.

AT&T licensed UNIX to several universities for educational purposes beginning in 1974 and made the operating system a commercial product a few years later. AT&T now sells UNIX source code licenses to computer manufacturers.

When a computer manufacturer develops a new kind of minicomputer, that company wants its new computer to run the most application software possible. How can the computer manufacturer do this if the computer is a new design? By licensing UNIX from AT&T, the computer maker ensures that its new computer will run UNIX applications, and the company saves time and money by getting the already-developed operating system from AT&T. The computer engineers can spend their time designing the computer hardware rather than worrying about developing a new operating system. A great number of minicomputers run UNIX, including some from IBM.

At its heart, UNIX is a time-sharing operating system *kernel*. The kernel, a set of services within the operating system software, controls the resources of a computer and allocates them to the applications running on that computer. A shell program interacts with you, the human, to enable you to run programs, copy files, log in, log out, and do other things. The shell may display a simple command-line prompt or present a graphical user interface with icons and windows. In either case, the shell and the applications you run on UNIX make use of the kernel's services to manage files and peripheral devices.

As distributed by computer makers, UNIX includes much more than the shell. You will find tens of megabytes of utilities and other software on a UNIX computer. Running many of these utilities requires quite a bit of expertise; this is why UNIX got its reputation as a cryptic, difficult operating system.

Defining the UNIX File System

Everything in the UNIX system is a file. This principle guided the development of UNIX and helped make it simple yet all-encompassing. A *file* is a sequence of characters (bytes).

The operating system imposes no special organization on files. The layout and meaning of the information in a file is strictly up to the software that accesses that file. Magnetic tapes, disk files, mail messages, keyboard characters, printer output—all of these *information containers* are a sequence of characters (a file) in the UNIX system. Even directories are just files that point to other files.

In most UNIX implementations, file names and directory names can contain up to 14 characters and are case-sensitive. For example, the files named memo.doc and Memo.Doc are two distinct files in UNIX. A file name such as memo.doc.may11 is valid under UNIX. The concept of file extensions, common under DOS, doesn't exist under UNIX. For security, each file has a set of permissions that tells UNIX who may use the file and how. A file's permissions specify your rights, the others in your group of accounts, and those of anyone not in your group. The permissions express who may read from the file, who may write to it, and (if the file is a computer program) who may execute it. If the file is a directory, the permissions express who may see what is in that directory.

Defining Communications and UNIX

You would expect a multi-user, time-sharing operating system to have excellent communications capabilities. UNIX fulfills your expectations. A person typically uses UNIX by dialing in through a modem from his or her terminal, or through a direct connection. The communications link is usually an asynchronous, serial connection between the terminal's RS-232 port and a similar port on the UNIX computer. Sometimes the link is a LAN cable.

Defining UNIX-Based Networks

Turning a UNIX computer into a file server is relatively simple. You run software at the UNIX host computer that accepts requests from workstations, processes those requests, and returns the appropriate response to the workstations. The file server software is just another computer program for the multitasking UNIX to manage. If the computer is fast enough, you also can run UNIX applications alongside the file server software and thus get the most from the computer system. Chapter 7, "Using Windows NT Server and Warp Server," discusses why these are such good environments for client/server architecture. UNIX is also a natural environment for client/server.

TCP/IP (explained in the following section as well as in Chapter 4, "Using Protocols, Cables, and Adapters") is a popular protocol for UNIX-based networks. Some software networking products, however, use NetBIOS to get information packets from computer to computer.

A workstation on a UNIX-based network sends file requests to the host computer and handles the responses as if they had come from the workstation's local hard disk. The workstation may run DOS, OS/2, UNIX, or (if it is a Macintosh) System 7. File redirection enables the workstation to store and retrieve UNIX files as if they were DOS, OS/2, or Mac files. Sometimes, however, you must perform some level of file translation to make a file accessible to different kinds of workstation computers. DOS text files provide a simple example. By convention, DOS ends each line of a text file with two characters: a carriage return and a linefeed. UNIX text files use only a linefeed.

Mac files are more complicated. On a Mac, a *resource fork* is an extension of the file directory that enables the Mac operating system and applications to store more information about the file besides its name, date, and length. The UNIX host may store the file name but not the *resource fork* portion of the file's directory entry. In this latter case, the resource fork does not get stored on the server, and a Mac file may lose some of its attributes when retrieved by another workstation.

Using TCP/IP

TCP/IP stands for *Transmission Control Protocol/Internet Protocol*. The Department of Defense designed TCP/IP for ARPANET, a geographically large network (not a LAN) that connected the sites of the Department of Defense's Advanced Research Projects Agency. TCP/IP is a layer of protocols, not a network operating system. IP provides datagram communications between nodes on a network (similar to Novell's IPX). TCP is similar to NetBIOS in that it provides point-to-point, guaranteed-delivery communications between nodes. TCP/IP usually comes with a set of standard utilities for transferring files (FTP), doing simple remote program execution (TELNET), and sending electronic mail (SMTP); these utilities are designed to work with TCP/IP. TCP/IP, even with these utilities, is not a network operating system. TCP/IP doesn't provide shared drive letters, folders, or file systems.

Because TCP/IP is a public, not proprietary, protocol, it has become extremely popular as the basis for interconnecting LANs from different vendors.

TCP/IP works on a peer networking concept. All computer systems connected by a TCP/IP network are peers from the network's viewpoint, although some computers will have more functions and capabilities than others because they run different operating systems. The designers of TCP/IP based its architecture on a layer of protocols and the *Internet address*, a standard computer-identification scheme.

The physical transport protocol underneath TCP/IP can be EtherNet, Token Ring, a serial (modem) link, or another physical medium for sending and receiving packets of information.

FTP Software sells one of the best TCP/IP products for DOS computers connected to a UNIX-based LAN:

> FTP Software
> 26 Princess Street
> Wakefield, MA 01880
> (617) 246-0900
> info@ftp.com

Using Internet Addresses

At the heart of TCP/IP is a scheme for routing messages that relies on unique, assigned addresses called *Internet addresses*. On a local or wide-area basis, TCP/IP routes messages between networks and between computer systems on each network. Every TCP/IP host and every workstation has an Internet address, consisting of a centrally assigned network ID and a locally administered local host address. This scheme enables the routing of messages between, as well as within, local area networks. The part of TCP/IP that has the job of recognizing Internet addresses is the *Address Recognition Protocol* (ARP).

An Internet address has four parts, in the form AAA.BBB.CCC.DDD. Each part, or field, is usually a decimal number. Periods separate the fields. The *class* of the Internet address is A if the first field is from 0 to 127, B if it is from 128 to 191, or C if the first field is from 192 to 255. The first field should not exceed a value of 255. An example of a class A Internet address follows:

> 89.1.10.2

The interpretation of an Internet address depends on its class. For class A addresses, the *network portion* of the address is the first field of the Internet address. For class B, the network portion is the first two fields. Class C addresses use the first three fields as the network portion of the address. The computer systems on a single network should all use class A, B, or C Internet addresses.

The *host address* portion of an Internet address consists of the remainder of fields after the network portion. Each field in the host address portion can have a value less than 256. You should not use 0 in all the host address fields; this can confuse host systems. TCP/IP software, by convention, assumes that at least one of the fields is non-zero.

As you can see, the size and range of the host address depend on the class. You may find the following Internet addresses already assigned on your network:

> 192.10.100.1
>
> 192.10.100.2
>
> 192.10.100.3

These three Internet addresses are class C addresses, because the first field is 192. The network portion of the addresses in the example is 192.10.100, and the host address portion is 1, 2, or 3.

You would find these numbers difficult to associate with individual workstations on the network, and so the numbering scheme enables you to assign a *host name* to each Internet address. This host name is easier to remember than the pure Internet address. This higher level naming method is called *domain naming*.

The DDN Network Information Center, a part of SRI International (333 Ravenswood Avenue, Menlo Park, CA 94025), assigns standard Internet network addresses and domain names. This ensures uniqueness and enables routing of TCP/IP messages among diverse companies and organizations. SRI imposes some structure on domain names as well as Internet addresses. IBM has several Internet addresses, for example. The domain name is ibm.com. The domain directory com includes all commercial users. The domain directories edu and gov include educational users and government users. Within IBM, different locations have different domain names. Two such domain names are austin.ibm.com and raleigh.ibm.com.

If you have access to a UNIX computer, you may want to display the list of host names on that computer. At a UNIX system prompt, type the *cat* command to reveal the contents of the hosts file in the /etc directory:

cat/etc/hosts

to view the list of host names and their Internet addresses.

If you plan to use Internet addresses on a TCP/IP-based network only within your company, without communicating with other companies or universities over the TCP/IP networks collectively known as the Internet, you can assign your own network and host IDs.

Using Protocols

TCP/IP does not specify the physical medium or protocol on which it runs. The most common TCP/IP physical protocols are EtherNet and serial (modem) connections, but you can use any physical transmission medium for TCP/IP as long as all devices that will communicate with each other use the same medium. Gateways can connect networks that use different physical protocols. Both local area networks and wide area networks can use TCP/IP to exchange information.

The *Internet Protocol* (IP) is the first, lowest layer of TCP/IP. The Transmission Control Protocol (TCP) and User Datagram Protocol (UDP) are two TCP/IP protocols that use IP. Another intermediate protocol that uses IP is the *Internet Control Message Protocol* (ICMP). ICMP enables the exchange of control and error messages between IP hosts. The Application layer occurs on top of TCP/IP, and consists of utility programs and application software.

Internet Protocol (IP). The basic unit of information exchange is a *datagram packet.* The Internet Protocol portion of TCP/IP provides for the routing of packets from computer to computer, and this is the only job it does. Higher level protocols and software do not concern themselves with the routing of packets. The IP protocol layer on a network can forward datagrams to their destinations without help from higher level protocols.

You may run across the acronym *SLIP* at some point. SLIP stands for *Serial Line IP ;* SLIP is an implementation of IP designed for serial communication links.

Like Novell's IPX protocol, IP does not guarantee delivery of packets.

Transmission Control Protocol (TCP). The Transmission Control Protocol uses IP to send and receive message packets. Like NetBIOS (discussed in Chapter 5), TCP provides the reliability factor—it guarantees successful reception of packets. TCP performs error checking to ensure that each packet's contents arrive intact, and TCP disassembles and reassembles packets to and from logical messages.

User Datagram Protocol (UDP). The User Datagram Protocol, like TCP, uses IP to send and receive messages. Unlike TCP, UDP (as a datagram-oriented protocol) does not provide for guaranteed delivery of messages. Computer programs that use UDP must implement their own checks for delivery, retransmission, and error recovery. However, UDP is faster than TCP. The programmer chooses TCP or UDP, depending on the requirements of the particular application.

TCP/IP Utilities. Networking vendors almost always offer a suite of utility software programs with TCP/IP. These utilities let you send and receive mail, emulate a terminal across a TCP/IP link, transfer files, log on to a different UNIX-based computer, run software on another UNIX-based computer, and do other tasks.

Using Simple Mail Transfer (SMTP). You can use the *Simple Mail Transfer Protocol* (SMTP) to send electronic mail on a TCP/IP network. You create your mail message with a text editor and use UNIX commands, such as sendmail, to format your outgoing mail. The addressee identification consists, naturally, of a domain name that TCP/IP converts for you to an Internet address. You can designate a mail relay host that will queue and forward your mail to remote destinations not directly connected to your LAN. SMTP is rudimentary, but it is simple to understand and use.

Using TELNET. The *TELNET* command enables you to access applications on another UNIX computer system as if you were directly attached to that system. TELNET behaves somewhat like a terminal emulator. Many implementations of TELNET are line-oriented and do not provide a full-screen mode of operation. You log on to the remote UNIX computer system through TELNET in much the same way you log on to your local UNIX computer system.

The TELNET command operates in two modes: command mode and input mode. When the TELNET command is issued without arguments, it enters command mode. You can also enter command mode by pressing Ctrl-T in input mode. In command mode, you can enter subcommands to manage the remote system. Some of these subcommands return you to the remote session upon completion. If a subcommand does not return you to the remote session, press Enter.

When you issue the TELNET command with arguments, it performs an open subcommand with those arguments and then enters input mode. The type of input mode is either character-at-a-time mode or line-by-line mode, depending on what the remote system supports. In character-at-a-time mode, most text typed is immediately sent to the remote host for processing. In line-by-line mode, all text is echoed locally and completed lines are sent to the remote host.

Networking Software

Typical TELNET commands appear in the following table:

Command	Function
?	Prints help information
Close	Closes current connection
Display	Displays operating parameters
Emulate	Emulates a VT100 or 3270 terminal
Mode	Enters line-by-line or character-at-a-time mode
Open	Connects to a site
Quit	Exits TELNET
Send	Transmits special characters
Set	Sets operating parameters
Status	Prints status information
Toggle	Toggles operating parameters
Z	Suspends TELNET

Using File Transfer (FTP). The ftp command is the interface to the File Transfer Protocol (FTP). This command uses FTP to transfer files between the local host and a remote host or between two remote hosts. The FTP protocol lets two hosts with different file systems transfer exchange data. Therefore, although the protocol provides a lot of flexibility for transferring data, it does not attempt to preserve file attributes specific to a particular file system (such as the protection mode or modification times of a file). Additionally, the FTP protocol makes few assumptions about the structure of a file system and does not enable you to do such things as recursively copy subdirectories. If you are transferring files between UNIX systems and need to preserve file attributes or recursively copy subdirectories, you should use the rcp (remote file copy) command.

The ftp command provides subcommands for tasks such as listing remote directories, changing the current local and remote directory, transferring multiple files in a single request, creating and removing directories, and escaping to the local shell to perform shell commands. The ftp command also provides for security by sending passwords to the remote host and letting you perform automatic login, file transfers, and logoff.

The following table shows some of the typical ftp commands:

Command	Function
account [Password]	Sends a supplemental password that a remote host may require before granting access to its resources.
append LocalFile [RemoteFile]	Appends a local file to a file on the remote host.
cd RemoteDirectory	Changes the working directory on the remote host to the specified directory.

Command	Function
cdup	Changes the working directory on the remote host to the parent of the current directory.
close	Ends the file transfer session but does not exit the ftp command.
delete RemoteFile	Deletes the specified remote file.
get RemoteFile [LocalFile]	Copies the remote file to the local host.
lcd [Directory]	Changes the working directory on the local host. If you do not specify a directory, the ftp command uses your home directory.
ls [RemoteDirectory] [LocalFile]	Writes an abbreviated file listing of a remote directory to a local file.
mkdir [RemoteDirectory]	Creates the directory, *RemoteDirectory*, on the remote host.
nlist	Prints a list of the files of a directory on the remote machine.
open HostName	Establishes a connection to the ftp server at the specified *HostName*.
pwd	Displays the name of the current directory on the remote host.
quit	Closes the connection and exits the ftp command.
rename [FromName] [ToName]	Renames a file on the remote host.
rmdir	Removes the directory *RemoteDirectory* at the RemoteDirectory remote host.
send LocalFile [RemoteFile]	Stores a local file on the remote host.
size	Returns the size of *filename* on the remote machine in bytes.
status	Displays current status of the ftp command.
user <user>	Identifies the local user as *user* to the remote ftp server.

Remote Access to UNIX Computers. The rlogin command logs you into the remote host and connects your local terminal to the remote host. The remote terminal type is the same as that given in the local environment variable TERM. The terminal or window size is also the same, if the remote host supports these sizes. All echoing takes place at the remote host, so, except for delays, the terminal connection is transparent. You can press Ctrl+S and Ctrl+Q to stop and start the flow of information, and the input and output buffers are flushed on interrupts.

The rcp command copies files between a remote host and your local UNIX computer. You would use rcp after logging in to the remote host with rlogin. By default, the mode and owner of an existing destination file are preserved. Normally, if a destination file does not exist, the mode of the destination file is equal to the mode of the source file as modified by the unmask command at the destination host. If the -p flag is used, the modification time and mode of source files are preserved at the destination host. If a remote host name is not specified for the source or the destination, the rcp command is equivalent to the cp command.

III

Networking Software

When copying files to or from a remote host, any remote file or directory name must be prefixed by the host of the remote host and a colon (:). Local file and directory names do not need to have a host specified. Because the rcp command assumes that a colon (:) terminates a host name, however, local file or directory names must have a backslash (\) inserted before any colons that are embedded in the name.

The user name entered for the remote host determines the file access privileges the rcp command uses at that host. Additionally, the user name given to a destination host determines the ownership and access modes of the resulting destination file or files.

The rsh command executes a command at a remote host or, if no command is specified, logs you into the remote host. The rsh command sends standard input from the local command line to the remote command and receives standard output and standard error from the remote command.

Because any input to the remote command must be specified on the local command line, you cannot use the rsh command to execute an interactive command on a remote host. If you need to execute an interactive command on a remote host, use the rlogin command or the rsh command with no command specified. If you do not specify a command, the rsh command executes rlogin instead.

The ping command sends an ICMP ECHO_REQUEST to obtain an ICMP ECHO_RESPONSE from a host or gateway, and is useful for determining the status of the network and various foreign hosts. You also can use the ping command to track hardware and software problems, as well as in network testing, measurement, and management. Ping is also useful for isolating problems.

The Host parameter is either a valid host name or Internet address. If the host is operational and on the network, it responds to the echo. Each echo request contains an IP and ICMP header, followed by a timeval structure, and enough bytes to fill out the packet. The PacketSize parameter indicates the number of bytes in each datagram, with 64 bytes used as the default. The optional Count parameter specifies a number of echo requests to send. The default is to continuously send echo requests until an interrupt is received (Ctrl+C).

When trying to isolate a problem, first run the ping command on the local host to verify that the local interface to the network is running. Then use the ping command for hosts and gateways that are progressively more distant from the local host. The ping command sends one datagram per second and prints one line of output for every response received. Ping calculates round-trip times and packet-loss statistics and displays a brief summary on completion.

If you are accustomed to working with UNIX, the commands and utility programs you have just learned about probably seem like natural extensions of your current UNIX environment. Also notice that with each command you had to think of the remote computer as a separate environment. When you use rlogin, for example, you have to remind yourself that you are logged in to a remote UNIX machine, not your local one. And you must use commands such as ftp or rcp to copy files from one computer to another.

If you use a DOS-based computer as a workstation, the UNIX commands and utilities may seem alien and cryptic. Arcane commands such as the ones you just covered are the Achilles' heel of UNIX.

Using the Network File System (NFS)

Network File System (NFS) is a popular network operating system for sharing file systems and directories across TCP/IP-based networks. Developed by Sun Microsystems, NFS is an application-layer protocol that sits on top of TCP/IP. All major vendors of UNIX-based systems offer NFS, and some vendors of non-UNIX computers offer software products that implement or work with NFS.

Understanding What NFS Does

The NFS protocol enables you to access a remote directory and its files as if that directory were on your local UNIX computer. Your UNIX applications use the files in the remote directory structure as if the files were local. Through file redirection, NFS transparently makes the remote machine's UNIX file systems available to you. When you use the UNIX command *mount* to gain access to a remote computer's directories, your computer becomes a *client* host. A remote computer that enables its directories to be mounted by other computers is a *server* host. A host may be a server for one or more clients and may at the same time be a client of one or more other servers. You mount the remote directories over local directory *stubs*—empty directories that exist just to facilitate remote access.

Using Remote Procedure Calls (RPC)

Sun Microsystems based its design of NFS on the *Remote Procedure Call* (*RPC*) concept, which enables software on different machines to communicate. If you have ever written a computer program or done some batch file programming, you know you can modularize your program so that separate sections of the software do different jobs. With RPC, these separate sections can reside on different kinds of computers. The Network File System uses RPC to redirect file input/output (I/O) operations across a network.

Remote Procedure Call enables programmers to treat a heterogeneous network of computers as if they were one big computer. With RPC, each part of an application can be targeted toward the kind of computer for which it is best suited. RPC is a good tool for building client/server systems.

What does a programmer have to do to use RPC? He or she codes each module in the C programming language, as usual. Each program module is designated as a *server* or *client*. Server modules are typically the back-end of the application (calculations, report generation, storage of permanent database records), while client modules manage the front-end user interface. The programmer creates an RPC compiler script that identifies the server and client modules. The programmer then runs the RPC compiler to generate the C source code that glues the modules together as if they were one executable program. Under the covers, the generated code creates a communication session between the client and server modules on the different computers. To the programmer, though, the server modules are called in the same way as any other subroutines that the client code might call. The fact that the client and server modules execute on different computers becomes transparent to the programmer's application.

The computers that participate in an NFS network may be different brands and models, and they likely represent data in different ways internally. NFS uses the *External Data Representation* (XDR) protocol to take care of these differences. With XDR, the information in the message packets is rearranged and translated to a computer-model-independent form.

NFS is a *stateless* protocol; servers and clients do not remember previous file operations. A workstation may open a file by sending the file name to the remote NFS server and receiving a response saying *the file is now open*. Later, when that workstation wants to read the file, the workstation sends a read-file request to the server. The read-file request contains the name of the file and the file position, so that the server does not have to remember the previous open-file operation it performed on behalf of the workstation. One consequence of NFS's statelessness is that NFS is somewhat slower than other network operating environments. The slower performance is the result of the extra LAN traffic from the larger packets (each one carries all the information necessary for that packet to stand on its own) and from the extra processing NFS has to do for each packet.

The statelessness of NFS avoids complicated crash-recovery handling on the part of the server and client. A client simply resends requests until a response is received. A client cannot tell the difference between a slow server and a server that has crashed. In the same vein, a server that has just been rebooted can resume honoring client requests without each of the clients also rebooting. NFS uses the User Datagram Protocol (UDP) described earlier to send and receive file requests and responses.

Using DOS Files and UNIX Files

The commands you use in an NFS environment to make resources available for sharing, or to share those resources, work in a way similar to the NET USE (NT Server, Warp Server) and MAP (NetWare) commands you've learned. However, you sometimes need to be aware of the differences between the way DOS, Windows, NT, and OS/2 treat a file and how UNIX treats the same file. The following sections explain these commands as well as the file handling differences.

Using NFS Commands. The NFS command SHARE makes a server resource (directory, file, or printer) available to other users. Using SHARE requires root-level administrative privileges on the server. To share a server directory named /server/scripts, for instance, you might use the following SHARE command:

```
share -o rw /server/scripts
```

In this example, "-o rw" specifies read-and-write access for people who access /server/scripts. Running the SHARE command with no parameters displays a list of resources currently available for others to connect to.

The NFS command UNSHARE removes a server resource from the list of those available for sharing.

Because the concept of file systems is central to UNIX (in contrast, DOS, Windows, and OS/2 computers use drive letters while Macintosh computers use folders), you use the MOUNT command to make a remote resource available to you on a client workstation. For example, issuing the following command at a client computer causes the shared resource /server/scripts to be mounted, for both read and write access, with a client name of /usr/scripts:

```
mount -o rw /server/scripts /usr/scripts
```

The UMOUNT command reverses the action of MOUNT, making the resource unavailable.

Differences Between DOS and UNIX Files. UNIX file names may contain up to 14 characters, they can have multiple periods in them, and they are case-sensitive (some UNIX implementations allow more than 14 characters in a file name). DOS file names, as you know, may contain up to eight characters of base name and have an optional one- to three-character extension. A single period separates the base name from the extension. DOS file names are not case-sensitive.

You will not have a problem with the differences between UNIX and DOS file-naming conventions if you only access DOS files from your workstation. If you use the CHDIR command to change to the root directory of the file server and type a DIR command, however, you will see typical UNIX directories such as USR, TMP, and LOST'UND. This last directory name is NFS's way of representing the ubiquitous UNIX lost+found directory in terms of the more restrictive DOS rules for file names. When a UNIX name does not map directly to a DOS file name, NFS substitutes special characters, such as apostrophes, in the name to help you access the file from DOS.

On the host computer, NFS stores files as UNIX files. File redirection makes the UNIX file versus DOS file difference transparent, however. The files you save from one DOS workstation can be accessed from other DOS workstations without your having to worry about the differences between the DOS and UNIX operating systems.

The only difference you have to be aware of is the way that DOS and UNIX each treat text files. UNIX uses a single linefeed character to end a line of text in a text file. DOS uses two characters: a carriage return followed by a linefeed. If you plan to share text files between DOS applications and UNIX applications, you can use a conversion utility to add carriage returns to UNIX files or delete carriage returns from DOS files. UNIX typically comes with such a utility, and several freeware versions are available.

Sharing UNIX Printers

You learned about NetWare's CAPTURE command in Chapter 6 and the NET USE command, for NT Server and Warp Server, in Chapter 7. Both commands redirect streams of print data that otherwise would flow through your computer's parallel port. Redirection diverts the print data to another computer's printer on the LAN. On a UNIX-based LAN, NFS provides a similar facility.

UNIX computers and their printers have administrator-assigned names, and you use these names to select which shared printer you want printouts to go to. The network operating systems spools your printouts, as separate print jobs, to the shared printer. Additionally, you can specify which UNIX command and associated command line parameters the network operating system should use on the print server computer. For example, in a LAN environment that uses the UNIX-based PC Interface network software product from Locus Computing, you might have the following:

```
PRINTER LPT1 HOST1 "lp -d hplaser -m"
```

This example redirects LPT1 printouts to the UNIX computer HOST1. It further specifies that HOST1 should use the UNIX "lp" command to do the actual printing. The command line parameter "-d hplaser" sends the printout to the printer device named hplaser, while the "-m" parameter instructs the HOST1 machine to send you a mail message when the printout finishes.

Using UNIX File Permissions

For security, NFS relies on standard UNIX protections. You use the NFS login program, which prompts you for a UNIX account ID and password, to gain access to the network drive. The network administrator must add each user to the UNIX system. You can be denied read or write access to files and directories on the UNIX host through the use of standard UNIX file permission masks. UNIX file and directory permissions masks are similar to NetWare's, NT Server's, and Warp Server's file and directory permissions. On a UNIX computer, you must have permission to read a file, write a file, or, for executable files, run a program.

Running Terminal Sessions

In addition to treating the UNIX computer as a file server, through a DOS drive letter and shared LAN printer, you can turn your personal computer into a terminal and log on to UNIX directly. The terminal emulator usually supplied with NFS operates across the LAN. You can emulate a VT220, VT100, or PC scancode terminal in your UNIX sessions. LAN-based terminal emulators support most of the characteristics of a standard Digital Equipment Corporation VT220 terminal, including multinational character sets, programmable function keys, numeric keypad cursor control, flow control, and the usual DEC control and escape sequences.

In 386-enhanced mode, Microsoft Windows can give you multiple, concurrent DOS sessions. In one session, you may treat the UNIX computer as a file server, running applications that access files on the network drive letter. In another DOS session under Windows, you can run the terminal emulator program to have a UNIX session with the UNIX computer. You can typically have only one terminal emulation session active at a time, however.

Using Yellow Pages

The *Yellow Pages* (*YP*) product (which in networking has nothing to do with the telephone company) complements NFS by providing a distributed network lookup service. Yellow Pages servers store databases called *maps* that client computers can query. Generally, these maps contain information about users, groups, network addresses, gateways, and other entities on the network. Yellow Pages comes with shell scripts to help you build the map files. One such script is *ypinit*, which can build Yellow Pages server maps from files available on your UNIX computer, including the local password, group, and TCP/IP configuration files.

As people share resources on a UNIX-based network, a Yellow Pages server resolves naming and addressing differences among the networked computers.

You sometimes will see Yellow Pages referred to as *Network Information Services* (*NIS*).

Other Network Operating Systems

NFS is pervasive in UNIX environments; however, some UNIX-based network operating systems such as SCO VisionFS use the same SMB protocol as NT Server, Warp Server, Windows for Workgroups, Windows 95, Warp Connect, and the old IBM PC LAN Program. While NFS requires that you use special NFS client software, VisionFS lets Windows for Workgroups, Windows 95, and Warp Connect users access a UNIX file server by using the SMB-based network software included with the base operating system. SCO VisionFS is a server-based solution for sharing file and print services from UNIX servers to Windows and OS/2 PCs. It runs on UNIX servers from SCO, Sun, and HP. VisionFS supports DOS file sharing and record locking to enable you to run multi-user applications on your UNIX-based network.

Chapter Summary

You have added an extra dimension to your knowledge of networking in this chapter: you now understand the basics of the UNIX operating system, and you know about the popular multi-vendor protocol TCP/IP. Network File System (NFS) is no longer a mystery to you.

In the next chapter, you turn your attention to using applications on your LAN.

III

Networking Software

Part IV

Expanding a Network

Chapter 10

Using Network Applications

Your individual personal computer exists to run software applications and help you get your work done. The network helps people in the office act as a team and get more work done. It does this by enabling people to share information and computer resources. Your LAN makes the personal computers in your office part of the team.

Your favorite applications may be LAN-aware and allow multiple concurrent use by the people in the office, or they may be single-user, stand-alone applications. Even in the case of single-user software, you may be able to share each application's executable and data files on the LAN. You may have to coordinate the sharing of specific files, however. This may involve telling others in your office that you have updated a particular spreadsheet file and that the file is now available for others to load and use at their workstations. On the other hand, your multi-user applications may help you share files in a way that makes it easy to know who updated a file last, why he or she updated the file, where the most recent file is located, and when the update took place.

A LAN-aware, multi-user application recognizes the presence of a network operating system and behaves accordingly. A single-user application treats the network drives the same as local drives and does not behave any differently when run on multiple, LAN-connected computers. This chapter shows you how to manage both multi-user software and single-user software on a LAN.

You start your exploration of LAN applications in this chapter by considering how DOS works on your computer when you are on the network. The various network operating systems implement rights and permissions for the sake of security, and this chapter shows how your applications behave differently according to how the network administrator grants or revokes these rights. You learn about *deadlocks*—a rare but data-damaging event in a multi-user environment.

In this chapter, you next look at the characteristics of a multi-user application. These characteristics include file sharing, record locking, user-specific configuration files, and multi-user printing. You cover the important issues of software licenses for multiple users. This chapter explains how to manage and use the different categories of application programs—word processing, desktop publishing, spreadsheets, and database managers—on a LAN.

Defining Single-User and Multi-User Operating Systems

DOS by itself is a single-user operating system. On a LAN, however, several users usually need to be able to run the same application on different workstations. A multi-user application, through DOS and the network operating system, coordinates the efforts of each user and workstation by understanding and manipulating the environment presented by the LAN. LAN-aware software extends DOS and adds an entirely new dimension to working with personal computers.

Using DOS

IBM, Microsoft, and Novell (in an independent sort of way) added functions to DOS to enable DOS computers to access a network. Microsoft and IBM, which obviously control what goes into DOS, placed these new and extended functions directly inside DOS. Because Novell is not a partner in the maintenance and programming of the DOS operating system, Novell originally supported these capabilities with functions provided by the NetWare Shell (NETx.COM). Novell, besides offering its own proprietary set of multi-user functions and DOS extensions, also recognizes and supports the Microsoft/IBM functions.

Looking at Different Versions of DOS. Microsoft and IBM added LAN-related functions to versions of DOS starting with 3.0. Computer programs running under DOS 3.0 can exercise file access control (exclusive or shared modes of opening files) and record locking. DOS 3.1 added the capability to obtain the identification of individual workstations, to determine which disk drives are remote (redirected/shared) and which are local, and to find out the network name of a remote disk drive. DOS 3.2 coincided with the release of IBM's Token Ring network adapter cards. DOS 3.3 added a function to enable programs to commit file data to disk (a sort of temporary close action). And DOS 4.0 makes the loading of the SHARE.EXE program mandatory rather than optional ("Using the DOS SHARE.EXE Program" describes the SHARE program later in this chapter).

Several years ago, more people were using Version 2.1 of DOS than any other version of DOS. (People do not necessarily upgrade to the next version of the operating system when each new version is released.) Because of the approach Novell took to create a LAN environment based on a separate layer of software above DOS, DOS 2.1 users who have the appropriate NetWare shell software were able to have access to a LAN without upgrading to a new operating system. This is one of the reasons Novell got an early toehold in the LAN marketplace. Today, of course, this is no longer a significant factor; most people have a later (LAN-compatible) version of DOS.

Using DOS Commands. DOS is not immune to file-sharing problems—even something as simple as issuing a COPY command to DOS can cause problems on a network. The problem does not happen often, fortunately. But the DOS command processor COMMAND.COM is not particularly LAN-aware. A file collision occurs if you tell DOS to copy a file that another workstation currently has open. It doesn't matter that the other workstation may be only reading from the file and the COPY command just wants to share the file by also just reading from it. In order to do the COPY, COMMAND.COM opens the input (source) file in compatibility mode, which, unless the file's directory entry is marked with the read-only attribute, asks for exclusive access to the file. The COPY command should open the input file with a mode that denies other workstations the capability to write to the file for the duration of the copy operation.

Novell supplies a file-copy utility of its own with NetWare, called NCOPY. Not only is NCOPY LAN-aware, but it also has a special feature for avoiding unnecessary message traffic across the LAN. If NCOPY detects that the source and destination files reside on the same file server, NCOPY performs the file copy directly at the file server instead of transmitting the file out to a workstation, which in turn would then have to transmit the file back to the file server under the destination file name.

Configuring DOS on a Workstation. The installation software for your network operating system will usually make whatever changes are necessary to your CONFIG.SYS and AUTOEXEC.BAT files. If the software is well-written, you will get a chance during the installation of the network to view, highlight, and perhaps modify the changes. The installation software also will put the workstation part of the network operating system on the hard disk of each of the personal computers in your office. The disk space required for these workstation files ranges from a few tens of kilobytes for NetWare to a few megabytes for NT Server.

If you use an 80386 or better personal computer and you have DOS 5 or later (or one of the memory manager products discussed in Chapter 5, "Using Workstations"), you can experiment with loading some or all of the network software into upper memory. Putting network driver software into upper memory is usually a trial-and-error process. If you are the analytical type, you can use the sets of documentation that came with your network adapter card and the other adapter cards in your computer to select likely areas of upper memory to use for TSRs and device drivers. You probably will wind up rebooting your computer several times, making changes each time to your CONFIG.SYS and AUTOEXEC.BAT files, before you find a combination of TSR and device driver upper memory usage that satisfies you. If you choose to go through this process, your reward is a much larger amount of memory in which to run your applications. You can free up substantial amounts of the 640K of conventional memory with DOS 5 or a memory manager product.

The Novell NetWare, NT Server, and Warp Server network operating systems can share an entire file server disk drive or, if desired, certain directories on the disk. The NetWare command MAP sets up drive mappings that specify the relationship between the drive letters and directories that a workstation sees on the network and the actual drive and directory structure on the file server. In a similar manner, for NT Server and Warp Server, the NET SHARE (at the file server) and NET USE (at a workstation) commands specify drive and directory relationships. Note that the drive letters and the directory structures visible to your applications depend on how these commands are used. Your application software may say a few words in the Installation section of the user documentation about how the application expects these drive mappings to be set up.

Using the DOS SHARE.EXE Program. SHARE.EXE enables file-sharing on a LAN. SHARE is distributed on the DOS distribution diskettes and consists of a terminate-and-stay-resident (TSR) program that inserts hooks deep into DOS. These hooks are so deep that you cannot remove SHARE from memory without rebooting the computer.

If SHARE is not loaded, DOS ignores the special file-access modes that a LAN-aware application specifies at the time it opens a file (to acquire exclusive access to a file, for example). In fact, it is possible to corrupt a network disk quite thoroughly if file collisions occur and SHARE is not in effect. This is one of the reasons that, beginning with DOS 4.0, SHARE is loaded automatically by DOS and is no longer something you can forget to run. SHARE is also automatically in effect under OS/2. SHARE is built into the OS/2 operating system, and you do not have to load SHARE if you use OS/2.

The user guide or reference manual that came with your application software probably will remind you to run SHARE before accessing the application. The best time to run SHARE is after you have loaded the network software but before you do any work. It does not matter whether SHARE runs before the logon process.

One interesting aspect of SHARE is that it enables file-sharing even on a stand-alone, single-user PC. Because you can have several TSR-type programs loaded underneath an application program running in the foreground, DOS needs to keep separate track of the file I/O performed by each background or foreground program. If SHARE is loaded on a single-user computer, the same file-sharing that occurs across the network can occur between two TSRs, or between a TSR and a foreground application.

If you are a Microsoft Windows user on a LAN, you should make doubly certain to load SHARE before starting Windows. Windows does not enable you to run SHARE in one of its enhanced-mode DOS sessions. Windows prevents SHARE from running by pretending that SHARE is already loaded. Windows does this because you can use the DOS EXIT command to end a DOS session, which would remove SHARE from memory. Windows cannot enable this to happen, because SHARE hooks itself into DOS. As an unfortunate side effect, multi-user software that you run in a DOS session will think that file sharing is enabled, when in fact SHARE is not present. File damage and corruption can result.

On a Windows for Workgroups computer running in 386-Enhanced mode, a replacement for SHARE.EXE (called VSHARE.386) takes over and manages concurrent file access and record locking. VSHARE is a Microsoft Windows *virtual device driver*, loaded via an entry in a Windows INI file.

Assigning Rights and Permissions

The concept of rights and permissions forms a significant part of the security offered by most network operating systems. These rights and permissions can protect data, but they can confuse application software (and you, too, when you run the applications).

An example of a situation that is unique to NetWare involves the Shareable/Nonshareable file attribute that you covered in Chapter 6's discussion of Novell NetWare. When a file is created on a NetWare file server, the network operating system gives the file a default attribute of readable, writable, nonshareable. This means that you or your application software will have to modify the attributes of the files that your applications expect to share among multiple users. If you have to modify the attributes manually, you can use the NetWare FLAG utility.

Searching Directories. Under Novell NetWare, Warp Server, and NT Server, situations can happen that would never occur on a single-user computer. You will recall, for example, the discussion in Chapter 7, "Using Windows NT Server and Warp Server," about the rights that can be associated with a directory on a NetWare server. A directory can be marked so that a program cannot even search it to see what files it contains. The files may actually exist (and be visible to users who have different NetWare trustee rights), but some users with insufficient rights may be restricted so that certain directories and files are invisible to the software they run and the DOS commands they issue. Because of this, an application may appear to behave differently when run on different workstations on the LAN.

Reading and Writing Files. It is generally a misuse of rights and permissions to mark a directory as searchable but not readable. Most network operating systems support this combination of rights, but you will find it highly frustrating. You can see the files in the directory when you issue a DOS DIR command, but your application cannot open and read the files.

On the other hand, turning off file-write permission for all users but one (or a few) is useful. This security technique makes the person who can write a file responsible for that file. Other people can read the file but cannot replace the information in the file.

Encountering Deadlocks

Deadlock is a gruesome but well-chosen word for a situation you very much want to avoid. Suppose that Workstation A and Workstation B are running different programs, but both programs need to update the same two files on the file server. Each program needs to lock the two files so that it can update the files with consistent data. At about the same moment, both programs reach the point in their processing at which they need to acquire the file locks. The sequence of events goes like this:

Program A locks file #1.

Program A writes data to file #1 that absolutely must be reflected in file #2.

Program B locks file #2.

Program B writes data to file #2 that absolutely must be reflected in file #1.

Program A tries to lock file #2. It fails.

Program B tries to lock file #1. It fails.

Another term for this situation is *deadly embrace*. This term sounds just as gruesome as deadlock, and is perhaps a bit more descriptive. Untangling the participants in a deadlock usually involves rebooting both workstations, which may leave inconsistent data in the files that were in use by the application.

If you encounter a situation that appears to be caused by a deadlock, you will want to notify the developer (vendor) of the application software. It is up to the programmer to avoid deadlocks. You sometimes can verify that a deadlock has occurred by going to the file server and looking at the network operating system's display of currently open files and active record locks.

Defining Characteristics of a Multi-User Application

In the next few sections of this chapter, you will gain an understanding of what makes multi-user applications different from single-user applications. LAN-aware software behaves differently on a LAN and recognizes the need to support several application users at the same time. Such software uses file sharing and record locking to preserve the integrity of its files. Well-written applications enable each person to have individual files of configuration and preference information. Multi-user printing, properly done, ensures that each print job appears on the shared LAN printer with the right fonts and page orientation, without being affected by the previous print job. Also, multi-user applications may have different licensing arrangements under which you purchase the software.

Learning How Software Behaves Differently on a LAN

You have seen how rights, permissions, and file attributes can cause an application to behave differently on a LAN. When an application does not handle the LAN environment very well, you will have to shoulder part of the job of coordinating file updates yourself. You will have to implement an office-wide strategy for notifying people when certain files can be accessed and updated, for example. Some software cannot be run on a LAN at all. Utility programs that sort directories fall into this category.

Depending on the extent to which a multi-user application is LAN-aware, the application software may mesh smoothly into the work your office does. The software may recognize that it is running on a workstation, know which person is using the software, and configure itself for each person's use.

Identifying Users. The account ID (user ID) you use to log on to the LAN is available to application software. (Your password is not, of course). In some instances, the software may use a *machine name* to identify each workstation. The application can use either piece of information in a wide variety of ways. The software may produce an audit trail of application activity on a user-by-user basis. Or the software may maintain separate configuration and preference files for each user.

It is not prevalent now, but years ago some application software stored configuration information inside the executable program file itself. The computer program had built-in defaults for the configuration. When you changed the configuration, the software simply changed its internal defaults by treating part of the executable file as a data file. This is one of the most devastating things a programmer can do on a network. The scheme has two problems. First, the application software cannot store multiple individual user configurations for everyone on the LAN. Second, you cannot mark the executable file as shareable and read-only (a useful file attribute on a NetWare LAN).

Better-designed applications establish a configuration file for each user. The account ID, user ID, or machine name probably will be the basis for the name of the configuration file.

If the documentation for the application software tells you that you must set up a machine name for each workstation (or each user login account ID), and if the documentation suggests guidelines for constructing the name (for example, it must be unique, between 1 and 8 characters, consist of alphabetic/numeric characters, and otherwise conform to the requirements for a valid file name under DOS), you can bet that the application is using this technique. Examples of such names are BARRY.CFG, SUSAN.CFG, SCOTT.CFG, CHRIS.CFG and JOEL.CFG.

Accessing Disk Sectors. You cannot run some utility programs on a network drive. The best example is CHKDSK. CHKDSK operates on disk sectors, and network operating systems do not provide the means for a program to lock a disk sector. Files may be locked during an update, but not sectors. In addition, CHKDSK only understands DOS-formatted disks. The file server disk drive may very well have an internal format that DOS does not understand. Attempting to run CHKDSK on a server typically results in the message, "Cannot CHKDSK a network drive."

Probably the most popular DOS-based hard disk utility product is Norton Utilities, from Symantec Corporation. This set of computer programs enables you to set your screen colors, search for text strings in files, find files, set volume labels, test your system's performance, change file attributes, print text files, and do a number of other useful things. It is these other things that do not work on a network drive. Norton Utilities contains computer programs for sorting directories, unerasing files, undeleting directories, and modifying the internal physical file location tables. These computer programs, while useful on a single-user DOS computer, are dangerous in a multi-user environment. If you were to sort a file server directory at one workstation while another workstation was using that same directory, you would "pull the rug out from beneath" the other user.

Other popular hard disk utilities that do not work on a network disk drive include PC Tools Deluxe, from Central Point Software; HDTest, from Peter Fletcher; SpinRite, from Gibson Research; OPTune, from Gazelle Systems; and Mace Utilities, from Symantec.

Using Root Directory Files. Some applications expect to be able to write files in the root directory of the current disk drive. The file may be a temporary file that holds work in progress while the software does its job. On a LAN, it is possible that you do not have sufficient permissions to be able to write files in the network drive's root directory.

For this reason, many network operating systems enable you to perform a special drive letter mapping that makes your personal directory on the LAN look like a root directory to applications. This feature is called *map root*. As an example of how this works, suppose that your name is Chris and your network administrator has created a personal network directory for you. The directory is F:\USERS\CHRIS. The network administrator may set up your drive letters so that F:\ is really F:\USERS\CHRIS. When your software thinks it is writing to the root directory of drive F, the files actually appear in F:\USERS\CHRIS.

Using File Sharing and Record Locking

Every open file on a file server is owned by the workstation that opened it. The ownership can be quite possessive ("No one touches this file but me.") or jointly communal ("If we cooperate, we can all own this file."). There are gradations between these ownerships. An application specifies how it wants to share a file when the computer program opens the file. Applications use file sharing and record locking to ensure that file updates occur on a consistent basis.

Examining the Need for File Sharing. What would happen if two workstations did not pay any attention to file-sharing concepts (did not load SHARE) and just went ahead and tried to change the contents of the same file? If the two workstations open the same file and attempt to update it at the same time, the results can be messy, to say the least. Here is an example of what can happen:

When workstation A reads a file or a portion of a file, the file server transfers the data from the file server hard disk into workstation A's memory for processing. Writing the data transfers it back to the file server. The same holds true, naturally, for workstation B. Suppose that workstation A reads a file and displays the file's data to user A. While user A is looking at his or her screen and keying in changes, workstation B also reads the file into B's memory and displays it to user B. User B types faster than user A and saves his or her changes first. User A, after pondering a few minutes, saves his or her changes (by writing the data from workstation memory to the file server). Clearly, the changes that user B made now are lost; they've been overwritten by those of the slower typist, user A.

An even more complicated situation arises when several *interrelated* files need to be updated. Because the contents of one file are supposed to have a certain correspondence to the contents of the other files, a helter-skelter series of updates from multiple workstations would be disastrous. Any relationships that existed before the several updates took place would quickly be destroyed.

File Sharing. At the time an application opens a file located on the file server, the software informs the server of its intention either to simply read from the file or perhaps both read and write to the file. The software also can ask the server to deny other workstations access to the file.

If the application signals an intention to only read from the file, and if the file is flagged with a file attribute of read-only, the server enables the application to access the file. If you have used the DOS ATTRIB command to mark a file as read-only, and an application indicates that it wants to write to the file, the network operating system will not enable the application to use the file, but will instead cause the application to produce an error message.

An application uses *sharing mode* to control how other workstations can concurrently open a file. The application specifies sharing mode at the time it opens a file. Sharing mode works by enabling the application at one workstation to restrict (or not restrict) how other workstations can use a file.

Applications express sharing mode in terms of denying certain capabilities to the other workstations that attempt to open the file. The restrictions an application can specify, as defined by the DOS Technical Reference manual the programmers use, are DENY_NONE, DENY_READ, DENY_WRITE, and DENY_READ_WRITE. In addition, there is a special mode called compatibility mode. The names for these modes seem odd because these are the names that programmers actually use as they develop the software. When a programmer instructs the computer program to open a file, he or she considers the file-sharing requirements for that file and chooses an appropriate mode. You will want to be aware of these modes so that you can recognize their behavior in the LAN-aware software you buy and use.

DENY_NONE grants full access to the file by applications at other workstations. In essence, DENY_NONE defers the protection of the file's integrity until later, when the application updates individual records. If a workstation opens a file with a sharing mode of DENY_READ, the network operating system enables other workstations to write to the file but not read it. DENY_WRITE is the opposite; if a workstation opens a file with a sharing mode of DENY_WRITE, the network operating system does not enable other workstations to update the file. The other workstations can, however, read from the file.

DENY_READ_WRITE confers exclusive access to the workstation that opens the file. Attempts by other workstations to open the file (with any value of sharing mode) will fail.

Compatibility mode is the default sharing mode. If an application does not specify otherwise, the network operating system uses compatibility mode to determine how other workstations can open a file. In general, this mode grants exclusive access to an application. Compatibility mode is also in effect for new files the application creates.

Record Locking. Because a file lock affects the entire file and extends from the time a file is opened until the time it's closed, the resulting *coarse granularity* (the system-wide effect on the group of people who are using the application at that moment) of the lock may be an awkward inconvenience to the people in the office. A lock that lasts for the entire time an application uses a file prevents others from accessing the file. A file lock does not enable file sharing.

A multi-user application uses record locking to protect the integrity of the data files. A record lock lasts only long enough to ensure that consistent data has been written to the file(s), and it usually affects only a small portion of the file.

A record lock specifies a certain region of a file by giving the region's location in the file (its offset) and its size (length). If the specified region cannot be locked successfully (another workstation opened the file in a mode other than DENY_NONE mode, or another workstation has locked the same record), the network operating system informs the application that the record is not available.

The locked region can encompass a portion of a data record, one data record, several physically adjacent data records, or the entire file. The choice is up to the application programmer. If each data record in a file is independent of all the others, the application simply locks the affected data record. However, if relationships exist among the records in a file (perhaps one record contains a pointer to another record, or the updating of the file implies that several records may need to be physically moved in the file), the application may lock the entire file as if it were a single large record. In either case, the record lock usually lasts only a few milliseconds.

Multi-User Printing

You would think that sending print data to a shared network printer would be easy, painless, and not nearly as much trouble as trying to share files and records. Unfortunately, this isn't so.

Suppose that a person on the network is running Lotus 1-2-3 and needs to print a spreadsheet in condensed (small) print because it is several cells wide. The person sends control codes to the printer, prints the spreadsheet, and walks away from the network printer with a nicely formatted printout in hand. The next person on the LAN to print a report receives a printout with data tightly bunched on the left side of the page in small characters. (The previous person's software left the printer in condensed print mode.)

Here is another example: you tell your application to print a lengthy, complex report. To your bewilderment, you find that other people's printouts are intermingled in the pages of your report. The page breaks occur nowhere near where they should. Yet the report prints correctly on a local (non-LAN-attached) printer. (The network software is inserting automatic page breaks and breaking the printout into multiple print jobs. In this example, the application performs lengthy processing steps between sections of the report. The network operating system senses these pauses and, at each pause, thinks the application has finished printing.) (See "The LAN Printer" in Chapter 5, "Using Workstations," for more on print jobs and print queues.)

NT Server and Warp Server try to detect when an application finishes printing. The workstation can set a time-out value to help the network operating system know when a pause in printing really means the end of a print job. In addition, NT Server and Warp Server come with the PRTSC utility that enables you to press Ctrl+Alt+Print Screen to signal the end of a print job.

You can create a file that NT Server or Warp Server uses to print job separator pages between printouts. The job separator page supports a wide variety of printer-control options, and you can use these options not only to say what the separator page should look like but also to reset the printer to a default mode before each printout is produced.

If you do not specify a job separator file, NT Server uses its DEFAULT.SEP file. You use the NET SEPARATOR command to specify whether separator pages should be in effect and the name of the job separator file.

NetWare offers somewhat more extensive control over the network printer through the use of the CAPTURE command (formerly the SPOOL command). You can control whether automatic form feeds are added to the end of a file of print data, whether a job separator page (Novell calls it a *banner page*) should be produced, whether tabs should be expanded into spaces and how many spaces to use, the number of copies that should be printed, the type of form that must be mounted in the printer, the variable text (user name or job name) that appears on the banner page, how NetWare detects the end of the print job (based on a time-out value or file-close operation), the lines per page, the width of each line, and some miscellaneous other items. Current versions of NetWare also provide the means to reset the printer between print jobs.

Buying Software Licenses for Multiple Users

Whether or not the software you use contains any sort of copy protection, you know that legally you must purchase a copy of the software for each person who will use it. You may interpret this to mean a single copy for everyone in the office, or you may interpret it to mean a copy for as many people as will use the software at one time. Either way, a LAN makes it too easy to share an application or utility from the file server's disk drive. Many companies buy too few copies of the software they use. Be aware that if you fall into this trap and are caught, the legal and financial penalties will be greater than the cost of the software.

Buying Software for Each User. Part of the problem of the multi-user license issue is that many software vendors have not come to grips with how to sell software to LAN users. These vendors insist that you purchase a single copy of the software for each LAN user. For one company in New York City, this means renting a small warehouse to store the unopened, still-shrink-wrapped copies of the software it purchases. The company buys a copy for each LAN user, but continues to use the first copy (installed on the file server). The other copies go into the warehouse. A site license for each of these software products would go a long way toward helping this company administer its LAN, but the company is frustrated by the single-user license agreements of many software vendors (see "Buying Site Licenses" later in this chapter).

Buying Network Packs. A few software vendors handle the multi-user license issue by selling network packs. You buy a license for simultaneous use by up to five or more people. The software resides on the file server, and you get the appropriate number of user manuals to supplement the software. Lotus Development offers a network version of 1-2-3 that takes this approach.

Buying Site Licenses. For more than five people, you really want a site license. This arrangement buys you the legal right for everyone in your office to use the software, and perhaps to make photocopies of the user manual. Not very many software vendors offer site licenses as of yet. If you are part of a large office, however, you should try to insist on a site license when you purchase software. If you can negotiate such an arrangement, both you and the software vendor come out winners. Eventually, you will see site licenses become more common.

Establishing Copy Protection on a LAN. You probably have run into copy-protection schemes before. With many of these schemes, you have to insert a key diskette (that cannot be copied under ordinary circumstances) to activate the software. Some copy-protection schemes put hidden files on your hard disk. Some schemes rely on *dongles*—special hardware keys you attach to the printer port of your computer. Still other schemes mark the location on the hard disk where files reside and do not enable you to copy these files to other locations.

All of these schemes have one objective. The software vendor wants to prevent software *piracy*—the theft of software by merely making additional copies of the application's files. All of these schemes have one common characteristic; they annoy the purchasers of the software.

On a LAN, it is possible to enforce software license agreements unobtrusively and gracefully. The application running at one workstation can communicate with other workstations through the LAN cable to determine if the same copy is being run at different workstations. The peer LAN product Personal NetWare, for example, does exactly this to make sure that you purchase one copy for each workstation. Some LAN management products include license metering functions and usage counters to help you avoid legal problems.

So far this chapter has explained what it means for software to be single-user or multi-user, and you have learned how a network operating system transforms single-user DOS into a multi-user environment on a LAN. You understand rights, permissions, file sharing, record locking, multi-user printing, and multi-user software licenses. In the remainder of this chapter, you focus on the applications. You first cover word processing and desktop publishing applications. You explore the sharing of spreadsheet files on the LAN. You also look closely at the class of personal computer applications known as database managers. DBMS applications are good candidates for multi-user access from LAN workstations because they usually involve great amounts of data entry.

Using Word Processing and Desktop Publishing Programs

You probably would not want another person's typing to mingle with your own as you prepare a memo, letter, or report with a word processing program. Perhaps GroupWare vendors (see Chapter 2, "Sharing Computer Resources") will someday find a good reason to implement concurrent, multi-user file sharing for word processor files, but until then, you will want to restrict your file sharing to loaning copies of your files to others after you have created the files. If you and the other people in your office produce hundreds or thousands of document files, however, you definitely will want to find a way to organize and keep track of all the files.

Sharing Files

On a peer-to-peer LAN, where your workstation is a file server to the other people in the office (and vice versa), you can share files simply by telling another person the name of the file and the directory it is in. If the other person has permission from the network operating system to read files in that directory, you can share your document files with him or her. You may want to set up three directories for document files. You can mark the first directory with permissions that enable other people to read and write files. Such a directory enables everyone to update files, so you must coordinate the updates within your office. The second directory for document files may be flagged with read-only permissions for other people. Such a directory enforces ownership of the files; you are the only one who can update them. Other people can copy the files and make use of their contents, but the read-only directory is your repository of original copies of documents. If you need a place to put private document files that you do not want others to read or write, you may create a third directory and flag it with appropriate permissions to keep prying eyes from peering into your files.

A server-based LAN is slightly different. To share a file, you must create the file on the shared network drive, or copy the file to the network drive after you create it. You may use a directory with read-only permissions (for other people) for serious communications and a second directory with read/write permissions for general correspondence.

Keeping Track of Documents

As document files proliferate in a single directory on the file server, the job of remembering what each one contains becomes monumental. You do not want your effectiveness to drop just because you cannot remember which file is which. When someone asks you for some information you have stored in a document file, you want to be able to find it quickly and easily.

The first thing you can do is houseclean regularly. There is no substitute for periodically (perhaps once a week) going through your document files to decide which ones you no longer need. (If you do happen to delete the wrong file, remember the backup copies your office makes each day. You can recover the file from the backup. Or, if you are on a NetWare LAN, you can use the SALVAGE (discussed in Chapter 6, "Using Novell NetWare") command to restore the file.)

The next thing you want to do is create more directories. You can use the directories on the file server as an outline structure that matches the work you do. By filing your documents in an appropriately named directory, you easily can remind yourself where certain documents are.

You may want to go beyond manual methods for keeping track of files. To automate the indexing of your documents, you will want software that is LAN-aware and easy to use. A good place to start your research is a product called InfoSelect, developed by

MicroLogic
P.O. Box 70
Hackensack, NJ 07602
(800) 342-5930

InfoSelect comes in a LAN version that enables you to share an office-wide Rolodex, schedule meetings, send electronic mail, maintain an office-wide electronic bulletin board, and—of course—index document files on the file server. Another resource is the list of GroupWare vendors in Chapter 11, "Using Electronic Mail."

As you do your research, you will find other products to evaluate—there are several in this category.

Using Spreadsheets

You can manage the sharing of spreadsheet files (worksheets) in a manner similar to the one you use for document files. The contents of spreadsheet files are somewhat more structured and organized than document files. You will want to implement well-known, consistent procedures within the office for sharing the information in spreadsheet files.

Worksheets lend themselves more to a multi-user, file-sharing environment than do document files. Although you still do not want other people's typing to mingle with yours as you enter data into a spreadsheet program, it's easy to see that a useful set of spreadsheet files can be the product of a team of people rather than an individual.

You may find that you want to share specific cells and ranges within a worksheet. You may want to form the habit of inserting remarks somewhere within the spreadsheet file to let others know which parts of the file they should use. You have learned to document your spreadsheets so that you can understand them after being away from them for a while. On a network, you need to extend this documentation to include the things that will help others to understand the information encoded in the files.

Lotus 1-2-3 and Microsoft Excel have features that encourage group usage of a spreadsheet file. These features let users do the following:

Communicate worksheet assumptions to others

Enable others to contribute to the model

Track who changed specific portions of the worksheet

Enable several people to work on a file concurrently

Using Database Managers

A *database* is any collection of related information in the form of lists, tables, notes, or other organizations of data. A database manager (DBMS) is the generalized software that enables you to enter, store, retrieve, process, and report the data. You design an application by telling the DBMS what data you want to keep track of, how it is laid out, how it should be processed, and how the data should be reported. You use the DBMS by subsequently entering data and by instructing the DBMS to process and report the data.

You easily can imagine a group of people entering data from many workstations into the same database. A database manager is a good candidate for LAN-awareness. With the proper file-sharing, record-locking, and workstation-identifying methodologies in place, the database manager becomes an essential tool for recording and processing information in your office. You want to make sure that you get a LAN-aware version of the software; using a single-user version of a DBMS on a LAN can be disastrous. You will find errors and inconsistencies creeping into the data as multiple users try to access the same file server files without the benefit of file sharing and record locking.

As you evaluate database manager products, you will want to apply the criteria in the following checklist:

Installation: You will want to discover how much memory the software uses, what types of memory, and whether you can run the DBMS under Windows or OS/2.

User interface: Decide if you like how the program is designed to interact with you.

Online help and documentation: Look for help screens and written documentation that seems useful to you. If you are new to the DBMS environment, ask if the product comes with a tutorial.

Data types: All DBMS programs enable you to define the data entry fields as numeric or text-based. Other data types you may use include memo/note, telephone number, Social Security, date, and time.

Query formation: A DBMS should offer pick lists and other aids to help you form queries.

Special reports: A DBMS should enable you to design your reports with a report generator, and you should be able to design specially formatted reports without a great deal of programming effort.

Import/export: Look for the capability of the DBMS to import and export a variety of file formats. Make sure that the software can interface with the other applications you use.

SQL usage: Structured Query Language (SQL) is an IBM standard for dealing with databases. If you need to access databases on host computers, or from products such as Microsoft's SQL Server, IBM's DB2 for OS/2, or Gupta Technology's SQLBase, you will want your DBMS to use SQL in a way that is compatible with these other products.

Application code generator: A menu-driven method of creating the procedural statements that make up the processing steps of the application is important, unless you are a professional programmer.

Distributable applications: You may want other people to be able to use the applications you develop. Determine how you can do this with the DBMS you are thinking of buying, and whether you have to pay extra for the capability.

Using Access

Microsoft Access is a Windows-based database manager that offers several interfaces. You can use the product's Windows interface to query and update your data, a computer language called Access Basic (similar to Visual Basic) to program your own applications, and Microsoft's Open Database Connectivity (ODBC) driver to allow Access to interface to other ODBC-compliant database tools and SQL servers.

Like most SQL databases, Access maintains a single disk file per database, storing multiple tables within that file. It's not a database server, however. In a multi-user situation, each Access client must fetch records from shared storage and process them locally. Access does not have FoxPro's blazing speed when querying single tables.

Access can attach and work with Paradox, dBASE, and Btrieve files. Access includes engines that understand Paradox, dBASE, and Btrieve file formats, and it will maintain foreign indexes in place. That means that, for example, Access and Paradox can enjoy concurrent multi-user access to the same shared files. Access's update capability is also a great enhancement to products such as Btrieve (a record manager programming tool from Novell) and FoxPro.

For more information about Access, contact

> Microsoft Corporation
> One Microsoft Way
> Redmond, WA 98052
> (800) 426-9400
> www.microsoft.com

Using dBASE

With Borland International's purchase of Ashton-Tate in 1991, the famed, best-selling dBASE won a new lease on life. When Ashton-Tate released the first version of dBASE IV two years behind schedule, dismayed developers found errors (bugs) in the product that made it virtually unusable. Later versions of dBASE IV contained fixes for the bugs as well as new features, but the product's reputation preceded it, and dBASE IV did not sell well. Other DBMS products offer more features and faster performance than dBASE IV. Application developers hope that Borland turns dBASE IV into a state-of-the-art DBMS.

For years, dBASE was a standard among database manager products. Other DBMS products measure themselves by the ability to import or export dBASE format files. To use dBASE IV to create such files, however, you must be a programmer and know the dBASE programming language. Other products use menus and prompts to help you write programs. dBASE IV comes with a menuing system called Control Center, but this does not help you write programs. Control Center is also not as easy to use as the menuing systems of Paradox or R:BASE.

dBASE does offer a helpful *query by example* (QBE) feature. With QBE, you build and store complex queries that help you find information in your database. The difficult task consists of designing and writing the database application.

The report-generator module of dBASE is similarly helpful. It enables you to quickly produce reports in several standard formats. Custom formats, however, require programming effort on your part. dBASE can have as many as one billion records per database, uses extended and/or expanded memory if present, and supports up to 256 fields per record.

For more information about dBASE, contact

> Borland International
> 1800 Green Hills Road
> Scotts Valley, CA 95067
> (800) 331-0877
> www.borland.com

Using FoxPro

FoxPro, a database manager that Microsoft acquired in its purchase of the Fox Software company, is the fastest-performing DBMS and one of the fastest-selling. These attributes probably account for Microsoft's purchase of Fox Software early in 1992—just a few months after Borland acquired Ashton-Tate's dBASE. Microsoft also offers the Windows-based Access database manager product, described earlier. It will be interesting to see how Microsoft positions Access and FoxPro in the marketplace.

The current FoxPro user interface is text-based rather than graphics-based. FoxPro uses character-mode windows to display data, however, and has a Windows-like set of pull-down and pop-up menus. You can use a mouse with FoxPro, and you can even move FoxPro's windows and press character-mode buttons on-screen to activate options. You can move database fields during a browse operation with click-and-drag mouse actions. Like FoxPro's file operations, the user interface is responsive and quick.

Fast indexing of files is the heart of FoxPro's performance. The relational query-by-example feature lacks most SQL commands but is flexible enough for almost any database inquiry you may want to make. FoxPro offers a range of application design tools to make your job easier. The procedural language is sophisticated, and you can use the optional compiler module to turn your application into executable (EXE) files.

FoxPro is not a simple tool for creating simple databases. This DBMS will likely stretch your programming skills a bit as you develop your first few applications. FoxPro's context-sensitive online help is rich with examples and explanations, but you will find the help text-oriented more toward programmers than novice computer users.

FoxPro can have as many as one billion records per database, uses extended and/or expanded memory if present, and supports up to 255 fields per record.

For more information about FoxPro, contact

> Microsoft Corporation
> One Microsoft Way
> Redmond, WA 98052
> (800) 426-9400
> www.microsoft.com

Using Paradox

Paradox is successful enough that many people wonder why Borland acquired Ashton-Tate and the dBASE products. Paradox is full-featured and easy to learn. You will find Paradox to be almost as fast as FoxPro, even on the largest of databases.

Speed notwithstanding, the Paradox user interface is its strongest selling point. Borland has paid a great deal of attention to the content and organization of the software's menus, help screens, and printed documentation. Borland also offers a Windows version of Paradox.

The straightforward, easy-to-understand approach Paradox takes to application development enables novices and experienced programmers to create sophisticated applications. You quickly can let Paradox build a standard column-oriented report for you, or you can step in and design a custom-formatted report. Paradox imports and exports a wide range of file types. Paradox offers a graphing tool to help you create 10 kinds of graphs, from pie charts to 3-D bar graphs, and contains a query by example module that enables you to simply check off the fields you want included in a query. A separate SQL Link module for accessing SQL database servers is available from Borland.

The Paradox Applications Language (PAL) is not difficult to learn. You even can create a simple application by letting Paradox record your keystrokes in a session; Paradox transforms your keystrokes into a script you can play back later. Experienced PAL programmers can use the script to create a complete application. The version of PAL that comes with Paradox for Windows, Object PAL, is highly object-oriented.

Paradox can have as many as two billion records per database, it uses extended and/or expanded memory if present, and it supports up to 255 fields per record.

For more information about Paradox, contact

> Borland International
> 1800 Green Hills Road
> Scotts Valley, CA 95067
> (800) 331-0877
> www.borland.com

Using R:BASE

R:BASE has been around for almost as long as dBASE. The years of competing with the former Ashton-Tate product have honed its features, help screens, and printed documentation into an easy-to-use DBMS. You can create useful, complete applications just by following R:BASE's application-generator menus. You certainly do not have to be a programmer to use R:BASE.

R:BASE contains a menu-driven query-by-example module that quickly leads you through the formation of a database inquiry. You can convert a query into a new database table if you want. Each R:BASE database can have up to 80 tables (files), and a query can use up to five databases.

R:BASE's menus help you build sophisticated applications. The application-code generator turns your data-entry screens and file descriptions into a custom-programmed application you can use in your office, even if you have never programmed before.

R:BASE comes with a procedural language that is easy to learn. Your application can make use of pull-down menus, help screens, and other features that make it easy to operate your application. The R:BASE programming language provides a full set of SQL commands. R:BASE can import and export dBASE format files.

R:BASE files can have an unlimited number of records per database, depending on the amount of free disk space you have. R:BASE uses extended and/or expanded memory if present, and supports up to 400 fields per record.

For more information about R:BASE, contact

> Microrim
> 15395 S.E. 30th Place
> Bellevue, WA 98007
> (800) 628-6990
> www.microrim.com

Using Relational Database Managers

For transacting with and storing core business data entities such as customers, products, orders, billings, and payments, an RDMS (Relational Database Management System) is an essential part of a business automation strategy. Putting the RDMS on a networked desktop PC is a key ingredient of client/server technology because you put the data (perhaps replicated to and from a central site) close to the people who use and own that data.

The next sections of this chapter examine Oracle (from Oracle Corporation), SQL Server (from either Microsoft or Sybase), and the LAN-based version of DB2 (from IBM). All three products are high quality software that you can trust, and all three companies offer good support and are likely to be around for a while. These products also offer such useful features as stored procedures, triggers, and constraints.

A *stored procedure* is a set of processing steps that execute on the database server PC rather than on the client. A *trigger* is a stored procedure that fires when a specified event (row insertion, deletion, or updating) occurs. A *constraint* is a business rule in the database that specifies acceptable values or relationships among data fields. Database constraints let you enforce referential integrity relationships among your database tables; you can ensure, for example, that no one can delete a customer's account in one table if billing records for that customer still exist in another table. Stored procedures, triggers, and constraints are big-league features that, along with higher capacity and performance, help distinguish these database managers from such products as Access and Paradox.

Performance is certainly a consideration when you're buying an RDMS, but one that's overshadowed by issues such as features, reliability, support, price, and even vendor financial health—you want a database vendor that's going to vigorously support and enhance its product for a long time to come. Performance takes a back seat for two reasons. First, the design of the database itself, rather than the database software, is by far the most important factor governing transaction and query processing times. Next, you can pick and choose different hardware on which to run your database software and thus appropriately scale the database according to the needs of each site that will run the application.

Using Oracle

Oracle runs on over 90 platforms (about 60 of which are UNIX environments). The database software is essentially the same code for each platform; the consistency in Oracle's behavior on the different platforms is amazing. Moving an Oracle database from one platform to another is a simple matter of using the supplied Export and Import utilities. Database administration and design are also consistent among platforms. The same DDL for creating an OS/2 Oracle database can also create a NetWare NLM database, an NT database, or a UNIX database.

Oracle takes advantage of SMP in environments that offer multiple CPUs (OS/2, NT, AIX, SCO). While the previous version of Oracle provided only "strict" data replication through two-phase commit or unsynchronized table snapshots, version 7.1 adds loose, time-delayed replication from a primary database site and optimistic replication that allows any one database site to update without waiting for other sites to catch up. You can configure Oracle to replicate table updates onto another (remote) Oracle database or a DB2 mainframe database.

Like DB2/2, Oracle offers user-defined datatypes and programming interfaces for a wide variety of computer languages, including C, C++, COBOL, and Fortran. Oracle clients can be any combination of DOS, DOS-plus-Windows, OS/2, and Macintosh System 7 LAN-attached computers. Oracle's SQL*NET over-the-wire SQL statement delivery system works with IPX/SPX, NetBIOS/NetBEUI, and TCP/IP transport-layer protocols. Computer programs can use embedded SQL, Oracle's callable programming interface (OCI), or Open DataBase Connectivity (ODBC) to issue SQL statements.

Administering Oracle is easy; Oracle for the OS/2 and NT platforms come with native GUI tools. You administer the NetWare NLM version of Oracle through an over-the-wire Windows interface. You can design an Oracle database to hold both text and image large objects. Oracle, through a separately available product, offers remote administration tools for remote sites that don't have their own database administrator.

Oracle supports the use of triggers, stored procedures, and database constraints through its PL/SQL database server programming environment.

In an effort to improve the processing of SQL statements, Oracle uses an optimizer to pre-digest SQL. As long as statistics exist in the database's data dictionary for at least one of the tables referenced by a SQL statement, the optimizer uses cost-based algorithms to consider the available access paths and determines the most efficient execution plan for that access. The optimizer offers a tuning feature, called HINTS, for those database administrators who want to tweak Oracle's performance. However, the optimizer doesn't offer as many tuning settings as DB2/2.

Oracle supports dynamic and, for embedded SQL, a form of static SQL. However, unlike DB2/2, there is no separate "bind" step the programmer performs during development. The following code fragment is an example that uses Oracle's OCI function call interface. Oracle header files establish new data types, such as text (representing strings) and sword (two-byte word integer), to ensure portability across Oracle-supported platforms. In the code, a call to orlon() performs a logon operation, establishing the link between the program and the database. The oopen() function opens a specific database cursor. And odefin()sets up a buffer to receive the results of a SELECT statement.

```
text *username = (text *) "SCOTT";
text *password = (text *) "TIGER";
text *insert = (text *) "INSERT INTO emp(empno, ename, job, sal, deptno) \
VALUES (:empno, :ename, :job, :sal, :deptno)";
text *seldept = (text *) "SELECT dname FROM dept WHERE deptno = :1";
text *maxemp = (text *) "SELECT NVL(MAX(empno), 0) FROM emp";
text *selemp = (text *) "SELECT ename, job FROM emp";
orlon(&lda, hda, username, -1, password, -1, 0)
oopen(&cda1, &lda, (text *) 0, -1, -1, (text *) 0, -1)
odefin(&cda1, 1, (ub1 *) &empno, (sword) sizeof(sword),
sword) INT_TYPE, (sword) -1, (sb2 *) 0,
(text *) 0, -1, -1,
(ub2 *) 0, (ub2 *) 0)
if (oexfet(&cda1, (ub4) 1, FALSE, FALSE)) {
if (cda1.rc == NO_DATA_FOUND)
empno = 10;
else {
err_report(&cda1);
do_exit(EXIT_FAILURE); } }
```

For more information about Oracle, contact

Oracle Corporation
Redwood Shores, CA 94065
(415) 506-7000
www.oracle.com

Using SQL Server

Microsoft licensed SQL Server for OS/2 from Sybase. In 1993, Microsoft switched SQL Server from OS/2 to its NT operating system and subsequently terminated its business relationship with Sybase. This latest version of SQL Server continues to look much like the Sybase database management products (which run on UNIX platforms), but Microsoft says that from 1993 to now about 60 percent of SQL Server has undergone changes and enhancements. We found that SQL Server's underlying architecture has changed considerably from prior versions. The programming interface and configuration of SQL Server, on the other hand, are very similar to both earlier versions of Microsoft SQL Server and the Sybase product.

One of the best-known ways to connect a SQL Server database to a mainframe DB2 database is MicroDecisionWare's MDI Gateway product. Interestingly, Sybase bought MicroDecisionWare in 1994. Microsoft SQL Server customers who use MDI hope that Microsoft and Sybase relax their strained relationship just enough to allow Sybase to maintain and enhance the MDI product.

SQL Server, which runs only on NT, has a new GUI administration tool called SQL Enterprise Manager (SEM). While previous versions of SQL Server used a text-mode Interactive SQL (ISQL) interface, SQL Server 6.0 has GUI administration tools for DBA (Database Administrator) tasks. The new features Microsoft added to version 6.0 include scrollable cursors, distributed management objects, and extended stored procedures. Before, you coded your SQL Server stored procedures in Microsoft's (Sybase's) Transact-SQL language, and you were limited both in performance and function to the design of Transact-SQL. Extended stored procedures allow SQL Server to use external programs to handle database events. SQL Server, like Oracle, uses a cost-based optimizer to examine and reformat SQL statements.

Microsoft has tightly integrated SQL Server into the NT environment. SQL Server is consistently the same database manager, from both architectural and user interface viewpoints, on Intel, MIPS, or DEC Alpha PCs. NT schedules individual SQL Server threads on different CPUs if your database server is an SMP machine.

SQL Server, like DB2/2 and Oracle, can automatically replicate database changes onto other remote databases. SQL Server 6.0 replication uses a publish-and-subscribe metaphor. A distribution server hosts a distribution database, which holds rows from published tables until SQL Server can copy the rows to the databases which subscribe to the published tables. A publication database can define publication tables and a subscription database can subscribe to those published items. Through SQL Server's SEM interface, replication is particularly easy to set up and configure. However, changes made on a remote SQL Server by means of a remote procedure cannot be rolled back (undone).

SQL Server offers user-defined datatypes and programming interfaces for several computer languages, including C, C++, COBOL, and Fortran. SQL Server clients can run DOS, Windows, or NT. Customers who use OS/2, UNIX, or Macintosh System 7 can purchase ODBC connectivity software from Visigenic Software (San Mateo, CA). You can link to SQL Server through IPX/SPX, NetBIOS/NetBEUI, or TCP/IP transport-layer protocols.

SQL Server supports declarative referential integrity, domain integrity (range validation), entity integrity (row uniqueness), constraints, triggers, and column-level rules and defaults. You can program database queries and updates through Microsoft's DB-lib function call interface or ODBC. Microsoft made substantial improvements to its Transact-SQL language for version 6, and SQL Server integrates especially well with Microsoft's Excel, Access, and Visual Basic products.

The following code fragment shows how to allocate a logon buffer with `dblogin()` and open the database with `dbopen()` and `dbuse()`. The code invokes `dbcmd()` to assemble a SQL statement, then uses `dbsqlexec()` to tell SQL Server to process the SQL. `dbresults()` begins the process of retrieving data, while `dbrows()` discovers how many rows in the table satisfy the SELECT statement. Calls to dbbind() connect program variables to fields in the database, and dbnextrow() lets the program access each returned row.

```
LoginPtr = dblogin();
dbsetlname(LoginPtr, DBLOGINNAME, DBSETUSER);
dbsetlname(LoginPtr, DBLOGINPW,   DBSETPWD);
dbsetlname(LoginPtr, DBLOGINAPP,  DBSETAPP);
dbproc = dbopen(LoginPtr, SERVERNAME);
dbuse(dbproc, "DatabaseName");
dbcmd(dbproc, "select CUST_NO, ");
dbcmd(dbproc, "CUST_NAME, ");
dbcmd(dbproc, "STATE_CD, ");
dbcmd(dbproc, "ZIP_CD, ");
dbcmd(dbproc, "from VCWS_TRIGGER ");
dbcmd(dbproc, "where TRANS_CD = \"1\" ");
rc = dbsqlexec(dbproc);
rc = dbresults(dbproc);
rc = dbrows(dbproc);
dbbind(dbproc,  1, STRINGBIND,  0, CustomerNumber);
dbbind(dbproc,  2, STRINGBIND,  0, CustomerName);
dbbind(dbproc,  3, STRINGBIND,  0, StateCode);
dbbind(dbproc,  4, STRINGBIND,  0, ZipCode);
result = dbnextrow(dbproc);
while (result != NO_MORE_ROWS)
  /* process retrieved data */
```

For more information about SQL Server, contact

Microsoft Corporation
One Microsoft Way
Redmond, WA 98052
(800) 426-9400
www.microsoft.com

Using DB2/2

IBM continues to make DB2 more consistent across PCs (OS/2), RS/6000s (AIX), AS/400s (OS/400), and mainframes. IBM has targeted other platforms for DB2 as well, including HP-UX, Solaris, SINIX (Siemens Nixdorf UNIX), and Windows NT. But DB2 is not yet one database product with a single code base for all these platforms. Slight differences exist among the different versions of the product, most notably in the Data Definition Language (DDL) statements you use to allocate and initialize a new database. You sacrifice a small amount of portability with DB2.

DB2/2 runs on OS/2 and supports Symmetric MultiProcessing (SMP) OS/2. DB2/2 supplies programming interfaces for a wide variety of computer languages, including C, C++, COBOL, and Fortran. IBM's own VisualAge and many third-party products (such as VX-REXX, from Watcom) are excellent add-on tools you can use with DB2/2. Clients for DB2 can be any combination of DOS, DOS-plus-Windows, OS/2, and Macintosh System 7 LAN-attached computers. DB2/2 works with IPX/SPX, NetBIOS/NetBEUI, APPC, and TCP/IP network protocols. Computer programs can use embedded SQL, DB2/2's callable programming interface, or Microsoft's Open DataBase Connectivity (ODBC) to issue Structured Query Language (SQL) statements to query or update the database.

You can configure DB2/2 to replicate data among a set of database servers, and DB2/2 can work through Distributed Database Connection Services (DDCS) or other middleware product to interface with a mainframe DB2 database. DB2/2 administration is easy, either locally or remotely, through GUI administration software. For remote sites that don't have their own database administrator, DB2/2 offers remote administration tools. A separate product, Visualizer, lets you build, update, or query your database (IBM previously shipped a Query Manager component with DB2/2). IBM supplies its Explain software with DB2/2; Explain is an optimization tool that reveals the detail of the steps DB2/2 uses during a database query or update.

DB2/2 2.1 subjects SQL statements to one of nine levels of optimization just prior to processing those statements. The nine levels, configurable by a database administrator or settable by application software, allow precise tuning of database response times. You would use level 0 or 1 for SQL that is already optimized by the programmer. Higher levels let DB2/2 examine and reformat SQL submitted by, for instance, a front-end query tool such as Microsoft Access.

DB2/2 supports both large text and large image objects, such as pictures, songs, and books. IBM uses Gradient Technology's license-tracking software in DB2/2 to help businesses manage the number of concurrent DB2 licenses they've purchased.

A programmer can design a program to emit either dynamic or static SQL to DB2. DB2 compiles dynamic SQL at runtime. *Dynamic* SQL can be a string of text, for instance, that someone types into a program at a command line prompt. In contrast, *static* SQL consists of statements, embedded directly in the program, that are fully known at program compile time. Pre-compile and post-compile steps, in a process IBM calls "binding," store the static SQL statements in files with a .BND extension. In general, static SQL executes much faster than dynamic SQL.

The following is an example of dynamic SQL in C. The EXEC SQL PREPARE statement causes DB2 to dynamically compile the SQL statement in the variable string. The sequence of CONNECT, PREPARE, DECLARE, OPEN, FETCH, and CLOSE statements shown in the code are typical of DB2/2 programs.

```
EXEC SQL BEGIN DECLARE SECTION;
    char   server[9];
    char   userid[9];
    char   passwd[19];
EXEC SQL END DECLARE SECTION;
EXEC SQL CONNECT TO :server USER :userid USING :passwd;
printf("Enter SQL statement: "); gets(string);
EXEC SQL PREPARE statement1 from :string;
EXEC SQL DECLARE pcurs CURSOR FOR statement1;
EXEC SQL OPEN pcurs;
EXEC SQL FETCH pcurs USING DESCRIPTOR :*sqldaPointer;
while (SQLCODE == 0) {
    display_da (sqldaPointer);
    EXEC SQL FETCH pcurs USING DESCRIPTOR :*sqldaPointer; }
EXEC SQL CLOSE pcurs;
```

The following shows an example of static SQL. The entire SQL statement is known at compile time.

```
EXEC SQL SELECT FIRSTNME INTO :firstname
         FROM employee
         WHERE LASTNAME = 'JOHNSON';
```

For more information about DB2, contact

IBM
Armonk, NY 10504
(800) 342-6672
(801) (914) 765-1900
www.ibm.com

SQL Compilers

The database engine's SQL compiler is arguably the most important part of an RDMS. The SQL compiler has to recognize and understand natural language (SQL), then turn the SQL statements into "instructions" that it gives to the database engine's retrieval and update processes. The SQL compiler's job is compounded by the fact that it has to operate in real time as quickly as possible.

An SQL compiler process an SQL statement in five basic steps. The first step parses the SQL, examines the SQL for syntax errors, then converts the SQL parse tree into an internal representation (IBM, which invented SQL, calls the internal format the Query Graph Model, or QGM). The second step examines the reformatted SQL to ensure that executing the statement won't violate referential integrity. The second step also notes whether the database engine should process a constraint or trigger for the SQL.

Next, the SQL compiler rewrites the SQL statement, replacing view references with actual column names and transforming the SQL for processing by the optimizer. The transformation eliminates redundant joins, adds implied predicates, and converts INTERSECT clauses to EXISTS subqueries. The optimizer itself, the fourth step, uses cost-based algorithms to determine the most efficient execution method for the SQL. The optimizer finds the best join order, for example, and decides whether the execution of the SQL statement will be CPU- or I/O-bound. The optimizer chooses an execution path for the SQL statement that will result in the quickest response from the database engine. The fifth step "remembers" the essence of the SQL for later comparison with other SQL statements—the SQL compiler keeps a history of how well it optimizes statements so it can "learn" the fastest ways to access the database. Finally, the SQL compiler's fifth step delivers the compiled, optimized SQL statement to the retrieval and update processes in the database engine.

Database Performance

The design of your database governs performance to a much greater degree than your choice of database software. Most databases can benefit from changes in table design, choice of index columns, and query design. If you focus first on these areas, you'll reap the most rewards from your efforts to make your database perform faster.

Normalizing the design of a database entails the elimination of redundant data, the avoidance of repeating data groups, and the creation of separate tables to hold different categories of data. A properly normalized database generally has many tables with relatively few columns in each. Normalization can improve database performance for the following reasons:

- Fewer columns in a table imply faster sorting and faster index creation.

- Indexes can be clustered because there are more tables.

- Indexes can be more compact.

- Fewer indexes per table suggest INSERT, UPDATE, and DELETE statements will process faster.

Choosing indexes and keys that help normalize the data can help performance. Simplifying long-running queries through the use of appropriate keys and indexes can reduce response times, and you might consider running complex queries that look at entire tables during times of the day when transaction volume is low.

Chapter Summary

This chapter brought you up to date on network applications and what makes them different from stand-alone software. You first covered how DOS behaves in a multi-user environment, and you then learned how the network operating system implements rights and permissions. After exploring the characteristics of multi-user applications—sharing files, locking records, identifying each user or workstation, and printing correctly on a shared LAN printer—you considered the software licensing issues you face on a LAN. You looked at word processing, desktop publishing, and spreadsheets from a multi-user point of view.

In the next chapter, you see how to manage your LAN so that it stays healthy and efficient.

Chapter 11

Using Electronic Mail

Electronic mail is the most popular add-on feature for local-area networks. You should have no trouble getting an e-mail product that is to your liking. Several commercial products exist. In some cases, the network operating system vendor bundles e-mail software with the network software. As you will see in this chapter, you can even find free e-mail applications to try out.

You learn how electronic mail works, and you find out how you can use it to your best advantage. You explore two of the industry standards for e-mail: Action Technologies' Message Handling Service (MHS) and the CCITT X.400 specification. Next, you become acquainted with the electronic equivalent of address lists (so you can send copies of a note to many people), and you discover the practical advantages of attaching files to your e-mail notes. You learn about several of the popular e-mail products. The chapter closes with a look at Groupware—the new class of software products designed to enhance the productivity of a team of people through e-mail and e-mail extensions.

An E-Mail Overview

Electronic mail can replace both voice mail (answering machines) and interoffice memos. In its simplest form, e-mail consists of a mechanism for transferring a file of text from you to one or more people. On a LAN, this may take the form of merely copying a text file into a personal post-office directory on the file server so the recipient can open and read his or her mail. This simplest of approaches does nothing for privacy and security, however. Most products elaborate greatly on this approach, using file encryption or directory and file permissions to enforce security.

Electronic mail offers several advantages over telephone calls and interoffice memos. These advantages let you do the following:

■ Send a message to one or more people quickly.

■ Send detailed information to someone who can store it for future reference.

- Put information in shared folders where others can read it and give comments.

- Allow recipients to read your message at a convenient time, without disrupting their productivity.

- Maintain copies of your electronic-mail correspondence.

Electronic mail does not need to be LAN-based. You can subscribe to a number of commercial services that offer e-mail. To use one of these services, you simply dial a number with your modem, log on to the service, and begin using that service's e-mail commands. You can compose your messages on-line, but, if the service charges on a connect-time basis, you may find it cheaper to compose your messages off-line and then quickly upload them to the service once on-line. These e-mail services include MCI Mail, CompuServe, BIX, Delphi, Prodigy, Western Union's EasyLink, AT&T Mail, America Online, the Internet, and others. Which service is best depends on your budget and, of course, on whether your correspondents are also on that same service.

Understanding E-Mail Components

E-mail products show off the best features of a LAN-based computer. You can easily compose and route mail to all your correspondents, whether they're across the hall or (through a modem) across the country. Under the hood, e-mail systems that use file servers are fairly straightforward. A central database contains the names and locations of all mail users. A second database holds individual mail messages and attached files. You will find that LANs are the most frequently used medium for routing e-mail from place to place. The more sophisticated packages also can send messages across longer distances—by way of a modem (over dial-up lines), through dedicated (leased) telephone lines, or through LAN bridges. Figure 11.1 illustrates one workstation sending an inter-office memo, electronically, to another workstation.

All e-mail software packages include a post-office component and a user-interface component. The software post-office component, like the real U.S. Postal Service, takes a completed mail message, decodes the address, and sends the message to its destination. Depending on the address, your message may be routed across the office through the LAN, through other computer systems in your office to another LAN, or across the country via gateways and bridges. Software post offices should be invisible. It is crucial that the software post office be reliable and prompt. And, if you expect people in your office to use e-mail instead of interoffice paper memos (or instead of Federal Express), the product must have a good interface.

The quality of the user interface is a primary factor in determining whether e-mail will fall into disuse or become an essential tool in the everyday operation of your office. If the software is obtuse, or if it lacks the features people need to enable them to communicate, the e-mail product will quickly gather dust.

The text editor within the e-mail system must be friendly and easy enough to use for infrequent, novice e-mail users, and it must be fast and powerful for those who use the e-mail system many times each day. If the text editor imposes constraints on the size of a mail message you can type, the e-mail system must enable you to attach longer files that you have created with a word processor or other application. The text editor must enable you to quickly correct typing mistakes—even those in the mail header, where the recipient's name and address show.

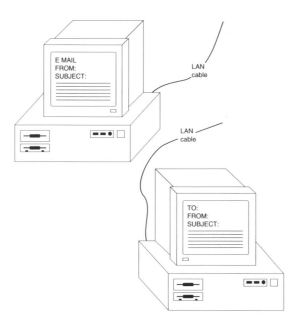

Fig. 11.1 Use electronic mail to send memos from PC to PC.

Looking at the Perfect E-Mail Package

Everyone knows that effective communications contribute positively to the bottom line. If a business does not communicate well (with a remotely-located sales staff, for example) profits may suffer accordingly. Successful companies have learned the value of communications, including tools such as electronic mail products.

Phone tag is a frustrating game that no one likes to play. A good e-mail package helps you to avoid the game by putting messages squarely on the desktop of the other person. With most e-mail packages, you can enclose (attach) files that contain graphics images, a software update (executable file), or a lengthy report (a document file).

Most e-mail products are somewhat expensive (although you will learn about two free ones later in this chapter). For a small LAN, price may be an overriding concern. In a large workgroup environment, however, where you are trying to establish electronic mail between different kinds of computers and networks, support and training will be your major expenses. If a vendor offers a product that connects all your computers, along with support and training, you probably will find yourself doing business with that vendor.

Some e-mail products may provide security when accessed across the network from workstations, but do nothing to prevent access from the server itself. You may need to lock your server in a secure place to prevent unauthorized tampering with the mail directories and files.

Generally speaking, electronic-mail products are not particularly easy to install or maintain. You should consider e-mail software to be in the same class as file-server software. Your network administrator should install the product, set up the user lists, and get the bridges connected (if appropriate). A system administrator should be able to easily manage an e-mail system, but for large installations that require bridges and gateways, help from an experienced installer is invaluable.

Another consideration is whether an e-mail system offers a mail front end for the different kinds of microcomputer systems and operating environments that everyone in your office is using. Some products offer front ends for Macintosh, OS/2, Windows 3, and even NewWave users, in addition to the DOS version that virtually every system comes with. (NewWave is a Windows 3.1 shell environment developed by Hewlett-Packard.) If you want to share mail with UNIX workstation users, you'll want to be sure the e-mail vendor offers a UUCP (UNIX-to-UNIX copy) or SMTP (Simple Mail Transfer Protocol) gateway. Through a UUCP or an SMTP gateway, UNIX users can send and receive e-mail to and from other computers.

Some e-mail products support a few specific types of network operating systems. Other products will work with any LAN that supports DOS file locking. All packages offer at least a rudimentary text editor, and some offer a graphics editor as well. Some products restrict the number and type of files you can attach. And not all e-mail programs encrypt files—an important consideration if you don't want your mail read by others.

Some electronic mail products have add-ons you may want. These include voice-mail capabilities (the capability to annotate an e-mail message with a short sound recording), on-line conferencing (the ability to "chat" between workstations), and the capability to set up bulletin boards where people can post public messages. Many products also enable you to call in and download your mail messages when you are out of the office.

Using Special Delivery

An e-mail bridge connects two similar e-mail systems. When your LAN post-office software realizes it has to send a message to a separate post office, the originating post office must put the message into a special envelope and do some extra work to deliver the message to the other post office. To send the mail across town or across the country, the sending post office uses a company-wide address list to find the phone number of the other office. It then dials up the other post office and transfers the message through a modem. The receiving post office, once it has received the message and opened the special envelope, treats the resulting mail message like all the others it deals with locally. The receiving post office simply routes the incoming message to the addressee on the local LAN.

In contrast to an e-mail bridge, an e-mail gateway translates between different message formats when the two post offices use different mail systems. Sometimes this translation is simply the rearranging of address (and return address) information. Or the translation process may be much more involved. The translation almost always has to convert from one format of account identification to that of the other mail system.

You may need such a gateway if you do business through commercial e-mail services, such as Western Union's EasyLink or AT&T Mail. The gateway collects your outgoing messages, dials the e-mail provider on a periodic schedule, sends the outgoing messages, and picks up any incoming messages. Some services also provide their own gateway software that routes messages between LAN-based e-mail systems by way of the e-mail service.

Deciding Whether You Need E-Mail

You may want to evaluate whether you actually need e-mail. Vendors of e-mail products will, of course, tell you that you need e-mail. E-mail can have a few drawbacks, however. For some products, for example, you need to be at your workstation to see the notification that you have something in your electronic in-basket. If you are away from your desk, you may miss the notification, and you will have to look in your in-basket to see what new mail you have. On a NetWare LAN, however, if the e-mail product uses the Send facility to notify you of incoming mail, the notification will sit at the bottom of your screen until you press Ctrl+Enter. On Macintosh-based e-mail systems, the Apple menu icons blink until you enter the e-mail system.

Another consideration is the size and organization of your office. If you have a fairly small office, with people who are located close to one another, e-mail may not be for you. Besides the cost of the e-mail product and the amount of file-server disk space allocated to e-mail, you will incur administrative costs. For the small office, you may well find that a sticky note or a tap on someone's shoulder is just as effective as e-mail. Technology for its own sake is not the answer.

If your company is geographically dispersed, if your office is large, if your workspace uses high partitions to separate people, or if you find it difficult to get the right people together to discuss your projects, e-mail may be the solution. In fact, if it sometimes takes more time to set up meetings in your office than the meetings themselves take, you will be interested in the workgroup-scheduling software mentioned later in this chapter.

Using MHS, X.400, and Other Standards

E-mail systems do not adhere to a universal standard for addressing and sending messages. Such a standard exists, in the form of the CCITT X.400 specification, but X.400 is difficult and cumbersome to administer and use. Most e-mail products instead use a de facto standard created by Action Technologies—Message Handling Service (MHS).

The X.400 Standard

The international e-mail interexchange standard, X.400, is so complex and costly to implement that currently only large enterprise-wide networks and commercial e-mail service providers use X.400 gateways.

X.400 is a CCITT standard; it defines how an intersystem mail message is addressed. When someone says "X.400," he or she usually is referring not only to the addressing standard but also a number of other CCITT e-mail standards. Among these are X.401, which describes the basic intersystem service elements, and X.411, which defines message-transfer protocols.

The most important member of the X.400 family of standards is X.410, which defines mail-handling protocols. X.410 deals with how Open Systems Interconnection (OSI) protocols work for e-mail applications. True e-mail interoperability is possible through these standards. Not all X.400 systems implement the standards properly, however. Some systems, for example, cannot reliably send binary files or Group 3 faxes (the most popular high-speed fax standard) from one network to another, even though such file transfer is part of the X.400 standard.

X.400 is becoming popular for international e-mail. U.S. Sprint, with its Telemail software, is a leader in providing overseas e-mail links. Administrators of Telemail networks, however, sometimes do not activate every connection with every possible e-mail domain, so you may not have access to overseas e-mail even if you use Telemail. On the other hand, some IBM proprietary e-mail systems do have X.400 gateways to Telemail.

Other obstacles to using X.400 exist. You must have a gateway from your LAN to an X.25 packet-switching network (like Telenet or Tymnet) to use X.400, and X.25 gateways are not common.

The X.400 Application Program Interface Association (APIA), founded in 1989, develops application programming interface standards between LAN e-mail systems, wide-area-network e-mail systems, gateways, and X.25 networks. Products using the X.400 API can connect your office's mail system to other mail systems. Such efforts are just beginning, and they will take years to bear fruit.

How do you address an X.400 e-mail message to someone? Basically, you format your text file with address elements that are defined in the standard. The e-mail system administrator assigns a unique originator/recipient name to every user. The format for an originator/recipient identifier follows:

keyword:value, keyword:value

Each keyword is an address element. Most e-mail systems use only a few address elements, but X.400 enables a system to use a dozen or more.

Every address contains certain common elements. For example, all X.400 addresses include an ADMD (Administrative Management Domain). An ADMD is a public-mail system (such as MCI Mail) that serves as a message-transfer system. A private mail domain (PRMD), such as a LAN e-mail system, can be attached to public networks like Telemail or MCI Mail.

A user name, user number, or a combination of first name and surname uniquely identifies an individual in his or her home mail system. A WidgetMail user, for example, who happens to work at the Widget Company, might be identified like this:

ADMD:MCIMail, PRMD:WidgetMail, FN:Barry, SN:Nance

The order in which the keywords and values appear does not matter.

As you can see from this scheme, keeping track of someone's e-mail address can require a sophisticated computer system and database. Knowing when you can use shortcut names and when you must use the elaborate form of the address is tricky. Fortunately, a new standard (labeled X.500 by the CCITT organization) addresses just this issue. A few years from now, X.500 will help you keep your mail messages from falling into a global dead-letter bin.

As defined by the CCITT, X.500 is a directory-assistance system for computers. X.500 database systems will contain the e-mail addresses of all users with accounts in X.400-type systems around the world. Such a global directory will take a long time to appear, of course.

The MHS Standard

Before the Message Handling Service, each electronic mail product stored its messages in files formatted in such a way that other products could not use the files. The addressing schemes used to identify recipients were proprietary. Action Technologies published the MHS standard to overcome these limitations. Action Technologies also wrote software that implements MHS on NetWare LANs, and Novell bundles MHS with each copy of NetWare it sells.

An MHS gateway requires its own dedicated server, but MHS is a convenient way of moving information between e-mail systems. Because many vendors of e-mail products support MHS, MHS has become the least common denominator for interconnecting workgroup e-mail systems.

MHS provides a standard directory-and-file structure on the file server, into which any mail application can drop messages. MHS puts the incoming messages in specific locations and manages the flow of messages between mail centers. When you install MHS, you create a publicly accessible server directory structure. Anyone on the network can create a message and give it to MHS for delivery. After you create the message, the MHS utility software sees the message and processes it.

A standard MHS packet is an ASCII text file containing several information items, each in a special format. A version number appears first and tells MHS that this is an MHS mail packet. The next line has the To field, and the following line has the From field. Your e-mail software has the responsibility of handling the addressing and providing complete MHS addresses.

If you address the message to a user on the same MHS server, the server simply copies the file to that user's MHS mailbox. Periodically, an MHS e-mail software module polls the mailbox, looking for new messages. When the module finds a new message, the MHS module copies it from the MHS mailbox to the e-mail mailbox. If the address is for another mail center, MHS moves the message to an out-basket directory for further processing. At a time determined by the MHS scheduler, the MHS server picks up the out-basket mail and sorts it by destination. The server uses the modem to establish a connection to the other mail center and then transfers the mail to the remote MHS site.

In turn, the remote MHS server collects the messages and sorts them by address. After a mail message is sorted, it is handled like all other messages on that LAN. As far as a user at the remote site is concerned, the only difference is that delivery of mail is not instantaneous. The e-mail software does not have to know about gateways and bridges. It just puts an address (in an MHS-recognizable format) on the mail message and hands the message to MHS.

The MHS scheduler can execute programs as part of its periodic, scheduled processing. These programs are usually file converters or message formatters that help the messages appear in a format another mail system can understand.

Action Technologies' Message Handling Service is less sophisticated than X.400, but MHS is more widely implemented in smaller workgroup environments that need to interconnect dissimilar e-mail systems. For more information on MHS, contact:

Action Technologies
2200 Powell Street
11th Floor
Emeryville, CA 94608
(800) 967-5356
(510) 521-6190
www.actiontech.com

Using Address Lists and Attached Files

You probably do not need an X.500 super phonebook yet, but you do need a simple way to address a mail message to a given group of people. Most e-mail products enable you to establish address lists. You can use the name of the group (Everyone, ProjectTeam, or Managers) to refer to all the people in that group when you address your mail. Sometimes, an e-mail product will use a network operating system's own groups. Pegasus Mail, a free electronic mail package from David Harris of Dunedin, New Zealand, is such a product (see the section "Pegasus Mail," later in this chapter).

You also need a way to attach files—perhaps a spreadsheet file or GIF or JPEG file containing a diagram—to the e-mail notes you send. Some e-mail applications support attached files directly by incorporating the actual binary file in the e-mail note. Such applications typically surround the attached binary file with internal markers that only the application recognizes, telling the recipient there's an attached file. Other applications specially encode the binary file in 7-bit ASCII form, using conventions such as base 64 notation or UUEncoding. Such ASCII-encoded files remain intact when traversing e-mail network paths that don't allow full 8-bit data transmission. The best example of a network path that often doesn't allow 8-bit character transmission is the Internet. Internet-aware e-mail applications make use of MIME headers to separate the body of an e-mail note from an attached file, as well as base 64 notation or UUEncoding to convert the attached file into 7-bit form.

Using a File Server as a Post Office

If the e-mail package your office selects becomes a frequently used, popular tool, you will find that the tons of interoffice paper mail that used to circulate in your office now reside on the file server. Your office will save on paper costs, but at the expense of some disk space on the server.

The network administrator will keep an eye on disk space usage for the mail system. When it grows beyond a reasonable threshold, he or she will circulate an e-mail message admonishing people to clean out their in-baskets and delete old mail.

Suppose that someone looks at his or her in-basket and sighs, "I have too many old messages to delete one by one; I'll go into the mail directory and do a DELETE *.* DOS command to save myself time." This is the time your security system should take over. If a person can use a DELETE or ERASE command in the mail directory, he or she also may have file-read rights and be tempted to read other people's mail. Or, if the person does not realize that other people's mail messages exist in that directory, a DELETE *.* command could wipe out everyone's mailbox in the post office.

The mail directory on the file server is as important as any other directory. The interoffice memos in that directory are an important part of your business, and they deserve the same backup procedures you would implement for the other directories on the server.

Using E-Mail Products

You have acquired a good understanding of e-mail concepts, standards, and practices. You are almost certainly curious about specific e-mail products. The next few sections of this chapter will satisfy your curiosity. You will learn about Pegasus Mail, cc:Mail, Da Vinci eMAIL, Higgins Mail, Microsoft Mail, and Lotus Notes.

Pegasus Mail

Pegasus Mail is free and works well. Pegasus Mail is easy to install and use. And Pegasus Mail uses NetWare's own user identification and group names to send and receive mail. Unless you have a nonNetWare workgroup environment, and unless you need MHS or X.400, you owe it to yourself to try Pegasus Mail. Look for Pegasus on bulletin boards in your area, on CompuServe, or on BIX (file name PMAIL21.EXE in LANs/Listings).

Pegasus works only on NetWare LANs. Using NetWare's own user identifications and groups, Pegasus needs no separate registration of mail users. You find out about incoming mail in either of two ways. The NewMail program, which a system administrator usually puts in everyone's log-in script so that it executes whenever you log on, informs you of new mail. While logged on to the LAN, you receive notifications of new mail through NetWare's Send facility. Send puts a message at the bottom of your screen; you press Ctrl+Enter after you have read it. Figure 11.2 shows the main Pegasus Mail screen.

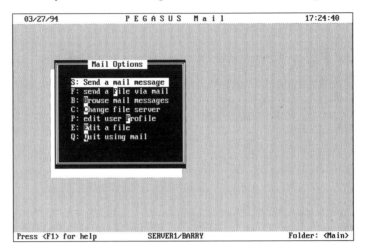

Fig. 11.2   The main Pegasus Mail screen lets you send and receive e-mail as well as select your e-mail preferences.

You can build personal address lists and distribution lists with Pegasus. Pegasus is highly configurable. Forwarding mail messages to other people is possible with Pegasus, as is archiving old mail. The text-mode version of Pegasus includes a capable text editor some-what reminiscent of WordStar in both appearance and keystroke commands. There's also a Windows version of Pegasus.

Installation of Pegasus is merely a matter of copying a few selected files into a public directory from which everyone can find and execute the software. You can begin using Pegasus immediately.

If you want to correspond with the author of Pegasus, David Harris, here is his address:

David Harris
Pegasus Mail
P.O. Box 5451
Dunedin, New Zealand

cc:Mail

cc:Mail comes in DOS, Windows, OS/2, and Mac versions. cc:Mail offers optional gate-ways to many other types of e-mail systems, and the software uses your network file server to provide mail services. It encrypts mail messages and stores them as data files on the server hard disk. Installation and administration are not easy. You follow the instruc-tions in the sizable administrator's manual to manually copy files during installation; cc:Mail does not come with an automatic installation program.

On a Macintosh, a desk accessory (DA) provides notification services, and a separate application program manages your mailbox. When you first run cc:Mail, the software gives you a Standard File dialog box you use to place the mail files on the server. cc:Mail then creates its Post_Office file. Thereafter, you simply double-click on this file to start cc:Mail. The software stores information (the path to the server and your user name) in this file to establish future connections. A set of icons on your Macintosh screen gives you buttons that you click on to provide mail services such as reading, composing, and deleting messages. Each button has an equivalent menu selection. You open highlighted mail entries by clicking the mouse or pressing the Return key. Attached files are document icons in a sub-window; double-clicking them tells cc:Mail to show you the file's contents. You can view graphics files sent from the PC on your Macintosh (cc:Mail saves them in PICT format). The Notify Desk Accessory running on the Macintosh computer polls the server at user-defined intervals for new messages. A small window or a chime tells you that you have new mail.

In contrast to their Macintosh counterparts, PC users run the Mail and Notify programs to manage their mailboxes. An optional TSR program alerts you to incoming messages. The Messenger module also can provide notification and sets up a hot key you can use to access mail services. Each time you run one of these cc:Mail modules, you supply the path to the mail directory, your mail name, and your password. Under Windows 3.1, an icon of a postage stamp represents the minimized Notify program. You use Notify to list the messages in your mailbox and to start cc:Mail.

The cc:Mail interface for IBM PC compatibles is different from the Mac interface, naturally. You navigate through a set of prompts and menu options to manage your mail. A built-in graphics editor enables you to draw images that you can attach to a message, and the Snapshot TSR enables you to capture and send screens from any application. Figure 11.3 shows the cc:Mail screen you use to send mail messages.

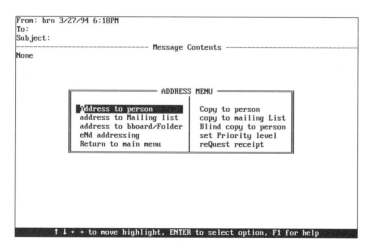

Fig. 11.3   The cc:Mail electronic mail product runs on several different platforms.

If you are interested in sending voice-mail attachments to your cc:Mail messages, you can buy VoxLink's VoxVoice (software, $2,000) or VoxMail (hardware and software,

$5,000). You use your telephone to call the voice-mail server to record messages, which VoxLink's software then attaches to cc:Mail messages.

For more information on cc:Mail, contact:

Lotus Development Corporation
55 Cambridge Parkway
Cambridge, MA 02142
(617) 577-8500

Microsoft Mail

You can get Microsoft Mail in one of three editions to suit an organization of almost any size. For small LANs, the Mail application that is part of Windows for Workgroups lets you point and click to send your memos to others. Windows for Workgroups Mail is useful when you have from 3 to 25 people in an office who need to stay in touch with one another. For larger groups or for groups dispersed geographically, you can get the Microsoft Mail and Schedule+ Extensions product. Or you may find that you need the complete Microsoft Mail product. Microsoft Mail provides electronic mail within a LAN, between LANs connected by modems, or between LANs and outside mail services such as MCI Mail. Microsoft Mail works with computers running the DOS, Windows, System 7 (Macintosh), and OS/2 operating systems.

To use Microsoft's electronic mail software products, you should first designate a member of your team as mail administrator. The administrator initializes the mail system by creating a post office on a file server computer and then adds the names of the team members to the address list for the post office. Thereafter, the administrator manages the disk space and the list of authorized mail-system users.

The computer you designate to hold the post office directory doesn't have to be the fastest machine in the office. You will, however, want to use a machine that stays powered on most of the time. If the post office computer isn't running when someone wants to send mail, the mail will be delayed.

Each person on the LAN manages his or her own disk space for saved mail messages; the mail administrator manages the disk space occupied by shared folders on the post office computer. A shared folder is a common, public access area that everyone in the workgroup can use. Each person on your team can open shared folders and view the mail messages in the shared folder, as well as create a new shared folder in the post office. The person gives other team members access to the new shared folder through access permissions (Read, Write, or Delete).

The mail administrator checks the status of shared folders to monitor the disk space those folders consume. When the mail administrator decides that the post office computer is low on available disk space, he or she can compress the space used by the folders. After compression, if the post office computer is still low on disk space, the administrator can encourage people to delete old mail messages or unused folders. The administrator can delete the entire post office, change the name of the post office, or move the post office directory to a new location.

Each workstation on the LAN has a private mail message file named MSMAIL.MMF. This message file is your private mailbox. When the Mail application software notices you have incoming mail, Mail retrieves it from the team's post office directory and stores the message in your mail message file. If you find you want to send mail but aren't connected to the LAN—perhaps you have a portable notebook computer and you're on a business trip—you can use Mail as you ordinarily would, even though you might be on an airplane or in a hotel room. Later, when you reconnect your notebook computer to the network, your Mail application can transmit your messages to the post office.

Windows for Workgroups electronic mail doesn't do a good job of allowing more than one person to access Mail from a single workstation. As noted, the MSMAIL.MMF file is a mailbox for all incoming mail on a workstation. You can set up a manual procedure for creating multiple instances of the MSMAIL.MMF file, but the procedure is somewhat tedious and error-prone. Microsoft recommends that two people who want to access Mail from the same workstation maintain their own MSMAIL files, using each person's initials as the file extension (MSMAIL.JJG and MSMAIL.RMY, for example). Microsoft recommends also that, before starting Mail, you copy the other person's MSMAIL file to MSMAIL.<initials> and then rename your copy of your personal MSMAIL file to MSMAIL.MMF. You must remember to do the copying and renaming operations before another person can access Mail.

You click the Compose icon or use the Compose Note menu item in the Mail menu to access the Send Note window. You use this window to address your message to one or more team members, indicate the subject of the memo, type the message, optionally specify how you want Mail to handle this particular message, and send the message to the recipient(s). When you send your note, the recipient's Mail application beeps, and the recipient sees a new message header appear in the inbox. The mail icon in the lower right corner of the Mail window becomes a picture of an envelope in a mail slot, and the summary information on the bottom line of the Mail window changes to show the recipient has a new, unread message. You can attach a file to your mail message, if you like. The file might be a spreadsheet, a chart, an image, or another DOS file related to your mail message. Figure 11.4 is the initial Microsoft Mail screen.

For more information about Microsoft Mail, contact:

Microsoft Corporation
One Microsoft Way
Redmond, WA 98052
(800) 426-9400

DaVinci eMAIL

DaVinci Systems has versions of eMAIL for DOS, Windows, OS/2, and NewWave environments. Under DOS, you can run eMAIL as a stand-alone application or as a pop-up TSR program. The micro TSR mode that DaVinci Systems designed into eMAIL uses a hard-disk swap file to store portions of the executable program. The result is that the eMAIL TSR takes up only 10K of RAM. You define a hot-key sequence that swaps out your current application and loads eMAIL. When you exit eMAIL, the TSR restores the interrupted application where it left off. eMAIL can use the NetWare Send mechanism to notify you of incoming mail, or you can load a TSR that presents a one-line message at the bottom of the screen. Windows alerts appear for a definable amount of time (the default is 20 seconds) and then disappear.

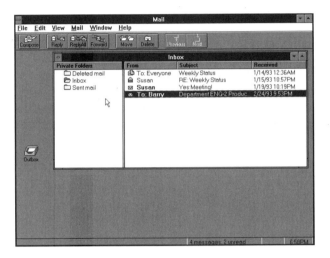

Fig. 11.4 Microsoft Mail, part of Microsoft Exchange, works on Windows-based computers.

The user interface of the DOS version is essentially a blank screen. You can press the F8 key to bring up option menus, but otherwise eMAIL presents you with little information to go on. You will want to keep the manual at your side if you are an infrequent user of eMAIL. The Windows version, on the other hand, is easy to use; it puts the mail functions into drop-down menus, just as you would expect.

eMAIL enables you to attach files to messages. Under Windows, you can send the contents of the Windows Clipboard to other Windows users. You copy some information to the Clipboard, attach the Clipboard data to your mail message, and the recipient simply pastes it into an application.

Security is not eMAIL's long suit, and you will want to take extra precautions for messages you send through eMAIL. The mail message files on the file server are easy for anyone to find. And messages are, by default, unencrypted. You must specifically request encryption when you send a mail message. Encrypted messages cannot be read by other people, and the recipient of such a message must supply a password to read the message.

You can configure eMAIL for each user. eMAIL maintains personal information files that define how eMAIL operates on users' systems. A person can change the polling frequency for incoming messages and the alert procedure, and he or she can customize the frequency and duration of the message-alert sounds by changing the MAIL.INI file. You may want to use this feature in an office where computers are close to one another, so that people can easily tell who has received mail.

For more information about eMAIL, contact:

DaVinci Systems
P.O. Box 17449
Raleigh, NC 27619
(800) 326-3556

Higgins Mail

Higgins Mail is a subset of Enable Software's workgroup scheduler software, and it runs on PC/DOS and OS/2 computers. Higgins Mail uses an electronic slip of paper metaphor to help you manage your mail messages.

If you have used Microsoft Word 5.0, with its Escape-for-menu, single-keypress-selects-option interface, you will be right at home with Higgins Mail. You press Esc to bring up the menu at the bottom of the screen, and then you press the appropriate key to choose a menu option. When you select an edit function, the menu disappears. Pressing Esc switches you from the editing window back to the menu. Context-sensitive help messages constantly tell you where you are, what you are doing, and what you can do next.

The shared Higgins Mail database on the file server uses a proprietary storage format, and Higgins Mail encrypts the messages in the database. It supports file attachments. Higgins Mail is quite popular, and a number of gateways exist to transfer mail between Higgins Mail and other e-mail systems.

You establish both nicknames (aliases) and full-user names when you install Higgins Mail. The software maintains a list of registered mail users. When you send a mail message, Higgins Mail shows you a list of people in what it calls the default domain. A domain is a group of people and resources on the LAN. You choose recipients from the default list or select a different domain of names. Your mailing address on the LAN consists of three items in the following format:

Domain:Workgroup:UserID

The Higgins Mail software module that notifies you of incoming mail is called *Mailcall*. This is a small (3.5K) TSR that displays a message for 10 seconds or until you press a key. If the new mail remains unread by you, Mailcall periodically displays the same message to remind you that you have mail. If you are away from your desk when mail arrives, Higgins Mail ensures that you will find out about it when you return.

For more information about Higgins Mail, contact:

Enable Software
Northway Ten Executive Park
Ballston Lake, NY 12019
(800) 888-0684

Other E-Mail Products

You may want to research other electronic mail products besides the ones mentioned in this chapter. If this is the case, you can use the following list of vendors as a starting point for your research:

Action Technologies
(The Coordinator)
1145 Atlantic Avenue
Suite 101
Alameda, CA 94501
(415) 521-6190
Fax: (415) 769-0596

Banyan Systems, Inc.
(Network Mail for Vines)
120 Flanders Road
Westborough, MA 01581
(508) 898-1000
Fax: (508) 898-1755

CE Software
(QuickMail)
P.O. Box 65580
West Des Moines, IA 50265
(800) 523-7638
(515) 224-1995
Fax: (515) 224-4534

Notework
72 Kent Street
Brookline, MA 02146
(617) 734-4317

Sitka Corporation
(InBox Plus)
950 Marina Village Parkway
Alameda, CA 94501
(800) 445-8677
(415) 769-9669
Fax: (415) 769-8771

SoftSwitch, Inc.
(Mailbridge and SoftSwitch Central e-mail gateways)
640 Lee Road
Wayne, PA 19087
(215) 640-9600
Fax: (215) 640-7550

VoxLink Corporation
(VoxVoice, VoxMail)
1516 Tyne Boulevard
Nashville, TN 37215
(615) 331-0275
Fax: (615) 331-2057

Going Beyond Electronic Mail

You can use your LAN (and its gateways) to save paper by implementing interoffice electronic mail; once you have done that, you will want more. The next set of problems you can solve with your LAN deals with scheduling meetings and managing projects. You can maintain an office-wide calendar of events on the LAN so that everyone knows when certain things will happen in the office ("Mr. Haynes of the California sales office will be here on Tuesday," for example). Beyond the simple calendar functions, some applications enable you to coordinate people's schedules and set up meetings. This type of application is known as Groupware, or workgroup software.

A group scheduler application acts as an electronic bulletin board. It provides a public place where you can post meeting announcements. If the software also knows each person's appointment calendar (the person keys appointments into the application, and keeps it up to date), the software can resolve meeting and scheduling conflicts. When you want to call a meeting, you enter an appointment in your calendar and give the names of the other people you need to talk to. Most group schedulers immediately notify the prospective attendees of the planned meeting. Each person can respond with, "Fine, I'll be there," or "Sorry, I can't make it then." Electronic mail is an essential component of the process; it enables you to tell people why you feel the meeting is necessary.

Group schedulers have different ways of handling meeting conflicts. Some examine the other participants' calendars and show you conflicts before you set a meeting time. Others find open times on everyone's schedule and propose a meeting time.

Most group schedulers work by organizing participants into teams. When you schedule a meeting, you can enter the team's name as the attendee rather than list all the individuals. The scheduler then inspects each team member's appointment calendar to determine the best time for the meeting. Some group scheduler applications support rudimentary project tracking as well. Two popular group schedulers are Schedule+ (discussed in Chapter 8, "Using Windows for Workgroups, Windows 95, and Warp Connect"), from Microsoft, and GroupWise, from Novell.

GroupWise

If you only have a few computers on a network, and those few machines are all Intel-based PCs, you probably won't need the power and functionality of GroupWise. However, if your network environment includes DOS clients, DOS and Windows clients, Macintosh clients, Windows NT clients, Windows 95 clients, OS/2 clients, and perhaps a Data General, UNIX, or VAX/VMS host computer, your LAN is a prime candidate for GroupWise. If you have more than 25 workstations, even if they all run the same operating system, you should look at GroupWise for your LAN.

GroupWise works on several types of networks: Novell NetWare, Banyan Vines, TOPS Network, Microsoft NT Server, IBM Warp Server, NOKIA PC-Net, 3Com 3+, 10Net, LANtastic, AT&T StarGROUP, DEC PCSA, and 3Com 3+ OPEN. A full installation of GroupWise consumes about 7M of disk space for the central (post office) portion, about 5.5M for DOS files, and about 5.5M for Windows files.

GroupWise gives the members of your organization electronic mail, a calendar, a calculator, an appointment book, a task list, team-oriented shared notes, a shell menu, a clipboard, a notebook with an auto-dial feature, a file manager, a macro editor, and a text editor. GroupWise integrates these functions across the LAN in a way that lets you and your coworkers coordinate smoothly despite the fact that you might be using different kinds of computers. The group scheduling software works across the LAN to help you make light work of setting up meetings and allocating resources, such as audio-visual equipment. GroupWise scans each person's (or resource's) appointment book to find acceptable meeting times. Invited attendees receive automatically generated e-mail requests to attend; each person can accept or decline with the click of the mouse.

You'll be right at home in GroupWise if you're familiar with the usual WordPerfect function key layout (F3 for help, F5 to list, F7 to exit, and so on). The GroupWise user interface is similar to WordPerfect's. If you don't use the WordPerfect word processor, you'll find the nearly CUA-compliant (CUA is Common User Access, a user interface standard) menus (Alt+F for File, Alt-E for Edit, and so on) easy to use. Version 4.0 added mouse support for the DOS text-mode application modules. Of course, the Windows and Macintosh modules let you point and click when you want to send notes or update your task list. For the most part, entering personal appointments and arranging group meetings is a simple fill-in-the-form process. GroupWise automates the job of searching for common free times when you want to hold a meeting. Personal appointments can be meetings, task list items you want to set aside time for, or other allocated blocks of time.

While using GroupWise is a breeze, installing and configuring the software is not. Your network administrator will spend a significant amount of time getting GroupWise ready for you to use. It may be time well spent, however; being able to share electronic mail and appointment books among different types of computers creates a level playing field out of what is usually a multi-platform mess.

The GroupWise shell is a DOS-menuing system that can be configured to manage all your applications, not just the suite of GroupWise modules. If you find you spend more time in one part of GroupWise, you can select a different view in GroupWise to give on-screen emphasis to that part—electronic mail, calendar, or perhaps the task list.

The electronic-mail gateway software that comes with GroupWise supports wide-area connections between GroupWise LANs in addition to MHS, SMTP, and X.400; you also get remote modem-based access to GroupWise when you're away from the office. If you write e-mail notes on a plane or in a hotel room without a modem, GroupWise will send the notes for you automatically when you return to the office and connect to the LAN.

Lotus Notes

Lotus Notes offers a unique blend of e-mail, conferencing, and client/server database technology. Notes is cross platform and includes support for Windows, OS/2, and Macintosh. It has features that will appeal to users (such as full-text indexing and background replication) and developers (such as macro functions and design templates).

Notes' security employs both passwords and physical tokens called ID files. During installation, you create a master ID file called the certifier ID. Then you use the certifier ID to stamp a certificate on each ID that you create on behalf of a server or a user. It's possible to register users in batches.

A Notes user (or server) can communicate with another server only when both hold a common certificate. Hierarchical certification, an X.500-like technique, permits you to create and manage a tree-like name space that reflects your company's organizational structure. It simplifies the exchange of Notes' data within and between organizations.

Notes uses public-key encryption technology to authenticate users and to affix digital signatures to mail messages. Notes' application builders can also create and distribute ad hoc keys that augment the server-, database-, document-, and section-level access controls with field-level encryption. It's an effective security system, but one that's quite complex. To protect a section of a document (for instance, a cluster of fields), you manipulate an access control list just as you would to protect a whole document or database. But to hide an individual field, you designate it encryptable, create a key, and then mail that key to the users you trust to access the field. They, in turn, must incorporate the key into their user IDs. Still another procedure governs regulation of access by roles, which are per-database groups of users that override public groups on an ad hoc basis.

A Notes server can use up to six protocols: NetBIOS, AppleTalk, Lotus' own dial-up protocol (called XPC), IPX/SPX, TCP/IP, and X.25. One of Lotus Notes' strengths is its similar look and feel on each of the platforms it runs on. Notes also takes advantage of specific platform features in certain cases. For instance, a System 7 Mac client can subscribe from within a shared Notes database to an edition published by a System 7 Mac. This arrangement makes the Mac-based edition visible not only to other Mac Notes clients, but to Windows and OS/2 Notes clients as well.

The client/server architecture of Notes has always accommodated remote access nicely, and Notes further improves matters by enabling workstations to run replication as a background task. Most e-mail and conferencing systems require special logic to support off-line reading and composition. Mail and conference messages are located in databases that replicate just like all other Notes databases.

Notes supports two kinds of version control, and the database designer can opt to record a complete change history for each document. One method makes the update subordinate to the original document; the other does the reverse. You can also now replicate selectively, regulating the bi-directional exchange with the same kind of formula you use to select the contents of a view.

Using the Verity text engine within Notes is productive and easy. If you have an unindexed database, the Find command leads to an ordinary text-search dialog box. On an indexed database, Find attaches a variety of full-text search tools to the window in which you view the database. You can create and execute complex queries that use wild cards, Boolean and proximity operators, and value-based expressions like Severity greater than = 5; save these queries for later use; and schedule them for automatic execution. You can order search results by relevance or by date.

The same forms through which you enter data into the views of a database serve double duty as query-by-example templates. You can also use these forms to specify updates to the result set. If you search across multiple Notes databases, however, you'll probably want to revert to the generic query builder, since one database's forms likely won't mean anything in the context of another database.

Lotus wants to position Notes as a general-purpose platform for applications that collect, organize, and distribute "semi-structured" information, route documents, and manage work flow. In support of that goal, Notes gives database designers new tools to process data and messages.

You build a Notes application—which is to say a heavily customized Notes database— around a set of forms and views. A form defines the fields that make up a document (for instance, a record) in a Notes database, and it handles data entry and queries. A view presents a selected subset of the documents in that database, typically sorted and often grouped by expandable categories. You can easily achieve relational effects by treating several views as tables related by a common key.

A significant enabling feature of Notes is the @MailSend function, which automates use of the Notes mail system. Of special importance is @MailSend's ability not only to attach copies of documents to messages but also to include links that point to shared documents. Table 1 identifies some other important features of Lotus Notes.

Table 11.1 Features of Lotus Notes	
Similar Client and Server Platforms	Windows, Macintosh, and dial-in users get remarkably similar client interfaces.
Hierarchical Certification	This administrative function lets you manage a hierarchical tree that represents your organizational structure.
Background Replication	Workstations can run replication as a background task, allowing you to synchronize databases even while sending and receiving mail.
Verity Text Engine	The integration of the Verity text engine adds search capabilities to indexed Notes databases.
Column Picklists	Notes' @DbColumn function delivers relational capabilities with the ability to generate picklists for forms from data in table columns.
Mail Automation	The @MailSend function gives programmatic control over Notes' mail functions, including attachments and links.

A Lotus Notes database contains only documents—its data records. But these data records are miles ahead of the conventional kind (for instance, "Given x bytes per record, record N must be at offset N x."). So, designer Iris Associates (which is now a part of Lotus Development) coined the term document for a dynamic data record of indeterminate size that can store any of seven different types of data: text, text lists, numbers, number ranges, times/dates, time/date ranges, and type composites.

A type composite, also known as a rich-text field, is a flexible, self-describing format that can store just about anything that you care to paste or embed into it. This includes word-processor files, spreadsheets, bitmaps, OLE objects, sounds, hypertext links (for instance, doclinks) to documents in the same or a different database, and even—if a C programmer using the Notes API so arranges—user-defined data types.

Views are windows for browsing through the database; they're sorted by pertinent data fields. Each column in a view either maps to a field in each note or shows the result of a Lotus 1-2-3-like formula. Using categories derived from the values in a database, a view can expand and contract in much the same manner as the outliner does in a word processor.

Forms are templates for entering and displaying a Note's data. A form can contain static text, bitmaps, data fields, and command buttons. The fields of a form map by name to the fields of a note, so a user can enter data with one form and view it using another.

From a user's perspective, you double-click on a Notes database icon to open a window containing a view. You then scroll through the view to the note that you want and double-click on it; another window opens to display the note's data in a form. It might contain, for example, an Ami Pro icon. Double-clicking on that launches the application and opens an embedded Ami Pro file for editing. When you quit Ami Pro, the file is stored safely back in the note. Because notes are such flexible containers, a database can store all the elements of its own user interface within itself—icons, forms, views, macros, and so forth. Thus, each database becomes a self-contained application.

Replication means cloning a Lotus Notes application (or database—the terms are usually synonymous). There's no restriction on how many replicas can exist, and no single replica serves as the master. Each replica accumulates its own unique additions and deletions (the latter are represented by deletion stubs). Replicas synchronize in two ways. Server-based replication is typically a scheduled affair; a task on one Notes server opens a dial-up or LAN connection to another. Client-based replication occurs intermittently at a user's discretion—perhaps from a laptop that dials into a Notes server from a hotel room.

Either way, the involved parties first establish each other's identity. Next, they consult their replication histories and build a list of the data notes, design notes, and ACL (access-control list) notes that have changed since the pair last replicated. Subject to each application's access permissions from the other, the applications then start to exchange notes. The first note to be swapped is the ACL, which can then govern access permissions for the rest of the exchange.

After all notes have been successfully swapped, both replicas update their replication-history records. Since an application doesn't know which other applications it will replicate with in the future, or when, all deletion stubs are kept intact. They're removed after the deletion-stub-purge interval, which is typically 90 days.

Typically, a large organization will start with one big Notes application, often a personnel-oriented one with a hybrid client/server architecture. Such an application enables smaller workgroups, typically driven by the need to manage documents, to build and use their own Notes applets. All organizations, large and small alike, have a standard document repository: the file server, a labyrinth of directories with thousands of files named in the DOS format. Users can more effectively classify, navigate, and search for those files if the files are placed under Notes' control. To create a simple Notes repository from the standard Document Library template, you only need about the same level of skill required to produce a useful spreadsheet.

For more information about Lotus Notes, contact the company:

> Lotus Development Corp.
> 55 Cambridge Parkway
> Cambridge, MA 02142
> (617) 577-8500

Microsoft Exchange

Microsoft also offers a Groupware product, called Microsoft Exchange, which is now part of Microsoft's Office 97 product. The Exchange application includes e-mail (Microsoft Mail), calendar (Schedule+), Internet and intranet gateway components (Exchange Internet Mail Connector), and a document-sharing component. Microsoft bundles the Exchange mail client in Windows 95. As with Lotus Notes, you can use Exchange to simply send e-mail or coordinate the activities of various people, or you can develop document-sharing applications that let a large organization distribute price lists and manage shareable documents.

Microsoft Exchange supports multiple connections between sites, so if one connection goes down, the system automatically reroutes messages through another. And it balances the load over the remaining connections to maximize performance. Local replication makes it possible to synchronize personal and public folders between your local machine and the server so that users can work off-line. And you can use the Remote Access Services (RAS) in NT Server for remote connectivity.

The significant features of Microsoft Exchange are the following:

- A Universal Inbox that enables users to store, access, and send messages, forms, faxes, and meeting requests from a single location.

- Public folders that enable users to share information with users in other locations and on other systems.

- Built-in support for Internet connectivity.

- A consistent user interface for the Windows, Macintosh, and eventually UNIX operating environments.

- Integrated security.

- Integrated support for remote computing.

- Sending and receiving fax documents.

Microsoft Exchange Server is part of the Microsoft BackOffice series of products. The Microsoft BackOffice software products include the Windows NT Server network operating system, SQL Server, SNA Server, Systems Management Server, and Exchange Server.

For more information about Microsoft Exchange, contact the vendor:

Microsoft Corporation
One Microsoft Way
Redmond, WA 98052-6399
(206) 882-8080
www.microsoft.com

Other Groupware Products

If you want to explore the class of software known as Groupware more fully, you will find the following list of companies a good place to start your research:

CaLANdar
Microsystems Software, Inc.
600 Worcester Road
Framingham, MA 01701
(508) 626-8511
Fax: (508) 626-8515

ClockWise
Phase II Software Corporation
444 Washington Street
Suite 407
Woburn, MA 01801
(800) 735-2557
(617) 937-0256
Fax: (617) 937-0098

The Coordinator II
Action Technologies, Inc.
1145 Atlantic Avenue
Alameda, CA 94501
(415) 521-6190
Fax: (415) 769-0596

Higgins Enable Software
Higgins Group
1150 Marina Village Parkway
Suite 101
Alameda, CA 94501
(800) 854-2807
(415) 865-9805
Fax: (415) 521-9779

Meeting Maker
On Technology, Inc.
155 Second Street
Cambridge, MA 02141
(617) 876-0900
Fax: (617) 876-0391

Network Scheduler II
PowerCore, Inc.
1 Diversatech Drive
Manteno, IL 60950
(800) 237-4754
(815) 468-3737
Fax: (815) 468-3867

OfficeWorks
Data Access Corporation
14000 Southwest 119 Avenue
Miami, FL 33186
(800) 451-3539
(801) (305) 238-0012
Fax: (305) 238-0017

OnTime
Campbell Services, Inc.
21700 Northwestern Highway
Suite 1070
Southfield, MI 48075

Schedule+
Microsoft Corporation
1 Microsoft Way
Redmond, WA 98052
(800) 426-9400
(801) (206) 882-8080
Fax: (206) 883-8101

Shoebox
R+R Associates, Inc.
39 Carwall Avenue
Mount Vernon, NY 10552
(914) 668-4057
Fax: (914) 668-9277

SuperTime
SuperTime, Inc.
2025 Sheppard Avenue E
Suite 2206
Willowdale
Toronto, Ontario
Canada M2J 1V7
(416) 499-3288
Fax: (416) 492-9192

Synchronize
CrossWind Technologies, Inc.
6630 Hwy. 9
Suite 201
Felton, CA 95018
(408) 335-4988
Fax: (408) 335-1086

Who-What-When Enterprise
Chronos Software
555 De Haro Street
Suite 240
San Francisco, CA 94107
(800) 999-1023
(801) (415) 626-4244
Fax: (415) 626-5393

Chapter Summary

This chapter introduced you to electronic mail, one of the more significant uses to which you can put your LAN after sharing files and printers. If you get the right e-mail product, you can dispense with the tons of interoffice mail that circulate through the office on paper. You can take a step towards the paperless office through e-mail. You will find your electronic files and notes much easier to organize than their physical, paper- and typewriter-oriented predecessors.

You have learned how electronic mail works and you know how to use it to your best advantage. You now understand two of the industry standards for e-mail: MHS and the X.400 specification. You have familiarized yourself with several of the more popular electronic mail products. And you have looked over the horizon to discover the new class of LAN-aware application software, Groupware.

In the next chapter, you turn to the subject of network management.

Chapter 12

Managing Your Network

Network management is more art than science. As networks grow to connect thousands or tens of thousands of workstations, the job of keeping the systems up and running requires considerable experience, in-depth knowledge, and thorough training. Novell started its Certified NetWare Engineer (CNE) program just to solve this problem, and both IBM and Microsoft offer certification programs. The Appendix in this book discusses certification programs in detail.

You are likely to see a variety of LANs in medium and large businesses. One department may run TCP/IP over EtherNet, with NFS on the departmental file server. Another part of the company may run NetWare over Token Ring, while yet another runs Warp Server over Fast Ethernet. Interconnecting LANs that use different cables and protocols are a big challenge in network management. When the network crashes, however, managing even a few nodes in a peer LAN can be a bigger job than you planned.

As you will see in this chapter, the designers of networks offer two special protocols just for network management—Simple Network Management Protocol (SNMP) and the OSI-compliant Common Management Information Protocol (CMIP). The protocols discussed in Chapter 4, "Using Protocols, Cables, and Adapters," enable workstations and file servers to communicate. The SNMP and CMIP protocols supply you with data that show the health of your network.

When problems occur on your LAN, you need to take a systematic approach to solving them. Diagnosing and identifying the problems are the most difficult steps. In this chapter, you learn how to recognize the causes of most LAN problems and become familiar with the tools that help you pinpoint network errors.

The network management protocols SNMP and CMIP, along with new versions of the network operating system software, someday will enable you to see and control an entire network without leaving your workstation. Hardware and software from different vendors will adhere to the new standards;

managing the LAN will be systematic and routine. Until then, however, you will need the information in this chapter to keep your LAN healthy.

Learning the Basics of Network Management

Networks are proliferating faster than people are gaining skills and training to manage them. The job of managing the network is growing in importance, yet not enough people can do the job. To understand what the job entails, you first must look at the basics of network management.

Keeping a LAN running is complicated by the dynamic, distributed nature of networks. Many LAN environments mix PCs, gateways, bridges, routers, minicomputers, and mainframes. The LAN may very well include software systems not designed for a large network, and, to further complicate the situation, the LAN may contain components from different vendors.

To manage a network, you need a plan. The system plan must change and grow as the network changes and grows. The plan must address such issues as cable diagrams, cable layout, network capacity, protocol and equipment standards, workstation growth, and new LAN technologies. The plan needs to stay abreast of new network management tools and products.

Examining Technical Issues

Most network operating systems keep track of LAN activity and track performance statistics, traffic volumes, error counts, and accounting information. You sometimes can control servers and bridges remotely. Many vendors are offering add-ons to existing systems. A simple upgrade to your network operating system may give you a wealth of information. Vendors of networking products are keenly aware of the need for management tools and information, and these vendors are working to overcome the technical issues of network management.

These vendors also are working on standards and conformance testing to ensure that their products will interoperate with the variety of hardware and software on today's heterogeneous LANs. The effort to provide management solutions compatible with the wide range of available LAN products, however, is not keeping up with the technological advances of the LAN industry.

You need some level of automated network management system if you are to view and control a large LAN. Such a system must consider several technical issues regarding how LANs fail.

Dealing with Common Mode Failures. Sometimes a failure in one LAN component will affect other components. Such an event is a *common mode failure*. The on-board logic of a network adapter, for example, may garble the interior portion of a received message packet. The network adapter will hand the result to the network operating system, which may not detect the error. If the network operating system puts the garbled data into a file, the file will be corrupt. Crosschecks and consistency checks help deal with such failures. A network management system must implement these checks.

Managing Traffic. A hardware or software failure may bring the LAN to a quiet halt, or the failure may cause more message packet traffic than the network is designed to handle. In the latter case, network adapters may detect the error and broadcast error message packets of their own, adding to the traffic. The overburdened network may give no outward sign of failure except for poor performance. A network management system must be able to detect and report such failures.

Determining Robustness. A LAN management system is likely to encounter unexpected or invalid (badly formed) message packets in its lifetime. How the system handles the unexpected message is important. The software must react properly to *duplicates*, or to messages from unregistered, off-line nodes. A robust LAN management system carries on by ignoring the bad message (letting the lower-level protocols handle the problem by resending the message) or by notifying an operator of the error and then issuing reset commands to the failing nodes.

Testing the LAN. You need to be able to tell the LAN management system how and when to test the network. The product must include built-in test points that enable you to exercise the LAN interfaces, perform an inventory of LAN facilities, and trace LAN activities.

Extending the LAN. The LAN management system will need to adapt to the network's growth. The growth may be the adding of new nodes, the connecting of the LAN to other networks, or the introduction of new technology. Unless it can adapt, the LAN management system itself will limit the growth of the network.

The LAN management system should have a long life span. Its adaptability to system changes depends on its ability to easily add new features and technology with minimal effect on the existing system.

Examining Administrative Issues

In addition to the technical issues, a LAN management system must handle a number of administrative issues. These include software distribution and version control, error determination and correction, system configuration management, and access control/ security.

Managing Software Distribution. You need to manage software distribution to prevent the introduction of non-licensed software and computer viruses into the network. One way to control software distribution is to handle it from a central location in the network. You copy software onto a file server from a single distribution point, and then remotely copy it to local hard disks. IBM's LAN Distribution Utility (LDU) is a product that automates this process.

You also want to synchronize all the workstations to ensure that everyone is using the correct version of the software. In some applications, such as those in the banking industry, you also have to synchronize remote software versions with central transaction-processing software versions. The simplest way to handle this synchronization is to make sure that all transactions include version information and that the central software rejects any out-of-date versions it receives.

Helping the Administrator. On small networks, the LAN administrator's job falls by default to someone in the office, probably as a part-time position. On larger systems (20 or more workstations), the administrator's job may be a recognized, full-time position. In either case, the administrator will need help finding and solving problems, making backups, keeping a vigilant eye on security, and monitoring performance. The LAN management software may report results to the administrator's workstation or, on LANs with hundreds of nodes, send the data up to a host system for further analysis and review.

Discovering Problems. The LAN management software records problems (events) related to network adapters, cables, and other LAN components. When an error such as a failed network adapter occurs, the software notifies the LAN administrator. If the management software is sophisticated enough, it may suggest alternative solutions to the administrator. The management software also should provide facilities for monitoring file server activity, print servers, and gateways. When there is a problem, the software typically alerts the LAN manager with an audible alarm and a highlighted indication of the problem on the display.

On a LAN with hundreds of workstations, the management software may forward the alert report to a host computer. The central site can use the information to maintain a centralized problem history file for each remote LAN. The alert log can contain vendor contacts for specific problems, generate trouble tickets, and include information about how the problem was resolved.

Logging and Reporting Events. The management software can log network events—such as peak network utilization times, new network addresses observed on the network, and error conditions—to a disk file or a printer. The administrator may import the logged events into a database for further filtering, reporting, and statistics-gathering. The LAN management software must be capable of writing a file in a format that can be imported into other applications. The software may offer its own facilities for reporting the data. Typically, you can generate reports from the information stored in the event log over a selected period of time. A network administrator, for example, often wants to review network utilization for the past 24 hours, and will want the software to provide that information.

Determining Operator Control. An administrator will want to query the status of a device attached to the network, such as a workstation, bridge, or gateway. The LAN management software should offer this capability. If the network adapters maintain a history of error statistics and traffic activity, the administrator will want to routinely gather this information from all or selected nodes on the LAN.

Another useful LAN management software function tests the status of the path between two workstations. This is especially handy when repeaters or bridges separate the workstations.

Managing the LAN's Configuration. Configuration management requires knowing what software is installed on which workstations and how those workstations are configured. For applications your company has developed internally, and which are distributed automatically and subject to strict version control, this is usually not a problem. But for off-the-shelf, shrink-wrapped software (spreadsheets and word processors), keeping track of which workstation accesses what software is a big job.

Large corporations most frequently take the approach of putting a certain collection of supported software packages on the network. Typically, the list includes one or two packages in each of the standard categories—word processing, database management, spreadsheets, and telecommunications.

If you use these packages, you can get help from the company's technical support personnel in the form of question answering and problem solving, tutorials and training, and data-conversion utilities. If you use other packages to do the same functions, the corporation may not offer technical support and may even remove the offending software from the file server.

In an environment of hundreds of workstations, such a corporate policy supports an organized, rational approach to managing the LAN. Version control, problem solving, training, and migration to new software can take place in an orderly, well-defined manner. The LAN management software may help enforce the corporate policy.

You typically can configure a workstation and its software to suit your personal preferences. In a large, corporate environment, this may hinder technical support. A configuration change involving screen colors is not important, but other workstation setup modifications may make the tasks of answering questions and fixing problems difficult. These modifications include unusual printer-control codes and default directory structures.

For shrink-wrapped software, it is essentially impossible to prevent you from changing your internal configuration for a particular product. You can use the software's configuration options to modify the product's printer setup and default directories to suit your personal preferences and work habits. If you have a technical support question, the person who tries to answer your question may have difficulty understanding your configuration. The best approach for a LAN encompassing hundreds or thousands of workstations is to have a prescribed configuration for each supported program. In the worst case, technical support personnel can return your workstation to the standard configuration as the first step in determining and correcting a problem.

Managing Access Control and Security

Controlling access to a small LAN is usually a function performed by the network operating system. On a large network connecting many LANs and mainframe computers, controlling access becomes a function of a LAN management facility.

Your account and password will log you on to your LAN, but you may need to pass through additional security checkpoints to access certain resources on the LAN. If your LAN is attached to a mainframe, this becomes especially true. You may find that certain applications require their own level of security before you can run them. The network administrator has the job of setting up security at the various levels. A LAN management product will support the administrator's role as security chief and may even provide the application-level password control.

A diskless workstation does not save money because it lacks disk drives, but it can be a useful tool if security is important in your office. Such a workstation prevents people from copying information on the file server to a transportable diskette. A diskless workstation also prevents someone from introducing foreign software and data files to the system.

Defining the Network Administrator's Role

Managing a LAN from a centralized location is a difficult task. As yet, you will not find a complete set of tools offered by vendors to help with all the administrator's tasks. The network administrator typically will have a mixed bag of partial-solution software and hardware tools to help get the job done. The administrator has to be an expert in using the available tools, often calling upon his or her own creativity to use the tools at hand to solve unusual problems. The administrator must understand the network's configuration, performance, accounting, planning, security, and applications in order to solve problems as they occur.

Using SNMP and CMIP—The LAN Management Protocols

A large part of network management consists of keeping track of the devices on your networks, checking on the network's performance, and diagnosing and correcting problems. Many of the LAN industry's efforts have been directed toward automating these tasks. These efforts have resulted in two distinct yet similar protocols for managing a network. These two protocols are designed by committees, not by specific vendors. (You learn about IBM's SNA Management Services in the section "Using IBM's Network Management Tools" later in this chapter.)

The Simple Network Management Protocol (SNMP) is an outgrowth of TCP/IP communications needs. Jeff Case, president of SNMP Research of Knoxville, Tennessee (a company that supplies software to SNMP vendors), and a group of other people authored SNMP to solve problems within such networks as the Internet (this is discussed in Chapter 9, "Using UNIX LANs").

The Common Management Information Protocol (CMIP), a part of the Open Systems Interconnection (OSI) standard, is a product of an international standards committee.

Both protocols have their advantages, and networking product vendors are developing LAN management systems that incorporate both. In the next few sections of this chapter, you will discover the similarities and differences between SNMP and CMIP.

Comparing CMIP to SNMP

CMIP and SNMP share a common goal: To bring network management details to the network administrator, so the administrator can make changes, find out where a fault lies, or just retrieve information from a node on the network. Both protocols help the administrator perform problem diagnosis, capacity planning, and report generation.

Both protocols use the concept of a *Management Information Base*, or MIB. An MIB consists of a set of variables, test points, and controls that all devices on the network support and that a network administrator can control. Both protocols also support vendor-specific extensions to the MIB. These extensions enable network devices with more intelligence to report or accept greater amounts of information, without requiring that all devices support the same intelligence.

As they develop network management products, vendors are merging the capabilities of SNMP and CMIP MIBs. By making SNMP and CMIP use compatible MIBs, vendors can create a network management product that can accept information from SNMP or CMIP but store the information in a common format.

Contrasting CMIP with SNMP

CMIP and SNMP differ in the ways they retrieve and report data across the network. The two protocols offer different functions, require different amounts of computer-processing power, and use different amounts of memory. Each protocol uses a different set of lower-level protocols to send and receive network management information on the network, and each protocol has the support of a different standards committee.

Data Access. SNMP and CMIP have data-retrieval functions that require a different outlook on the part of the retriever. SNMP is better at accessing specific individual items of information, while CMIP is oriented more toward retrieving collections of information. With SNMP, you ask for the particular item you want. CMIP requires you to make a general request and then qualify that request with specifics about what you do not want. SNMP operates in a more focused manner, while CMIP deals with classes of data that you constrain with stated qualifications.

Both approaches have their advantages. For some problems, you know exactly what information you want; SNMP's approach would be quite satisfactory in such cases. At other times, you want the broadest possible answer to a query so that you can see all relevant bits of information.

Polling Versus Reporting. SNMP works by *polling*—a central management processor (perhaps your workstation) regularly asks each device on the network for its status. CMIP uses *reporting*, in which the device only informs your central management station about changes in the device's status.

With the SNMP approach, a large number of network devices will cause a great deal of message traffic. This may slow down the network. With SNMP, however, you can have devices on the network that are not intelligent enough to detect and report problems. SNMP makes it simpler to detect a device that has failed completely and that is unable to report its failure. The implementation of SNMP in the remote device only has to be large enough to answer "Yes" or "No" when it is polled.

Size and Performance. A network management system built on SNMP can be smaller, faster, and less expensive than a CMIP implementation. CMIP requires a faster computer and more memory to do its job. This is logical, because polling requires less intelligence from the devices being managed than reporting does.

In most cases, a vendor can easily implement SNMP in a TSR program on a DOS-based personal computer. It would be difficult to do this with CMIP.

CMIP is broader in scope and has more features and capabilities than SNMP. But, as mentioned in the preceding section, you pay the price in terms of memory and speed to have CMIP's functions. You may not want or need all of CMIP's functions on your network.

Vendors of network management systems that are primarily SNMP-based will have to be more creative, but they can accomplish almost the same tasks as with CMIP.

Transport Layer Protocols. To send a network management request or response across the network, SNMP uses simple datagrams. As Chapter 4, "Using Protocols, Cables, and Adapters," mentioned, datagrams are connectionless, and there is no guarantee of delivery. The two communicating devices must consider the possibility that a datagram will not get to its destination. This means the sender will retry the send operation several times before declaring that the receiver has died. SNMP can use simple communications protocols such as IPX or IP and UDP to route messages.

The difference between datagram- and session-oriented communications is best seen by contrasting a letter and a phone call: The phone call sets up a two-way circuit, but the letter simply gets sent. Letters require less equipment and overhead than phone calls, and this is also true for datagrams.

Its use of connection-oriented communications sessions makes CMIP better at retrieving large amounts of data. It also can make the network harder to manage when problems occur, however. If the network is failing and is almost nonfunctional, SNMP will retry its network management requests until one of them gets through. The session-oriented connections that CMIP depends upon may no longer exist as a result of the network failure.

Protocol Standards. CMIP, like other OSI protocols, is an international standard controlled by international standards bodies such as the ISO. Vendors can test their implementations against a conformance test suite from the Corporation for Open Systems (COS), which also performs conformance tests for other OSI protocols.

SNMP, in contrast, is not an international standard. Like TCP/IP, however, SNMP is controlled by the Internet Activities Board.

Assessing CMIP and SNMP Product Availability

If practicality is the most important principle to you, SNMP has one undeniable advantage: There are many more products supporting it than CMIP. Despite the considerable interest in CMIP, it has not been implemented in as many network products. Products based on SNMP—routers, EtherNet hubs, fiber devices, and EtherNet devices—are common. Part of the reason is that SNMP is older. Many companies are developing network management systems that use CMIP or a combination of CMIP and SNMP.

Choosing SNMP or CMIP for Your LAN

Should your network management system be based on SNMP or CMIP? SNMP is more oriented toward managing specific devices, while CMIP is better at communicating information between two or more network management systems. In this light, SNMP and CMIP play complementary roles. Depending on the size and complexity of your network, you may find that the best network management system for your office uses both CMIP and SNMP. The system may use SNMP to manage specific devices on a particular LAN. The same software may use CMIP to help a network administrator in New York manage a wide area network of LANs in Chicago, Los Angeles, and Dallas.

Using IBM's Network Management Tools

Large, wide area networks are not uncommon among IBM customers. It should come as no surprise to you that IBM offers network management products for such networks. Token Ring and IBM's own Systems Network Architecture (SNA) are the foundation upon which LAN Network Manager and NetView are built.

Managing Token Ring LANs

Token Ring has always had special capabilities in the areas of internal diagnostics and ring management, capabilities that have gone largely untapped by network management software. Unlike ARCnet and EtherNet, Token Ring LANs circulate a constant stream of Medium Access Control (MAC) frames that provide a wealth of information regarding the network's status. The network adapter cards use these MAC frames privately to keep the network running, but network management applications can intercept the frames to reveal the status and health of the network.

Few vendors offer software tools that capture these MAC frames for network management purposes. One vendor, IBM, augments the MAC frames with another protocol layer of management services as defined by Systems Network Architecture. In large companies,

Token Ring LANs often are part of SNA networks. SNA is an IBM standard for networking that encompasses just about everything. Terminals, PCs, LANs, controllers, mainframes, and even remote printers come under the SNA umbrella. An SNA network node is characterized as an *entry point* or a *focal point*. An entry point can generate SNA statistics and status information; a focal point receives the data and presents it to an operator.

Within SNA, IBM has defined a Management Services standard that defines how network management products communicate with one another. The IBM standard, for example, says that an *alert* (a record of an error or other significant event) contains such data fields as the address of the node at which the error occurred, the date and time of the error, the ID of the management component reporting the error, the probable cause, and a recommended action. (Of course, the node initiating the alert may not be able to fill in all these items.) Although it was developed by IBM, SNA is nonetheless a well-known and fully documented standard that many computer manufacturers adhere to so that their hardware and software are IBM-compatible.

Not all Token Ring workstations are peers. One workstation is designated as the *active monitor*, which means it assumes additional responsibilities for controlling the ring. The active monitor maintains the ring's timing control, issues new tokens (if necessary) to keep things going, and generates diagnostic frames under certain circumstances. The active monitor can be any one of the workstations on the network and is chosen when the ring is initialized. If the active monitor fails, there is an automatic procedure by which the other workstations (the standby monitors) negotiate with one another to choose a new active monitor.

The IEEE 802.5 Token Ring standard defines six types of MAC frames. A workstation sends a Duplicate Address Test frame when it first joins the ring to ensure that its address is unique. To tell other workstations that it is still alive, the active monitor periodically sends an Active Monitor Present frame. Other workstations periodically send a Standby Monitor Present frame. A standby monitor sends Claim Token frames when it suspects that the active monitor may have died. A workstation sends a Beacon frame in the event of a major network problem, such as a broken cable or a workstation transmitting without waiting for a token (for example, going out of turn). A Purge frame is sent either after a ring initializes itself or after a new active monitor is established.

Network management software locates the active monitor on the LAN by looking for the Active Monitor Present MAC frames. Software watches for Beacon frames and uses them to trigger diagnostic actions. Using the standard ring-polling technique defined in the IEEE 802.5 Token Ring specification, the software also can determine the status of each network adapter card on the network. If an adapter is found to be disabled and the Token Ring LAN is part of an SNA network, an alert can be generated. When errors occur on a Token Ring workstation, the real culprit is sometimes a different workstation. The *nearest active upstream neighbor (NAUN)* workstation—the node responsible for passing a token or frame downstream to this workstation—may have malfunctioned and corrupted the data. Network management software can detect the NAUN relationship and use it to point you in the right direction.

Using SNA on Token Ring

Above the MAC layer, a focal point or an entry point that needs to perform management tasks can use SNA Management Services. If SNA-aware support software is loaded into a workstation, that workstation can be queried, tested, and diagnosed from a remote location. SNA is rich in management and maintenance functions. It defines services for performing traces, recording memory snapshots (even from a remote system), requesting or responding to tests, and generating and recording statistics.

To trace events on one segment of the network, for example, the focal point issues an Activate Link (ACTLINK) request. It follows up with an Activate Trace (ACTTRACE) request, records the resulting Record Trace Data (RECTRD) events, and finally issues a Deactivate Trace (DACTTRACE) request. The RECTRD messages contain the link address, the trace type, and the trace data. An ACTTRACE request may specify that the trace include data for an entire segment (transmission group) or for a specific link.

A Request Maintenance Statistics (REQMS) request asks an SNA node to report resource maintenance statistics and specifies whether those statistics counters should be reset after being reported. A Token Ring workstation on an SNA network can respond to this request with *adapter engineering change level data* (version information about the network adapter), network software version data, traffic counts, and error counts. If error counts exceed predetermined thresholds, the workstation can send these statistics even without receiving an REQMS message.

As you can see, SNA is not lacking in services for network maintenance and management.

Using IBM's LAN Network Manager

IBM's LAN Network Manager is a network management product. It helps network administrators manage Token Ring LANs, especially those that are part of larger SNA networks. The software provides a simple menu interface that works with NetView (a mainframe IBM product) or by itself on a single- or multi-segment Token Ring network. Do not confuse IBM's LAN Network Manager with Microsoft's LAN Manager: The IBM offering is a true network management application, while Microsoft's product is a network operating system.

IBM LAN Network Manager is Systems Application Architecture-compliant, and runs under OS/2 Presentation Manager. It uses OS/2 Database Manager to store and retrieve network configuration data and network error-event histories (alerts).

Version 1.1 of LAN Network Manager incorporates 80 NetView commands, uses the CMIP and SNMP protocols, and can display a graphical representation of your LAN.

Running alone, LAN Network Manager acts as a focal point on a network. When used with NetView, though, it is also an entry point (an agent) to the mainframe product NetView. When used as an entry point, LAN Network Manager is, in SNA terms, a System Services Control Point node. It uses an SNA SSCP-Physical Unit communications session to talk to NetView. Usually, several SSCPs exist in an SNA network, and they provide essential management services: helping to activate or deactivate the network, allocating network resources, managing the recovery of the network from communications failures, collecting traffic data, interacting with network operations people and executing their commands, and coordinating the interconnection of the different segments of the network. NetView itself is an SSCP node that offers central management of a large, geographically diverse network.

What does this mean to you? You can initiate and control network management operations from any terminal or workstation on the network, whether or not it is physically part of the Token Ring network being managed. This is especially useful to network administrators who are geographically remote from the LANs they care for.

Using IBM's NetView

The mainframe-based product NetView incorporates and combines the features of several other IBM mainframe products. Network Communications Control Facility (NCCF) works across multiple-domain networks to record alerts, divide management responsibilities among several network operators, and run command-script programs. Network Logical Data Manager records session and routing information, including response-time data. Network Problem Determination Application analyzes network problems and presents the results at several levels of detail. At the lowest level, NPDA reveals the probable cause of an error or failure.

NetView integrates these and other functions into a simple menu-driven management application. A NetView operator easily can look at a particular SNA node's health and analyze statistics or reconfigure or reset network devices. A LAN Network Manager or NetView operator, for example, can reconfigure a LAN bridge to have a different network address or a different *hopcount limit* (the maximum number of bridges through which a message frame can pass). From NetView or LAN Network Manager, you can collect performance and traffic statistics from LAN bridges (including a count of the frames that have been discarded or not forwarded because of error conditions) and a count of broadcast frames intended for reception by all workstations.

You also can use NetView's NCCF to query or command LAN Network Manager without being at a LAN Network Manager workstation. You can ask for the status of a Token Ring node, remove the node from the network, perform a point-to-point test between two nodes, reset LAN Network Manager, and ask for a display of the configuration of a LAN segment.

You can programmatically control NetView or obtain network status and event history information from it in two ways. NetView incorporates a script file processor that an administrator can use to automate the system's response to certain events. Programming the script language facility embedded in NetView is much like writing scripts for a PC communications program. You easily can write a program that wakes up when a particular alert is received, for example. Your program may try to recover automatically from the error by sending a reset-device command to the problem node.

The application programming interface to NetView is more complicated, but it enables custom-written programs in a high-level language to access NetView configuration data files and alert histories. An application program also can use the NetView API to trigger an alert of its own—perhaps to signal a problem with a database file. NetView records the resulting alert in its history file and takes an appropriate action (as you define it). This action may consist, for example, of a notification that operator intervention is required.

A recent aspect of the NetView API is an LU 6.2 (peer-to-peer communications) facility. LU 6.2 is a dialog-oriented protocol within SNA. With simple verbs such as allocate, receive-and-wait, send-data, confirm, and de-allocate, the LU 6.2 protocol makes it easy to query NetView or perform custom network management tasks (implemented by your company's staff of programmers, of course).

Another IBM product, NetView/PC, provides an API to NetView that other vendors can use to interface with their equipment. Such companies as Bay Networks, Synoptics, AT&T, Paradyne, and Codex have products that work with NetView and are based on the NetView/PC interface. The devices that use this interface include EtherNet adapters, modem-management hardware, and T-1 network resources.

Auditing Your IBM LAN

LAN Network Manager works with other IBM products to control access to the network. It enables you to set up rules defining when certain workstations can log on. With the IBM LAN Station Manager and 8230 Token Ring Controlled Access Unit, LAN Network Manager can detect intruder log-ons, generate an alert, and automatically remove the offender from the network by reprogramming or resetting the 8230 CAU. LAN Network Manager itself is, of course, password protected.

Do you know exactly where all your company's PCs are? LAN Network Manager, LAN Station Manager, and the CAU work together to help you map your LANs as they change.

The CAU incorporates a data-reporting function that notifies LAN Network Manager of adapter, lobe, and segment identifications for the workstations on the LAN. LAN Station Manager, available for DOS and OS/2, collects device information from each workstation and sends the information to LAN Network Manager. LAN Station Manager maintains a station database of user-specific information, such as room number, serial number, and a symbolic machine name. IBM suggests that you install LAN Station Manager on each workstation. LAN Network Manager (or NetView) can trigger the CAU or LAN Station Manager to report what they know and correlate a workstation with a building location. You can use the resulting information to track down all your company's PCs.

IBM uses CMIP in its network-management products, but IBM's CMIP and SNMP usage is fairly limited. One of the few places CMIP comes into the picture is between the new CAU device and LAN Network Manager. Other diagnostic and management functions within the network generally will not be CMIP-compliant. The primary protocol that IBM uses in its network management products is defined in SNA's Management Services, and this will remain true for years to come. An IBM spokesperson has said that future CMIP support will be added as the definition of CMIP becomes clearer.

Using IBM Network-Management Applications

Token Ring has hidden strengths, and you soon will see more network-management applications that take advantage of these strengths. In the meantime, the IBM products discussed in this chapter can give you an inside look at the health of your network. LAN Network Manager and NetView are sophisticated yet simple. They also are somewhat expensive. You will not want to purchase these tools for a small office LAN. If you have at least a medium-size Token Ring LAN, you may consider getting LAN Network Manager. Budgets notwithstanding, when you need tools like these, you need them badly.

Using General LAN-Management Tools

In the following sections of this chapter, you learn about specific tools you can use to help manage your network. These tools range from Time-Domain Reflectometers (TDRs) to Integrated Management Systems. Some of these tools can be quite expensive. If your network is important to your business, however, you may find these tools a wise investment. You also discover how to use these tools.

Estimating the Cost of Downtime

In recent studies, major corporations reported sizable financial losses when problems occurred on their networks. One study calculated the lost productivity resulting from network problems to be more than $3 million per year, on the average. The same study found that the average network is completely or partially disabled about twice a month, and the downtime lasts more than half a business day.

Network *downtime*, the time that the network is down or degraded, can be expensive. This is particularly true for a business that runs its day-to-day operations on a network. As companies recognize the increased importance of their networks, they demand better tools from vendors to help keep the networks running. The biggest network application of the 1990s may be network management.

Setting Network Management Goals

Network management has two goals. First, proper LAN management tries to reduce the number of network problems. If problems occur, the second goal is to minimize inconvenience and localize the damage. With these goals in mind, the International Standards Organization (ISO) identified five management categories a LAN management system should include: fault, configuration, performance, security, and accounting. Descriptions of these management categories follow:

Accounting management	Records and reports network resource utilization data.
Configuration management	Understands and controls the parameters that define the state of the network.
Fault management	Detects, isolates, and controls problems on the network.

Performance management	Analyzes and controls the rate at which the network can process data.
Security management	Controls access to network resources.

Four types of network management products exist to deal with the five ISO categories: physical-layer tools, network monitors, network analyzers, and integrated network management systems. Each kind of product offers different benefits to the people who manage today's heterogeneous networks.

Defining the Types of Tools

Physical-layer tools include Time-Domain Reflectometers (TDRs), oscilloscopes, breakout boxes, power meters, and similar products that find problems such as cable breaks, short circuits, unterminated cables, and bad connections.

Using the Time-Domain Reflectometer. Years ago, cable testers were bulky, awkward devices. However, microminiaturization has produced relatively inexpensive handheld devices you can carry to check individual cables. These small devices sometimes come with portable printers you can use to produce a report on the health of each cable in your system. All such devices are battery-powered, and a few use rechargeable NiCad batteries. Figure 12.1 shows popular LAN diagnostic products from the Microtest company.

A cable tester contains a Time-Domain Reflectometer (TDR) and, perhaps, additional test circuits. A TDR works by sending sonar-like pulses through the LAN cable. The TDR detects the reflections, analyzes them, and displays the result. A cable tester typically can tell you the length of a cable, whether the cable is correctly wired internally (pin-to-pin wire mapping), whether the cable contains a short circuit (wires touching each other through damaged or missing insulation), whether the cable contains a broken wire (an "open"), and whether the cable suffers from electrical crosstalk (interference). Any of these problems can bring down a network.

The Future of Cable Testers. Manufacturers of cable testers are pushing the technology of cable analysis. New devices extend cable testing into the realm of protocol analysis. The Fluke 670 LANMeter and Scope Communications FrameScope units go beyond the physical layer of the OSI reference model (the usual domain of cable testers) into layers 2, 3, and even 4. The Fluke 670 costs about $6,000 and the FrameScope costs about $4,000—both quite a bit below the price of a protocol analyzer.

Different models of both devices attach to a live EtherNet or Token Ring LAN. The devices accumulate and display statistics showing the health and performance of your network. Generally, the statistics show message frame counts, either total or by type of frame, in relation to elapsed time. For EtherNet LANs, the devices reveal excess collisions (indicating a jabbering network adapter), late collisions (your cables are too long), and error frame counts (the result of faulty connections). On a Token Ring LAN, each device can recognize and count Media Access Control (MAC) layer frames.

Fig. 12.1 Cable testing tools from companies like Microtest are invaluable to a LAN administrator diagnosing a connectivity problem.

These frames show neighbor relationships (in terms of MAU connections), receiver congestion errors (network adapters whose buffers can't handle incoming traffic), line errors, CRC errors, and the dreaded beaconing LAN. Even when your LAN is beaconing, these new cable testers can be inserted into the ring and determine the network addresses of the affected nodes. When an MAU port gets "stuck," the tester informs you of the condition and lets you reset the port remotely from the enhanced cable tester. You also can determine whether a Token Ring cable is experiencing phase jitter (a difficult-to-sense noise condition that often indicates a bad MAU).

These devices don't decode and display particular LAN message frames. Instead, the devices take a snapshot of each frame as it goes by, determine the type and meaning of the frame, and increment appropriate counters in the cable tester's memory. Both units have flash ROM and over 256K of RAM for frame buffers and statistics.

You can choose to watch overall network traffic, certain kinds of error situations, or traffic to and from a given node. You can determine which node is sending or receiving the most LAN traffic. You can "ping" a file server or other LAN node to determine the active presence of that node. Pinging is the sending of a LAN message to a node and waiting for a response. If you determine that a particular cable or network adapter is adversely affecting the LAN, you can cause that network node to remove itself from the ring. You can monitor the status of bridges and routers, and even determine token rotation time on a ring.

The units let you associate workstation names or individuals' names with network addresses, making it easy to see who is active on the LAN and whose connections are healthy. You won't have to know that node "10005A123456" is Sue's PC. The units have serial ports through which you can download upgrades into the flash ROM chips. Also, of course, these new devices can perform the more mundane cable tests you'd expect of a TDR device.

These enhanced cable testers have sizable LCD displays and remind you at first glance of a Nintendo Gameboy. Don't be fooled, though; these new handheld cable testers are just what the doctor ordered for ailing networks. One such tester may find its way into your bag of network tools someday.

Short circuits and open connections can happen months or years after installation, especially if cheap insulation dries out, becomes brittle, and cracks. Conversely, a water-soaked cable won't carry LAN traffic very well. During installation, a person sometimes will pull a wire around a corner, and part of the insulation will scrape off (a condition called a *shiner*). This cable problem might not cause a network outage for several months.

Some wiring problems happen during cable manufacture and connection. Occasionally, the factory or the installer will put connectors on the cable with the wrong wire leading to the wrong pin, and the new cable won't work at all. Or, the person may mix up the wire pairs by attaching connectors in a way that causes one of the wires to carry a signal that the other wire pair should carry (a condition known as *reversed pairs*). Even with perfectly manufactured, carefully connected wire, you might inadvertently cause a cable problem. In planning a network installation or enhancement, you might overlook the published limitations of the wiring specification; the result is a LAN segment with cables that are too long or have too many nodes in a segment. It's easy to overlook distance and number-of-nodes limitations when you are concentrating on giving people access to the network.

Before you attach the cable tester to your LAN, you must know the type of cable your LAN uses. Electricity travels at different speeds in different types of cable. The testing device must know the "nominal velocity of propagation" (NVP) for your cable before the tester can make accurate distance determinations. NVP, expressed as a fraction or sometimes a percentage of the speed of light in a vacuum, can vary from .60 to .90.

For example, Level 3 UTP cable has an NVP of .62, Level 5 UTP has an NVP of .72, RG-58 has an NVP of .80, RG-62 has an NVP of .84, and Type 1 has an NVP of .78. The cable tester will display incorrect results if you don't supply the tester with the right information about the cable type. Even the difference between foam and non-foam insulation in the cable can throw off the tester's results. The first thing you do with a new cable tester is calibrate the unit in relation to the type of cable you use. The cable tester often comes with a chart or table expressing the NVP for popular cable types,b you'll want to calibrate the tester anyway, in relation to the exact type of cable in your LAN. Calibration is a matter of trying different NVP values until the tester displays the correct cable length for a cable whose length you've measured.

You also need an up-to-date, accurate diagram of the topology (layout) of your LAN. When you think you've found a wiring fault, you will want to pinpoint the bad cable on your diagram to make sure that you understand how the symptoms of the problem (a particular group of workstations being dropped from the LAN, for example) relate to the wiring fault you've identified.

The basic procedure for using a cable tester is simple. After you detach both ends of the cable from the network, you connect the cable tester to one end and, for unshielded twisted pair (UTP), you connect a loopback device to the other end. The genderless data connector on shielded twisted pair (STP) is its own loopback device. You then run through the tester's diagnostic steps to see whether the cable is healthy.

You can and should use a cable tester to check a new LAN cable installation. When you build a LAN or add a cable segment to an existing LAN, you'll want to know that the new wires can carry noise-free LAN signals before you log on to a file server. If a contractor installs and maintains your LAN wiring, insist that the contractor perform cable tests during the installation. If you install your own wiring, use a cable tester to check your work.

Using Network Monitors. A *network monitor* is a computer device that attaches to a network and monitors all or a selected portion of the network traffic. By examining frame-level information in each packet, network monitors can compile statistics on network utilization, packet type, number of packets sent and received by each network node, packet errors, and other significant information.

Network monitors are relatively inexpensive, and you can use several on a large LAN— one for each network segment. You generally would let your network monitors run continuously, allowing them to collect data and search for problems. A network monitor does a reasonably good job of detecting errors, and most such tools can be part of an integrated management system. Network monitors cost from several hundred dollars (for software-only products) to about $10,000. Figure 12.2 shows the relatively inexpensive TXD product from Thomas-Conrad ($195 for a site license). TXD reveals statistical and diagnostic information about Novell NetWare LANs.

Fig. 12.2   Thomas-Conrad, now a part of Compaq Computer, offers diagnostic tools such as TXD.

Using Network Analyzers. While network monitors can detect network problems, *network analyzers* (sometimes called *protocol analyzers*) can help you track down and fix those problems. Network analyzers contain sophisticated features for real-time traffic analysis, packet capture and decoding, and packet transmission. Some even include troubleshooting expertise in the form of test suites. Network analyzers sometimes feature a built-in TDR. The most sophisticated network analyzers use special-purpose hardware to detect problems not visible to standard network controllers. Recently, manufacturers of network analyzers have begun adding artificial intelligence (AI) to their products.

Network analyzers are complicated, expensive tools for detecting certain kinds of LAN problems. You would use an analyzer to identify a failing device, configuration error, or LAN bottleneck. These tools are more sophisticated than cable testers or software-only network utilities. When you are faced with a problem that requires you to examine the detailed contents of your data frames, you are like a doctor who reaches for a microscope to view cells in a blood sample. The analyzer is the microscope; as the doctor, you have to know what normal cells look like and how many of each type you should see.

Network analyzers passively listen to all the frames flowing across the LAN and give you a picture of their health. The analyzer selects those frames that meet your filtering criteria, captures them in a file, and summarizes the frames or decodes them to show their contents. You can tell a network analyzer to show just error frames, frames from (or to) a certain workstation or server, frames of a certain type or that contain a given pattern of data, or frames that exceed size and frequency thresholds that you establish. Some analyzers enable you to inject extra traffic on the LAN, enabling you to simulate the addition of more nodes.

Once you know what to look for, a network analyzer can show you exactly which network adapter is causing a broadcast storm, help identify a misconfigured gateway that is causing routing errors, or show you the interpacket arrival rate of those frames involved in a performance problem. The network analyzer is not a substitute for your own experience and knowledge. You need to be a networking expert to use a network analyzer well.

Prices for network analyzers start at about $10,000, and they can cost more than $30,000 with support for multiple physical media and protocol decoding. Analyzers are sold as kits or complete products. The kit consists of a network adapter and software you install in one of your PCs. If you buy the complete product, you get the adapter and software preinstalled in a PC of the vendor's choice. The Sniffer, from Network General, is a popular network analyzer. Figure 12.3 shows a typical Sniffer PC. Figure 12.4 illustrates the Sniffer family of products.

Fig. 12.3 The Network General Sniffer typically consists of a portable computer with the Sniffer software preinstalled.

Looking at the Hewlett-Packard Network Advisor. The HP (Hewlett-Packard) Network Advisor is a PC with a monochrome or color LCD screen and a LAN interface designed for data acquisition. The HP software runs on top of DOS. Its graphical user interface is different from Windows or Presentation Manager, but it is not hard to get used to. The AI portion, Fault Finder, is written in Prolog and contains more than 100 rules.

When you invoke Fault Finder on a Token Ring LAN, it offers you these categories:

- Monitor for Station Insertion Failures
- Monitor for Hard Errors
- Monitor for Beacon MAC Frames

- Monitor for Congested Station Receivers

- Monitor for Ring Beaconing

The Network Advisor then asks which fault(s) to investigate. You can ask Fault Finder to explain itself. If you ask for a definition of the last category, for example, Fault Finder tells you, "The ring is considered to be beaconing if a station has transmitted 8 consecutive Beacon MAC frames."

Fig.12.4   Network General offers several models of its Sniffer.

You can see from the simple nature of the categories and the explanation that Fault Finder is not yet a genius at finding problems on your LAN. HP started at the lowest (physical) layer of the LAN with its AI product and expects to move up the protocol ladder into more complicated scenarios as time goes on. The list of symptoms you can give Fault Finder eventually will grow from "Can't Connect" to such problems as "Sporadic Slowdowns," "Can't Access Server 3," and "Corrupted Server Files."

Beyond its Fault Finder component, the Network Advisor sports the same features and functions as other network analyzers. You can capture frames for a specified period, using filters you set up. The Advisor decodes MAC-layer frames, AppleTalk frames, IBM PC LAN Program frames (NetBIOS and SMBs—System Message Blocks), Novell NetWare frames (IPX, SPX, and NCP—NetWare Core Protocol), IBM System Network Architecture (SNA) frames, and TCP/IP frames. To get more information on the Network Advisor, contact

Network Advisor
Hewlett-Packard Company
5070 Centennial Boulevard
Colorado Springs, CO 80919
(719) 531-4497
Fax: (719) 531-4505
www.hp.com

Looking at the Network General Sniffer. The Sniffer can decode and interpret frames from more protocols on more networks than other products, but it does not offer as many ways to categorize network activity on a NetWare LAN as does Novell's LANalyzer, nor is it as easy to use. If you want to know how many directory search requests a workstation issued, for example, you first must tell the Sniffer what data pattern to look for—that is, which bytes in which frame locations identify a directory search frame. The information is easy to pick out of the Sniffer display, but you must describe the search pattern in terms of bytes and byte offsets. On the LANalyzer, you simply select the Directory Search category.

Sniffer can show you statistics on LAN traffic to help you understand the health of your LAN. To give you an idea of what these figures look like, Figure 12.5 shows absolute traffic statistics on a Sniffer screen.

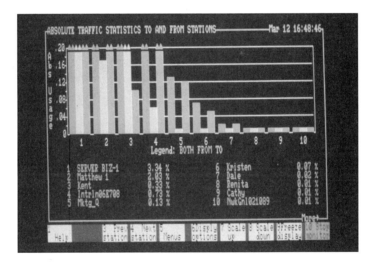

Fig. 12.5   The Sniffer can show absolute traffic statistics by network node.

On a Token Ring LAN, a failing network adapter often passes garbled data to the next node on the token ring, which in turn begins beaconing an alarm on the network. All activity stops on the LAN until you find and replace the faulty card. The Sniffer can notify you that the network is beaconing and correctly report the address of the faulty node.

Finding hardware errors and frame errors in the lower layers of the LAN is one job for a network analyzer. But you also can isolate performance bottlenecks. Sniffer can capture frames between specific nodes (a workstation and a server, for example) and display network utilization, frame counts, and the total number of bytes captured. During later analysis of this data, Sniffer shows you when each frame appeared on the network and what that frame contained.

If you kept notes describing what the workstation operator did during the capture, you can correlate the work being done to the timings of the different kinds of frames.

Suppose that the workstation loaded a 250K executable file from the file server. Sniffer would show 250 requests from the workstation interspersed with the 250 responses (assuming 1K packets) from the server. Unfortunately, Sniffer cannot explicitly tell you that the server hard disk, CPU, or disk controller is too slow. Sniffer looks only at the message traffic as the traffic appears on the LAN. You have to perform controlled experiments—varying the number of active workstations, the type of workstation, and other parameters—to get clear implications on which to base your conclusions. For more information on Sniffer, contact

> Network General Corporation
> 4200 Bohannon Drive
> Menlo Park, CA 94025
> (415) 688-2700
> (800) 952-6300
> Fax: (415) 321-0855
> www.sniffer.com

Looking at Novell LANalyzer. It goes without saying that Novell knows NetWare better than anyone else. LANalyzer does many of the same things as Sniffer, but on fewer networks and for fewer protocols. One of those protocols is, of course, NetWare. If you're a NetWare user, you'll find that LANalyzer characterizes your LAN activity in highly useful ways.

LANalyzer comes with preset templates, called *applications*, that you use to filter, interpret, and display the frames on your LAN. The applications for the Token Ring physical layer, for example, include Devices, ErrMon, Map, Priority, RingChng, and RingMon. These applications, especially ErrMon and RingMon, help you determine the health of your network adapters and cabling system. At a higher level, the applications called BridgeVu, FileView, NodeView, OverView, and ServerVu show you the LAN traffic in terms of server, workstation, and bridge functions. You can tell LANalyzer that you want to see just file-open activity and/or directory-search activity, if, for example, you want to see if someone's PATH statement is causing too many wrong directories to be searched for an executable file.

LANalyzer is a PC board and software you install in one of your PCs. The text-mode user interface looks and feels like the other NetWare utilities (SYSCON, FILER, and so on) that NetWare users are familiar with. For more information on LANalyzer, contact

> Novell, Inc.
> LANalyzer Products Division
> 2180 Fortune Drive
> San Jose, CA 95131
> (408) 434-2300
> (800) 243-8526
> www.novell.com

Using the Integrated Network Management System. The fourth and final type of product available for managing a network is the *Integrated Network Management System*. Using the INMS, you can monitor and control your entire network from a central location. The INMS addresses all five ISO network-management categories: fault, performance, configuration, security, and accounting. You use the INMS through a console device that provides a graphical user interface. The console device is integrated with a network management station that communicates with network agents—special workstation software, for example—on remote computer devices to determine the state of the network. Agents collect interesting information—such as the number of packets the device has received—and make it available to the INMS upon query. When a problem occurs, agents also can send alarms to the console to immediately alert the network manager. INMSs are the most expensive network management products.

Using the Tools

You learned at the beginning of this chapter that network management is both a science and an art. You must be a logical scientist and a creative artist to use these tools. As a scientist, you must understand how networks function and know the relationships between the symptoms of a problem and the list of possible causes. As an artist, you must think your way through the diagnostic process, drawing on your experiences with similar problems to solve a problem. The diagnostic process consists of four steps you repeat until you find and fix the problem: observing the symptoms, developing a list of possible causes, performing tests to isolate the cause, and analyzing the results.

Observing Symptoms. You first observe the symptoms of the problem. You may be tempted, in the rush to fix the problem, to begin experimenting with solutions before you finish a thorough examination of the symptoms. If you give in to temptation, you probably will wind up spending more time and money to fix the problem than if you had considered all the symptoms and their ramifications.

The most obvious symptoms are not always the key to understanding the problem. To know why this is true, you have to understand one of the primary characteristics of network protocols. Network protocols are designed to hide network problems, not expose them. Most network protocols incorporate retry logic and other techniques to support automatic recovery from problems. This causes most network problems to display a single obvious symptom: Slow response from the network. Although the network's attempts to retry a failing operation increase network reliability, the retries also make network troubleshooting more difficult. You see a common symptom for many problems.

In your analysis of the symptoms, you need to go beyond the slow response symptom. You need to ask yourself questions that help you focus on the behavior of the LAN. Does this problem affect everyone, everyone in a given area, or random individuals? What is the percentage of time the problem occurs? Is the problem continuous or intermittent? Does it occur regularly? What has changed recently? Has a computer device been added to the network? Have any internetworking devices been reconfigured? Which vendor's products may have produced these symptoms? What are the vendor and version numbers of the computer systems, network adapter cards, hubs, routers, bridges, application software, and network operating system software?

After you gather this information, you can begin the second step in the diagnostic process—the development of a list of possible causes for the symptoms you have observed.

Knowing What Is Normal. You have to sift through the observed symptoms and facts, looking for the cause of a problem. To recognize the symptoms, however, you must know what is normal and what is not normal on your network. The process of determining the normal characteristics of an individual network is called *baselining*.

Baselining is not one of the four steps in the diagnostic process. You must perform the baselining before the problem occurs. Of course, once a problem occurs, it is too late to determine the normal behavior of the network. If you have a clear, complete picture of the normal behavior of your LAN, you can answer the following questions: What is the average network utilization? How does it vary during the business day? What are the primary applications on the network? What protocols are running on the network? What are the performance characteristics of these protocols? Who manufactured the network interface controllers, media attachment units, hubs, and other network connection hardware? What are their performance characteristics? Who manufactured the repeaters, bridges, routers, and gateways on the network? What versions of software and firmware are they running? What are their performance characteristics?

Making a List of Possible Causes. With the baseline information at your fingertips, you can begin to ask how the observed symptoms relate to the normal operation of the network. You can distinguish unusual behavior and look for its cause. Experience and knowledge are your tools in this step.

To develop your list of possible causes, you must know how each network component can fail and what that failure can do to the entire network. As you make your list, visualize the dynamic nature of the LAN. Imagine how each component (network adapter, network operating system, cabling, or other unit) interacts with the rest of the network. Use your knowledge of protocols and network software to see how a network component's failure may cause the problem at hand. Excessive traffic, for example, can cause high collision counts on an EtherNet LAN, but a cable segment that is too long, or a malfunctioning transceiver, also can cause frequent collisions.

Isolating the Cause and Analyzing Results. In the third step, you test the LAN to see which of the items on your list is the culprit. You will use any and perhaps all of the tools covered earlier in this chapter, but you may find that the tool you use most is the network analyzer. The analyzer enables you to monitor the network's behavior interactively, and the analyzer gives you more views of what is happening.

Once you think you have found the failing component, you test your hypothesis. You simply may remove the failing component from the network to see if the problem disappears, or you may reconfigure or reset the component. Because diagnosis usually requires 80 percent of the problem-solving effort, and implementing a solution only 20 percent, you probably will find this last step the most straightforward.

Dealing with Common Problems

A typical network administrator spends a great deal of time solving problems and trying to understand the network's performance. Different parts of a network experience different kinds of problems and exhibit different symptoms.

Dealing with Network Hardware Problems. The most frequent network problems occur in the physical layer—the lowest layer of the Open Systems Interconnection model. Because hardware is subject to physical stress, electrical connectivity problems are the most common fault type. These problems include cable breaks, cable shorts, breaks elsewhere in the circuit, and malfunctions in the actual network adapter circuitry.

Dealing with Cabling Problems. You can isolate cable problems with a network analyzer or TDR. You often can find problems with hardware circuitry by examining error traffic on the network using a network analyzer. At other times, you must attack these problems with a process of elimination to isolate the cause. A cable-management system may help you locate the problem (see "Managing Cables" later in this chapter).

Practicing Performance Tuning

Network monitors and analyzers enable you to compile statistics on your LAN's message traffic. You can use these figures to understand your LAN's performance as it relates to the traffic. You can view the daily network utilization patterns, identify the heaviest users, determine the various percentages of different protocol traffic, find network bottlenecks, and perhaps even recognize why those bottlenecks exist.

This analysis may suggest to you that you need to partition the network into multiple segments, add file servers, or upgrade your network adapters to obtain better performance. The performance tuning task is not a small one, however. You will need to spend a significant amount of time gathering statistics and relating those statistics to the particular components of your LAN.

Performance Tuning Your LAN. Network management is both an art and a science, but finding a bottleneck on a LAN can require the skills of a magician with a Ph.D. in electrical engineering. You may get advice like "Put a faster hard drive in the server," "Switch to Token Ring," "Switch to EtherNet," "Switch to NetWare," or "Switch to Warp Server." What if you take the advice and discover that performance does not change? The part you replaced was not the bottleneck; something else was.

You can use the information in the following sections to make your LAN faster, spending wisely in the process.

Performance Factors. When you run an application that resides on the file server and that in turn reads and writes files on the server, a flurry of activity takes place. First, COMMAND.COM looks in each of your PATH directories for the executable file. This searching of server directories causes a dialog of LAN messages. For each directory, your workstation sends a "Find File" request message, and the server sends back a response. The executable file loads into your workstation's memory through another series of LAN messages, usually in 512- or 1024-byte packets (LAN packets have size limits). Once loaded, the application program issues open, read, write, and close requests that become LAN messages sent to the server. The server responds to each request by sending back an "OK" or a "Here's the data" message. On NetBIOS-based networks, the receiver separately acknowledges each message. On NetWare networks, however, the acknowledgment and the response message are the same.

The server must manage a queue of requests from the many workstations on the LAN, and the queue can get quite long. If you use the server for remote printing, two problems can occur. Multiple print jobs may keep the file server busy reading and writing spool files, thus delaying other file-service requests. The file server also has to devote time and effort to managing the shared printer. In addition, workstation and server messages (both for file service and print spooling) may have to cross one or more bridges, which creates another delay.

The upper layers of the network software (such as NetWare's NET*x*.COM) filter each file and print request and create one or more message records that the network software hands to a lower layer (IPX.COM). This layer in turn gives the request message to the network device drivers. Through an 8-, 16-, or 32-bit slot, these drivers tell the network adapter to send the request to the server. When it can use the LAN cable, the network card sends the request. At the server, the network support software hands the request up through more layers of support code before the network operating system finally processes it. If the request cannot be satisfied from server memory (the RAM cache), the server waits for the hard disk to rotate into position to access the data. The response travels back to the workstation through the support software, server network adapter, LAN cable, workstation network adapter, and workstation support software. A 250K executable, using 512-byte message packets, requires the interchange of more than 500 requests and 500 responses just to load the program. (Larger packets cause less server overhead.) When many people try to use the file server at the same time, the server is the Grand Central Station for LAN traffic and file requests.

The network bottleneck may be at the workstation, in the network drivers, network TSRs, or network adapter. The transmission rate of the LAN also may be the bottleneck. At the server, you have several suspects. The server CPU may not be executing the network operating system software quickly enough. The network software may not be efficiently coded. Too little RAM in the server for file-caching purposes means that the server frequently must take the time to access the hard disk drive. The server may spend an inordinate amount of time acting as a print server. Perhaps your server's overhead would be less if you could configure it to use larger packets. Could the speed of the bus be holding you back? Perhaps the server and the network adapter have trouble communicating through a confining 8-bit slot. The network adapter may not contain enough RAM to buffer all the LAN messages. Are your bridges slowing you down? The list of potential bottlenecks is a long one, and the picture is further complicated by the interactions that can occur between the components. As you look for performance bottlenecks on your LAN, you will need to keep these factors in mind.

Managing Cables

The cable-management system is a fairly new tool for the network administrator that documents and displays the physical layout of your network. For a small LAN, your first documentation efforts may be a pencil-drawn map of the office that shows LAN cables and other components. A large LAN requires more sophisticated documentation. You can use a cable management system to find and track cables and other *network assets*— a term made popular by vendors of such cable-management software.

Cable-management systems offer a range of features that track the complete physical infrastructure of a network. The system stores data about each component, including its location, in a database. On demand, the system displays a graphical picture of the network. A cable-management system also can report on the network assets.

You can view the entire network, or you can zoom in on a part of the network. By clicking an icon that represents a network component, you can quickly locate specific information such as cable routes, the available outlets on a given floor, or all items on a given circuit.

The database contains detailed information on the network assets—from the location of cables to the administrative information associated with each piece of equipment, cable, and cableway. The cable-management database also stores characteristics such as the brand of equipment, costs, model numbers, location within the facility, and connectivity and wiring schemes.

In addition to using a cable-management system to document your LAN, you can use it to generate work orders for equipment moves and changes as well as repair orders for failed components. The system also keeps a history of changes made to the network.

Using the Resource Guide

Several companies offer products to help you manage a network. You will find the following list a good starting place in your evaluation of network management products.

> 3Com Corporation
> 5400 Bayfront Plaza
> Santa Clara, CA 95052
> (800) 638-3266
> (408) 764-5000
> Fax: (408) 764-5001

> AT&T Computer Systems
> 1776 On the Green
> Ninth Floor
> Morristown, NJ 07960
> (800) 247-1212
> (904) 636-2314
> Fax: (904) 636-3078

Automated Design Systems
375 Northridge Road
Suite 270
Atlanta, GA 30350
(404) 394-2552

Banyan Systems, Inc.
115 Flanders Road
Westborough, MA 01581
(508) 898-1000

BICC Data Networks, Inc.
1800 West Park Drive
Westborough, MA 01581
(800) 447-6526
(508) 898-2422
Fax: (508) 898-3739

Blue Lance, Inc.
1700 West Loop S
Suite 700
Houston, TX 77027
(713) 680-1187
Fax: (713) 622-1370

Brightwork Development
P.O. Box 8728
Red Bank, NJ 07701
(800) 552-9876
(201) 530-0440
Fax: (201) 530-0622

Daystrom Data Products
15 Sunrise Hill Road
Fishkill, NY 12524
(914) 896-7378

Digilog, Inc.
1370 Welsh Road
Montgomeryville, PA 18936
(215) 628-4530
Fax: (215) 628-3935

Digital Equipment Corporation
30 Proter Road
Littleton, MA 01460
(508) 562-4521

Bytex
120 Turnpike Road
Southborough, MA 01772
(508) 480-0840

Cabletron Systems, Inc.
35 Industrial Way
Rochester, NH 03867
(603) 332-9400
Fax: (603) 332-4616

Certus International Corporation
13110 Shaker Square
Cleveland, Ohio 44120
(800) 722-8737
(216) 752-8181
Fax: (216) 752-8188

Cheyenne Software
55 Bryant Avenue
Roslyn, NY 11576
(800) 243-9462
(516) 484-5110
Fax: (516) 484-5110

Chipcom Corporation
118 Turnpike Road
Southborough, MA 01772
(800) 228-9930
(508) 460-8900
Fax: (508) 460-8950

Computer Tyme, Inc.
411 North Sherman
Suite 300
Springfield, MO 65802
(800) 548-5353
(417) 866-1222
Fax: (417) 866-0135

Connect Computer Company
9855 West 78th Street
Eden Prairie, MN 55344
(612) 944-0181
Fax: (612) 944-9298

Data General Corporation
4400 Computer Drive
Westborough, MA 01580
(508) 366-8911

Dolphin Software
6050 Peachtree Parkway
Suite 340-208
Norcross, GA 30092
(404) 339-7877
Fax: (404) 339-7905

ETI Software, Inc.
2930 Prospect Avenue
Cleveland, Ohio 44115
(800) 336-2014
(216) 241-1140
Fax: (216) 241-2319

Frye Computer Systems, Inc.
19 Temple Place
Boston, MA 02111
(617) 247-2300
Fax: (617) 451-6711

Gazelle Systems
42 North University Avenue
Suite 10
Provo, UT 84601
(800) 233-0383
(801) 377-1288
Fax: (801) 373-6933

Hewlett-Packard Company
Vancouver Division
18110 Southeast 34th Street
Camas, WA 98607
(206) 254-8110

Microcom, Inc.
500 River Ridge Drive
Norwood, MA 02062
(617) 551-1000
Fax: (617) 551-1898

Microtest, Inc.
3519 East Shea Boulevard
Suite 134
Phoenix, AZ 85028
(800) 526-9675
Fax: (602) 971-6963

Horizons Technology, Inc.
3990 Ruffin Road
San Diego, CA 92123
(619) 292-8331
Fax: (619) 292-7321

Hughes LAN Systems
1225 Charleston Road
Mountain View, CA 94043
(415) 966-7300

IBM Corporation
1000 Northwest 51st Street
Boca Raton, FL 33432
(407) 443-2000

International Data Science
7 Wellington Road
Lincoln, RI 02865
(401) 333-6200
Fax: (401) 333-3584

Internetix, Inc.
8903 Presidential Parkway
Suite 210
Upper Marlborough, MD 20772
(301) 420-7900
Fax: (301) 420-4395

Isicad, Inc.
1920 West Corporate Way
P.O. Box 61022
Anaheim, CA 92803
(714) 533-8910

J.A. Lomax Associates
659 Adrienne Street
Suite 101
Novato, CA 94945
(800) 225-6629
(415) 892-9606
Fax: (415) 898-0867

LAN Support Group, Inc.
P.O. Box 460269
Houston, TX 77056
(800) 749-8439
(713) 622-4900

Network & Communication
   Technology, Inc.
24 Wampum Road
Park Ridge, NJ 07656
(201) 307-9000
Fax: (201) 307-9404

Network Computing, Inc.
1950 Stemmons
Suite 3016
Dallas, TX 75207
(214) 746-4949

Network General Corporation
4200 Bohannon Drive
Menlo Park, CA 94025
(415) 688-2700

Network Interface Corporation
15019 West 95th Street
Lenexa, KS 66215
(913) 894-2277
Fax: (913) 894-0226

Network Management, Inc.
19 Rector Street
15th Floor
New York, NY 10006
(212) 797-3800
Fax: (212) 797-3817

Novell, Inc.
122 East 1700
South Provo, UT 84606
(801) 429-5900
Fax: (801) 377-9353

Standard Microsystems Corporation
35 Marcus Boulevard
Hauppauge, NY 11788
(516) 273-3100
Fax: (516) 273-2136

StarTek, Inc.
100 Otis Street
Northborough, MA 01532
(508) 393-9393
Fax: (508) 393-6934

Optical Data Systems
1101 East Arapaho
Richardson, TX 75081
(214) 234-6400
Fax: (214) 234-1467

Palindrome Corporation
850 East Diehl Road
Naperville, IL 60653
(708) 505-3300

Proteon, Inc.
Two Technology Drive
Westborough, MA 01581
(508) 898-2800
Fax: (508) 898-2118

ProTools, Inc.
14976 Northwest Greenbrier Parkway
Beaverton, OR 97006
(503) 645-5400
Fax: (503) 645-3577

Retix
2644 30th Street
Santa Monica, CA 90405
(213) 399-2200
Fax: (213) 458-2685

Saber Software Corporation
5944 Luther Lane
Suite 1007
Dallas, TX 75225
(800) 338-8754
(214) 361-8086
Fax: (214) 361-1882

SoftShell Systems
1163 Triton Drive
Foster City, CA 94404
(800) 322-7638
(415) 571-9000
Fax: (415) 571-0622

Spider Systems, Inc.
12 New England Executive Park
Burlington, MA 01803
(800) 447-7807
(617) 270-3510
Fax: (617) 270-9818

SynOptics Communications, Inc.
4401 Great American Parkway
P.O. Box 58185
Santa Clara, CA 95952
(800) 776-8023
(408) 988-2400
Fax: (408) 988-5525

Technology Dynamics, Inc.
145 15th Street NE
Suite 624
Atlanta, GA 30361
(800) 226-0428
(404) 874-0428

Telebit Corporation
1315 Chesapeake Terrace
Sunnyvale, CA 94089
(800) 835-3248
(408) 734-4333
Fax: (408) 734-3333

TGR Software, Inc.
2 Ravinia Drive
Suite 330
Atlanta, GA 30346
(404) 390-7450
Fax: (404) 390-7455

Thomas-Conrad Corporation
1908-R Kramer Lane
Austin, TX 78758
(800) 332-8683
(512) 836-1935
Fax: (512) 836-2840

Ungermann-Bass, Inc.
3900 Freedom Circle
Santa Clara, CA 95052
(408) 496-0111
Fax: (408) 970-7343

Unisys Corporation
2700 North First Street
P.O. Box 6685
San Jose, CA 95150
(408) 434-2848
Fax: (408) 434-2131

Vitalink Communications Corporation
6607 Kaiser Drive
Fremont, CA 94555
(800) 523-9550
(415) 794-1100
Fax: (415) 795-1085

Wang Laboratories, Inc.
One Industrial Avenue
Lowell, MA 01851
(800) 225-0654
(508) 459-5000

Wollongong Group, Inc.
1129 San Antonio Road
Palo Alto, CA 94303
(800) 872-8649
(415) 962-7100
Fax: (415) 969-5547

Chapter Summary

In this chapter, you rounded out your exploration of local area networks by considering the issues, techniques, and tools of network management. After covering the basics, you learned about the Simple Network Management Protocol (SNMP) and the Common Management Information Protocol (CMIP).

You then turned your attention to IBM's network management products, concentrating on the special capabilities of Token Ring. You understand the purpose and use of general tools such as a time-domain reflectometer, network monitor, network analyzer, and integrated management system. You learned about cable management. Also, you have a resource guide you can use to research specific products and companies.

In the next chapter, you look at the issues you will face when vendors offer you additional LAN products, claiming they will *interoperate* with your existing network.

Chapter 13

Analyzing Interoperability

Vendors of LAN products like to claim that their products work on many types of networks. Both hardware and software vendors use the word *interoperability* to describe the degree to which a product can be used on different networks, in different situations, and for different purposes. However, you have to take these claims with a grain of salt if you try to treat the products as building blocks on your LAN.

Have you ever stared at a printed word a little too long and watched it turn into a strange, foreign-looking object? In the LAN industry, everyone seems to have stared at interoperability for too long. In this chapter, you'll take an analytical look at the word *interoperability* to see what it really means. The word has been overworked and misused—it's time to put some meaning and substance back into interoperability, so you can use the word constructively and productively in discussions of which LAN products actually work well together.

Interoperability pertains to nearly everything in your day-to-day life, to one degree or another. As you may imagine, most of the examples in this chapter deal with local area networks, but you'll also touch on other ways of making computer components talk to one another. Modems, serial ports, printers, printer ports, application software, e-mail links, musical instruments, telephones, and even fax machines exemplify degrees of interoperability.

Learning What Interoperates

The more you hear and read about interoperability, the more skeptical you need to be. This is a cynical observation, but a useful one. You'll learn why in this chapter.

The first thing you'll notice about interoperability is that people don't use the word to refer to things that actually *do* interoperate. You've probably gone to the store, bought a telephone and some phone cord with RJ-11 jacks (or a modular plug) at either end, plugged the phone into a wall jack in your house, and immediately picked up the handset to make a call. You didn't once use the word *interoperability* when you described the job to your friends.

Here's an even better example: you had a few extra dollars while you were at the store, so you bought a small electrical appliance (a toaster, perhaps). As soon as you got home you plugged it into a wall outlet and used it, without thinking once of the word *interoperable*. The degree of interoperability with telephone companies and utility companies is exceedingly high.

On the other hand, have you ever tried to merge several LANs into one? Suppose you have a mixture of networks, each using different network operating systems—IBM LAN Server, Novell NetWare (perhaps with some Macintosh workstations), LANtastic, and Network File System (NFS). You want to set things up so that all the LAN users get to share the same resources and files on all the servers. You'll quickly begin using *interoperable* as an expletive while you try to make it work.

If you buy all your hardware and software from a single manufacturer, your concern for interoperability is eased somewhat. IBM, for example, produces charts and tables to show which of its products work together and which don't. You still may run into things that don't work well together, however.

You could say IBM is just another computer manufacturer. IBM is large enough, though, that its specifications and guidelines often become industry standards. This affects interoperability. Looking at things from the other direction, you can buy IBM modems that use the Hayes command set, which itself is a standard. Interoperability is closely linked to the existence of adhered-to standards.

Examining the OSI Protocol Stack

To impose some organization on the subject, you can use the Open Systems Interconnection (OSI) model as a guide. You can work your way up the OSI model protocol stack as you explore interoperability. Note that the OSI model is only a guide, because many products are still not OSI-compliant. Still, the OSI model is an important reference point for discussions about LANs. As you analyze interoperability at the different layers of the OSI model, one of the things you'll discover is that interoperability gets fuzzier and fuzzier as you get near the top of the stack. Vendor claims notwithstanding, interoperability isn't always easily achieved, especially at the higher layers of the OSI model.

The OSI model defines seven protocol layers and specifies that each layer is insulated from the others by a well-defined interface. Figure 13.1 shows the seven layers.

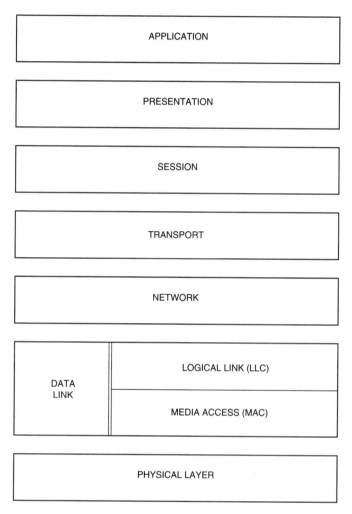

Fig. 13.1   The seven layers of the OSI Reference Model provide a theoretical framework for evaluating specific protocol stack implementations.

The Open Systems Interconnection (OSI) reference model organizes local area network connectivity into seven independent pieces, or layers. The following list explains these layers:

■ *Application:* The Application layer is the highest level. It interfaces with users, re-trieves information from databases, and transfers whole files. It is the part of the OSI model visible to you. It turns your LAN accesses into work requests it passes to the next level down, the Presentation layer. The Application layer doesn't do any real work itself, instead delegating all tasks to the lower layers. A work request to be sent across the network enters the OSI model protocol stack at the Application layer, travels downward toward the first layer (the Physical layer), zips across to the other workstation or server, and then travels back up the protocol stack until the work request message reaches the application on the other computer through its own Application layer.

■ *Presentation:* The Presentation layer receives work requests from the Application layer, or it delivers responses to the Application layer. This layer exists to hide differences between different kinds of computers. When IBM, Apple, DEC, NeXT, and Burroughs computers all want to talk to each other, some translation and byte-reordering is necessary. This layer converts data into (or from) a machine's native internal numeric format. The Presentation layer also compresses the messages into an encrypted form, for security purposes. (When delivering messages, the Presentation layer decrypts the messages.) Once its job is finished, the Presentation layer submits its results to the next layer.

■ *Session:* Computers on local area networks use names or numbers to identify each other. The Session layer uses each computer's identification to call another computer, in the same way you use telephone numbers to make telephone calls. The Session layer makes the initial contact and manages the progress of the call. The call itself is a *session*—an exchange of messages (or a dialog) between two workstations. The functions in this layer enable applications running at two workstations to coordinate their communications into a single session. The Session layer, like a telephone company, doesn't say anything during the dialog.

■ *Transport:* The Transport layer is the only layer that concerns itself with making sure the information sent by one computer on the network is received properly by another computer. The Transport layer knows the maximum size of each LAN packet and breaks up a work request message (or response) into smaller packets as necessary. When more than one packet is in process at any time, this layer controls the sequencing of the message packets and regulates inbound traffic flow. If a duplicate packet arrives (perhaps the result of a retransmission), this layer recognizes and discards it. The Transport layer delegates the work of routing packets to the next lower layer.

■ *Network:* The Network layer plans the routing of the packets. The message packets may need to travel through several LAN segments to get to their destinations. The Network layer keeps track of the different routes that a message packet may need to travel. The Network layer inserts this routing information into each message packet to help the intermediate computers and devices forward the message packet to its destination. This layer takes responsibility for addressing and delivering messages, end-to-end, from source computer to final destination.

■ *Data Link:* The Data Link layer is the most complex. It encompasses the sending of the characters that make up a message packet on a character-by-character basis. Because of its complexity, the Data Link layer is broken into a Media Access Control (MAC) layer and a Logical Link Control (LLC) layer. The MAC layer manages network access (token-passing or collision-sensing, for example) and network control. The LLC layer, operating at a higher level than the MAC layer, sends and receives the user data messages and packets (typically file service requests and responses). If the Data Link layer detects an error, it arranges for the sending computer to retransmit the message packet. The error detection is only point-to-point; the sending computer may be only forwarding a message from the originating computer. (The Transport layer has control and responsibility for end-to-end delivery.)

- *Physical:* The Physical layer only needs to turn the characters in a message packet into electrical signals. This layer doesn't need to process routing information, computer names, or the other contents of a message packet. Because the other layers have done their supervisory work already, the Physical layer merely has to send or receive the electrical signals through the LAN cable. This part of the OSI model specifies the physical and electrical characteristics of the connections that make up the network. It encompasses things like twisted-pair cables, fiber-optic cables, coaxial cables, connectors, repeaters, and so on. You can think of it as the Hardware layer.

Interoperability—the degree to which LAN hardware and software products from different vendors work well with each other—varies considerably as you consider each of the layers of the OSI model. In the next few sections, using the OSI model as a guide, you'll look at the criteria and the obstacles for interoperability on local area networks.

The Physical and Data Link Layers

Within each type of cable, physical interoperability is pretty well defined. If you tell someone you've connected some computers with an RG-58 A/U coaxial cable, there's a good chance he or she will immediately think of thin EtherNet (ThinNet). If you mention shielded twisted-pair (IBM Type 1) cable, Token Ring will likely come to mind. Unshielded twisted pair may be Token Ring or EtherNet's relatively new 10BASET. Fiber optics? FDDI (Fiber Distributed Data Interface) is new enough that you may just get puzzled looks.

In each case, though, the simple mention of the type of cable is nearly enough to define the entire physical appearance of the network components, and to specify what will connect to what (interoperability). If your computer has a Token Ring card and you want to connect to a Token Ring LAN, you can ask two questions to find out if it's possible: "Does the LAN operate at 4 or 16 megabits per second?" and "Does the LAN use shielded or unshielded twisted-pair cable?" Once you know your Token Ring adapter is using the right speed and can connect to the LAN's cabling system, you can reliably join the ring. This level of interoperability is made possible by the Institute of Electrical and Electronic Engineers (the IEEE). The 802.3 (EtherNet) and 802.5 (Token Ring) standards specify *exactly* how the Physical layer of the network should behave, and these standards extend their reach into the Data Link layer.

Other physical standards are highly interoperable. The best example is a parallel printer cable (the Centronics Interface). If you buy a printer with a parallel interface and the printer doesn't work with a computer and cable that are known to be good, it's certain that the printer isn't working.

The standard for serial cables, RS-232, is as exacting as the Centronics parallel printer interface. This standard defines Data Terminal Equipment (DTE) and Data Communications Equipment (DCE), and it specifies how to connect DTE and DCE to make them work (interoperate). You can buy a modem with an RS-232 interface, connect it to your RS-232 serial port with an RS-232 serial cable, and you'll know everything will work.

Suppose you get out some spare chips and a soldering iron and somehow manage to connect your Token Ring-equipped computer to your EtherNet LAN so that the EtherNet message packets (frames) successfully enter the Token Ring card. Can you "interoperate" your new network adapter on your LAN? Of course not.

First, your Token Ring adapter needs to see a three-byte token it can claim before the adapter can send data on the network. The adapters in the other workstations rely on collision sensing to get their message across. But even forgetting about tokens and collision sensing, the basic format of the data is different.

Pascal programmers call the data format of a message packet a *record*. In C, it's a *struct*. Assembler programmers may use a struc <> notation to define the data format. COBOL programmers think of it in terms of a record description. Basically, the data format is the layout of the data in memory—the organization of the data bytes into fields within a data record. Not only is an EtherNet data record (frame) laid out differently than a Token Ring frame, but IEEE 802.3 EtherNet is slightly different than what some call True EtherNet (Fig. 13.2 shows the differences). Within each standard (IEEE 802.3 EtherNet or IEEE 802.5 Token Ring), though, the degree of interoperability is quite high.

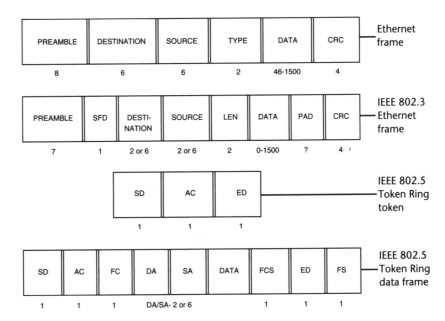

Fig. 13.2   Essential data elements, such as destination and source network addresses, appear in different positions within different protocols.

ARCnet data records (frames), FDDI frames, and StarLAN frames are laid out differently, too—just as you would expect. The essential point, though, is that your hybrid, jury-rigged Token Ring card won't work with your EtherNet LAN because these record layouts are understood by the ROM program code burned into each adapter. If you did manage to modify the Token Ring card enough to make it work, you wouldn't have a Token Ring card anymore—you'd have the world's most expensive EtherNet adapter.

In Figure 13.2, the following parameters are used:

AC	Access control
CRC	Cyclic redundancy checksum
DA	Destination address
ED	End delimiter
FC	Frame control
FCS	Frame check sequence
FS	Frame status
PAD	Filler bytes to bring the frame to a minimum length
SA	Source address
SD	Start delimiter
SFD	Start frame delimiter

What about non-LAN examples? If interoperability is such a slippery thing, how is it that you can use your fax machine to send documents and pictures to someone else, no matter what type of fax machine they have? The answer, of course, is standards. Group III FAX is a standard understood around the world.

9600-baud modems took a while to catch on, mostly because the standard for data representation was still evolving. Now you have CCITT V.32 modems from different manufacturers that reach out and touch each other constantly. Some modems, made just as the CCITT standard became official, don't always speak clearly to other 9600-baud modems. An example is the U.S. Robotics Courier HST modem; before USR's Dual Standard, its modems didn't operate well with other 9600-baud modems. (The original HST used a proprietary modulation scheme, which provides a 9600-bps forward channel and a back channel running at 1200 bps.)

Higher-speed 28.8kb modems interoperate if they adhere to the CCITT V.34 standard.

The Network and Transport Layers

People talk a lot about interoperability at the Network and Transport layers. Remember, the more people talk about interoperability, the more skeptical you have to be. Interoperability is sporadic and elusive at these levels.

IPX.COM implements the IPX protocol. IPX is the layer of NetWare workstation protocol software between NET*x*.COM (above) and network adapter software (below). IPX (internetwork packet exchange) has its own API, and application software on one NetWare workstation can talk through this interface to other NetWare workstations. The workstation dialog takes place in a unique dialect of network languages, however; other workstations may use the same cables and network adapters, but they cannot participate if they don't speak the IPX language.

If you're confused by this talk of layers, protocol stacks, and interfaces, look back at Figure 13.2 for a moment. See the field in the EtherNet and Token Ring frames labeled DATA? The data field is yet another record layout. The fields in this encapsulated data record are defined by the software in the Network and Transport layers. If you send your NetWare workstation an EtherNet frame with a data field (record) containing bytes laid out a certain way, your IPX-based workstation will recognize the frame. If you put wrong values in those bytes, your workstation won't know what to do with the frame, even if the EtherNet portion is filled out correctly. At the Network and Transport layers, interoperability is defined mostly in terms of the definition of the data within the message packet.

IPX is a close adaptation of a protocol developed by Xerox: the Xerox Network Standard (XNS). Novell uses it, of course, but there are no other "major players" whose LAN products implement IPX directly. One way around this stumbling block is to use the Clarkson Packet Drivers. Supported by Novell, FTP Software of Wakefield, Massachusetts, much of the academic community, and other groups, the Clarkson Packet Drivers enable multiple protocols to use the same network adapter. IPX data packets are routed to IPX, NetBIOS packets to NetBIOS, TCP/IP packets to TCP/IP, Network File System (NFS) packets to NFS, and so forth. These drivers take up a little extra RAM, but they do a good job of providing interoperability at the Network and Transport layers—if, of course, you have multiple upper layers that all need to use the same network adapter.

TCP/IP, which stands for *Transmission Control Protocol/Internet Protocol*, is in the public domain because it was developed by the federal government. (In general, the government cannot have copyrights.) This is one big reason for the popularity of TCP/IP. TCP can be considered a Session layer definition, and will be discussed later. IP fits more into the Transport layer. TCP/IP is yet another piece of the interoperability puzzle. If everyone used TCP/IP (or IPX, or NetBIOS), you would have a much easier time making networks interoperate. The different Transport layer definitions (record layouts and data field meanings) are the biggest obstacles to interoperability.

Another term people use at the level of the Transport layer is *transport independence*. This is another way of saying *interoperability*. Suppose you're a programmer and you want to develop an application where some modules run under OS/2 on an IBM PS/2, some run on an Apple Macintosh (a Mac would be a good place to put the application's user interface component), and some run on a UNIX computer. You want to design the modules so the *calling interface*—one module passing parameters and control to another—is completely transparent to the programmer. You need special "glue" to put these pieces together. The "glue" is called *remote procedure calls*, or RPC.

RPC is like Crazy Glue because it lets different kinds of computers process different parts of the same application. Companies like SunSoft (a subsidiary of Sun Microsystems),

NetWise, Novell, Hewlett-Packard, and Momentum Software are doing amazing things with RPC. American Airlines, for example, is using Xipc from Momentum Software to develop a cargo-routing system that runs on a variety of computers.

Transport independence means that all the machines making up the entire application system are using the same Transport layer definition—IPX, NetBIOS, TCP/IP, or something else. RPC works well when the same Transport layer is available for all the kinds of computers you want to use. You segregate your application program modules by target machine, and voilà—you've incorporated the best characteristics of each kind of computer into one system.

So far we've concentrated on IPX and TCP/IP. Where does NetBIOS fit into the picture? Because much of NetBIOS works at the Session layer, you'll learn about NetBIOS next as you work your way up the OSI model.

The Session Layer

IPX.COM actually contains two protocols: IPX and SPX (sequenced packet exchange). As you would expect, SPX is a layer on top of IPX and uses IPX to send and receive its data messages. SPX is session-oriented, like NetBIOS, but the similarity ends there. The degree of interoperability between IPX/SPX and NetBIOS is exceedingly low.

Novell supplies a NetBIOS.EXE program with NetWare that you would think would solve the problem. It doesn't, however. If the various implementations of NetBIOS were interoperable, you could construct a protocol stack of network adapter support software, IPX.COM, NetBIOS, and different redirector modules from Novell (NetWare NET*x*.COM), Artisoft (LANtastic), IBM (DOS LAN Requester), and other vendors, and you would be able to access just about any file server ever created. (You'll learn about redirector software in the next section.)

Even if you had enough RAM to hold this protocol stack, you still couldn't use it to access anything. Each vendor expects its LAN software to work with the NetBIOS *it* implemented. You've climbed only five-sevenths of the way up the OSI model, and already interoperability is out of focus and getting fuzzier by the minute.

Although there are some differences in the programming interfaces of each of the implementations from various vendors, a bigger problem is the different data record layouts used to shuttle NetBIOS packets across the network. On a DOS-based workstation, IBM's NetBIOS module is the device driver DXMT0MOD.SYS (part of the IBM LAN support program). Novell's NetBIOS module is NETBIOS.EXE. Artisoft's NetBIOS for LANtastic is AILANBIOS. Performance Technology's POWERLan NetBIOS module is named for the adapter it supports. For each of these NetBIOS modules, the format and content of the data record (encapsulated inside the data field of the EtherNet or Token Ring frame) are different.

The Presentation and Application Layers

The software on your LAN that gives you access to the file server is the network shell, or redirector. On a NetWare network, this is NET*x*.COM, where *x* denotes the DOS version. Or you may use the DOS-version-independent NETX.COM. On an OS/2-based IBM LAN

Server network, this layer is represented by DOS LAN Requester at DOS-based worksta-tions. Other vendors' redirector software usually is called REDIR or simply NET.

You can also talk about electronic mail interoperability and the software mechanisms for sharing data in the OS/2 Presentation Manager and Microsoft Windows environments in a discussion about the Presentation and Application layers.

It goes without saying that NetWare LANs, OS/2 LANs, Banyan LANs, and peer-to-peer LANs aren't easily interoperable at the Presentation and Application layers. Just as you would suspect from the discussion of lower layers of the protocol stack, the lack of com-munication among different vendors' redirector software modules is mostly a matter of data definition.

NetWare workstations use the NetWare Core Protocol (NCP) to request file services; serv-ers respond in kind. NCP was proprietary until early in 1991, when Novell announced it would license the NCP specification for a fee. It's uncertain how the Network General people managed to decode the NCP data packets some years ago. Network General's Sniffer is a protocol analyzer capable of interpreting and displaying the interior of LAN packets on a variety of networks. Perhaps Network General reverse-engineered the NCP protocol. If this is true, you have to admire the Network General programmers. It's a huge, tedious job to make sense of streams of bytes flying back and forth across a LAN.

IBM created the Server Message Block (SMB) protocol for use with the PC LAN Program. One of the best documents for understanding the SMB protocol is Volume 2, Number 8-1 of the IBM Personal Computer Seminar Proceedings. Printed all the way back in 1985, it's nonetheless a useful introduction to how SMBs work.

IBM uses the SMB protocol in OS/2 Warp Server and Warp Connect. Microsoft also uses the SMB protocol in its NT Server, Windows for Workgroups, and Windows 95 environ-ments. A few vendors of peer-to-peer products (such as Performance Technology) also support SMBs. With some limitations—the result of minor differences in how these ven-dors use the SMB protocol—IBM's network software products and Microsoft's do interoperate.

Examining Interprocess Communications

Beyond the OSI model, new products and new standards for application-level interprocess communications come into being so often that it's hard to get a handle on the current state of affairs. *Interoperable* is the word used to describe each new product and standard. As this chapter suggests, the frequent use of the word is significant, but not in the way the vendor intends. A vendor's claims regarding interoperability should always be taken with a grain of salt.

Microsoft and IBM designed Dynamic Data Exchange (DDE), an application-to-application protocol for use in the Windows environment, for the spreadsheet program Excel. DDE is described in the Windows SDK (software developer's kit) and is available to other applications that want to talk to each other. In addition, Microsoft offers Object Linking and Embedding (OLE), also co-developed by IBM and Microsoft, for applications to use under Windows 3.1, Windows NT, and Windows 95. DDE has five mechanisms that applications can use:

- *Execute:* One application controls the execution of another.

- *Hot link:* A server application sends data to a client application whenever data changes.

- *Poke:* A client transfers data to a server.

- *Request:* Equivalent to a copy-and-paste operation between the server application and the client, without the need for the intermediate clipboard.

- *Warm link:* The server notifies the client that data has changed and the client then can request it.

For two applications to use DDE, they must agree on the format of the data to be exchanged. If the applications are from different vendors, the vendors must publish detailed specifications.

OLE is a layer on top of DDE that insulates the application programmer from some of DDE's tedious detail. One application puts data into a container located in the other application. The second application only needs to know how to display the data. If changes to the data are required, the second application invokes the first through a special interface.

Hewlett-Packard's New Wave is object-oriented. New Wave uses the concept of agents, and it contains an intelligent link manager that resolves object names into file system names. Version 3.1 of New Wave incorporates OLE.

Interoperability among the various providers of interprocess communications facilities probably won't happen for a long time. Even within a single protocol like DDE, interoperability will be highly application-dependent. Two applications from separate vendors can claim to use DDE or OLE, yet won't be able to share data through DDE/OLE because each application defines different interprocess commands and data formats.

Examining Electronic Mail Interoperability

Commercial electronic mail products often adhere to the Message Handling System (MHS) or the X.400 standard. MHS messages, for example, have a header, a body of text, and perhaps an attached file. The header contains a destination address, a return address, a postmark, and other information. Both addresses have a particular format: <username>@<workgroupname>. Applications that define data in this same format can interoperate with MHS. Similarly, applications that use X.400 conventions can interoperate with other X.400 applications and users. For Internet e-mail interoperability, many mail reader software products support MIME encoding of file attachments. MIME encoding is an e-mail convention that surrounds each portion of an e-mail message—message body and file attachments—with identifying text that describes that portion.

Of course, many electronic mail standards exist. Western Union has EasyLink, Telenet offers Telemail, and a rather popular one is PROFS from IBM. Interoperability among these systems is mostly a matter of reformatting data to look the way the other system expects.

Chapter Summary

Interoperability is such a big issue that an annual trade show—Interop—is devoted to it. Run by the Advanced Computing Environment people, Interop has one overriding criterion for its exhibitors: products must successfully interoperate with other products on a network. Interop is one of the best shows, with little fluff, good seminars, and good access to the technical people who sweat bullets to turn *interoperable* into a word you won't have to hear much anymore.

In the next chapter, you'll broaden your horizons to discover how you can connect multiple LANs to form a wide area network—a WAN.

Chapter 14

Building WANs from LANs

You learned in Chapter 1 that a local area network can encompass a small geographic area, such as a department-sized office or small building. Table 4.1 in Chapter 4, "Using Protocols, Cables, and Adapters," revealed the distance limitations of popular local area networks (Ethernet, Token Ring, and ARCnet). Someday your organization may need to exceed these distance limitations to allow people in different locations to share files. In this chapter, you'll learn how to connect several local area networks (LANs) into one wide area network (WAN).

You'll first cover the basics of wide area networks. You'll learn how to connect geographically dispersed LANs, and you'll find out what bridges, routers, and gateways are. You'll consider the differences between sharing files on a LAN and sharing files on a WAN. You'll discover the factors that influence where you should place shared files in a WAN. You'll learn how to print remotely across a WAN, and you'll gain an understanding of how a WAN affects the administrative tasks you perform on the WAN-connected LANs.

You'll then move on to a detailed description of the protocols you can choose to use as you build your WAN. You'll learn the advantages and disadvantages of each protocol, and you'll find out that state and federal regulations can sometimes dictate which protocol you choose.

Exploring WAN Basics

Within your own office space, you own your LAN. You can purchase new workstations, cables, repeaters, and hubs, and add these components to the LAN. You can diagnose and correct the problems that happen on your LAN.

With a WAN, however, the situation is different. You must contract with a communications services provider (your telephone company, for instance) to connect two LANs that are across the street or across the country from one another. The telephone company will lease a special kind of phone line to you. You'll probably purchase the WAN hardware that connects your LANs to either end of the phone line, but you'll rely on the phone company to make sure the phone line is continuously available and noise-free.

WAN hardware consists of routers, bridges, and gateways. The "Using Bridges, Routers, Brouters, and Gateways" section of this chapter describes this hardware in detail. Basically, the WAN hardware provides a path between LANs, over which two or more LANs can share frames and packets. This communication of frames and packets between LANs allows a workstation on one LAN to access a file server or print server on another LAN.

WANs don't use Ethernet, Token Ring, or ARCnet. At the physical layer, WANs use protocols that typically encapsulate the Ethernet, Token Ring, or ARCnet frames. An encapsulated frame travels across the WAN link to the other LAN, where the WAN turns the frame back into a LAN packet. The WAN hardware decides which frames need to travel to another LAN, and the type and configuration of the WAN hardware determines which WAN protocol is used.

Different WAN protocols carry information at different speeds (and at different costs). You'll explore these protocols in detail later in this chapter. In general, the WAN equipment (router, bridge, or gateway) uses one or more of these protocols to transport frames and packets between LANs. Because these WAN protocols typically operate more slowly than the LAN protocols described in Chapter 4 ("Using Protocols, Cables, and Adapters"), you'll notice that accessing files across a WAN takes more time than accessing the same files on your local area network.

Connecting Distant LANs

You must do two things to connect different LANs into one network. First, you must create a physical path between the LANs. Next, you must enable the flow of information between the LANs. This means that you must establish a common protocol the LANs can use to exchange information. Most vendor products for connecting LANs use a common high-level protocol such as TCP/IP, IPX, or NetBIOS. At a layer below the high-level protocol, the WAN uses a protocol designed for use over high-speed telephone lines to transport the TCP/IP, IPX, or NetBIOS packets.

You can think of interconnected LANs in terms of layers connected by these common protocols. The bottom layer consists of individual LANs, each with its own file servers and workstations. The common protocol ties the bottom layers through special communications devices. Such a device does not change the individual LANs; the device simply transports message packets between the LANs.

If communications devices connect two LANs that are geographically distant from one another, you'll probably use services and equipment offered by your telephone company to make the connection. Depending on which states and which area codes the two LANs are in, you may find that federal or state regulations limit your choice of vendors, communications equipment, and available protocols. For example, Southern New England Telephone (SNET) offers T1 lines and SMDS lines, at least through 1996, but does not offer ATM or Frame Relay. (You'll learn about these WAN protocols later in this chapter.)

Between two LANs that are both within the 203 (Connecticut) area code, only SNET can provide private telephone line services. These kinds of restrictions may greatly affect how you set up WAN connections between your LANs.

If you must connect two LANs, the job will be easier if they both already use the same topology and network operating system. If the topologies or network operating systems are different, you must look for products that specialize in connecting those particular topologies or network operating systems. Interconnecting LANs is easier if your organization has adhered to widely accepted standards instead of proprietary topologies and protocols. If your organization has LANs that aren't compatible, you can leave the LANs unconnected, or you can replace one or the other LAN with hardware and software that does enable interconnecting LANs.

Using Bridges, Routers, Brouters, and Gateways

Bridges, routers, brouters, and gateways let you connect different LANs into a single heterogeneous system. The following sections describe each of these connectivity devices.

Using Bridges. Bridges operate at a high level and allow you to link LANs you could not otherwise link, regardless of distance limitations. Bridges can interconnect network segments that use different physical media. It's not uncommon to see a bridge between LANs that uses fiber-optic and coaxial cable, for example. Such a bridge has a fiber-optic connector at one end and a coax connector at the other end. Internally, the bridge translates between the two cabling schemes. In addition, bridges can tie together dissimilar low-level (Physical and Data-Link layer) protocols. You may use bridges to connect similar LAN segments, such as two EtherNet segments, or to mix dissimilar segments, such as a Token Ring segment and an EtherNet segment.

Bridges often feature high-level protocol transparency. Bridges can move traffic between two segments over a third segment in the middle that cannot understand the data passing through it. As far as the bridge is concerned, the intermediate segment exists for routing purposes only. Finally, bridges enable devices and segments using the same high-level protocol (TCP/IP or NetBIOS, for example) to communicate, regardless of the physical layer each LAN uses.

Bridges are intelligent. They learn the destination addresses of traffic passing on them and direct the traffic to its proper destination. This explains their importance in network partitioning. When you find that a physical network segment has excessive traffic and its performance is beginning to degrade, you can break it into two segments with a bridge. The bridge directs the traffic to its destination on the other LAN segment, limiting traffic that isn't intended for a given segment. Bridges use a process of learning, filtering, and forwarding to keep traffic within the physical segment it belongs in.

Because bridges must learn addresses, examine packets, and make forwarding decisions, they're often slow. However, they offer special connectivity advantages and options that make them useful in mixed-protocol environments.

Using Routers. The router is, in some respects, more intelligent than the bridge. Routers don't have the same ability to learn as bridges do, but they can make routing decisions that determine the most efficient data path between two network segments.

Routers don't care what topologies or access-level protocols the network segments use. Because routers operate at the next layer above bridges (the Network layer of the OSI Model), they're not affected by medium or access protocols. Routers often are used between network segments that use the same high-level protocol. The most popular transport layer protocol that routers handle is Novell's IPX.

Bridges make a forward or discard decision on each packet of data, depending on whether the packet is destined for an address on the other side of the bridge. Routers choose the best route for the packet by checking a routing table. They see only the packets addressed to them by the preceding router, while bridges must examine all packets passing on the network.

Most large internetworks can make good use of routers. You should remember, however, that routers need to have the same high-level protocol in all the network segments they connect. If you're connecting networks in a multi-protocol environment, you're probably better off using bridges. The same is true if you want to segment a network to control traffic loads.

Using Brouters. Brouters are a kind of hybrid of bridges and routers. Often referred to as *multi-protocol routers*, brouters provide many of the advantages of bridges and routers for very complex networks. True multi-protocol routers don't contain the bridging advantages of brouters; they simply enable the router to do what routers do with more than one protocol. Brouters actually decide whether a packet uses a protocol that is routable. Brouters then route the packets they can and bridge the rest.

Brouters are complex, expensive, and difficult to install, but for very complicated heterogeneous networks, they often provide the best internetworking solution.

Using Gateways. Gateways operate at the top layers of the OSI model. They provide the most sophisticated method of connecting network segments and networks to hosts. You select a gateway when you have to interconnect systems built on totally different communications architectures. You would use a gateway to interconnect a TCP/IP LAN to an SNA mainframe, for example. The two architectures have no commonalties, so the gateway must translate the data passing between the two systems.

The Spanning Tree. Using a technique called the *spanning tree algorithm* (part of the IEEE 802.1 internetworking standard), you can place bridges between distant LANs. A spanning tree is another term for a switchable path between two devices on a network.

Under the spanning tree algorithm, the bridges making up the alternative routes between Chicago and Dallas, for example, conduct a series of bridge-to-bridge negotiations. The result is that one bridge (the one that sees the best path) is in a *forwarding* state. The other bridge is *blocked* and will not forward packets. If the open path degrades, the other bridge opens and the first one closes, maintaining optimum traffic rates across the internetwork. This technique isn't reserved for wide area networks; you also can use it to provide traffic-flow management locally or within a large office building.

Sharing Distant Resources

The WAN hardware creates an environment that allows a network operating system (Novell NetWare, for example) to function the same across the WAN link as the NOS does on the LAN. You can copy files, share files, run network utility software, and print through the WAN link just as you can on your LAN. However, the WAN can't transport data between workstations and remote file servers as fast as the LAN does. You'll notice that accessing data on a remote (WAN-linked) file server happens more slowly than accessing data on a local file server. Your application software, utilities, and operating system commands (such as COPY and DIR) will work over the WAN, but the difference in performance will be apparent.

Transferring and Sharing Files. A high-speed WAN connection to a remote file server can give you access that's faster than the floppy disk drive in your computer. Depending on how many other people are using a high-speed WAN link at the same time you are, you may even find that remote file server access is nearly as fast as your local hard disk. A slow, less expensive WAN connection will provide access that's slower than your floppy disk drive.

You'll want to analyze the different kinds of file operations that happen on your LAN and decide which of these file operations you'll allow across the WAN link. Electronic mail is a good candidate for WAN connectivity, but copying large files across the WAN may not be.

Deciding Where Files Should Go. Each LAN in a wide area network will need its own file server (or servers). You'll want to make the WAN link as efficient as possible by grouping files on each file server in a way that puts the files that a person uses most frequently on a local file server. You can thus minimize WAN traffic. Shared, multi-user files will naturally have to exist in a central location for everyone to use. But you can prevent the WAN link from becoming overburdened by intelligently locating files near the people who use them the most. You might even consider putting duplicate files on the file servers at both sites, where appropriate. You can run a batch file after hours to synchronize the data between the WAN-linked file servers.

Printing Remotely. Even a few pages of printed output can represent a considerable amount of data. While it's possible to connect to a shared printer across a WAN link, the stream of print data might consume the capacity of the WAN link for several minutes (or longer). Streams of print data containing downloadable fonts, PCL commands (for Hewlett-Packard LaserJet printers), or Postscript commands are the worst culprits. You'll want to carefully limit printing across the WAN link to just those printouts that must be produced at the remote site. Instead of printing through the WAN link, you might consider changing the workflow procedures at each site to instead copy the related files through the WAN link. People can then initiate the print operation on the local area network the printer is attached to.

Administering the Remote LAN. You manage a wide area network (WAN) in much the same way you administer one of the LANs, except that you must take into account the different network topologies and protocols the LANs use. You also have a few new devices on the LAN that create the special communications links, and that you need to manage.

A heterogeneous network contains several network segments that differ in topology, protocol, or network operating system. The network may contain PCs operating on Ethernet or Token Ring, UNIX workstations running TCP/IP, and mainframes using IBM's Systems Network Architecture (SNA). The bridges, routers, and gateways create a heterogeneous, interconnected network. From an administrative perspective, you may need to have a LAN administrator at each remote site. If two WAN-connected LANs are in the same building or across the street from one another, you may not need to hire additional LAN administrators. In this case, though, the LAN administrator will definitely want to assemble a toolbox of transportable tools, such as diagnostic diskettes, boot diskettes, cable testers, screwdrivers, and, perhaps, a protocol analyzer.

You can use remote access and remote control software products like those mentioned in Chapter 2 ("Sharing Computer Resources") to help administer a remote LAN from a central site. And some versions of the LAN management products described in Chapter 12 ("Managing Your Network") are intended for wide area networks.

A large network, connecting many LANs in a wide area network, contains many additional components that can cause network problems and failure. Because these products exist at intersections within the network traffic pattern, they can cause significant problems when they malfunction. Complex products such as routers, brouters, and gateways are subject to hard-to-locate configuration errors (see "Using Bridges, Routers, Brouters, and Gateways" earlier in this chapter). To isolate the problem, you may determine if nodes on only one side of an internetworking product are affected. If this is the case, you can start the search with that product. Ask yourself what has changed recently and what unplanned side effects that change may have had.

Learning WAN Protocols

You learned about the Ethernet, Token Ring, and FDDI physical layer protocols in Chapter 4 ("Using Protocols, Cables, and Adapters"), and you also learned about the transport layer protocols IPX and NetBIOS. Wide area networks use protocols designed for high-speed telephone lines, and these protocols are different from what you covered in Chapter 4.

When you select the WAN hardware and type of telephone line that will link your local area networks, you can choose from a variety of protocols. Connecting two LANs in different area codes may let you select from a wider variety of options, depending on the regulatory agencies that control your telephone company. You'll need to consult with the telephone companies that offer services in your area to find out which protocols you can select. The following sections describe several ways to create wide area networks; not all services or products may be available from all telephone companies.

Using Dial-Up Modems

The least expensive and slowest type of WAN link uses dial-up modems over a voice-grade telephone line. The NetWare Asynchronous Remote Router from Novell is an example. You can create one or more connections between LANs with the Asynchronous Router. Through a regular voice-grade dial-up telephone line, the router allows two NetWare LANs to share file and print services. You install the software on two PCs, one at either location. Both PCs contain network adapters and serial (COM) ports. You might use the serial ports built into the PCs or purchase serial communications adapters from Novell, called Wide area network Interface Modules (WNIM) boards. You connect the PCs' serial ports to modems and the network adapters to each LAN. Once you have one modem dial the other modem's telephone number, the router software in each PC uses the connection to send and receive NetWare IPX packets. You typically use 9.6, 14.4, or 28.8 kilobaud modems with the Asynchronous Router software.

Using X.25

An X.25 network consists of a number of components, called packet switches, that switch and route packets to their destinations. The network breaks up the transmitted data into a collection of small packets, transmits the packets through data paths between the source and destination nodes, and then reassembles the data at the destination. The path between the nodes is a *virtual circuit*. To higher layers of software, the virtual circuit appears to be a single, continuous, logical connection. However, the X.25 protocol lets the packets travel different paths between the source node and the destination. The equipment that breaks up or reassembles the packets is a Packet Assembler/Disassembler (PAD). X.25 packets are usually 128 bytes, but the source and destination nodes can negotiate a different packet size when they establish the virtual circuit. The X.25 protocol can support a theoretical maximum of 4,095 concurrent virtual circuits across a physical link between a node and the X.25 network itself. In practice, the network will have fewer virtual circuits because most physical links can't send or receive data fast enough to have a large number of virtual circuits. An X.25 network typically uses a data transmission speed of 64 Kbps.

Using Frame Relay

Engineers developed Frame Relay to support Broadband Integrated Services Digital Network (B-ISDN). B-ISDN is a high-speed protocol intended primarily for several kinds of information: voice, video, and data (including LAN data). Frame Relay typically offers higher data transmission rates than X.25 networks by avoiding much of the overhead inherent in an X.25 network. A Frame Relay environment switches and routes packets, but at the lower data link layer. X.25 switching occurs at the higher network layer. Frame Relay doesn't provide the flow control and error correction components of an X.25 network, but instead relies on the higher layers of protocol software to verify and retransmit data as necessary. Frame Relay assumes the physical layer of the network is a reliable link between nodes. Frame Relay operates at transmission rates up to 2 Mbps—slower than a LAN, but not much so.

Using T1 Circuits

A T1 circuit, or link, is a point-to-point full-duplex digital circuit designed originally to carry digitized voice signals. T1 circuits use a variety of media, including copper wire, coaxial cable, fiber-optic cable, infrared, microwave, and satellite links. Almost every telephone company offers T1 circuits. Each T1 link operates at a data transmission rate of 1.544 Mbps. You might lease several T1 links from the telephone company and multiplex them to support several concurrent voice and data sessions.

Using Synchronous Optical Network (SONET)

Bellcore, a telephone company subsidiary, first proposed the data transmission characteristics of SONET, Synchronous Optical Network. SONET is now an international standard accepted by ANSI and the CCITT. SONET provides a point-to-point link over fiber-optic cable and operates at a multiple of 51.84 Mbps. The different rates are identified as OC-1, OC-8, OC-48, and so forth. The "OC" portion of the designation stands for Optical Carrier and the number is the multiple of 51.84 Mbps at which the network transmits data. OC-8, for example, operates at a rate of 2,488.32 Mbps. Frames within SONET consist of Synchronous Transport Signals (STS). An STS-1 frame is 810 bytes represented in matrix form. The matrix has 90 columns and 9 rows, with each cell of the matrix a byte. 27 bytes of the STS-1 frame contain network overhead, and the remaining 87 columns (minus 9 bytes for row-level transport overhead) contain the data. An STS-1 frame can thus carry 774 bytes of information. SONET sends an STS-1 frame every 125 microseconds, which is 8,000 frames per second.

Using Asynchronous Transfer Mode (ATM)

Asynchronous Transfer Mode (ATM) is a technology built on top of SONET. Each packet, called a cell, is 48 bytes and is the fundamental unit of ATM data transfer. Because each cell has a five-byte header containing the destination address, the total cell size is 53 bytes. In the case of LAN message traffic, LAN Terminal Adapters break the LAN messages into ATM cells at the source node and reassemble them at the destination node. The packet switching services of ATM can be used to support Frame Relay as well as other wide area network transport services. The multiplexing of cells in an ATM network provide good use of the available bandwidth. The network allocates cells on demand when traffic is high. The network flexibly responds to the needs of the LANs as the LANs send and receive LAN messages.

Comparing WANS and MANs

Metropolitan area networks (MANs) are similar to WANs. A city-wide network is a MAN if that network adheres to a standard being promoted by the IEEE 802.6 committee. The standard provides for data transfer rates of up to 155 megabits per second; MANs use fiber-optic technology to achieve the high data communication rate. The protocol used in a MAN is called Dual Queue Dual Bus (DQDB) and consists of two loops of fiber-optic cable connecting the network nodes. A DQDB-based network forms a ring so that a central node or station can provide clocking and synchronization information to control and manage the proper transmission of frames. DQDB uses two loops of fiber to allow nodes to put requests to transmit in a distributed queue; this helps the network provide consistent response rates, regardless of the physical size of the network.

Using Switched Multi-Megabit Data Service (SMDS)

In addition to inventing SONET, Bellcore developed a WAN protocol called Switched Multi-Megabit Data Service (SMDS). SMDS uses a three-layer approach to interface to LANs. These layers are the SMDS Interface Protocol. The top layer, level 3, provides a datagram service whose packets are up to 9,188 bytes. At level 2, SMDS breaks the data into 53-byte ATM cells. Level 1, the physical (lowest) level, usually consists of a metropolitan area network link.

Talking to the Phone Company

You should consider the foregoing discussion of WAN protocols to be pure theory; some of the protocols represent relatively new technology and may not be available in your area. You'll need to talk to one or more phone companies to find out which of these services and products you can choose from. Prices vary widely from vendor to vendor, but achieving the most important goal—creating a reliable, effective link between LANs—will depend on your getting compatible components. In addition to talking to telephone company sales representatives, discuss your needs with vendors of high-speed communications equipment, including companies such as Cisco, Bay Networks, 3COM, Microcom, and Andrew.

Looking at Special Kinds of Phone Lines

Leased line service can be expensive, but renting a private telephone line from a phone company is often the only way to connect remote locations if you have a great deal of data to send and receive. WANs typically use leased lines to connect two or more LANs. Almost every telephone company, including AT&T, Sprint, MCI, and Cable and Wireless, offers leased line services.

The following description of some of the AT&T services gives you a general idea of the services you can choose from. Other companies provide similar services, but costs vary widely among the telephone companies. Be sure to compare the services and prices of different long distance providers. Note particularly that rates and services change from time to time, based on both technological advances and government regulation modifications. Also note that, while I use AT&T services as an example in this chapter, this book doesn't endorse one particular phone company.

AT&T's ACCUNET Spectrum of Digital Services (ACDS) is a digital private line service for data, video, and voice at 9.6, 56/64, 128, 256, 384, 512, 768, and 1,544 kilobits per second. The rates slower than 1,544 kbps are *intermediate bit rates*, while the 1,544 rate is *T1 Service*. ACDS customers can pay for the exact transmission speed needed to meet their communications requirements.

AT&T typically charges a fee for ACDS that's based on several factors. The three major factors are the following: the cost of the *local channels* (the paths to your local phone company at each site), the *access coordination fee*, and the cost of the *interoffice channel* (the long distance path between the two sites). If the same local phone company serves both sites, fees are based on rates filed with

(continues)

(continued)

the Public Utility Commission (PUC). For long distance service, the rates are filed with the Federal Communications Commission (FCC). In particular, Tariff 9 (available from the FCC) identifies the interoffice channel rates. Tariff 11 identifies the local channel rates and the access coordination fees.

Another AT&T service, ACCUNET T1.5 Service, is a digital private line service that transmits high volumes of data, video, and voice at 1.544 megabits (millions of bits) per second. ACCUNET T45 Service is a digital private line service that transmits data, video, and voice at 45 megabits per second.

AT&T offers yet another service, one that is highly reliable. The DATAPHONE Digital Service is rarely unavailable or unusable. The service offers line speeds of 2,400, 4,800, 9,600, 19,200 and 56,000 bits per second. The popularity of this service has waned considerably because of the advent of error-correcting modems and the improvement in regular phone lines—they now rarely fail.

Chapter Summary

You learned how to build wide area networks (WANs) in this chapter. You explored the basic principles of wide area networking, and you looked at WAN hardware (bridges, routers, and gateways). You now understand that most WANs are slower than the LANs they connect, and you know to modify your usage of the LANs accordingly. You also understand the different WAN protocols that vendors offer.

Understanding LAN Certification

Novell, Microsoft, and IBM have training courses and knowledge-verification tests that you can use to gain professional recognition of your LAN skills. These programs give you greater status and might help you increase your salary. Employers in the computer industry are well aware of these certification programs and often look specifically for people who've achieved one of the levels of certification from these programs.

Getting Certified by Novell

The Novell program offers three levels of certification. You can become a Certified NetWare Engineer (CNE), an Enterprise Certified NetWare Engineer (ECNE), or a Certified NetWare Administrator (CNA). Additionally, Novell offers a special level of certification for the people who teach courses leading to one of the other levels. People in this last category are Certified NetWare Instructors, or CNIs.

Novell created the Certified NetWare Engineer designation to tell Novell's customers whether a person is qualified to install and maintain a Novell NetWare LAN. You become a CNE by passing a series of rigorous tests. Novell designed these tests to reveal your knowledge of local area networking and the NetWare products in particular. CNEs enjoy a special relationship with Novell's technical support staff, one not available to the general public. If you're familiar with PCs, PC networks, and Novell NetWare, you may want to undergo the tests to become recognized as a CNE.

You can take the CNE tests in any order, and the certification process begins when you take your first test. You have one year from the date you first take a CNE test to complete the program.

The tests cover your skills and your knowledge in several areas, including the inner workings of personal computers, the configuration and use of DOS, and the use and configuration of NetWare versions 2.2, 3.12, and 4.11. CNE candidates plan their own curriculum, within Novell guidelines. The Drake Authorized Testing Centers (DATC) administer the tests.

Novell itself offers many training courses you can take; the courses are designed specifi-cally to give you the knowledge you'll need to pass the CNE tests. You can call (800) 233-3382 to find out more information about the Novell Authorized Education Centers near you. To contact Drake, call (800) RED-EXAM. You take the test at a computer; the testing software accepts your responses and scores the result. Each Drake Authorized Testing Center downloads the test before the test session and then uploads the results to a cen-tral Drake location after you finish the test. Novell receives the score results from Drake within 48 hours; you receive your test results immediately, before you leave the test center.

A question you might encounter during the CNE test is, "Describe the tables, perfor-mance features, blocks, and buffers important to the workings of file server memory." Another possible question is, "Identify the NetWare 3.12 memory pools and describe the features, content, resource use, and effect of each."

In addition to the recognition that the CNE designation will bring you, you get other benefits. Novell supplies CNEs with a free CD-ROM containing the Network Support Encyclopedia. This resource is a database of technical information regarding Novell prod-ucts. The information in the database includes the following:

- Installation, maintenance, and troubleshooting techniques

- Technical bulletins and manuals

- Patches, fixes, and driver software

- Technical notes from manufacturers of PC hardware and software

Novell also gives each CNE two free "support incidents," which is Novell's term for tele-phone technical support to help you solve a problem. CNEs can purchase additional support incidents at half the regular rate. You also get to use the CNE logo on your busi-ness card and stationery. Novell encourages CNEs to join CNEPA (the CNE Professional Association), a nonprofit organization devoted to helping CNEs keep up with new hard-ware and software technologies.

The Enterprise Certified NetWare Engineer designation is for CNEs who wish to achieve an even higher level of certification. To become an ECNE, you must first be a CNE. A person certified as an ECNE possesses an in-depth knowledge of many areas of network-ing, including TCP/IP, troubleshooting difficult LAN problems, and communications technologies and theories.

A Certified NetWare Administrator (CNA) is an expert in managing NetWare LANs. A CNA doesn't require the technical skills of a CNE or ECNE, but he or she must be famil-iar with the administration, configuration, and tuning of NetWare. The test a CNA can-didate takes reveals his knowledge in the following areas:

- Adding, changing, and deleting account IDs and groups

- Configuring printers

- Writing login scripts

- Setting up NetWare security

- Managing workstation network software

- Troubleshooting

- Making backup copies of server files

Achieving IBM Certification

IBM has a certification program similar to the one Novell offers, and the Drake Authorized Testing Centers also administer the tests you take. The IBM program leads to three different designations for people interested in local area networking: Certified LAN Server Administrator, Certified LAN Server Engineer, and Certified LAN Server Instructor. While Novell's program emphasizes knowledge relating to Novell NetWare, the IBM program focuses on the LAN Server network operating system. To find out more about the IBM certification program, call (800) IBM-TEACH or (800) 959-EXAM.

Like a Novell CNA, a Certified LAN Server Administrator is an expert in the day-to-day support of a local area network. He or she knows how to manage logon accounts, make backup copies of server files, maintain security, and perform other network tasks.

A Certified LAN Server Engineer knows how to design, install, maintain, troubleshoot, and tune a local area network based on LAN Server.

A person who's achieved Certified LAN Server Instructor status is proficient both in local area network technology and explaining that technology to other people.

People certified through the IBM program receive special recognition in the computer industry and attain a special status. If you're one of these people, IBM will list you in the Professional Certification Program Directory (with your permission), which IBM supplies to its customers. IBM gives certified professionals priority status when they call for technical support. IBM distributes the Technical Library/Personal Systems CD-ROM disk to certified engineers, as well as free subscriptions to newsletters and magazines that help the professional keep his or her skills current. The certified professional is also entitled to use a special certification logo on business cards and stationery.

The tests, administered by Drake, are similar to those in Novell's program. In fact, IBM will give you credit in the IBM program for some of the CNE, ECNE, or CNA tests you've already passed. IBM offers educational courses through its Skill Dynamics subsidiary, and those courses are available on a self-study basis.

Microsoft Certification

Soon after Novell and IBM established certification programs, Microsoft also began offering its Microsoft Certified Professional Program. Like the other two programs, Microsoft's program aims to assess and verify software-related skills for technical computer professionals. Microsoft's certification program evaluates a computer professional's ability to design, develop, implement, and support solutions with Microsoft products.

Four Microsoft-sponsored certifications are currently available. They are Microsoft Certified Systems Engineer (MCSE), Microsoft Certified Solution Developer (MCSD), Microsoft Certified Product Specialist (MCPS), and Microsoft Certified Trainer (MCT). Of these four, the Microsoft Certified Systems Engineer designation is the one appropriate for network professionals. MCSEs are qualified to effectively plan, implement, maintain, and support information systems in a wide range of computing environments with Microsoft Windows NT Server and Microsoft's other network-related products.

The Microsoft Certified Solution Developer credential is suited for programmers, while the Microsoft Certified Product Specialist designation recognizes expertise with a particular Microsoft product. A Microsoft Certified Trainer is qualified to deliver Microsoft Official Curriculum courses at Microsoft Authorized Technical Education Centers.

To become a Microsoft Certified Systems Engineer, you must pass four operating system exams and two elective exams that provide a measure of technical proficiency and expertise. An independent organization, Sylvan Prometric, administers the Microsoft certification examinations at more than 800 Authorized Prometric Testing Centers.

The operating system exams require candidates to prove their expertise with desktop, server, and networking components. The elective exams require proof of expertise with Microsoft products such as SQL Server and SNA Server. Examples of course and examination titles in the program are Networking Essentials, Networking with Microsoft Windows for Workgroups 3.11, Microsoft SNA Server, Implementing and Supporting Microsoft Systems Management Server 1.0, Implementing and Supporting Microsoft Windows NT Server 4.0 in the Enterprise, and Microsoft SQL Server Database Implementation.

To inquire about Microsoft's certification programs, you can call an Authorized Prometric Testing Center. The telephone number in the United States and Canada is (800) 755-EXAM (755-3926). Outside the United States and Canada, you should contact your local Sylvan Prometric Registration Center.

Summary

Many employers consider these certification programs a good way to qualify job candidates, as well as a means of keeping employee skills up to date. However, the price of the courses and exams is higher than some individuals can afford. Be aware that an employer's tuition reimbursement policy may help defray some or all certification costs.

Some people achieve certification in all three programs, while others concentrate on a specific vendor's technology. Fortunately, many concepts in one vendor's technology apply generally to other vendors' technologies. The differences, as you learned in Chapters 6 ("Using Novell NetWare") and 7 ("Using Windows NT Server and Warp Server"), are in the details of operating system architecture, user interface design, and protocol usage.

Glossary of Terms

Access method A way to determine which workstation or personal computer will be next to use the LAN. A set of rules used by network hardware to direct traffic over the network. One of the main methods used to distinguish various LAN hardware. How a LAN governs users' physical (electrical) access to the cable significantly affects its features and performance. Examples of access methods are token passing and carrier sense multiple access with collision detection (CSMA/CD). *See* CSMA/CD.

Address A set of numbers that uniquely identifies something—a workstation on a LAN, a location in computer memory, or a packet of data traveling through a network.

ANSI Abbreviation for American National Standards Institute, a volunteer organization that helps set standards and also represents the United States in the International Standards Organization (ISO).

AppleTalk Apple Computer's proprietary LAN for linking Macintosh computers and peripherals. AppleTalk is a CSMA/CD network that operates at 115 kilobits per second and accommodates up to 32 devices.

Application layer The seventh and highest layer of the open systems interconnection data communications model of the International Standards Organization. The Application layer supplies functions to applications or nodes, enabling them to communicate with other applications or nodes. File transfer and electronic mail work at this layer. *See* OSI model.

ARCnet Abbreviation for attached resource computer network. One of the earliest and most popular LANs. A 2.5-megabits-per-second LAN that uses a modified token-passing protocol. Developed by Datapoint, ARCnet adapter cards now are manufactured by many vendors, including Standard Microsystems, Thomas-Conrad, and Pure Data, Ltd.

Back-up server A program or device that copies files so that at least two up-to-date copies always exist.

Balun An impedance-matching transformer. Baluns are small, passive devices that convert the impedance of coaxial cable so that its signal can run on twisted-pair wiring. Often baluns are used so that IBM 3270 terminals can use twisted-pair wiring. Baluns work for some types of protocols and not for others. They can be bottlenecks that slow down your network.

Bandwidth   The difference between the highest and lowest frequencies of a transmission channel. A measure of the information capacity of the transmission channel. Often expressed in hertz (cycles per second), but sometimes expressed in bits per second.

BNC   An acronym for Bayonet-Neill-Concelnan. A bayonet-locking connector for thin coaxial cables, like those used with EtherNet.

Bridge   Equipment that connects LANs, enabling communication between devices on separate LANs. Bridges are protocol-independent but hardware-specific. Bridges connect LANs with different hardware and different protocols. A device that connects an EtherNet network to a Token Ring network is an example of a bridge. With this bridge, you can send signals between the two networks. A bridge differs from a gateway or a router. Routers connect LANs with the same protocols but different hardware. Gateways connect two LANs with different protocols by translating between them, enabling them to talk to each other. The bridge does no translation. Bridges are best used to break a large network into smaller networks, while allowing the individual networks to share the same resources.

Broadcast message   A message from one user sent to all users. On LANs, all workstations and devices receive the message.

Bus network   A one-cable LAN in which all workstations are connected to a single cable. On a bus network, all workstations hear all transmissions on the cable. Each workstation selects those transmissions addressed to it based on the address information contained in the transmission. The simplest and most common LAN topology.

Cabling   The medium by which nodes on a LAN are connected to each other. Cabling can be twisted-pair, coaxial, twinaxial (cable used to connect 5250 terminals to System/36, System/38, or AS/400 IBM computers), or fiber-optic.

Coaxial cable   A type of electrical cable in which a solid piece of metal wire is surrounded by insulation, which in turn is surrounded by a tubular piece of metal. The axis of curvature of this piece of metal coincides with the center of a piece of wire, hence the term coaxial. Coaxial cables have wide bandwidths and can carry many data, voice, and video signals simultaneously. *See* Bandwidth.

Collision   The result of two workstations trying to use a shared transmission medium (cable) simultaneously. The electrical signals "bump" into each other, corrupting both signals. Both parties then have to retransmit their information. In most systems, a built-in delay ensures that the collision does not occur again. The whole process takes fractions of a second.

Collision detection   The process of detecting that simultaneous (and therefore damaging) transmissions have taken place. Typically, each transmitting workstation that detects the collision will wait some period of time and try again. Collision detection is an essential part of CSMA/CD access method. Workstations can tell that a collision has taken place if they don't receive an acknowledgment from the receiving station within a certain amount of time (usually fractions of a second).

Communications server   Also called an asynchronous server or asynchronous gateway. A communications server handles different asynchronous protocols and enables nodes on a LAN to share modems or host connections. Usually, one machine on a LAN will act as a gateway. People on the LAN can go through this machine to access modems or a host.

Contention   A way to determine how separate workstations can access the same cable, which is a shared transmission medium on a LAN. Each workstation tries to access the network at will. If the network is busy, the workstation must wait and try again.

CSMA/CD   Abbreviation for Carrier Sense Multiple Access with Collision Detection—a method of having multiple workstations access a transmission medium (multiple access) by listening until no signals are detected (carrier sense), and then transmitting and checking to see whether more than one signal is present (collision detection). Each workstation attempts to transmit when it thinks the network is free. If there's a collision, each workstation attempts to retransmit after a preset delay, which is different for each workstation. CSMA/CD is one of the most popular access methods for PC-based LANs. EtherNet-based LANs use CSMA/CD.

Cyclical redundancy check   A method of detecting errors in a message by performing a mathematical calculation on the bits in the message and then sending the results of the calculation along with the message. The receiving workstation performs the same calculation on the message data as it's received and then checks the results against those transmitted at the end of the message. If the results don't match, the receiver asks the sender to send again.

Database server   A specialized computer that serves database data to PCs on a LAN the way a file server serves files. With a regular file server, all the database data must be downloaded over the LAN to your PC so that the PC can pick out the information your application wants. With a database server, the server itself does the selecting, sending only the data needed to your PC.

Datagram   A transmission method in which sections of a message are transmitted in scattered order, and the correct order is reestablished by the receiving workstation.

Data Link layer   The second layer of the open systems interconnection data communications model of the International Standards Organization. The Data Link layer is the level that puts messages together and coordinates their flow. Also refers to a connection between two computers over a phone line. *See* OSI model.

DECnet   Digital Equipment Corporation's proprietary EtherNet LAN.

Diskless PC   A PC without a disk drive. Used on a LAN, a diskless PC runs by booting DOS from a file server. The PC does this via a read-only memory chip on its network adapter card called a remote boot ROM. Diskless PCs are cheaper, more compact, and offer better security than PCs with disks.

Distributed data processing   The processing of information in separate locations equipped with independent computers. The computers are connected by a network. Often, this is a more efficient use of computer processing power because each CPU can be devoted to a certain task. A LAN is a perfect example of distributed processing.

Electronic mail   A messaging system that operates over some sort of communications medium, often a LAN. Most e-mail systems enable users to type out messages and send them to other users on the system. Some e-mail systems are dial-up services, like MCI Mail or CompuServe. Others are applications running under a network operating system on a LAN.

EtherNet   A CSMA/CD, 10M-bit-per-second network using coaxial cable. Developed at Xerox, EtherNet is one of the most popular LANs in use.

Fault tolerance   A method of making a computer or network system resistant to software errors and hardware problems. A fault tolerance LAN system, as marketed by Novell under the System Fault Tolerant (SFT) name, tries to ensure that even in the event of a power failure, a disk crash, or a major user error, data isn't lost and the system can keep running. Cabling systems also can be fault tolerant, using redundant wiring so that even if a cable is cut, the system can keep running. True fault tolerance is very difficult to achieve.

FDDI   Short for fiber distributed data interface. FDDI is an emerging ANSI standard for a 100-megabits-per-second fiber-optic LAN. FDDI is compatible with the standards for the physical layer of the OSI model.

Fiber optics   A data transmission medium consisting of glass fibers. Light-emitting diodes send light through the fiber to a detector, which then converts the light back into electrical signals. Fiber optics will be the predominant media for LANs in the future. Fiber-optic LANs offer immense bandwidth, as well as protection from eavesdropping, electromagnetic interference, and radioactivity.

File locking   A method of ensuring data integrity. With a file-locking system, only one user at a time can update a file. Other users are locked out, unable to access the file. Contrast this system with record locking.

File server   A computer containing files shared by everyone connected to a LAN. In some LANs, the server is a dedicated personal computer. In other LANs, any PC can be a file server.

Frame   A group of bits sent over a communications channel, usually containing its own control information, including address and error detection. The exact size and makeup of a frame depends on the protocol.

Gateway   A computer system and its software that enable two networks using different protocols to communicate with each other. Common gateways hook PC-based LANs into IBM mainframes (SNA gateways) or to X.25 packet-switched public network systems (X.25 gateways).

Hub   The center of a star topology network or cabling system. File servers often act as the hub of a LAN. They house the network software and direct communications within the network. They may also act as the gateway to another LAN.

Hybrid network   A LAN with a mixture of topologies and access methods. For example, a network that includes both a token ring and a CSMA/CD bus.

IEEE   Abbreviation for the Institute of Electrical and Electronic Engineers, a publishing and standards-making body responsible for many standards used in LANs, including the 802 series.

IEEE 802.2   A Data Link layer standard used with the IEEE 802.3, 802.4, and 802.5 standards.

IEEE 802.3   A physical layer standard specifying a LAN with a CSMA/CD access method on a bus topology. EtherNet follows the 802.3 standard.

IEEE 802.4   A physical layer standard specifying a LAN with a token-passing access method on a bus topology. ARCnet works this way.

IEEE 802.5   A physical layer standard specifying a LAN with a token-passing access method on a ring topology. Used by IBM's Token Ring hardware.

Interrupt request line (IRQ)   The communications channel through which devices issue interrupts to the interrupt handler of a PC's microprocessor. The IRQ is the channel through which these devices get the microprocessor's attention. Different IRQs are assigned to different devices. This assignment pattern differs from PC to PC. Many LAN adapter cards use an IRQ to get to the microprocessor. You must be sure that your LAN adapter card isn't trying to use the IRQ assigned to another peripheral, such as the hard disk controller or VGA card.

Local area network (LAN)   A data communications network spanning a limited geographical area (a few miles at most). A LAN enables you to share disks, printers, communications, and other devices, as well as files.

Log in   The process of identifying oneself to a computer system. Used to control access to computer systems or a network. Sometimes "log on."

NetBIOS   Short for Network Basic Input/Output System, IBM's LAN communications protocol. NetBIOS has been adopted as an industry standard. It offers LAN applications a variety of ways to carry out interapplication communications and data transfer. To run an application that works with NetBIOS, a non-IBM network operating system or network adapter card must offer a NetBIOS emulator. More and more hardware and software vendors offer these emulators. They aren't always perfectly compatible, however.

Network adapter card   Electronic circuitry that connects a workstation to a network. Usually a card that fits into one of the expansion slots inside a personal computer. A network adapter card works with the network software and computer operating system to send and receive messages on the network.

Network layer   The third layer of the OSI model of data communications. It involves routing data messages through the network using alternative routes. *See* OSI standards.

Network operating system (NOS)   The software side of a LAN, a NOS is the program that controls the operation of a network. A NOS enables users to communicate and to share files and peripherals. It provides the user interface to the LAN, and it communicates with the LAN hardware or network adapter card. Note that a network operating system is different than a network adapter card: IBM's Token Ring, for example, is an adapter card, not a NOS.

Nodes   The points in a network where service is provided, service is used, or communications channels are interconnected. "Node" is used interchangeably with "workstation."

Noise   Random electrical signals, generated by circuit components or by natural disturbances, that distort transmitted data and introduce errors. Noise can come from lightning, crossed cables, and electrical motors.

OSI model   Abbreviation for open systems interconnection, a logical structure for network operations standardized within the ISO. *See* OSI standards.

OSI standards   The International Standards Organization (ISO) has established the open system interconnection (OSI). OSI provides a network design framework, enabling equipment from different vendors to communicate. The OSI model is a design in which groups of protocols, or rules for communicating, are arranged as layers. Each layer performs a specific data communications function. Each of these steps, or OSI layers, builds on the one below it. Although each step must be performed in order, within each layer there are several options. In the OSI model, there are seven layers. The first three layers are Physical, Data Link, and Network, all of which are concerned with data transmission and routing. The fourth layer, Transport, provides an interface between the first three layers and last three layers. The last three layers are Session, Presentation, and Application. These layers focus on user applications.

Packet   A group of bits, including address, data, and control elements, that are switched and transmitted together. Think of a packet as one sentence or one group of numbers being sent at the same time.

Plenum   A type of cable jacket commonly used in forced air plenums, or ducts. If plenum cable catches fire, it doesn't circulate toxic smoke throughout the ventilation system.

Presentation layer   The sixth layer of the OSI model of data communications. This layer controls the formats of screens and files. Control codes, special graphics, and character sets work in this layer. *See* OSI standards.

Printer server   A computer or program providing LAN workstations with access to a centralized, shared printer. Print requests from each workstation go to the printer server, which segregates the requests into individual print jobs. Print jobs usually are handled in the order they're received.

Protocol   A set of rules for communicating among computers. These rules govern format, timing, sequencing, and error control.

Protocol analyzer   A specialized computer or program that connects to a LAN and analyzes its traffic. Good protocol analyzers can record and display data on all levels of traffic on a LAN cable, from the lowest media access control packets to NetBIOS commands and application data. Protocol analyzers are excellent for diagnosing network problems, but they require some expertise because their data output is rather obscure.

Record locking   The most common and sophisticated means for multiuser LAN applications to maintain data integrity. In a record-locking system, users are prevented from working on the same data record at the same time. That way, users don't overwrite other users' changes and data integrity is maintained. Although record locking doesn't enable users to work with the same record at the same time, it does enable multiple users to work on the same file simultaneously; each workstation locks a particular record (a small part of the file) for only a brief time. Compare record locking with file locking, which enables just a single user to work on a file a time.

Repeater   A device that amplifies signals from one piece of cable and passes them on to another piece of cable without changing the signals' contents. Repeaters increase the maximum length of LAN connections.

Ring   A LAN topology (organization) where each workstation is connected to two other workstations, forming a loop (or ring). Data is sent from workstation to workstation around the loop in the same direction. Each PC acts as a repeater by resending messages to other PCs. Rings have a predictable response time, determined by the number of PCs.

Router   A router is like a bridge, but more protocol-dependent. A router usually can link only LANs with the identical protocol (such as two LANtastic LANs or two NetWare LANs). Like bridges, routers restrict a LAN's local traffic to itself, passing data on the bridged (routed) LAN only when that data is specifically intended for it. Compare a router to a repeater, which indiscriminately passes all data along, regardless of its destination. *See* Bridge.

Security   A way of ensuring that data on a LAN is protected from unauthorized use. Network security measures can be software-based, where passwords restrict users' access to certain data files or directories. Usually this kind of security is implemented by the network operating system. Audit trails are another software-based security measure, in which an ongoing journal is maintained of file usage.

Server   A computer providing a service to LAN users, such as shared access to disks, files, a printer, or an electronic mail system. Usually a combination of hardware and software. *See* File server and Printer server.

Session   A logical network connection between two workstations (typically a user station and a server) for the exchange of data. Also a data conversation between two devices, such as a dumb terminal and a mainframe. It's possible to have more than one session going between two devices simultaneously.

Session layer   The fifth layer of the OSI model of data communications. The Session layer does the log-keeping, security, and administrative tasks.

Shielding   The process of protecting a cable (consisting of one or more plastic-coated conductors) with a grounded metal sheath so electrical signals from outside the cable cannot interfere with transmission inside it.

Star   A LAN topology in which all workstations are wired directly to a central workstation that establishes, maintains, and breaks connections between the workstations. The center of a star is called the hub. The advantage of a star is that it's easy to isolate a problem node. If the central node fails, however, the entire network fails.

TCP/IP   Short for Transmission Control Protocol/Internet Protocol. TCP/IP is an important and established internetworking protocol that works at the third and fourth layers of the OSI model. Developed by the Department of Defense, TCP/IP is designed to be rugged and robust, and to guarantee delivery of data in the most demanding of circumstances. TCP/IP is becoming more popular with networking and computer vendors who want to connect their equipment to a variety of other systems and protocols.

Thin EtherNet   An EtherNet technology that uses a smaller diameter coaxial cable than standard EtherNet. Also called CheaperNet because of the lower cabling cost. Thin EtherNet systems tend to have transceivers located on the network adapter card rather than in external boxes. PCs connect to the Thin EtherNet bus via a "T" connector.

Token   A unique combination of bits. When a LAN workstation receives a token, it's given permission to transmit. *See* Token passing.

Token bus   A LAN with a bus topology that uses token passing as its access method.

Token passing   An access method in which a token is passed from workstation to workstation, giving permission to send a message. When you have the token, you can send. You attach your message to the token, which "carries" it around the LAN. Every station between you and the recipient "sees" the message, but only the receiving workstation accepts it. When the receiving station gets the message, the station generates another token.

Token Ring   A LAN with a ring topology that uses token passing as its access method.

Topology   The description of the physical connections of a network. Or, the description of the possible logical connections between nodes, indicating which pairs of nodes are able to communicate. Examples of topology are bus, ring, star, and tree.

Transport layer   The fourth layer of the OSI model of data communications. High-level quality control (error checking) and some alternate routing is done at this level.

Tree   A LAN topology in which there is only one route between any two of the nodes on the network. The pattern of connections resembles a tree, in which all branches spring from one root.

Twisted pair   Two insulated wires twisted around each other. The pair of wires may be surrounded by a shield, a jacket, additional insulation, or similar pairs of wires. Most twisted-pair wire is not shielded, which makes it susceptible to electromagnetic interference. However, twisted-pair wiring is easier to install and change than coaxial cable, although its bandwidth (information-carrying capacity) is usually much smaller.

Wide area network   A data communications network designed to serve an area of hundreds or thousands of miles. Public and private packet-switching networks and the nationwide telephone network are good examples of wide area networks.

Workstation   A personal computer attached to a LAN; a client. *See* Server.

Index

Symbols

Check out Que® Books on the World Wide Web
http://www.quecorp.com

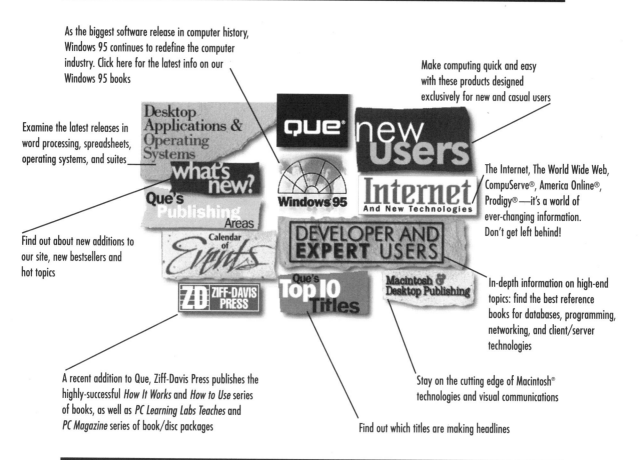

As the biggest software release in computer history, Windows 95 continues to redefine the computer industry. Click here for the latest info on our Windows 95 books

Make computing quick and easy with these products designed exclusively for new and casual users

Examine the latest releases in word processing, spreadsheets, operating systems, and suites

The Internet, The World Wide Web, CompuServe®, America Online®, Prodigy® —it's a world of ever-changing information. Don't get left behind!

Find out about new additions to our site, new bestsellers and hot topics

In-depth information on high-end topics: find the best reference books for databases, programming, networking, and client/server technologies

A recent addition to Que, Ziff-Davis Press publishes the highly-successful *How It Works* and *How to Use* series of books, as well as *PC Learning Labs Teaches* and *PC Magazine* series of book/disc packages

Stay on the cutting edge of Macintosh® technologies and visual communications

Find out which titles are making headlines

With 6 separate publishing groups, Que develops products for many specific market segments and areas of computer technology. Explore our Web Site and you'll find information on best-selling titles, newly published titles, upcoming products, authors, and much more.

- Stay informed on the latest industry trends and products available
- Visit our online bookstore for the latest information and editions
- Download software from Que's library of the best shareware and freeware

Complete and Return this Card
for a *FREE* Computer Book Catalog

Thank you for purchasing this book! You have purchased a superior computer book written expressly for your needs. To continue to provide the kind of up-to-date, pertinent coverage you've come to expect from us, we need to hear from you. Please take a minute to complete and return this self-addressed, postage-paid form. In return, we'll send you a free catalog of all our computer books on topics ranging from word processing to programming and the internet.

Mr. ☐   Mrs. ☐   Ms. ☐   Dr. ☐

Name (first) ☐ (M.I.) ☐ (last) ☐

Address ☐

City ☐   State ☐   Zip ☐

Phone ☐   Fax ☐

Company Name ☐

Email address ☐

Please check at least (3) influencing factors for purchasing this book.

Front or back cover information on book .... ☐
Special approach to the content .... ☐
Completeness of content .... ☐
Author's reputation .... ☐
Publisher's reputation .... ☐
Book cover design or layout .... ☐
Index or table of contents of book .... ☐
Price of book .... ☐
Special effects, graphics, illustrations .... ☐
Other (Please specify): _____ ☐

How did you first learn about this book?

Saw in Macmillan Computer Publishing catalog .... ☐
Recommended by store personnel .... ☐
Saw the book on bookshelf at store .... ☐
Recommended by a friend .... ☐
Received advertisement in the mail .... ☐
Saw an advertisement in: _____ ☐
Read book review in: _____ ☐
Other (Please specify): _____ ☐

How many computer books have you purchased in the last six months?

This book only .... ☐   3 to 5 books .... ☐
2 books .... ☐   More than 5 .... ☐

4. Where did you purchase this book?

Bookstore .... ☐
Computer Store .... ☐
Consumer Electronics Store .... ☐
Department Store .... ☐
Office Club .... ☐
Warehouse Club .... ☐
Mail Order .... ☐
Direct from Publisher .... ☐
Internet site .... ☐
Other (Please specify): _____ ☐

5. How long have you been using a computer?

☐ Less than 6 months   ☐ 6 months to a year
☐ 1 to 3 years   ☐ More than 3 years

6. What is your level of experience with personal computers and with the subject of this book?

	With PCs	With subject of book
New	☐	☐
Casual	☐	☐
Accomplished	☐	☐
Expert	☐	☐

Source Code ISBN: 0-7897-1158-3

7. Which of the following best describes your job title?

Administrative Assistant .... ☐
Coordinator .... ☐
Manager/Supervisor .... ☐
Director .... ☐
Vice President .... ☐
President/CEO/COO .... ☐
Lawyer/Doctor/Medical Professional .... ☐
Teacher/Educator/Trainer .... ☐
Engineer/Technician .... ☐
Consultant .... ☐
Not employed/Student/Retired .... ☐
Other (Please specify): _____ ☐

8. Which of the following best describes the area of the company your job title falls under?

Accounting .... ☐
Engineering .... ☐
Manufacturing .... ☐
Operations .... ☐
Marketing .... ☐
Sales .... ☐
Other (Please specify): _____ ☐

9. What is your age?

Under 20 .... ☐
21-29 .... ☐
30-39 .... ☐
40-49 .... ☐
50-59 .... ☐
60-over .... ☐

10. Are you:

Male .... ☐
Female .... ☐

11. Which computer publications do you read regularly? (Please list)

_____
_____
_____
_____
_____
_____
_____
_____
_____
_____

Comments: _____
_____
_____

Fold here and scotch-tape to ma

MACMILLAN COMPUTER PUBLISHING USA

A VIACOM COMPANY

Technical ----- Support:

If you need assistance with the information in this book or with a CD/Disk accompanying the book, please access the Knowledge Base on our Web site at **http://www.superlibrary.com/general/support**. Our most Frequently Asked Questions are answered there. If you do not find the answer to your questions on our Web site, you may contact Macmillan Technical Support **(317) 581-3833** or e-mail us at **support@mcp.com**.